Nixon in New York

The Fairleigh Dickinson University Press Series in Law, Culture, and the Humanities

Series Editor:
Caroline Joan "Kay" S. Picart, M.Phil. (Cantab), Ph.D., J.D., Esquire Attorney at Law; Adjunct Professor, FAMU College of Law; former English & HUM professor, FSU

The Fairleigh Dickinson University Press Series in Law, Culture, and the Humanities publishes scholarly works in which the field of Law intersects with, among others, Film, Criminology, Sociology, Communication, Critical/Cultural Studies, Literature, History, Philosophy, and the Humanities.

On the Web at http://www.fdu.edu/fdupress

Recent Publications in Italian Studies

Victor Li, *Nixon in New York: How Wall Street Helped Richard Nixon Win the White House* (2017)
Marouf A. Hasian, Jr., *Kafkaesque Laws, Nisour Square, and the Trials of the Former Blackwater Guards* (2017)
Michaela Stockey-Bridge, *The Lure of Hope: On the Transnational Surrogacy Trail from Australia to India* (2017)
Ted Laros, *Literature and the Law in South Africa, 1910-2010: The Long Walk to Artistic Freedom* (2017)
Peter Robson and Johnny Rodger, *The Spaces of Justice: The Architecture of the Scottish Court* (2017)
Doran Larson, *Witness in the Era of Mass Incarceration: Discovering the Ethical Prison* (2017)
Raymond J. McKoski, *Judges in Street Clothes: Acting Ethically Off-the-Bench* (2017)
H. Lowell Brown, *The American Constitutional Tradition: Colonial Charters, Covenants, and Revolutionary State Constitutions 1578–1786* (2017)
Arua Oko Omaka, *The Biafran Humanitarian Crisis, 1967-1970: International Human Rights and Joint Church Aid* (2016)
Marouf A. Hasian, Jr., *Representing Ebola: Culture, Law, and Public Discourse about the 2013–2015 West Africa Ebola Outbreak* (2016)
Jacqueline O'Connor, *Law and Sexuality in Tennessee Williams's America* (2016)
Caroline Joan "Kay" S. Picart, Michael Hviid Jacobsen, and Cecil E. Greek, *Framing Law and Crime: An Interdisciplinary Anthology* (2016)
Caroline Joan "Kay" S. Picart, *Law In and As Culture: Intellectual Property, Minority Rights, and the Rights of Indigenous Peoples* (2016)

Nixon in New York

How Wall Street Helped Richard Nixon Win the White House

Victor Li

FAIRLEIGH DICKINSON UNIVERSITY PRESS
Vancouver • Madison • Teaneck • Wroxton

Published by Fairleigh Dickinson University Press
Copublished by The Rowman & Littlefield Publishing Group, Inc.
4501 Forbes Boulevard, Suite 200, Lanham, Maryland 20706
www.rowman.com

Unit A, Whitacre Mews, 26-34 Stannary Street, London SE11 4AB

Fairleigh Dickinson University Press gratefully acknowledges the support received for scholarly publishing from the Friends of FDU Press.

British Library Cataloguing in Publication Information Available

Library of Congress Cataloging-in-Publication Data Available

ISBN 978-1-68393-000-6 (cloth : alk. paper)
ISBN 978-1-68393-001-3 (electronic)

∞™ The paper used in this publication meets the minimum requirements of American National Standard for Information Sciences Permanence of Paper for Printed Library Materials, ANSI/NISO Z39.48-1992.

Printed in the United States of America

To Kelly and Bernie.

Contents

Acknowledgments

Writing a book about a subject as complex as Richard Nixon was daunting, and there are so many people I'd like to thank for making this possible. First and foremost, my wonderful wife, Kelly, was extremely supportive, as well as instrumental in helping me do my research. She even helped me photocopy documents from the Nixon Library after I had a near panic attack over how many boxes I had to go through. Mostly, she encouraged me to follow my dream and to not worry too much about how it turned out. There were times when I questioned whether I should even do this, but she always cheered me on and kept me from getting in my own way. Thank you, my dear. I love you, and I'm very lucky to have you as my wife.

I'd also like to thank my family. My mom and dad have always supported me, no matter what, and they didn't get angry after I told them I was turning my back on my expensive legal education and becoming a journalist. My mother is also the only person I know who has read every single one of my articles and stories—going all the way back to the eighth grade when I reviewed movies for my middle school newspaper. My brother, Herman, an economics professor, is no stranger to doing scholarly writing and has been a good sounding board for me during this long process. I'd also like to thank my grandmother and my Aunt Sandy for giving me support from afar. Thanks, also, to my brother-in-law Scott Ruffcorn and sister-in-law Violet Yuen for helping me out and letting me stay with them during research trips to New York City.

I owe a tremendous debt of gratitude to the late Tom Evans and his two daughters, Heather and Paige. The genesis of this book came when I tried to interview Tom Evans for a retrospective article about Nixon's arrival at the Mudge firm. Unfortunately, I never got to speak with him, as he passed away shortly after I reached out. When I decided to write this book, I got in touch with Heather to ask her, out of the blue, if I could go through her father's papers. She was extremely gracious and even gave me free run of her house in Brooklyn. I hit a veritable goldmine of information, as he had been working on a manuscript about Mudge and had conducted interviews with several important figures, both at the firm and with the Nixon Administration, before their deaths. He had also held on to a lot of his memos from that time period, and this information was crucial and invaluable to me as I embarked on my project. Paige was also very helpful and, like Heather, opened up her home to me and helped me with her father's files. Based on everything I learned while writing this book, as well as talking to people who knew him, Tom Evans seemed like a thoroughly impressive lawyer and educator, and an even better man.

My colleagues at the *ABA Journal* have been very understanding and accommodating, as I've had to balance writing this book with my full-time job covering the business of law and legal technology. I'd especially like to thank managing editor Reginald Davis and editor-in-chief/publisher Molly McDonough, who have been supportive of me and have given me time and space to pursue this project. They are the best bosses I could have asked for, and I'm blessed to work with so many excellent journalists, editors, and designers for such a fantastic and prestigious publication.

I especially want to say a hearty "thank you" to my former boss, Allen Pusey. He reviewed my manuscript thoroughly—devoting a lot more time to this project that I had any right to expect. He has been nothing but supportive of me ever since the day I met him, and I only wish I could have spent more time as one of his reporters.

Another big "thank you" goes to my good friend Owen Lipsett. Like me, Owen is a fugitive from the legal industry, and he took time out of his busy schedule to review my manuscript and give me some much-appreciated insight. Now if I could only get him to root for Manchester United instead of Arsenal.

The folks at the Richard Nixon Presidential Museum and Library were very friendly and helpful to me. Thanks to the staff at the research room for your patience and diligence.

There are many reporters, editors, and professors that I'd like to thank for molding me into the journalist that I am today. In addition to my wonderful colleagues at the *ABA Journal*, I'd like to thank Jack Cavanaugh, Tom Edsall, and Ruth Padawer of Columbia University Graduate School of Journalism, and Monica Bay, formerly of *Law Technology News*.

I am especially grateful to Aric Press, my former boss at ALM, for his insights and advice regarding how to promote this book. I'm not a natural when it comes to marketing, so his suggestions were extremely helpful.

Thanks, as well, to Jeffrey Frank for speaking with me as I contemplated whether I should write this. I greatly enjoyed his book, "Ike and Dick: Portrait of a Strange Political Marriage" and saw that he had spoken with Tom Evans about Nixon's law firm days. I emailed him one day and he, very kindly, shared some of his notes with me.

Thank you, as well, to Jon Lindsey, partner at legal recruiting giants Major Lindsey & Africa, for answering questions I had about Mudge and helping me interpret some financial documents relating to the firm.

I'd also like to thank Caroline Picart and Harry Keyishian at Fairleigh Dickinson University Press for believing in me and guiding me through this process. Writing this book has been a tough, grueling, humbling, and ultimately rewarding experience, and I'd like to thank them for giving me this opportunity. Thanks, also, to Zachary Nycum at Rowman & Littlefield.

Since this is a book about the law, I'd be remiss if I didn't thank my lawyer, Chad Nold of Saper Law, for helping me with the book contract.

Finally, I'd like to thank my sweet dog, Bernie, for keeping me company while I slaved away behind the computer. He even made sure to give me regular tummy rub breaks—tummy rubs for him, not me, of course.

Prologue

"I was talked into this campaign by amateurs," Richard Nixon said to journalist Theodore White about the 1968 presidential election.[1]

Nixon had a compelling narrative heading into that campaign. Seemingly finished as a politician following two successive electoral defeats and one public temper tantrum during what was supposed to be a concession speech, Nixon was in the midst of a self-imposed exile from his home state and political base of California. He was happily ensconced nearly 2,800 miles away, living and working in New York where he made lots of money and traveled the world representing the Wall Street law firm that bore his name. Then one day, Leonard Garment, Thomas Evans, and John Sears, the three amateurs in question who happened to work at his law firm, convinced the reluctant Nixon to pick himself up off the mat and ride to the rescue of a country on the verge of implosion. With their help, Nixon would undertake an impressive and unprecedented comeback, culminating with victory in the 1968 presidential election.

As was the case at several points in his life, Nixon's version of the facts didn't quite match up with what actually happened.

Richard Nixon had never really given up on his White House ambitions and was probably the last person his law firm "amateurs" needed to talk into running for president. If his so-called wilderness years proved anything, it was that he would never be truly happy as a private citizen, and that being a wealthy corporate lawyer and the public face of a major Wall Street law firm would never fill the void in his soul the way electoral politics did. No matter what Nixon may have said in public—and even to his own family—he was hardly finished as a politician. Almost from the moment he arrived in New York in 1963 to join the Wall Street law firm of Mudge, Stern, Baldwin & Todd as the firm's new senior partner and primary rainmaker, he was hoping and planning on running for president again. In fact, within months of his name going on the shingle, he was back in the political arena, making a half-hearted, poorly executed, ultimately futile bid for the 1964 presidential nomination. After that, there was no going back, and the rest of his time at the firm was spent positioning himself for the 1968 contest.

Where Nixon's narrative was consistent with what actually happened was in relation to the role his law firm "amateurs" played in getting him ready to run again. Big law firms have an abundance of certain resources, such as money, intellectual heft, access to deep-pocketed potential donors, and, most importantly, labor—all of which can be vital for a large-scale political campaign. Nixon's firm, which had been renamed Nixon, Mudge, Rose, Guthrie & Alexander, provided its leader with all of those resources and played a central role in helping Nixon come back from political oblivion.

This book will look at the role Nixon's legal career and law firm played in getting him ready to run for, and win, the presidency in 1968. The firm provided him with a deep reservoir of young, tireless, and vigorous acolytes, lending a Kennedy-esque flavor to his fledgling campaign, albeit from a more conservative angle. The infusion of new talent also gave Nixon, who had made catastrophic errors during his two electoral defeats while earning a well-deserved reputation as a micromanager, important insights and perspectives that allowed him to avoid the mistakes of the past. Being a corporate lawyer also allowed him to build a network of well-heeled potential donors—several of whom had been close friends and had been begging him to make another run for the presidency for years. Several of these close friends did their part to help keep Nixon afloat, sending a constant stream of work to him—first when he was a lawyer with the California law firm of Adams, Duque & Hazeltine after the 1960 election, and then at Nixon Mudge.

Nixon's time on Wall Street gave him a chance to reinvent himself. Long suspicious of intellectuals, especially those from the "Eastern Establishment," Nixon had to become one of them in order to sign up clients for his law firm. It was an important step in remaking his image from brooding, underhanded, awkward opportunist to something voters could respect, if not admire.

In the meantime, he established himself as a pretty good lawyer and public partner for a Wall Street firm that had been stuck in neutral for decades. He brought in several high-powered clients with him, most notably Pepsi-Cola, and proved to be a magnet for business. His firm thrived and expanded, becoming one of the largest on Wall Street. While he served, primarily, as a rainmaker, he also demonstrated his worth as an attorney by ably arguing a landmark First Amendment case before the Supreme Court.

Excelling at his new job also allowed Nixon to rebuild his shattered confidence after his devastating electoral losses. But it wasn't enough for him to feel better about himself. He needed to get rid of the dreaded "loser label" that had, seemingly, been tattooed to his forehead—and his firm provided a vital helping hand. His colleagues would put their own ambitions and careers on hold in order to help Nixon, shielding him from politically sensitive legal matters and allowing him to take the spotlight on matters that would help him if he ever ran for office again. In another important instance, his colleagues, unlike Nixon, understood the power of television as a transformative medium and devised a strategy for using it as a weapon in 1968. In doing so, they managed to turn a perceived weakness of Nixon's into a strength that went a long way toward erasing his "loser" image.

His Nixon Mudge colleagues, led by the firm's newest named partner John Mitchell (who had merged his small but lucrative municipal bond firm with Nixon Mudge in late 1966) had carefully built up the infrastructure that the campaign would rely on. Like his fellow lawyers at Nixon Mudge, Mitchell was a political novice who had never run a campaign before becoming Nixon's campaign manager. However, he had amassed an enviable network of political contacts throughout the country, thanks to his municipal bond practice—making Mitchell the obvious choice to run Nixon's campaign. The Nixon Mudge–based staff experienced a high point during the New Hampshire primary, laying the groundwork for Nixon's impressive victory in the state and setting the tone for the rest of the prenomination stage of the election.

As longtime Nixon aide John Ehrlichman would later say about Nixon's law firm staff:

> Between wars a campaign is more like an organism which can live for years in the national ganglion hidden from sight. On the twenty-fourth floor, amidst the five floors leased to Nixon, Mudge, Rose, Guthrie and Alexander at 20 Broad Street, in a back corner by the door to Richard Nixon's office, there incubated the incipient virus of a presidential campaign. . . . No larger than a total of six people and a few filing cabinets, typewriters and telephones, the embryonic campaign fed on the ambition of Richard Nixon, the money of several wealthy political speculators, and the optimistic loyalty of a few people who admired Richard Nixon.[2]

But like many viruses, Nixon's law firm–based campaign staff eventually ran its course. As Nixon moved closer to securing the GOP nomination, he began to rely more on his experienced political staffers who had worked with him on prior campaigns. Other than Mitchell, who remained influential, Nixon's law firm crew saw themselves elbowed out of the picture once the general election campaign began.

After Nixon's victory, the firm would reap the benefits of being associated with the newly elected president. Now known as Mudge, Rose, Guthrie & Alexander, the firm was widely perceived as having access to the president, as well as to Mitchell, who had become attorney general. The firm also courted controversy, as questions popped up about preferential treatment from the Nixon Administration for several firm clients. Despite that, the firm thrived during the early years of the Nixon Administration, expanding, yet again, when it came to both real estate and personnel. Mudge had become one of the ten largest law firms in the country when it came to attorney head count, and firm partners took home more in pay than all but a few other firms on Wall Street. It was not an exaggeration to say that Mudge had become, in the words of journalist Paul Hoffman, "the firm to see."

But if "amateurs" helped bring about the Nixon Administration, it's certainly true that amateurs helped bring it down. The botched break-in at the Watergate Hotel would eventually snowball into the defining political scandal of its era, and Mudge would not escape the avalanche unscathed. The post-Watergate years were tough for the once vibrant firm, making Mudge, to borrow another one of Hoffman's phrases, "the firm to flee."

Their fates would remain intertwined for the rest of their lives. In the mid-1980s, both Nixon and the firm he once led were on the verge of yet another comeback. Nixon had reinvented himself as an author and respected foreign policy advisor to several of his successors in the White House while Mudge had returned to its pre-Watergate size. However, their triumphs would be short-lived. Nixon was never the same after his wife died in 1993, and the former president would follow her to the grave less than a year later. In 1995, his former firm would also die as Mudge closed its doors after several years of declining revenue and mass partner defections.

When Richard Milhous Nixon enrolled at Duke University School of Law in 1934, he, no doubt, got the same wake-up call that all law students get the moment they step foot into the place they'll call home for the next three years. Law schools don't teach you how to be a lawyer. They barely even teach you about the law itself. Instead, the main objective of law school is to teach you how to think like a lawyer. In fact, law schools are quite open about this, and even if they aren't, the entire curriculum is centered around learning case law and studying legal precedents rather than learning practical skills and studying statutes. For most lawyers, it's a hard habit to break; when they first take on a case or matter, the very first thing they'll do is look up similar cases from the past to see if they are controlling or binding.

In order to fulfill his lifelong ambition of becoming president, he had to break with precedent and do something that had never been done before—or since. This is the story of how he did it—and the lawyers who helped him.

NOTES

1. Theodore H. White, *The Making of the President 1968* (New York: Atheneum Publishers, 1969), 46.
2. John Ehrlichman, *The China Card* (New York: Warner Books, Inc., 1987).

Chapter One

"You Won't Have Nixon to Kick Around Anymore!"

Richard Nixon was in a foul mood when he took to the stage inside the ballroom of the Beverly Hilton on the morning of November 7, 1962. Sometimes, it could be hard to tell how he was feeling. He was an enigma even to his friends and admirers, while his enemies—well, his enemies were so numerous and varied that, one day, he would have his own official "Enemies List" that consisted of hundreds of names yet still seemed incomplete. On this morning, though, his feelings were pretty obvious to anyone with a pulse. He was so furious that one could almost see the proverbial steam coming from his ears as feelings of bitterness and failure permeated from his pores.

Worse, he'd have to face perhaps his greatest enemy: the press. He had once been their darling, harnessing their approval and acclaim to facilitate a rapid rise through the Republican ranks to become one of the most famous politicians in the country. Now he considered the media to be an implacable foe that was largely responsible for his current predicament.

It was the day after the California gubernatorial election, and Nixon had just gotten humiliated at the polls. Only two years earlier, the two-term vice president had nearly fulfilled his lifelong ambition when he came within an eyelash of winning the presidency in one of the closest elections in American history. That race, against John F. Kennedy, had also been one of the most controversial, marred by accusations of voter fraud, ballot box stuffing, and Mayor Richard Daley of Chicago playing the part of Victor Frankenstein by resurrecting thousands of dead men to vote Democratic.

After returning to California to plot his next move, he had decided to throw his hat in the ring for the governorship. His victory in 1962 had been considered a fait accompli—a savvy move by a smart, calculating, and shrewd politician in advance of another run at the ultimate prize, the White House. Nixon had challenged sitting governor Edmund "Pat" Brown, and while it's never easy to unseat an incumbent, Nixon was still supposed to win. However, when all the ballots were counted, Nixon had lost by five percentage points in a state where he had only known victories. Unlike the race against Kennedy, the gubernatorial contest was such a definitive loss for Nixon that the electoral magicians were not needed. For Nixon, who loved football almost as much as he loved politics, it was like he had come within a few yards of winning the Super Bowl, and in his zeal to get back to the big game played poorly during the following season and missed the playoffs entirely.

He had never even wanted to run for governor.[1] He, admittedly, cared little for local issues and knew almost nothing about state politics, having served his entire political career in Washington. His strengths, particularly his deep knowledge of foreign policy, would be next to useless in a gubernatorial race. His wife, Pat, had also warned him against taking the race, making the prescient argument that it was the wrong job for him, it was the wrong time to run because it was too soon after his presidential defeat, and it was the wrong place. "We had been away from California for 14 years, and she knew how difficult it would be to build a political organization, particularly at the county, city and precinct levels," Nixon reflected.[2]

However, Nixon had been under a constant stream of pressure, almost from the moment he arrived home after his term as vice president ended, to run against Brown.[3] Dwight D. Eisenhower, J. Edgar Hoover, and Thomas Dewey had all encouraged him to run, telling him that he needed a strong electoral base from which to mount another campaign for the White House. He chose to listen to them and not to the likes of Herbert Hoover, Douglas MacArthur, and ex–*LA Times* publisher Norman Chandler—to say nothing of his wife—who all encouraged him to stay away from the race. "MacArthur put it in his usual characteristically oracular way: 'California is a great state but it is too parochial. You should be in Washington, not Sacramento,'" Nixon recounted.[4]

The one saving grace for Nixon was that the job seemed to be his for the taking. Brown had a reputation as a lightweight and, in a state where Republicans had dominated the political scene for much of the century, his incumbency seemed like a fluke. In fact, when Brown first won the governor's mansion in 1958, defeating then-US Senate Minority Leader William Knowland in a massive upset, he became only the second Democrat to win a gubernatorial election in California in the twentieth century.

Furthermore, Nixon had essentially cleared the field when he entered the Republican primary as none of his rivals in the GOP dared tangle with the former vice president. The only candidate of any significance was Joe Shell, a state assembly member and former captain of the University of Southern

California football team. Compared to Nixon, Shell was a nobody (initial polls in 1962 had him at 2 percent[5]), and his intemperate, outspoken nature made him borderline unelectable as a statewide candidate. Indeed, he wouldn't have been out of place in the modern-day Tea Party. For instance, during the gubernatorial race, he told *Time* magazine: "I've gotten sick and tired of calling people liberals when they're basically socialists."[6]

Shell, however, had tapped into the growing divide between conservative and moderate Republicans and slowly chipped away at Nixon's lead. He had even picked up some endorsements, including one from the ultraconservative John Birch Society (Nixon, who was running as a self-proclaimed "progressive conservative,"[7] had disavowed and denounced the Birchers as a bunch of "kooks and nuts"[8]), and had financial support from A. C. "Cy" Ruble, former chairman of Union Oil Company of California.[9] When it came time for the primary, Shell shocked the state, taking one-third of the vote—a strong showing against the two-term vice president who had never lost an election in his home state other than a student body president race when he was in high school.[10] After a futile attempt to wring concessions out of Nixon in exchange for an endorsement, Shell ultimately backed Nixon, but in such a tepid and unenthusiastic manner that his supporters on the right flank immediately caught on. In fact, Caspar Weinberger, who was serving as chairman of the California Republican Party, later wrote that the Shell/Nixon contest helped cost Nixon the general election.[11] "Nixon won the primary but he did so without generating much GOP enthusiasm, which was deadly given that he was running against an incumbent Democratic governor who had not done anything particularly iniquitous," Weinberger wrote in his memoir *In the Arena.*[12]

Even though Nixon had limped into the general election, he was still favored to win, and most polls put the former vice president well ahead. Brown, however, proved to be a much more formidable candidate than Nixon had anticipated. Jolly and stocky, with a thinning head of hair and a thick set of spectacles, the self-effacing Brown was like everyone's grandpa—in stark contrast to the brooding Nixon. Beneath that nonthreatening exterior, however, was a shrewd operator who, smartly, used his "bumbler"[13] image as both a shield and sword. Brown's opponents routinely underestimated him while voters embraced his everyman appeal. Even the *Los Angeles Times*, known as a pro-Republican newspaper, liked him and gave him favorable coverage.[14]

As Nixon soon found out, Brown and his backers could punch with the best of them. One leaflet that was, purportedly, distributed by the "Independent Voters of California" contained a copy of a property deed signed by Nixon when he was still living in Washington, D.C., that included a restrictive covenant forbidding the resale of the property to blacks or Jews. Those kinds of covenants were common back then, and Ehrlichman had encouraged

Nixon to say that he had simply signed the contract without reading the fine print (admittedly, not a great position for any lawyer to take). Nixon demurred, reasoning that "most of the people who would vote for him approved of such covenants."[15]

Perhaps his biggest handicap was that his initial lack of interest in the job had never really gone away. While he was, undoubtedly, a formidable politician who knew more about national and international affairs than almost any other politician in the country at the time, when it came to issues important to California, he lacked that same level of knowledge, especially in comparison to Brown. Having spent his entire career in Washington, Nixon's unfamiliarity with his home state hampered him and forced him to talk in vague generalities about cleaning up Sacramento without going into specifics. The press picked up on this and began questioning whether he actually knew anything about the state he sought to lead.[16] Nixon even fell back on a tried-and-true tactic: accusing his opponent of being soft on communism. However, this only prompted more skeptical questions from reporters—something that annoyed Nixon greatly.

He also had to swat away speculation that he was planning on running for president in 1964 and was only using the job to stay relevant until then. When he announced his candidacy for governor in September 1961, he had pledged not to be a candidate for president in 1964.[17] Brown, however, had done a good job convincing voters that Nixon would break that pledge on day one in Sacramento. Nixon had added fuel to the fire by committing an unforced error, telling reporters that he was running for "governor of the United States."

Finally, in a race that was characterized by Nixon's focus on national and international issues at the expense of local ones, it was, ironically enough, an international issue that helped condemn him to defeat. The Cuban Missile Crisis resulted in President Kennedy's popularity hitting the stratosphere, and Democrats throughout America, including Brown, benefitted from Kennedy's bounce in the polls.[18] Brown surged ahead, and Nixon knew it was over well before polls opened on the morning of November 6, 1962.[19]

As the returns came in and the realization set in that he had lost another race, Nixon decided to drown his sorrows.[20] His resentment grew as his wife wept bitterly in the bedroom of his hotel suite at the Beverly Hilton where his campaign had set up shop to monitor the returns, and his campaign team was scattered throughout the living room trying to recover from the shellshock of losing a race that had seemed like a mere formality. H. R. (Bob) Haldeman, who served as Nixon's campaign manager in 1962 and would go on to greater infamy as White House Chief of Staff under Nixon, recounted that, when his boss was tired, "one beer would transform his normal speech into the rambling elocution of a Bowery wino."[21]

The drinking hadn't clouded his judgment too much, as he had telegrammed Brown a gracious note of congratulations. When he woke up the next morning, however, he was bitter and hungover and was no longer in a conciliatory mood. With reporters waiting for him in the Hilton ballroom, ready to conduct a postmortem of his campaign, Nixon had initially decided not to speak with them. It seemed like the right call. After all, nothing good could possibly come from him going in front of a live microphone with a dark cloud of failure, resentment, and alcohol swirling around him.

"I had not had time to shave," Nixon recalled.[22] "I felt terrible, and I looked worse."

Originally, he had planned on leaving it to his press secretary, Herbert Klein, to feed the pigeons. But like a guy who just couldn't resist pressing the gigantic red button marked "danger," Nixon couldn't stay away from the throng of reporters. According to Nixon's recollection, he had made up his mind not to speak to the reporters and was about to start heading home when he looked at the television screen in his suite and saw that the press conference was already underway. Then he heard overheard one of the reporters on the screen ask, "Where's Nixon?" Thinking that this reporter sounded disrespectful and rude, Nixon, who was already spoiling for a fight, abruptly changed his mind and decided to face off with the media after all.

Others recalled that Nixon was goaded into confronting the reporters by a couple of his aides. Klein himself has stated that he believed Nixon was resigned to going home without incident until two of his aides, Ray Arbuthnot and Jack Drown, changed his mind. "You can't let the press chase you out the back door," they told him.[23] "You ought to face them."

Either way, Nixon had decided he wasn't going to go quietly into the night. "I was holding this briefing, and the next thing I saw was Bob Haldeman waving at me, so I thought this was the signal," Klein recalled.[24] "I said 'the Vice-President has just left to go to his home.' About ten seconds later, I heard applause coming across the hotel lobby and [Nixon emerged] through the door."

Wearing a blue suit, shirt, and tie that matched his mood, Nixon took the stage and peered imperiously at the crowd of reporters.[25] He thrust his left hand in his pants pocket and walked up to the microphone. Editorial cartoonists and satirists enjoyed drawing Nixon as a scowling or brooding man with dark circles around his eyes, a perennial five-o-clock shadow on his face and a large nose that became more and more prominent as his career progressed (his enemies likened it to Pinocchio's nose—only they believed that Nixon's telltale sign of lying was that his lips were moving). He was like a mean version of Droopy the Dog, a sad-sack cartoon pooch who had long, prominent jowls and a permanent hangdog expression on his face. Campaign staffer Ehrlichman later described Nixon as "hung-over, trembling and red-eyed" as he launched into one of the more astonishing postcampaign tirades in American political history.[26]

"Now that Mr. Klein has made his statement, and now that all the members of the press are so delighted that I have lost, I'd like to make a statement of my own," Nixon said, immediately putting the stunned reporters in attendance on notice.[27] After asserting that he had "no complaints about the press coverage," he then spent the next few minutes reeling off a laundry list of complaints, singling out the dominant Los Angeles newspaper, the *LA Times*, for treating him unfairly. Nixon angrily laid into all of the reporters present, complaining that they misrepresented him on the campaign trail and refused to accurately report what he had said. He asserted that his few flubs, including the one where he had said he was running for "governor of the United States," had been blown out of proportion while reporters had given Brown a free ride. He also lectured them about how to do their jobs, maintaining that if they were going to back one candidate over the other, they should do it on the editorial pages rather than as part of their news coverage.

Nixon then launched into his concession speech. Except, rather than fall back on the usual vague platitudes that are standard components of almost all concession speeches, such as moving forward together and being grateful to God and family, Nixon launched into an attack on the man that had just defeated him by nearly 300,000 votes out of nearly 5.8 million cast.

> I congratulate Governor Brown, as Herb Klein has already indicated, for his victory. He has, I think, the greatest honor and the greatest responsibility of any Governor in the United States . . . I believe Governor Brown has a heart, even though he believes I do not. I believe he is a good American, even though he feels I am not . . . I am proud of the fact that I defended my opponent's patriotism. You gentlemen didn't report it, but I am proud that I did that. I am proud also that I defended the fact that he was a man of good motives, a man that I disagreed with very strongly, but a man of good motives. I want that—for once, gentlemen, I would appreciate if you would write what I say, in that respect. I think it's very important what you write it—in the lead—in the lead.[28]

After some general observations about election results throughout the country, Nixon then dropped the bombshell. He was finished with electoral politics. The Republican Party would have to continue on without him—preferably with one of the men who had actually won on Election Night as its new titular head. Nixon specifically mentioned governors Nelson Rockefeller of New York and Jim Rhodes of Ohio, who had been reelected, and governors-elect George Romney of Michigan and William Scranton of Pennsylvania, who had just won their first terms, as four men that could vie for the presidential nomination in 1964. "In 1964, the Republican Party will be revitalized," Nixon noted.[29] "Now, it will be revitalized, of course, provided the Republicans in California also can under new leadership—not mine—because I have fought the fight and now it's up to others to take this responsibility of leadership, and I don't say this with any bitterness, because I just feel that that's the way it should be."

He also thanked his staff and his volunteers, telling them that they did a magnificent job—kind of. "I only wish they could have gotten out a few more votes in the key precincts, but because they didn't Mr. Brown has won and I have lost the election," he said.[30] He weighed in on domestic and foreign affairs while noting that President Kennedy had a lot of things he needed to do in order to keep the country safe while revitalizing the economy.

He also said "one last thing" multiple times as he looked for the right note to go out on. First, he went the personal route. "One last thing," Nixon said.[31] "What are my plans? Well, my plans are to go home. I'm going to get acquainted with my family again. And my plans, incidentally, are, from a political standpoint, of course, to take a holiday. It will be a long holiday." A few moments later, he tried, once again, to wrap things up. This time, he tried the magnanimous route. "One last thing. People say: 'What about the past? What about losing in '60 and losing in '62?'" he said again.[32] "I did not win. I have no hard feelings against anybody, against my opponent, and least of all the people of California. We got our message through as well as we could."

Ultimately, he decided to wrap up by hitting the press one last time while seemingly writing his own epitaph.

> One last thing. At the outset, I said a couple of things with regard to the press that I noticed some of you looked a little irritated about. And my philosophy with respect to the press has really never gotten through. And I want to get it through. This cannot be said for any other American political figure today, I guess. Never in my 16 years of campaigning have I complained to a publisher, to an editor, about the coverage of a reporter. I believe a reporter has got a right to write it as he feels it. I believe if a reporter believes that one man ought to win rather than the other, rather it's on television or radio or the like, he ought to say so. I will say to the reporter sometimes that I think well, look, I wish you'd give my opponent the same going over that you give me. And as I leave the press, all I can say is this: For 16 years, ever since the Hiss case, you've had a lot of—a lot of fun—that you've had an opportunity to attack me and I think I've given as good as I've taken. It was carried right up to the last day.[33]

Finally, Nixon signed off with one of the most infamous and repeated lines in political history. "You won't have Nixon to kick around any more, because, gentlemen, this is my last press conference and it will be one in which I have welcomed the opportunity to test wits with you," he said.[34]

When he finally ended his speech, there were no smiles and no handshakes. There was no defiant "victory" pose like there would be twelve years later when Nixon boarded the White House helicopter after resigning the presidency. Instead, he left the ballroom unceremoniously and went home to face an uncertain future and a family that suddenly had their patriarch all to themselves.

It wasn't supposed to be this way.

Richard Nixon had enjoyed a meteoric rise to power that had seemed destined to land him in the White House. Instead, as he returned home from the Beverly Hilton a deflated and devastated man, he was forced to confront a new reality: he was finished as a politician, and he hadn't even turned fifty yet. His wife, Pat, and his two daughters, Tricia and Julie, had watched his defiant stand against the press on television and had cheered him on. When he arrived home, however, reality set in and all four Nixons started to absorb the full magnitude of the defeat. Pat's voice quivered as she tried to suppress tears, and all she was able to say was: "Oh, Dick!" Nixon then brushed past her and went to the backyard, where he broke down and wept. Seeing their parents in emotional turmoil was a new experience for the Nixon girls, and Tricia recalled that the dark cloud over the family, particularly between her parents, didn't dissipate for a long time. "There was a sadness," Tricia said.[35] "And the sadness went on for years."

The one thing the four Nixons agreed on was that they needed to get out of California. For Nixon, it wasn't a hard sell. As the *LA Times* would write after he passed away in 1994, Nixon had always had an ambivalent relationship with his home state. "Richard Nixon was *from* California but not really *of* California [original emphasis]," the paper wrote.[36] This ambivalence was reciprocated, as Californians never really embraced the man who, by all rights, should have been their proud standard-bearer.

He was born in 1913 in Yorba Linda to devout Quakers Francis and Hannah Milhous Nixon. For a party that values people who pull themselves up by the bootstraps and gets ahead by working hard, Nixon was the Horatio Alger of his era. He had grown up poor—so poor that he couldn't join the local Boy Scout troop because his father couldn't afford to pay the troop's dues and couldn't afford to buy Richard a uniform.[37] His parents couldn't even spare a few quarters to let Richard and his four brothers buy small twenty-five-cent firecrackers to celebrate the Fourth of July.

The reason why they were in such dire straits was because the family ranch had failed in 1922. As a result, the Nixon family was forced to leave Yorba Linda and relocate to nearby Whittier, where Frank opened a small grocery store and gas station.[38] Richard and his brothers all pitched in and helped run the store. At an age when most children have trouble getting out of bed in time to make homeroom, Richard would accompany his father to the Los Angeles vegetable market at 4:30 every morning and help him load fresh produce into his truck. Upon returning home, he'd have to wash all of the vegetables before the school bus came around at 8:00 a.m. After school, he'd go to the store where he had regular chores, like doing inventory or waiting on customers.[39] Slowly, but surely, the family's finances improved somewhat. Indeed, Nixon later said he knew things had gotten better when he and his brothers could actually go to a professional barber for their haircuts instead of relying on their father's unskilled hands.

"We were poor, but the glory of it was, we didn't know it," Nixon said to Eisenhower about his childhood.[40]

His childhood was hardly idyllic, though. Tuberculosis had struck down Richard's younger brother, Arthur, at the young age of seven. By all accounts, Arthur's death had a profound impact on Richard, who recalled crying every day for weeks after Arthur's funeral.[41] Nixon later called Arthur's death the "first sad moment in an otherwise very happy childhood."[42] Several years later, the disease reared its ugly head once again, killing Richard's older brother, Harold, when he was twenty-three years old. Because Harold's medical bills had overwhelmed his parents, Richard could not afford to attend Harvard University, even though he had been offered a full scholarship.

Instead, he enrolled at nearby Whittier College, where he was an outstanding student and active on campus. He joined the football team, the Glee Club, the debate team, and helped organize numerous on- and off-campus activities including ski trips and picnics.[43] Most notably, one of the first things he did when he enrolled at Whittier was to form his own antiestablishment student society. It was a play that he would run many decades later, and on a much larger scale, during the 1968 presidential campaign when he spoke about a "silent majority" that was sick of the antiwar movement and yearned for a return to "law and order." In his 2000 book, *Nixonland: The Rise of a President and the Fracturing of America*, Rick Perlstein writes, at length, about the social scene at Whittier and how Nixon upended the traditional order of things by forming his own power base. "Richard Nixon was a serial collector of resentments," Perlstein wrote.[44] "He raged for what he could not have or control." One of those was the fact that he just didn't fit in with the Franklins, who were the preeminent social club at Whittier. Comprised of your usual collection of "big men on campus," the Franklins were handsome, witty, rich, graceful, well spoken, and, most importantly of all, exclusive. Basically, if JFK had decided to enroll at Whittier College as an undergrad, he would have won the presidency of the Franklins in a landslide.

What Nixon realized was that the Franklins' exclusivity was also their biggest weakness. Simply put, there were more non-Franklins than Franklins, and many non-Franklins, like Nixon, resented the fact that they weren't allowed to join. So, Nixon formed his own power base at Whittier by creating the Orthogonians. "Nixon's new club, the Orthogonians, was for strivers, those not to the manner born, the commuter students like him," Perlstein wrote.[45] "He persuaded his fellows that reveling in one's unpolish was a nobility of its own." Nixon, himself, recalled that the Orthogonians lived by the "Four B's": beans, brawn, brain, and bowels, and that while the Franklins posed for their yearbook photos in tuxedos, Orthogonians wore open-necked shirts.[46]

What differentiated Nixon's base from an 1980's high school comedy where the unpopular kids rise up against the football team and cheerleaders is that Whittier's jocks actually made up much of the Orthogonians' power base. As Perlstein notes, Nixon understood sports and knew that the Franklins versus Orthogonians divide existed on every single team. After all, any team usually has, at most, a small handful of stars. Everyone else is a role player that toils in the shadows, like the lineman who blocks for the quarterback or the backup who only plays when the starter gets hurt. By winning the support of this athletic silent majority, Nixon was able to grow his power base to the point where he defeated a Franklin for student body president in a major upset. "The unpolished, after all, were everywhere in the majority," Perlstein wrote.[47] "Ever-expanding circles of Orthogonians, encompassing all those who ever felt their pride wounded by the Franklins of the world, were already his constituency."

After graduating from Whittier, Nixon enrolled at Duke University School of Law. His fascination with the law had begun during his childhood with, ironically enough, a political scandal. Frank had taken a special interest in the Teapot Dome scandal as it unfolded in 1924, which threatened to take down the administration of Warren Harding, and he would routinely condemn crooked politicians and lawyers. Dick, who followed the scandal by reading the newspapers, would proclaim to his mother one day that he wanted to be a lawyer—an honest, incorruptible lawyer whose integrity would be beyond reproach and not for sale.[48]

At Duke, he was known for having a tireless work ethic and spent almost every waking moment studying. Driven, in large part, by fear of losing his scholarship and returning home as a failure, Nixon put his studies before everything, including friendships, comfort, and his own health (he was known to eat a Milky Way candy bar every day as breakfast). In a school full of achievers and hard workers (one of his classmates, Charles Rhyne, would become a famous litigator who served as president of the American Bar Association and played a role in helping Nixon prepare for his 1968 presidential campaign), Nixon stood out from the pack. He even earned the nickname "Iron Butt" for his ability to sit in a chair inside the law library for hours hunched over books and notepads.[49]

His work ethic paid off. He earned his Juris Doctor degree in 1937, finishing third in his class while serving on the law review. These days, Duke is one of the best and most prestigious law schools in the country, and Nixon's class rank and credentials would have been enough for him to waltz into any big law firm in the country and ask when did they want him to start. In 1937, however, Duke Law was not as highly regarded as it is today. In fact, when Nixon matriculated, the school was in the middle of an aggressive campaign to increase its prestige by giving out scholarships to talented students—which is why he was able to attend in the first place.

Another strike against Nixon was the fact that the elite white-shoe Wall Street firms were very selective—and some would say discriminatory—about whom they hired. For some perspective, future Supreme Court Justice Ruth Bader Ginsburg couldn't get a single New York law firm job after graduating from Columbia Law School in 1959 despite finishing first in her class (Supreme Court Justice Felix Frankfurter even turned her down for a clerkship, saying he wasn't ready to hire a woman).[50] Meanwhile, Joseph Flom, a Harvard Law grad who was in the top 5 percent of his class, couldn't convince any of the top firms in New York to hire a Jewish lawyer like himself.[51] As such, he joined a small four-man firm in 1948 and rapidly established himself as a top transactional lawyer and a pioneer in the field of hostile takeovers. Today, his firm, Skadden, Arps, Slate, Meagher & Flom, is one of the largest, richest and most prestigious law firms in the United States.

When Nixon failed to get a job with any of the big firms he interviewed at, he was quick to blame his modest roots and pedigree. "I knew that these firms were virtually closed shops which hired only from the establishment elite of the Ivy League law schools, but I thought it would be worth a try," Nixon said.[52] "I must have looked pretty scruffy sitting in those plush polished mahogany and leather reception rooms in my one good suit." He recalled getting a cold reception from Sullivan & Cromwell, a prestigious law firm whose managing partner, John Foster Dulles, would serve as secretary of state under Eisenhower.[53] He made more headway at now-defunct Donovan, Leisure, Newton and Irvine and was offered a second interview by named-partner George Leisure.[54] However, by this point, Nixon had decided not to go the law firm route and, instead, had his eye on joining J. Edgar Hoover's FBI.

Perhaps part of him knew that the level of commitment required of a big law firm lawyer would preclude him from doing what he really wanted to be doing. "If they had given me a job I'm sure I would have been there today, a corporation lawyer instead of Vice President," Nixon said in 1959.[55] Or maybe Nixon believed that being a G-Man would be a better springboard into politics than being a Wall Street lawyer. After all, it was an exciting time to be an FBI agent. When Nixon applied, the bureau was three years removed from leading the Lindbergh baby kidnapping investigation and had also taken down several important underworld figures such as Machine Gun Kelly in 1933 and John Dillinger the following year.

However, much like his corporate law endeavors, his FBI application was also unsuccessful. Despite a glowing recommendation from H. Claude Horack, dean of Duke Law School, Nixon came up empty handed without so much as an explanation from the bureau. Years later, after Nixon had been elected vice president, Hoover told him that his application had been accepted but budget cuts had caused the appointment to fall through.

Without any options on the East Coast, Nixon had no choice but to return home to Whittier. "Richard Nixon had passionately hoped to escape Whittier and was dejected to find himself, after his prodigies at Duke University and his efforts at job-hunting in New York and at the FBI, back where he started," Conrad Black wrote.[56] In fact, he was elected president of his law school bar association after running on a platform promising to focus on finding jobs for graduates.[57] One of his ideas had been to get various local newspapers to print stories and photographs of Duke Law graduates in hope of getting them some publicity as they entered the job market. While it did make him into something of a celebrity back home in Whittier, it didn't seem to help Nixon much when it came to landing a job with a New York law firm or with the FBI.[58]

Nixon begrudgingly moved into his parents' house and, in 1937, took a job with Whittier's oldest law firm, Wingert and Bewley. He was, more or less, a country lawyer, handling a range of services including real estate transactions, divorces, leases, wills, and others.[59] According to the *LA Times*, his first client was a woman named Emma Wygal, who paid Nixon $5 to collect $700 in back payments owed to her. It was a far cry from Wall Street, and Nixon's starting salary was only $250 a month.[60]

It was also a far cry from public service, although he was able to represent the city in his capacity as assistant city attorney under the supervision of Thomas Bewley, his firm's named partner, who doubled as Whittier city attorney. Otherwise, Nixon had an up and down five years with the firm. Divorce cases made him uncomfortable, especially when female clients revealed their most intimate details to him. He was also responsible for the firm getting hit with a malpractice suit after he made a mistake filing a deed (the suit ended up settling for $4,800).[61] Nevertheless, his partners thought enough of Nixon to make him a full partner in the firm in 1939. It was a proud moment for the young lawyer, as he later recalled: "Now for the first time, I was no longer Frank and Hannah Nixon's son—I was Mr. Nixon, the new partner in Wingert and Bewley."[62]

According to Bewley, Nixon soon emerged as the top trial lawyer at the firm and was particularly skilled at conducting cross-examinations. The firm didn't handle too many trials, focusing, instead, on what Bewley called "preventative medicine." However, whenever they had a case that went to trial, Bewley found that Nixon's work was first rate. "He always seemed to be way ahead of the witness, and could anticipate the answers the witness would make," Bewley said.[63] "And he had courtroom psychology. He could talk so that butter wouldn't melt in his mouth, or he could take hold of a cantankerous witness and shake him like a dog." Nixon's trials tended to be small-dollar affairs—his first nine cases brought in fees ranging from $10 to $87.50.[64]

He also distinguished himself as a hard worker. Carrying over his work ethic from law school, Nixon frequently worked sixteen-hour days and was known to stay late—long after his co-workers had all gone home for the day. Bewley, with his busy social schedule, would often return to his office late at night where he would usually see Nixon "pacing up and down the room" with his shoulders "hunched over in his characteristic fashion" silently working through a legal issue or dictating a memo to his secretary.[65]

In some areas, however, his record was less than stellar. A partner's other major responsibility is bringing in business, and on this front, Nixon's talents were somewhat deficient. Nixon had opened a branch office for the firm in La Habra in 1939, and was tasked with signing up clients in the small town that only had two other practicing attorneys. Nixon, however, seemed clueless when it came to drumming up business for his firm. "So they sent Dick out here, and he was in an old abandoned hardware store," one La Habra lawyer recalled.[66] "He stayed out there for days on end waiting for business."

Nixon had much better luck with his love life. As the story goes, the year was 1938 and Nixon had decided to give acting a shot and joined the Whittier Community Players production of *The Dark Tower*. He was cast opposite Thelma Catherine ("Pat") Ryan, a high school teacher who immediately stole his heart. "I thought I knew everyone in Whittier, but that night a beautiful and vivacious young woman with titian hair appeared whom I had never seen before," he wrote in his memoirs.[67] "I found I could not take my eyes away from her." According to Nixon, he knew he wanted to marry her immediately, but Pat took some convincing. Eventually, they married in 1940 and soon had two daughters, Tricia and Julie.

By the end of 1941, both Nixons felt that they had outgrown Whittier and were looking to get out. Pat always enjoyed traveling, and Dick was hoping to break into politics. When Dick received a job offer from the Office of Price Administration in Washington, D.C., the Nixons packed their bags and moved to D.C. in the beginning of 1942—mere weeks after the United States entered World War II.[68] Nixon ultimately joined the U.S. Navy Reserve and served during the war, albeit in a noncombat role.

After the war, he returned to California to begin his political career. In 1946, he signed up to run for US House of Representatives for the 12th District of California and ended up defeating the incumbent, Democrat Jerry Voorhis. Nixon quickly made a mark in D.C. thanks to his work on two important committees. As a member of the Education and Labor Committee, he helped draft and pass the groundbreaking Taft-Hartley Act of 1947, which restricts the power of labor unions.

But it was on the House Un-American Activities Committee where Nixon would become a national figure. In 1948, Nixon launched an investigation into espionage allegations against Alger Hiss, a prominent attorney and diplomat who had helped establish the United Nations.[69] Nixon backed Whittaker Chambers, a reporter and former Communist spy, who had accused Hiss of passing some confidential documents to him and brought Hiss before the committee where Hiss denied Chambers's allegations under oath. After Chambers dramatically produced the documents, which, at one point, had been hidden inside a hollowed-out pumpkin on his property, Hiss lost credibility. Worse, he was on the hook for perjury and was convicted in 1950 and sentenced to five years imprisonment.

Nixon was now a star, but his newfound fame came with a cost. He recalled in his memoirs that taking on a liberal hero like Hiss had caused several influential papers to turn on him—even though he had uncovered enough evidence and testimony to prove that Hiss had, at the very least, lied under oath when testifying about his alleged ties to the Communist Party. "The Hiss case just stayed with him and never went away, and the wounds and the feeling about the press that happened there are very basic to him," Nixon's friend and aide Robert Finch said.[70] "There was, for a long time, a corrosive effect. And there was genuine anger there, I mean real anger . . . real hostility, something that went so deep as to make a man embattled."

Famed journalist David Halberstam disputed this interpretation, noting that Nixon's press coverage had been quite favorable throughout the Hiss investigation and that reporters liked Nixon because he was a constant and reliable source for them.[71] He also noted that the press, particularly the *LA Times*, favored Nixon during his contentious Senate race in 1950 against liberal Democratic congresswoman and former actress Helen Gahagan Douglas. The high-profile race is still regarded as one of the nastiest and most vicious in American history. Both candidates embraced their inner middle-schoolers and engaged in vicious name-calling and insults. Douglas became known as "The Pink Lady," after a line in one of Nixon's stump speeches where he linked her to communism by alleging that she was "pink right down to her underwear." For this and other hardball tactics, including multiple instances of push-polling, where an anonymous caller would ask voters if they were aware that Helen Douglas had married a Jew named Melvyn Hesselberg (known better as Hollywood star Melvyn Douglas), as well as an infamous campaign flier printed on pink paper comparing Douglas's voting record to radical New York congressman (and suspected Communist) Vito Marcantonio, Douglas responded by hitting Nixon with a nickname that his opponents would use on him for the rest of his life: "Tricky Dick."[72]

The *LA Times* also did its part, attacking Douglas in editorials and refusing to challenge Nixon's allegations. The *Times* focused on the Communist angle while ignoring issues that were more favorable to Douglas. The paper would report any positive development in the Nixon campaign, such as Democrats crossing party lines to support him or volunteer groups working overtime to help him, while virtually ignoring Douglas, refusing to even print her campaign schedules.[73] In the end, the high-profile race between two rising stars wasn't much of a contest. Nixon won in a landslide, and Douglas never ran for political office again.

Instead, it wasn't until 1952, when Nixon earned, and nearly lost, the opportunity of a lifetime, that his relationship with the media reached its point of no return. In September 1952, two months after he was nominated for vice president, several newspapers began running stories about a previously undisclosed political fund set up by Nixon's former campaign manager, Murray Chotiner, and others. The fund was, ostensibly, set up to collect donations to reimburse Nixon for various expenses beyond his Senate allowances. In reality, however, it was to allow Nixon to continue campaigning throughout his Senate term so that he'd be well placed to run for reelection (a race that became moot when he was elected vice president in 1952). For instance, the fund would allow Nixon to travel to and from California more frequently and be reimbursed beyond his Senate mileage allowance. Nixon could also send out more mail and make more telephone calls if he had funds in addition to his Senate expense account.[74]

The fund, which contained approximately $18,000,[75] was legal, but it reeked of impropriety. The *New York Post*, which was one of the first papers to report on the fund, used the following headline: "Secret Rich Men's Trust Fund Keeps Nixon in Style Far beyond His Salary." Other newspapers started calling for his resignation from the ticket, including the *Washington Post* and *New York Herald Tribune*.[76] Eisenhower and his advisors seemed to be leaning toward kicking Nixon out, and Nixon himself was concerned that his place as vice presidential nominee was in danger.[77]

Unlike how he would handle the Watergate break-in twenty years later, Nixon decided to get in front of the burgeoning scandal and put all of his cards out on the table. The Republican National Committee and the national senatorial and congressional campaign committees paid $75,000 for half-an-hour of television time, and on the evening of September 23, before an audience of nearly sixty million, Nixon went about making his case to the American people. Armed with documents from the law firm of Gibson, Dunn & Crutcher confirming the legality of the fund, Nixon wrapped his defense of the fund around a compelling narrative about his family finances. "Every penny of it was used to pay for political expenses that I did not think should be charged to the taxpayers of the United States."[78] Nixon also made sure to point out that he had not gotten rich as a result of his fund, and laid out, in painstaking detail, his family's finances, which included two mortgages and a couple of outstanding loans, a 1950 Oldsmobile, and no stocks or bonds.

Nixon said that his modest means extended to his family, pointing out that his wife, Pat, "doesn't have a mink coat"—instead she wore "a respectable Republican cloth coat." Nixon did say that he got one gift that he decided to keep—a cocker spaniel from a donor in Texas that his daughters fell in love with and decided to name Checkers.

The "Checkers speech," as it became known, did wonders for Nixon. He was mobbed by well wishers and supporters as he walked back to his hotel after delivering the speech. Telegrams started pouring into the RNC headquarters at a rate of some four thousand an hour—most of them were in support of the embattled Nixon.[79] While Eisenhower reserved his final judgment for a few days, in the end, the general decided to stick with Nixon.[80]

Even though things had worked out, Nixon remained bitter toward the media for the rest of his career. "I regarded what had been done to me as character assassination, and the experience permanently and powerfully affected my attitude toward the press in particular and the news media in general," Nixon wrote in his memoirs.[81] William Safire, a speechwriter who worked on Nixon's presidential campaigns, later wrote that, during the 1968 presidential race, Nixon would often remind his senior aides "the press is the enemy."[82] He was even less charitable to Leo Katcher, the *New York Post* reporter that had originally written the story about Nixon's fund. "Tell your brother he's a son of a bitch," Nixon later told Katcher's brother, Edward.[83]

Perhaps that's why the media seemed keen to take a victory lap after Nixon's defeat and self-implosion. *Time* magazine declared Nixon's political career to be dead,[84] while James "Scotty" Reston of the *New York Times* called Nixon "unelected and unmourned, an unemployed lawyer."[85] ABC inadvertently lent Nixon a helping hand when it broadcast "The Political Obituary of Richard Nixon" on the Sunday after the election. Journalist Howard Smith hosted a documentary that included interviews with two Nixon allies, Murray Chotiner and Republican congressman (and future Nixon vice president) Gerald Ford, as well as two Nixon enemies, Jerry Voorhis and Alger Hiss. The appearance of Hiss on the program resulted in an uproar as viewers took umbrage with Smith's decision to provide the convicted perjurer with a platform to denounce the guy who got him. "[Nixon] was less interested in developing the facts objectively than in seeking ways of making a preconceived plan appear plausible," Hiss said when asked about Nixon's conduct toward him. "I regard his actions as motivated by ambition, by personal self-serving."

According to Smith himself,[86] ABC was flooded with nearly sixty thousand angry letters. The pressure was such that James Hagerty, the network's vice president in charge of news (and former White House press secretary under Eisenhower), felt compelled to defend his network's use of Hiss, while emphasizing that he was "against Hiss and everything he stands for."[87] Instead, Hagerty pointed out that Hiss was a newsmaker and that he had, undoubtedly, played a major role in Nixon's political career.

ABC stood by Smith but couldn't find companies to sponsor the program following the season, and Smith's show was eventually cancelled. Smith's career didn't recover for six years, ironically enough, right around the time a certain ex-politician was preparing to run for president.[88]

Nixon, meanwhile, played the incident perfectly and even got some sympathy as a result of Hiss's comments. "What does an attack by one convicted perjurer mean when weighed on the scale against thousands of wires and letters from patriotic Americans?" Nixon said in a statement at the time.[89] In his memoirs, he reflected: "The immediate uproar of this remark helped to turn me from the sore loser of the 'last press conference' into something of an injured party."[90]

Indeed, Nixon's 1962 loss and subsequent meltdown may have actually helped pave the way for his comeback in 1968. For one thing, it took him out of the running in 1964, avoiding what he assumed, then, would be a rematch with Kennedy. Nixon knew how hard it was to unseat an incumbent president, and the last thing he wanted was to become the next Adlai Stevenson, who had waged two consecutive losing campaigns to Eisenhower and was finished as a national politician even before all of the ballots were counted the second time around. "Far from wanting to use the state-house in Sacramento to launch another Presidential bid in 1964, as Brown successfully charged in the 1962 campaign, Nixon actually hoped to use it as a four-year hiding place, from which he could avoid making another losing race against Kennedy," Jules Witcover wrote in *The Resurrection of Richard Nixon.*[91] "Inherent in his decision to run for governor was a Presidential timetable not of 1964, but of 1968, when he finally did make his second try."

Nixon, himself, would eventually subscribe to this view, saying that the 1962 loss helped him because, otherwise, he would have either been drafted as the candidate in 1964 and lost to the unbeatable Lyndon Johnson that year, or he would have suffered a humiliating defeat at the 1964 GOP National Convention to eventual nominee Barry Goldwater, ending his national ambitions once and for all. "There is no question that running for governor was a bad risk," Nixon said.[92] "But the road to victory is sometimes paved with defeat."

In fact, Stephen Ambrose argued that the "last press conference" was actually the start of his presidential race—the reporters just didn't know it because they were too busy watching the train wreck unfold before them. "The story that the reporters had missed was that Nixon had just made the press an issue," Ambrose wrote. "Nixon knew that the national press did not speak for or to millions of Republicans. He understood and enunciated a point of view: that the press was liberal, Democratic, do-gooder, pro-big government and big labor for high taxes, yet craven in the face of the Communist menace, and always out to give the shaft to Republicans."[93] Indeed, it's a play that many Republicans continue to run today, and it's one of the main reasons for the overwhelming success of Fox News, a network that was launched by former Nixon media consultant Roger Ailes.

It's possible that Nixon, at the time of his on-stage meltdown, truly believed he was finished as a politician. He was under no illusions about how damaging the loss to Brown, as well as his temper tantrum, had been to his political prospects. "He felt as though he were through with politics," Chotiner said many years later.[94] "Not by choice, but by outcome." He knew he had come across as a poor sport and that no one liked a sore loser. As he was leaving the stage, he had said to Klein: "Damn it, I know you didn't want me to do that, but I had to say it!"[95]

However, as Witcover argued, Nixon was, by nature, a political animal, and he was never going to be content being away from the game. "Nixon never permitted the thought to enter his mind that he would get out of politics—public life, party activity, discussion of issues—altogether," Witcover wrote.[96] As such, Nixon may not have been thinking about the White House as he arrived home from the Beverly Hilton that November morning—except that his ultimate goal seemed further away than ever.

Nevertheless, given his subsequent moves and choices, it was clear that he had decided to position himself so that he would remain an important voice on national and international issues. Nixon likened the political world to "the big leagues," and he was determined to stay in the game—even if he didn't get to be the star player anymore. If he couldn't be president, and as Witcover noted, it certainly looked that way, there were many other roles within the party or country that he could fill.[97] And who knew? American politics were always changing, and just because things looked bleak for him in 1962 didn't mean that they would remain so.

Years later, Nixon remarked that the press conference had "served a purpose." "The press had a guilt complex about their inaccuracy," he argued.[98] "Since then, they've become more accurate and respectful." In fact, he admitted that he had gone on his tirade to serve notice that he was done being the media's whipping boy and that he wished he had done it sooner.[99] "I believe that it gave the media a warning that I would not sit back and take whatever biased coverage was dished out to me," Nixon said.[100] If he were truly finished as a politician, then this begs the question why he would care about his press coverage in the future. Instead, as Ambrose argued, Nixon knew he would run for president again and all he had to do was be ready to seize the opportunity when it came around. "He used his assets shrewdly, and succeeded with the qualities that had made him successful in the past—hard work, boldness, risk taking and attacking the Democrats," Ambrose wrote.[101]

Most importantly, Nixon had learned his lesson about the price of losing his temper. "From the moment of his disastrous 'last press conference,' the man embarked on a determined effort never again to inflict damage on himself through lack of self-discipline," Witcover wrote.[102] In that regard, being a lawyer helped him because, if there's anything they teach you in law school, it's that every word matters and lawyers must choose them carefully.

In the meantime, he needed a break—from everything. Politically, his reputation was toxic, and after two consecutive losses, the only race he could have possibly won was for county coroner—and only because the voters probably would have gotten a kick out of seeing him surrounded by corpses who were as dead as his White House ambitions. He was a divisive figure who seemed to inspire suspicion, distrust, and even hate. Moreover, many of his biggest and most serious professional wounds had been self-inflicted. A move to the private sector would allow him to leave the echo chamber of electoral politics, broadening his horizons while giving him access to intelligent minds and different points of view. In other words, leaving politics, if only for a little while, could allow Richard Nixon to think differently. And everyone was pretty much in agreement that Nixon, if he ever wanted to have a future in electoral politics, needed to be different.

And he had to get out of California. Luckily, he had some friends in high places that would help him find a nice landing place.

NOTES

1. Richard Nixon, *RN: The Memoirs of Richard Nixon* (New York: Simon & Schuster, 2013).
2. Richard Nixon, *In the Arena: A Memoir of Victory, Defeat and Renewal* (New York: Simon & Schuster, 1990), 196–97.
3. Nixon, *RN*.
4. Nixon, *RN*.
5. Kurt Schuparra, *Triumph of the Right: The Rise of the California Conservative Movement, 1945–1966* (Armonk, NY: M. E. Sharpe, 1998).
6. Valerie Nelson, "Ex-Legislator Challenged Nixon," *Los Angeles Times*, April 11, 2008, accessed on January 15, 2016, http://articles.latimes.com/2008/apr/11/local/me-shell11.
7. "Nation: Progressive Conservative." *Time*, June 15, 1962, accessed on January 20, 2016, http://content.time.com/time/magazine/article/0,9171,873594,00.html.
8. Keith Wheeler, "The Campaigns Get Cracking," *Life*, October 5, 1962. Also: Rick Perlstein, *Nixonland: The Rise of a President and the Fracturing of America* (New York, Scribner, 2010), 60.
9. F. Clinton White and William Gill, *Suite 3505: The Story of the Draft Goldwater Movement* (Ashland, OH: Ashbrook Press, 1967).
10. Jonathan Aitken, *Nixon: A Life* (Washington, DC: Regnery History, 1993), 29-30.
11. Nelson, "Ex-Legislator Challenged Nixon."
12. Caspar Weinberger with Gretchen Roberts, *In the Arena: A Memoir of the 20th Century* (Washington, DC: Regnery Publishing, 2001), 130.
13. George Skelton, "Sacramento's Savvy Sophomore," *Los Angeles Times*, September 4, 2000, accessed on January 20, 2016, http://articles.latimes.com/2000/sep/04/news/mn-15350.
14. David Halberstam, *The Powers That Be* (New York: Open Road Media, 2012), 350.
15. Stephen Ambrose, *Nixon: Volume 1, The Education of a Politician, 1913–1962* (New York: Simon & Schuster, 1987), 661–65.
16. Halberstam, *The Powers That Be*, 346.

17. Nixon, *RN*.
18. Matt Lait, "Looking Back at the 1962 Gubernatorial Race: Debate: Edmund G. (Pat) Brown and Ex-President's Former Campaign Manager Discuss the Election at Richard Nixon Library & Birthplace," *Los Angeles Times*, March 22, 1992, accessed on January 20, 2016, http://articles.latimes.com/1992-03-22/local/me-7477_1_richard-nixon.
19. Jules Witcover, *The Resurrection of Richard Nixon* (New York: G. P. Putnam's Sons, 1970), 31.
20. Halberstam, *The Powers That Be*, 348.
21. Maarja Krusten, "Speculating about Slurred Speech," *Washington Post*, December 7, 1996, accessed January 29, 2017, https://www.washingtonpost.com/archive/opinions/1996/12/07/speculating-about-slurred-speech/e4aa96a7-4c86-4967-9f38-7abcf52cd4af/.
22. Brian Williams, "The 'Last Press Conference,'" *NBC News Daily Nightly*, November 7, 2007, accessed January 29, 2017, http://dailynightly.nbcnews.com/_news/2007/11/07/4373652-the-last-press-conference.
23. Nixon, *RN*.
24. Herbert Klein, exit interview by John R. Nesbitt and Terry W. Good, July 13, 1973, accessed January 29, 2017, http://www.nixonlibrary.gov/virtuallibrary/documents/exitinterviews/klein-exit.pdf.
25. Roger Stone, *Nixon's Secrets: The Rise, Fall, and Untold Truth about the President, Watergate, and the Pardon* (New York: Skyhorse Publishing, 2014), 189–92.
26. John Ehrlichman, *Witness to Power: The Nixon Years* (New York: Simon Schuster, 1982), 33.
27. " Transcript of Richard Nixon's 'Last Press Conference,'" University of Pennsylvania, accessed March 4, 2016, http://languagelog.ldc.upenn.edu/myl/RichardNixonConcession.html.
28. " Transcript of Richard Nixon's 'Last Press Conference.'"
29. " Transcript of Richard Nixon's 'Last Press Conference.'"
30. " Transcript of Richard Nixon's 'Last Press Conference.'"
31. " Transcript of Richard Nixon's 'Last Press Conference.'"
32. " Transcript of Richard Nixon's 'Last Press Conference.'"
33. " Transcript of Richard Nixon's 'Last Press Conference.'"
34. " Transcript of Richard Nixon's 'Last Press Conference.'"
35. Julie Nixon Eisenhower, *Pat Nixon: The Untold Story* (New York: Simon & Schuster, 1986), 216.
36. Bill Stall, "Richard Nixon: 1913–1994: Nixon's Relations with California Ran Hot and Cold," *Los Angeles Times*, April 24, 1994, accessed January 10, 2016, http://articles.latimes.com/1994-04-24/news/mn-49906_1_richard-nixon.
37. Aitken, *Nixon: A Life*, 13.
38. "Biography of Richard M. Nixon," Richard Nixon Presidential Library and Museum, accessed January 10, 2016, http://www.nixonlibrary.gov/thelife/nixonbio.pdf.
39. Aitken, *Nixon: A Life*, 21.
40. Aitken, *Nixon: A Life*, 13.
41. Nixon, *RN*.
42. Aitken, *Nixon: A Life*, 26.
43. Aitken, *Nixon: A Life*, 32.
44. Perlstein, *Nixonland*.
45. Perlstein, *Nixonland*.
46. Nixon, *RN*.
47. Perlstein, *Nixonland*.
48. Ambrose, *Nixon, Volume 1*, 29.
49. Ambrose, *Nixon, Volume 1*, 74. Also Evan Thomas, "Did Nixon Start the Politics of Hate?" *Newsweek*, May 8, 2008, accessed August 26, 2017, http://www.newsweek.com/evan-thomas-did-nixon-start-politics-hate-89829.
50. "Rejected by the Firm," Makers, accessed January 10, 2016, http://www.makers.com/moments/rejected-firm. Also Neil Lewis, "The Supreme Court: Woman in the News; Rejected as a Clerk, Chosen as a Justice: Ruth Joan Bader Ginsburg," *New York Times*, June 15, 1993,

accessed January 10, 2016, http://www.nytimes.com/1993/06/15/us/supreme-court-woman-rejected-clerk-chosen-justice-ruth-joan-bader-ginsburg.html.

51. Victor Li, "Joseph Flom, Pioneering M&A Lawyer and Skadden Name Partner, Dies at 87," *Am Law Daily*, February 23, 2011, accessed January 10, 2016, http://amlawdaily.typepad.com/amlawdaily/2011/02/flomobit.html.

52. Aitken, *Nixon: A Life*, 76.

53. Ambrose, *Nixon: Volume 1*, 81.

54. Aitken, *Nixon: A Life*, 76.

55. Ambrose, *Nixon: Volume 1*, 81.

56. Conrad Black, *Richard M. Nixon: A Life in Full* (New York: PublicAffairs, 2007), 38.

57. Black, *Richard M. Nixon*, 37.

58. Black, *Richard M. Nixon*, 38.

59. Paul Carter, "Before He Was President, He Was a Local Attorney," *OC Lawyer*, March 2011, accessed on February 1, 2017, http://www.virtualonlineeditions.com/display_article.php?id=650716.

60. Janice Jones, "Nixon's Law Office," *Los Angeles Times*, July 18, 1990, accessed on January 10, 2016, http://articles.latimes.com/1990-07-18/news/vw-785_1_law-office.

61. Black, *Richard M. Nixon*, 38–40.

62. Ambrose, *Nixon: Volume 1*, 90.

63. Ambrose, *Nixon: Volume 1*.

64. Carter, "Before He Was President, He Was a Local Attorney."

65. Ambrose, *Nixon: Volume 1*, 88.

66. Ambrose, *Nixon: Volume 1*, 90.

67. Nixon, *RN*.

68. Aitken, *Nixon: A Life*, 95, and Roger Morris, *Richard Milhous Nixon: The Rise of an American Politician* (New York: Henry Holt & Co., 1991), 124–26.

69. Aitken, *Nixon: A Life*, 134–35.

70. John A. Farrell, "When Nixon Met the Press," *Politico*, August 6, 2014, accessed January 10, 2016, http://www.politico.com/magazine/story/2014/08/nixon-and-the-media-109773_Page2.html -ixzz3HCGflm9C.

71. Halberstam, *The Powers That Be*, 259.

72. Sally Denton, "'Tricky Dick' vs. The Pink Lady," *Daily Beast*, November 16, 2009, accessed on January 10, 2016, http://www.thedailybeast.com/articles/2009/11/16/tricky-dick-vs-the-pink-lady.html.

73. Halberstam, *The Powers That Be*, 262–63.

74. Lee Huebner, "The Checkers Speech after 60 Years," *The Atlantic*, September 22, 2012, accessed on January 12, 2016, http://www.theatlantic.com/politics/archive/2012/09/the-checkers-speech-after-60-years/262172/.

75. Gladwin Hill, "Nixon Leaves Fate to G.O.P. Chiefs," *New York Times*, September 24, 1952, accessed on January 12, 2016, http://events.nytimes.com/learning/general/specials/elections/1952/featured_article1.html.

76. Nixon, *RN*.

77. Nixon, *RN*.

78. "Primary Resources: Checkers Speech, 1952," PBS.org, accessed January 9, 2016, http://archive.li/C1pFS.

79. Jeffrey Frank, *Ike and Dick: Portrait of a Strange Political Marriage* (New York: Simon & Schuster Paperbacks, 2013), 55.

80. Nixon, *RN*. According to Nixon, Thomas Dewey had told him that Eisenhower's advisors wanted him to resign from the ticket at the end of his speech. Dewey, however, hadn't confirmed it with Eisenhower, and Nixon refused to resign without that bit of confirmation. After the speech, Eisenhower gave a speech supporting Nixon but said he'd wait until he met with Nixon face to face before making a decision. An enraged Nixon then dictated a resignation telegram but never sent it. Ultimately, the two met in Wheeling, West Virginia, and Nixon remained on the ticket.

81. Nixon, *RN*.

82. William Safire, *Safire's Political Dictionary* (London: Oxford University Press, 2008), 114.

83. Morris, *Richard Milhous Nixon*, 762.

84. "Nation: California: Career's End," *Time*, November 16, 1962, accessed January 9, 2016, http://content.time.com/time/magazine/article/0,9171,829391,00.html.

85. Stone, *Nixon's Secrets*, 197.

86. James Kates, "Kicking Nixon: Howard K. Smith and the Commentator's Imperative," ARNet, accessed on January 24, 2016, http://www.americansc.org.uk/Online/Nixon.html.

87. "ABC's Hagerty Defends Use of Hiss on TV Show," *Evening Independent*, November 19, 1962, accessed on January 24, 2016, http://news.google.com/newspapers?nid=950&dat=19621119&id=dEdQAAAAIBAJ&sjid=-lYDAAAAIBAJ&pg=6595,2424225.

88. Harold Jackson, "Howard K. Smith," *The Guardian*, February 19, 2002.

89. "Richard Nixon Sends a Message," *Chicago Tribune*, November 18, 1962, accessed on February 22, 2017, http://archives.chicagotribune.com/1962/11/18/page/1/article/how-u-s-probers-tripped-alger-hiss.

90. Nixon, *RN*.

91. Witcover, *The Resurrection of Richard Nixon*, 22–23.

92. Nixon, *In the Arena*, 196–97.

93. Stephen Ambrose, *Nixon, Volume 2: The Triumph of a Politician, 1962–1972*, (New York: Simon & Schuster, 1989), 12.

94. Witcover, *The Resurrection of Richard Nixon*, 32.

95. Stone, *Nixon's Secrets*, 194.

96. Witcover, *The Resurrection of Richard Nixon*, 32.

97. Witcover, *The Resurrection of Richard Nixon*, 33.

98. Ambrose, *Nixon: Volume 2*, 13.

99. "Frank Gannon's Interview with Richard Nixon, Part 1," University of Georgia, September 7, 1983, accessed March 29, 2017, http://www.libs.uga.edu/media/collections/nixon/ohms/sept7part1.html.

100. Nixon, *RN*.

101. Ambrose, *Nixon: Volume 2*, 13.

102. Witcover, *The Resurrection of Richard Nixon*, 34.

Chapter Two

"A Politician Does Not Change His Base."

Four months after his "last press conference," Richard Nixon seemed to be making good on his vow to leave politics. A few days before St. Patrick's Day in 1963, he had a job interview with several partners from the Wall Street law firm Mudge, Stern, Baldwin & Todd. The last time he had interviewed with a white-shoe law firm in New York, he had been a law student and, like many aspiring lawyers before and after him, he had squeezed into an interview suit he hardly ever wore and sat, nervously, in the waiting room of the managing partner's office hoping to distinguish himself from the hundreds of competitors equally desperate for the job.

This was a different type of interview.

The former vice president and his future law partners played a round at the Baltusrol Golf Club in New Jersey in a game that was part job interview, part recruiting pitch from the firm that would soon bear his name. The interview was hardly a formality, though. John Alexander, tax group leader at the firm and one of Mudge's most important partners, was skeptical. After all, this wasn't Nixon's first go-around in the legal field. After losing the presidential election in 1960, Nixon had returned home to California and joined the firm of Adams, Duque & Hazeltine. While there, he had spent more time writing his memoirs and campaigning for governor than practicing law or bringing in clients. Alexander was worried about history repeating itself and wanted to know what the firm would get out of hiring Nixon.

"Dick," Alexander said while enjoying a round of drinks with the former vice president on the so-called nineteenth hole at the golf course. "I've always admired you and feel that you are a man of great competence—except on the golf course." After some good-natured laughter from the rest of the party, Alexander then got to the point. "You could bring a lot to our firm. But

I wouldn't be honest with you or myself if I didn't say that I have a significant reservation about your coming with us." Alexander then brought up the Adams Duque experience and told Nixon that "scant attention was paid to the practice of law" and that "the experience was a huge disappointment to most of your partners." Alexander then paused before driving home his main point. "We don't want to go through that here."[1]

It was a stunning moment for Nixon and Elmer Bobst, the CEO of pharmaceutical company Warner-Lambert Corporation, Mudge's biggest client. Bobst, a close friend of Nixon's, had been the one who had suggested the union between Nixon and Mudge in the first place. Neither was used to being questioned, and Bobst, who had come to Baltusrol thinking that deal was already done, sat in stone-faced silence as Alexander conducted his inquiry. The other Mudge partners sat, grim faced and stoic, as they watched Nixon, intently, to see how he might react.

Nixon, however, handled the situation deftly. His tenure with Adams Duque had been distorted, he argued. For one thing, he and law firm leader Earl Adams had agreed, beforehand, that Nixon would be allowed to juggle his law practice with writing his memoirs and running for governor. As for his main point, however, Nixon understood where Alexander was coming from. "Do I intend to spend my time practicing or will I be dabbling in politics?" Nixon asked rhetorically.[2] "The answer is I intend to devote my full time to the firm." Nixon then referenced the last press conference and reiterated that he was through with politics. "John, if you knew anything about politics, you would know that a politician does not change his base," Nixon said.[3] "I made my intentions known fairly emphatically in my 'last press conference.' Those words were crystal clear, John, but my actions are even more so. A politician does not give up his base."

The answer seemed to satisfy Alexander, who promptly dropped his reservations about Nixon joining the firm. It's not clear whether he noticed that Nixon's answer was hardly unequivocal in its nature, and gave him plenty of wiggle room should he decide to make a political comeback in the future. In other words, it was a perfect response from a lawyer.

The idea that Nixon would give up his political base to move to a city that, almost literally, belonged to Nelson Rockefeller, his biggest rival in the Republican Party, was a shocking move. For one thing, California was one of the best and most powerful bases to have for any politician who had presidential aspirations. Along with Pennsylvania, the state was the joint second largest in terms of electoral votes during the 1960 presidential election, and would be alone in second place by the 1964 contest. California was quickly becoming the most populous state in the country, and it was hardly a stretch to say that the road to the White House would, one day, go through Sacramento.

Plus, Nixon was a student of history. He was aware that the political world had been littered with comeback stories and second acts. Franklin D. Roosevelt survived polio and a landslide loss as a vice presidential candidate in 1920 to win four terms in the White House. Grover Cleveland had been drummed out of the White House in 1888, only to come back four years later and win another term. Even Herbert Hoover, one of the most unpopular and maligned presidents in American history, tried for the White House again, making it to the fifth ballot at the 1940 Republican National Convention before losing to eventual nominee Wendell Willkie. History showed that Nixon was far from finished as a politician, and conventional wisdom held that if he wanted to launch any sort of comeback, even after his loss to Brown and subsequent temper tantrum, then he would have to find a job in California where he could make a living while still being active in politics.

Nixon, however, had other ideas. Many of his friends and political colleagues were encouraging him to move East, and Nixon immediately saw the advantages of setting up shop in the Big Apple. "I think Nixon felt that the West Coast was like a cow town and that the big league was in New York, and he was big league," said future Nixon appointments secretary Dwight Chapin.[4] Besides the bitterness and disappointment from the 1962 loss, Chapin noted that New York, not Los Angeles, was a worldwide hub for important business people, as well as public officials from both home and abroad. "So, in order to really keep his contacts and to maximize his earning power . . . the New York strategy makes sense—outside of the political," Chapin said. New York also made sense for Nixon considering its importance on the world stage. "There was no foreign policy angle in California," a Nixon aide said to Witcover.[5] "It had to be the east. He had to have his cake (money) and eat it too (his interest in foreign policy)."

Mostly, Nixon was bored living on the West Coast and, to paraphrase Frank Sinatra, wanted to live in a city that never sleeps. "New York is very cold and very ruthless and very exciting," Nixon said to the *LA Times*.[6] "It's a place where you can't slow down."

Once New York became a possibility, it seemed to lift the Nixons' collective spirits. Dick and Pat Nixon may have had a storybook start to their relationship, but by the time of the 1962 gubernatorial contest, their marriage was at its nadir. Pat, the dutiful wife, had been a loyal soldier for Dick during all of his political campaigns. But her enthusiasm for the spotlight, which had never been all that high to begin with, had shrunken to an all-time low by the time Nixon was wrapping up his 1962 campaign. Pat had always been firmly against the gubernatorial race, and had even told *Ladies' Home Journal* in November 1962 that she wanted Dick to sit this one out, hinting at the strain that his constant campaigning had put his family under. "As nearly as I can define my attitude, [it was]: Let's stay home," she had said.[7] "Let's be a private family. Let's take a vacation trip when we want to. Let's not be leaders but instead, make our contribution in other ways."

Nixon wrote that he felt he owed his family one after he had run for governor over their objections and recalled that Pat was especially in favor of the move, believing that it would preclude him from running for office again. "I was reluctant to uproot Pat and the girls again, but since the election California held much less charm for them, and I found they were quite excited by the prospect of living in New York," Nixon said.[8] Nixon promoted the idea that it had been Pat and his family that had made the call to move to New York, telling well-known political columnist (and Republican) Roscoe Drummond of the *LA Times* that he agreed with his wife that he had to leave California or else he would be under constant pressure to run for office again.[9] Within a few weeks of moving to New York, Pat seemed happier than she had been in years. "I hope we never have to move again," she told her husband during dinner two weeks after moving in their new twelve-room, $135,000 apartment at 810 Fifth Avenue.[10]

There were also compelling political reasons to leave California. For one thing, he could avoid getting dragged even further into the intraparty civil war that was going on between conservatives and moderates in the state. Nixon was already carrying some battle scars as a result of his clash with Shell in the 1962 gubernatorial primary, and he would only get more if he continued to lead the party. His only real rival within the state GOP was Thomas Kuchel, a moderate-to-liberal senator who seemed to relish in bucking his party.[11] He had already crossed Nixon by refusing to endorse him in the 1962 gubernatorial race, and would run into more trouble when he wouldn't endorse Barry Goldwater, the GOP presidential nominee, in 1964. Kuchel's battles with the rising conservative tide in his party would lead him into a collision course with the person who ultimately replaced Nixon as the leader of the California GOP: Ronald Reagan.

"Had I stayed in California, I would still be this titular head of the Republican Party," Nixon noted.[12] "Now, being titular head is about as useful as being the fifth tit on a cow."

Moving to a new state would allow him to remain above the fray—commenting only on important national and international issues while ignoring state and local issues he cared little for, and avoiding intraparty politics. Likewise being untethered to a particular geographic base would allow him to weigh in on matters he wanted to without worry as to how it might play to his constituents back home. Being in New York, under the thumb of Rockefeller, would also allow him to avoid the pressure of running for office, something he had been unable to do in California. After all, how could he possibly try to compete with the longtime governor of New York, who was first elected in 1958 and wouldn't leave office until 1973 when he became vice president of the United States under Gerald Ford, and was the prohibitive favorite for the GOP presidential nomination in 1964? "Despite my defeat by Brown, I could still play an important, if not uncontested, leadership role in the Republican Party in California," Nixon recalled.[13] "But leaving my political base and moving to a state in which all political power was firmly held by Nelson Rockefeller, my principal rival, would be an announcement that I was ruling myself out as an active political figure for the foreseeable future."

Plus, if Nixon ever doubted the extent of Nelson Rockefeller's power in New York, all he had to do was take a ride in the elevator all the way to the top of his new apartment building. Rockefeller may have been Nixon's new neighbor, but just because they shared the same roof didn't mean that Nixon was in Rockefeller's league when it came to finances or living space. In fact, calling Rockefeller "wealthy" was almost understating it. With access to the kind of fortune most people only read about or see on screen, Rockefeller could, pretty much, do whatever he wanted. Having originally purchased a luxurious thirty-room triplex that took up the top three floors of the building, when Rockefeller and his first wife, Mary, got divorced in 1962, they worked out an agreement so that they'd both keep the apartment. Mary got the top two floors while Nelson and his new wife, Margaretta (she was nicknamed "Happy"), kept the other floor. As it turned out, this wasn't nearly enough space for the governor and his new wife, so he did what any man with near-unlimited resources and political power would have done. He purchased the corresponding floor of the building next door, 812 Fifth Avenue, knocked down the wall between the buildings, and built a staircase to connect the two suites together.[14] By doing this, he and his ex-wife could minimize their contact with one another since he would use the entrance at 812 Fifth Avenue while Mary would continue using the one at 810.

Rockefeller's wealth and influence weren't limited to his domicile. A quick jaunt around New York City only underscored just how much clout Rockefeller and his family had. Twelve blocks to the south of Nixon's new apartment was Rockefeller Center. Rockefeller Institute was seven blocks east. The Rockefeller Foundation was on West 50th Street, a stone's throw from the theater district that Nixon enjoyed going to. The old Standard Oil building, home to the oil behemoth founded by Rockefeller's grandfather, John D. Rockefeller, was a quarter-mile from Nixon's law firm. Rockefeller had even helped secure funding, as well as the land, for the United Nations building located near the East River. If any family owned New York City, it was the Rockefellers.

Obviously, Nixon wasn't looking to steal Rockefeller's base from under his nose. Instead, his move to New York—the "fast track" as he called it, was all about finding a well-paying job that would allow him to remain active in politics, as well as travel the world.[15] Nixon had several options on the table before he ever met with the folks from Mudge; Chrysler Corporation was looking at him to be their next chairman, while two major universities had offered him their school presidencies.

Nixon, however, had come to the conclusion that working for a big law firm was an ideal way for him to continue engaging in partisan politics while traveling the world and augmenting his foreign policy credentials. All he had to do was find a law firm that would give him a nice salary, as well as plenty of time to do what he wanted to do. Thanks to some deep-pocketed friends in high places, Richard Nixon and the lawyers at what would soon be Nixon, Mudge, Rose, Guthrie & Alexander found that they were a match made in heaven.

"NEW BLOOD AT THE TOP."

Long before Pepsi had the likes of Michael Jackson, Madonna, or Shaq as a celebrity endorser, it had Nikita Khrushchev and Richard Milhous Nixon.

Their commercial for Pepsi didn't include pyrotechnics, choreographed dancing, catchy jingles, or sex appeal—unless you consider a debate over the merits of capitalism versus communism between the vice president of the United States and the premier of the Soviet Union sexy. In 1959, Nixon was visiting Moscow when he and Soviet leader Khrushchev made a joint appearance at the American National Exhibition at Sokolniki Park. The exhibition was held to promote cultural understanding between Russians and Americans, but the two leaders took the opportunity to engage in an impromptu debate that started inside the kitchen of an American-style display house and continued all over the showroom floor, with the two men gesticulating and jabbing fingers at one another while reporters and cameramen recorded everything. When they got to the Pepsi-Cola stand (which featured two different Pepsi drinks: one made in the United States and one made with Russian water), that's when it happened.

> The company's new slogan was "Be Sociable! Have a Pepsi!" What better ad than a picture of America's foremost adversary (and the scourge of Coca-Cola, which the Party in Europe equated with capitalist decadence) acting sociable over a Pepsi made in the USSR?[16] "Don't worry about it Don," Nixon is said to have told Pepsi's CEO, Donald Kendall. "I'll bring Khrushchev by and we'll get a Pepsi in his hand."[17]

Pepsi's photographer got numerous shots of Khrushchev drinking Pepsi-Cola. Obviously, the Soviet leader preferred the one with Russian water, and touted its superiority over the American version, calling it "quite refreshing."[18] It may not have had the same cultural impact of Joanie Sommers singing "It's Pepsi, for Those Who Think Young," but it was no less effective. After all, in a totalitarian society like the Soviet Union, if the leader drank something, then everyone drank it.[19] As such, Kendall was able to negotiate a fifteen-year exclusive deal with the USSR shortly after the expo ended—a deal that, effectively, shut Coke out of the Communist stronghold.[20]

Kendall was grateful to Nixon for his role in making it happen. "We got front-page publicity all over the world, 'Khrushchev learns to be sociable,'" Kendall recalled.[21] "The publicity was unbelievable. It saved my job." So when Nixon started job hunting in 1962, Kendall paid him back by giving him a very important chit to play with potential employers. He made it known that whichever firm hired Nixon would also get Pepsi, with its annual billings in excess of $3 million,[22] as a client.[23]

Despite that, there weren't a whole lot of firms lining up to hire the former vice president. After all, Nixon's demands were steep. He was looking for an annual salary in the neighborhood of $250,000 with time off to engage in politics, as well as travel the world.[24] The top firms didn't need to bend over backward to accommodate him since they had no trouble making money and landing top clients on their own. Conversely, most smaller firms were priced out of a move for Nixon, and even if they could have afforded him, they wouldn't have been able to provide him with the kind of platform he needed to maintain his high political profile. "There just weren't too many places where he could get $250,000 and all his time," one member of his future firm told Witcover.[25] Another Mudge associate noted Nixon's reputation as a political animal and opined that many firms simply "didn't want a tiger in their midst."[26]

Nixon had spoken with William Rogers, a former US Attorney General, about joining his firm, Royall, Koegel & Rogers. (The firm, later known as Rogers & Wells, merged with Clifford Chance in 2000.) Rogers had a strong relationship with Nixon that went back several years. He had served as counsel on the House Un-American Activities Committee and had helped convince Nixon to go after Alger Hiss. He had also provided some advice to Nixon during the Checkers episode and helped him maintain his spot on the ticket.[27] In 1969, Rogers would become Nixon's secretary of state, serving until 1973, whereupon he returned to his law firm. "Bill felt very strongly that I should come to his firm," said Nixon.[28] "But we talked about it and we had a good frank talk. And we both agreed that having two political lawyers in the firm would be just one too many."

Additionally, Nixon didn't really have much of a legal resume to speak of. He had spent much of his adult life running for office and serving in Washington. While he was a lawyer by training, he had only practiced law for approximately seven years. Four-and-half of those years had been spent at Wingert and Bewley in Whittier, while his time as a lawyer with the Office of Price Administration had lasted a mere eight months before World War II hit and he enlisted in the navy. The other two years came after his defeat in the 1960 presidential race when he returned to California and worked at Adams, Duque & Hazeltine.

"When I first ran for Congress, [Adams Duque lead partner] Earl Adams had lived in my district," Nixon recalled.[29] "And he said: 'In the event you lose, I will give you a place in my firm.' This was in 1947. So, when I went to Adams Duque fourteen years later, I said: 'I'm finally accepting your offer because I now find myself qualified.'"

As Alexander had alluded to during that initial meeting with Nixon at the Baltusrol Golf Club, Nixon had, essentially, been a part-timer at Adams Duque. Nixon's response to Alexander had also been correct. He had chosen to join Earl Adams's firm, in large part, because Adams, a prominent, politically connected lawyer,[30] had offered a less demanding "of counsel" role instead of a full partnership, giving him plenty of time to write his memoirs and prepare for another run for office, either as governor in 1962 or president in 1964. It was an offer Nixon couldn't refuse. In fact, he even turned down an offer from Thomas Dewey to join Dewey Ballantine,[31] as well as an equity partnership with Gibson, Dunn & Crutcher, the firm that had given his Senate political fund a clean bill of legal health. "Gibson Dunn made a very, very good offer," said Nixon.[32] "Full partnership and so forth and so on. But it required [me to work] full time." He also turned down another intriguing possibility: Major League Baseball. Both the players and the owners were considering him to be the next commissioner. "That was very tough to turn down because I was a sports man," Nixon recalled.[33] "But I finally decided not to do that."

"I DID VERY LITTLE ON THE LEGAL SIDE."

As a result of his arrangement with Adams, the firm would never be Nixon's main priority. "I did very little on the legal side," Nixon admitted.[34] "I was running for governor, and I had very little time for law." One area where Nixon did help the firm was on the business end. During his short tenure at Adams, Duque & Hazeltine, Nixon brought in a tremendous amount of business that, under different circumstances, would have put him on the fast track to making partner.

In fact, the Nixon who seemed clueless about how to drum up business for Wingert and Bewley was now a bona fide rainmaker. He had begun accumulating business even before the expiration of his term as vice president, making him an attractive recruit for any number of top California firms. Much of it came from friends and political allies. For instance, John Clifford Folger, an investment banker who had served as chairman of the Republican National Finance Committee during the Eisenhower Administration, reached out to Nixon in early January 1961 and offered to retain Nixon and whatever firm he ended up at for $10,000 a year. "I can't tell you how pleased and honored I am that the first checks I received after entering law practice again were from you," Nixon wrote Folger on March 18, 1961,[35] less than a week after he joined Adams Duque.[36] "Needless to say, Earl Adams and my other colleagues at the firm look forward to the opportunity of representing some of your interests on the West Coast."

Frank Rackley, president of Pittsburgh-based Jessop Steel Company, was another early client. Rackley and his wife, Marguerite, had been longtime friends and confidants of Nixon's, and Frank offered to hire Nixon before the former vice president had even finalized his employment plans. In 1959, Jessop Steel had acquired a California-based company named Chase Steel & Supply Company and combined it with some other companies to form Jessop Steel of California. Rackley asked Nixon to be the attorney for Jessop's new West Coast operations, writing the former VP in February 1961: "I would like to ask that we be one of your first clients, and after you have settled, I will be on the Coast and discuss with you at that time the matter of your firm acting as our counsel on the West Coast."[37] Nixon's relationship with Rackley was especially warm. The steel magnate often sent letters of encouragement to Nixon, telling his attorney in March 1961: "It is nice to do business, but really fun to do business with friends."[38] Rackley even enclosed a copy of Juliet Wilbor Tompkins's poem "For All These" that included lines such as:

> I thank Thee that as yet I need not know,
> Yet need not fear the mystery of end;
> But more than all, and though all these should go
> Dear Lord, this on my knees . . . I thank thee for my friend.

Nixon's other friends were less effusive, but still came calling once he started at Adams Duque. Mutual fund pioneer Jack Dreyfus, who had a close relationship with Nixon and had previously offered the former VP the CEO position at his own Dreyfus Corporation, sent work to Nixon and the firm. Publishing magnate and friend Walter Annenberg also reached out, writing Nixon two months after he was officially announced as the newest member of Adams Duque, retaining him as his outside counsel.[39] Annenberg suggested a $10,000 yearly retainer for "mutual advice and counsel in California as may be appropriate from time to time." Besides hiring Nixon for legal advice, Annenberg also agreed to carry Nixon's columns and articles in the *Philadelphia Inquirer*—a nice platform for the former VP, especially if his name ever appeared on the ballot in Pennsylvania again.

Robert Abplanalp, CEO of Precision Valve Corporation, who was close friends with both Nixon and Charles "Bebe" Rebozo, a Florida millionaire and one of Nixon's closest confidants, also put Nixon and Adams Duque on an annual retainer of $10,000. In addition to legal advice, Nixon also served as a sounding board and conduit for Abplanalp's tax proposals. The CEO was convinced that the United States could reverse its unfavorable balance of trade by offering tax incentives to American-based companies to increase the dollar-volume of exports, and he asked Nixon to weigh in. Nixon expressed some skepticism of his client's proposals, but out of respect for his friend, he ran it past his economic advisers from the 1960 campaign, who were also unconvinced.[40]

Prominent Republicans led several of the clients Nixon brought in to Adams Duque. Richfield Oil Corporation (which merged with Atlantic Refining Company in 1966 to form ARCO), hired Nixon and Adams Duque in May 1961 for an annual retainer of $10,000.[41] Richfield's president, Charles Jones, had been friends with both Eisenhower and Nixon and had gone to bat for Nixon before, chiding Ike after the president had toyed with the idea of dropping Nixon from the ticket in 1956.[42] Another one of Ike's good friends, W. Alton Jones (no relation to Charles), made it clear that he was hiring Nixon first and his firm second. Jones, a prominent Republican who was president of oil and gas company Cities Service Company (now Citgo), wrote Nixon three days after Kennedy's inauguration with an offer to put him on a $10,000 yearly retainer. When Nixon landed at Adams Duque, Jones wrote again, making the representation official while expressing hope that he might meet the other members of Nixon's new firm in due time.[43] Securities firm Kidder Peabody & Company, which retained Nixon in June 1961, had a number of prominent executives who were active within the Republican Party, including vice president Lloyd Waring (a former Massachusetts GOP chair) and chairman Albert Hamilton Gordon.[44]

His political ties came in handy in other ways for the firm. Nixon forged a strong working relationship with Royall, Koegel & Rogers. One of the biggest cases the two firms worked on at the time was a long-running lawsuit involving one of the biggest movie stars of all time and one of the most troubled productions in film history. When 20th Century Fox decided to produce the big-budget sword-and-sandal epic, *Cleopatra*, it had, seemingly, scored a major coup by casting Academy Award–winning actress and bona fide sex symbol Elizabeth Taylor. However, by the time the film was released in 1963, Fox stood on the verge of bankruptcy thanks to delays and overruns that saw the movie's official budget swell from $2 million to an estimated $44 million, making it the most expensive film in history at the time.[45] One of the biggest delays took place right after filming commenced in September 1960 when Taylor suffered a near-fatal illness. Later that year, as Taylor was recovering and unable to work, Fox got into a dispute with Lloyd's of London over how much insurance to pay out to cover her unavailability. Fox turned to Royall, Koegel & Rogers, who, in turn, contacted Nixon and Adams Duque for help. Nixon suggested in an August 1961 letter that he could reach out to then-chancellor of the exchequer Selwyn Lloyd of the United Kingdom for help in resolving the matter (Chancellor Lloyd was not affiliated with Lloyd's of London). The British, Nixon wrote in a letter to Royall Koegel partner Otto Koegel, depend on income from their insurance ventures, and they would be loathe to develop a reputation for slowness and delays in settling claims. "If you believe an approach to [Chancellor] Lloyd would be appropriate, I should be glad to write him since I have a friendly personal relationship with him which would enable me to put the request on a proper basis," Nixon wrote.[46] Ultimately, the case settled once filming resumed, as Lloyd's agreed to pay Fox part of what it had been demanding.[47]

In general, Nixon was there to generate business, and it was up to the other attorneys at Adams Duque to handle the actual legal matters for the clients he brought in. In less than two years at the firm (it was even less time, if you consider the fact that he was also writing a book and running for governor), Nixon had proven he had a deep Rolodex of rich, powerful, and prominent business leaders who were willing to entrust their legal matters to him. As it happened, there was a New York firm that was looking for the exact set of skills he brought to the table. It was a prestigious, well-known firm that had fallen on hard times and needed a big-time player like him to boost its business and profile. It was also a place where he could have his time to travel the world and remain involved with politics, and he wouldn't have any competitors at the office to be wary about.

Mudge, Stern, Baldwin & Todd was that firm.

"MUDGE, SLUDGE, FUDGE AND WON'T BUDGE."

In retrospect, it's ironic that, for a guy who professed to hate Harvard and the Eastern Establishment as much as he did, Richard Nixon went to work on Wall Street. After all, Wall Street was crawling with Harvard grads, as well as Yale grads, Columbia grads, and even some Oxford grads. That was especially true in 1963, when Nixon joined the Mudge firm, just as it had been true when Nixon had applied to several Wall Street firms during his third year of law school only to return home, empty-handed, to Whittier. In fact, between 1950 and 1965, over 70 percent of lawyers on Wall Street came from three schools: Harvard, Yale, and Columbia.[48]

Nixon had long been suspicious of intellectuals, liberals, elites, and other members of the so-called Eastern Establishment, and, if there were any one institution that epitomized the establishment, it was Harvard. After all, Harvard Yard had been like a second home to all four of Joe Kennedy's sons (as well as Joe himself). Another former nemesis, Alger Hiss, had graduated from Harvard Law, while several of his future antagonists, including Daniel Ellsberg, Archibald Cox, and US senator Sam Ervin, were also Harvard alums. Harvard men were among the most common entries on his vaunted

"Enemies List," as several of the university's professors, officials, and trustees made the cut, including Law School dean Derek Bok and economics professor John Kenneth Galbraith.

"None of them in the Cabinet, do you understand?" Haldeman recalled Nixon telling him after his election to the presidency.[49] "None of those Harvard bastards!"

Yet as mentioned earlier, Nixon had almost been a Harvard man. Indeed, maybe his attitude toward the school, and toward Eastern elites, in general, would have been different had he been able to spend his formative years at Harvard Yard. Nixon may not have been a Harvard alum, but he sure seemed to surround himself with them. As political journalist Theodore White pointed out, Nixon hired more Harvard men than the five Harvard alumni that had served as president before him (John and John Quincy Adams, Theodore and Franklin Roosevelt, JFK). To Henry Kissinger, Nixon's contradictory attitude toward Harvard was a microcosm of his feelings toward the Eastern Establishment. Like the kid who didn't want to go to the dance but desperately wanted someone to invite him, Nixon may have hated Harvard and the people who went there, but he also wanted their acceptance. "Nixon was afraid of Harvard, and he was attracted to it," Kissinger told Evan Thomas.[50] "He aspired to it." Herbert Klein agreed, saying that Nixon seemed more jealous than hateful toward the Eastern Establishment. "If you look at the people he was close to, a lot of them were in the Eastern Establishment," Klein said, pointing out that Nixon moved to New York, one of the main pillars of the Eastern Establishment.[51] "It was the feeling of a poor boy from a small store in a small town who wished he had some of the trappings that go with being a Yale graduate."

Years after he had been driven from the White House in disgrace, Nixon reflected on his conflict with the Eastern Establishment as a whole. "What starts the process, really, are the laughs and snubs and slights you get when you are a kid," Nixon told an aide.[52] "But if you are reasonably intelligent and if your anger is deep enough and strong enough, you learn you can change those attitudes by excellence, by personal gut performance, while those who have everything are sitting on their fat butts." His belief that he could earn everyone's respect with hard work and determination explained how he approached his entire political career—as well as his time as a lawyer in New York during his "wilderness years."

In the meantime, Nixon would have to figure out a way to survive, and thrive, in a place where elite Ivy League graduates ran the show. Nixon could thank Paul Cravath for that. Cravath almost single-handedly changed the law firm world and created the system that we still live with today.

Born in 1861, Cravath graduated from Columbia Law School in 1886. In 1899, he joined the politically connected New York City law firm of Blatchford, Seward & Griswold.[53] The Blatchford in the firm name referred to

Samuel Blatchford, a prominent lawyer who left the firm in 1882 after being appointed to the Supreme Court by President Chester Alan Arthur. The Seward was William Seward, former governor of New York, US senator, and secretary of state, who died in 1872.

When Cravath joined Blatchford, Seward & Griswold, the law firm world was very different than it is today. Associates usually served apprenticeships with solo practitioners and were paid based on how much business they brought into the firm.[54] Cravath came up with a new system whereby law firms turned into law factories. Essentially, the firm would hire only the best law students from the top schools and give them a salary and training for about ten years before they would either move up to become full partners entrusted with guiding the firm over the next decade or they would be shipped out.[55] Associates would all make the same amount of money and would be promoted in lockstep so they could collaborate and work together for the benefit of the firm rather than competing with one another for promotions or raises (there would be still be competition, obviously—only one-out-of-twelve associates would make partner).[56]

In order to compete with Cravath's firm, today known as Cravath, Swaine & Moore, other large firms in New York had to do the same thing. While some firms have moved away from the system in recent years, the Cravath System remains alive and well and firmly in place at most large law firms today. In fact, Cravath continues to serve as the bellwether for most large firms. These days, most law firms wait until Cravath announces its end-of-the-year bonuses before announcing theirs.[57]

The immediate effect of the "Cravath System" on Wall Street was to create an elite class of lawyers that came from the best schools and were well paid and well connected. The top firms on Wall Street became known as "white shoe" firms in reference to the white buckskin shoes that were in vogue at Ivy League institutions. In his history of Cravath, Swaine & Moore, Robert Swaine noted that, as of 1948, fifteen of his firm's twenty-three partners had been Phi Beta Kappa as undergrads and fifteen had edited the *Law Review*.[58] When Emory Buckner ran the prestigious firm of Root, Clark, Buckner & Howard (later Dewey Ballantine) during the late 1920s and early 1930s, every person who became a partner during those years, bar one, came from either Harvard or Oxford. Root Clark was one of the first Wall Street firms to promote a Jewish lawyer to the partnership—in this case, it was 1925 and the person in question was Leo Gottlieb of Harvard Law School.[59] It wasn't an exaggeration to say that Wall Street had, essentially, become a finishing school for Ivy Leaguers—and that, after clients, elite, top-notch law students had become the new currency on Wall Street.

The firm that became Nixon, Mudge, Rose, Guthrie & Alexander wasn't immune to such conditions. Like many of its competitors, the firm started out with several completely different names on the masthead. Nixon Mudge traced its history back to 1869, when Simon Hunt Stern, a prominent New York lawyer, opened up his own practice near Wall Street.[60] Stern's biggest client was the Bank of the Manhattan Company (now part of JPMorgan Chase & Co.), and in 1892, he brought in another New York lawyer, Charles Rushmore, to help him handle the bank's litigation matters. The two men became full partners, and Stern & Rushmore was born.[61]

Perhaps it was destiny, then, for Nixon to join this firm. After all, in addition to being a prominent lawyer, Rushmore's claim to fame was that he had been the namesake for Mount Rushmore in South Dakota. Rushmore was an avid outdoorsman and visited the (then unnamed) site so often that, when he asked locals what it was called, they joked that it should be known as "Mount Rushmore."[62] The name stuck, and the United States Board of Geographic Names officially recognized "Mount Rushmore" in 1930. Eleven years later, the monument officially unveiled the now familiar busts of George Washington, Thomas Jefferson, Abraham Lincoln, and Theodore Roosevelt.

Rushmore had established himself as a top trial lawyer in New York and frequently represented underdogs against more powerful opponents, such as women going against their husbands in divorce or support proceedings or individual shareholders taking on large corporations.[63] Stern died in 1906, and his son, also a prominent lawyer, took his dad's place on the masthead. The younger Stern combined with Rushmore and another corporate lawyer, Eldon Bisbee, to form one of the largest firms on Wall Street, and as Wall Street boomed throughout the 1920s, so did Rushmore, Stern & Bisbee. As of 1930, the firm boasted fourteen partners, making it one of the largest firms on Wall Street based on partner head count.[64]

The stock market crash in October 1929 and the onset of the Great Depression had the effect of causing a downturn in the firm's fortunes, albeit indirectly. Albert Wiggin, the chief executive for firm client Chase National Bank, had been lauded for his actions in restoring stability to the stock market after Black Thursday by leading a group of bankers in buying stocks at higher-than-market prices. However, a few years later, his reputation took a hit when it came out during a US Senate investigation into the stock market crash that he had profited by selling short in the months leading up to the collapse. The Senate commission (known informally as the Pecora Commission after Ferdinand Pecora, a former Manhattan prosecutor and the chief counsel to the US Senate Committee on Banking and Currency, which held the hearings) found that Wiggin had sold short on 42,506 shares of Chase and made a tidy $4 million profit. Additionally, by using a Canadian shell company to buy the stocks, he had avoided US taxes.[65]

Wiggin did nothing illegal when he sold short on his own stocks. Short selling is a common tactic for investors and is an important feature of hedge funds. But selling short on your own stocks has always seemed unethical and even nefarious—in fact, nearly eighty years after Black Thursday, short sellers were widely blamed for helping trigger the Great Recession of 2008, the worst economic disaster in American history since the Great Depression. The Pecora Commission, in particular, had harsh words for Wiggin. "In the entire investigation, it is doubtful if there was another instance of a corporate executive who so thoroughly and successfully used his official and fiduciary position for private profit," the commission found.[66]

Wiggin's travails had a deleterious effect on Rushmore, Bisbee & Stern, which had represented him before the Commission. The firm's lawyers were seen as not merely being advisors but active aiders and abettors for Wiggin. Bisbee, in particular, came under scrutiny for having served as a director for the corporation Wiggin had used for his short sales. "With the disclosures of the Pecora hearings, the preeminence of Rushmore, Bisbee & Stern as a leading banking firm was shattered," Thomas Evans, who served as managing partner of Mudge for a decade starting in 1969, recalled.[67] "The firm had committed the cardinal sin of one who holds himself out to be a counselor—the advice that it had given had turned out, in retrospect, to be wrong."

The damage to the firm's prestige was only part of the reason why it underwent a decline during the 1930s. The other reason was the simple passage of time. Rushmore died in 1931, and Bisbee retired in 1934. The firm lost some clients because it had paid too much attention to Chase, most notably the Bank of the Manhattan Company, and when Wiggin retired from Chase in 1932, the firm lost its close relationship with its biggest client.[68]

Alfred E. Mudge stepped up and filled the void at the firm. Mudge was able to hold on to most of Chase's business, and he soon became the senior partner at the firm, which was renamed Mudge, Stern, Williams & Tucker in 1934.[69] Mudge was well respected for being a problem solver who had a knack for figuring out how to avoid conflict. Despite that, it was a personal conflict that helped cause his firm to lose Chase as a client. Chase had merged with the Equitable Trust Company in 1930, and the merged entity's largest shareholder, John D. Rockefeller Jr. (Nelson Rockefeller's father), decided to flex his muscle. Rockefeller's brother-in-law, Winthrop Aldrich, took over as the bank's president while Rockefeller's lawyer, Albert Milbank, started handling most of the bank's legal affairs. Mudge still held on to some of Chase's work, but he and Aldrich clashed. "I don't think [Aldrich] and Mudge got along very well," future Mudge name partner Randolph "Bob" Guthrie said.[70] "One thing led to another, and Mudge was so stupid—also not thinking of the firm—that he told [Aldrich] to take the business and stick it."

As Evans pointed out, Mudge's angry outburst was similar to how Nixon conducted himself during his "last press conference"—only in the case of the firm, Mudge's intemperate remark cost his firm its biggest client and started it on a lengthy decline. During the 1940s and 1950s, institutional rot had set in, and new blood was desperately needed. "The firm was very sloppy," Guthrie said.[71] "It didn't pay very much attention to its clients. The people who had the business were getting old and not worrying about it. And they were rich enough so they didn't care." Guthrie noted that the firm leaders seemed content to stand pat and were oblivious to the need to generate more business. "For example, Chase owned about 98 odd percent of American Express," Guthrie said.[72] Bisbee could have at any time with his friend Wiggin, just called up on the phone—and I'm sure Mr. Wiggin would have written a memorandum directing business be handled by this firm . . . He never bothered. He thought the firm had enough work to do and it was overcrowded here for him. And the boys were growing older. They had enough from their point of view."

As a result, the firm had acquired an unflattering nickname within legal circles: "Mudge, Sludge, Fudge & Won't Budge."[73]

THE PUBLIC PARTNER.

One way that law firms can boost their revenue and size is by merging with, or acquiring, another firm. Law firms continue to do it to this day, and in 1955, Mudge decided to go this route by merging with Baldwin & Todd, a smaller firm that specialized in trusts and estates.[74] Law firm experts always say that integration of two separate firms is the hardest part of a merger, so it helps if the lawyers involved already know each other and have a strong relationship.[75]

That was the case between Mudge Stern and Baldwin & Todd. The two firms had worked together on prior matters, notably dividing up the R. J. Reynolds estate after the tobacco magnate's death, as well as representing heiress Dorothy Whitney Straight Elmhirst. Most notably, John Alexander had worked at both firms, moving from Mudge to Baldwin in 1936 to head the latter's tax practice. After Alfred Mudge died in 1945, Alexander was offered the opportunity to return to his old firm and head its tax department, which was twice as large as Baldwin's. Alexander accepted, but maintained positive relations with Baldwin & Todd, in particular his friend, Baldwin partner Milton Rose. Alexander and Rose continued to work together on Elmhirst trust matters and frequently traveled together, with the topic of the futures of their respective firms a popular subject of discussion. In 1954, when Alexander and Guthrie, now coheads of the Mudge firm, started looking for merger partners, Baldwin & Todd was a natural choice.[76]

The new firm, Mudge, Stern, Baldwin & Todd, was now one of the largest on Wall Street. The firm had kept the names of its legacy partners, but Guthrie, Rose and Alexander, along with Matthew Herold of Baldwin & Todd, were the ones in charge. Guthrie, in particular, had a tremendous amount of influence at the firm and was commonly seen by the other partners as the driving force at Mudge.[77] As Leonard Garment, a Mudge partner that joined the firm in 1949 and eventually became Nixon's closest friend at the firm, recalled, on the surface, things had never been better at the firm:

> Over a hundred lawyers occupied five floors of the New York Stock Exchange building at 20 Broad Street, with all the usual status trappings—internal elevators, numerous conference rooms, period furniture, collector-quality ship prints, a look of purposeful busyness and a huge library displayed to clients through floor-to-ceiling glass walls.[78]

However, looks only went so far, and Mudge wasn't the big-time law firm that it aspired to be. "Despite the air of success, however, the firm seemed stuck," Garment observed.[79] "It had good clients, good lawyers and interesting business, but not quite enough of each." Plus Garment noted that the firm was routinely passed over when it came to getting huge bet-the-company trials or complicated corporate transactions involving more money than most people saw in a lifetime. Those are the types of cases or deals that define you as a law firm and, as Garment observed, "something, or someone, seemed to be lacking."[80]

What it lacked was a big-name public partner to bring in business and recruit the best and brightest law students in America (or, at least, from Harvard, Yale, and Columbia). As journalist Paul Hoffman put it, the public partner is someone with a big name and reputation that comes to Wall Street from government or politics in order to serve as a magnet for business. Public partners aren't there to run the day-to-day affairs of a firm, nor are they supposed to practice much law. Instead, Hoffman claimed public partners are really there to perform two services: consulting with clients and boosting the firm's profile. "It even helps if he keeps a hand in politics or civic projects," he said.[81] "Every time he gets his name in the papers, it's another advertisement for the firm." Indeed, law firms continue to do this today, and one of the busiest recruiting windows in Washington takes place right after an election, when retiring and defeated representatives and senators are leaving office and looking for their next jobs. "Even though they're not walking in with business right away, they are magnets for business," said Ivan Adler, a legal recruiter in Washington, D.C., noting that foreign clients especially love getting the opportunity to speak with an ex-politician.[82]

Prior to the merger with Baldwin & Todd, the Mudge firm had tried to install John Francis Brosnan, a former chancellor of the State University of New York and chairman of the State Board of Regents, as public partner.[83] Brosnan, however, was already in his mid-sixties and was winding down his practice rather than gearing up to try to compete with Wall Street lawyers who were younger and better connected than him.[84] The only other firm lawyer that had the kind of political connections necessary to be a public partner was Hiram C. Todd, a former US Attorney for the Northern District of New York who had been the name partner at Baldwin & Todd. If Brosnan had been too old, then Todd was downright ancient—by the time of the merger, he was already seventy-eight years old[85] —so he was never really considered for the role.

Elmer Bobst, however, knew that those names weren't good enough, at least not if Mudge wanted to get out of second gear. Warner-Lambert Pharmaceutical Company (which had been a legacy Baldwin Todd client) was Mudge's biggest client, so when its CEO spoke, Mudge's leaders listened. Bobst told them, in no uncertain terms, that they needed a giant to serve as the public head of the firm. "You need new blood at the top," Bobst told Rose.[86] "Someone who can serve to bring the firm into the eyes of Wall Street and to the attention of industry throughout the country."

The most effective public partners on Wall Street had been men of stature and power who had accomplished great things in national politics and could open doors and prompt immediate return calls or letters simply through the power of their names. Some of the most well-known and successful public partners include former US Speaker of the House Thomas Brackett Reed (known as "Czar Reed" for the way he wielded near-absolute power in the House), who joined the firm known today as Simpson Thacher & Bartlett in 1889,[87] and 1916 Republican presidential nominee and associate justice of the Supreme Court Charles Evans Hughes, who headed the firm known today as Hughes Hubbard & Reed before becoming Chief Justice of the Supreme Court in 1930.[88]

There were three public partners that were most relevant to the situation Nixon found himself in as he left California. Lead partner John W. Davis, a former congressman from West Virginia and a famed US solicitor general, joined the firm known today as Davis, Polk & Wardwell in 1921. Davis was a top trial lawyer and had argued more cases before the Supreme Court than all but a handful of lawyers, but he was, perhaps, better known for having been the Democratic nominee for president in 1924. A dark-horse candidate who was not well known throughout the country, Davis lost in a landslide against the popular incumbent Calvin Coolidge. Indeed, it was such a shellacking that Davis only won 28.8 percent of the popular vote—the lowest percentage by a Democratic presidential nominee (not counting the 1860 presidential election, when the Democratic Party was split in two).

Despite his loss, Davis remained a top lawyer and a big draw for his firm. He represented ten Hollywood movie studios in an antitrust case that went all the way to the Supreme Court. He lost the case, but Louis Mayer, cofounder of MGM, was so impressed with his work that he named Davis as his outside counsel.[89] Davis also represented JPMorgan & Co. in the aforementioned Pecora Hearings. Later on in his illustrious career, he argued two landmark cases before the Supreme Court. He won the Youngstown Steel case in 1952, in which the Supreme Court found that President Harry Truman's seizure of private steel mills in Ohio was an unconstitutional usurpation of power. On the other hand, two years later, he lost, perhaps, his most infamous case when the Supreme Court ruled against racially segregated public schools in *Brown v. Board of Education.*[90] Davis died a year later, but his firm continued to prosper and is today one of the largest in the country in terms of both gross revenue and attorney head count.[91]

In 1941, another failed GOP nominee for president found a nice landing spot on Wall Street when Wendell Willkie joined Miller, Boston & Owen one year after losing to Franklin Delano Roosevelt.[92] Willkie was a lot like Nixon in that he had done well in the 1940 presidential race (FDR had a commanding majority in the Electoral College, but Willkie won more popular votes than any other Republican presidential candidate up to that point—a record that would stand until Eisenhower in 1952) and was still seen as a viable presidential candidate in the future. The parallels between Willkie and Nixon get even deeper when looking at Willkie's activities while serving as lead partner for the firm that eventually became Willkie Farr & Gallagher. Like Nixon, Willkie spent a lot of time traveling abroad and established himself as statesman and titular head of the Republican Party. Like Nixon, he represented high-profile clients—in Willkie's case, he defended several top Hollywood studios when they were called before the Senate and accused of spreading propaganda in order to lure the United States into World War II.[93] Also, like Nixon, Willkie had no intention of quitting politics and fully intended on running for president again. Indeed, he was one of the front runners in 1944, but he did poorly in the primaries and ultimately lost the nomination to Thomas Dewey.

Dewey provides the other main parallel for Nixon and the Mudge firm. Like Nixon, Dewey had made his reputation as a young crusader taking on a public menace. While Nixon had gone after the Reds, Dewey had targeted organized crime. As a special prosecutor for Manhattan, and later, as Manhattan district attorney, Dewey made his bones as a gang buster by bringing down numerous Mafia figures, including the titular "Boss of Bosses," Charles "Lucky" Luciano, in 1936.[94] Dewey was so highly regarded as a lawyer that a popular, and possibly apocryphal story, from that time period was that a girl wanted to sue God in order to stop a rainstorm. "You can't sue God and win," the girl's dad told her. "I can if Dewey is my lawyer," she responded.[95]

Dewey rode his reputation all the way to the New York governor's mansion, serving in that capacity from 1943 to 1954. Much like Nixon, Dewey had been the GOP standard-bearer in spite of some serious personality defects. In Dewey's case, his magic with juries did not extend to the campaign trail, as he was widely perceived to be uncharismatic, stiff, pompous, and unlikeable.[96] With his pencil-thin mustache and short stature (he stood somewhere between 5 foot 6 inches and 5 foot 8 inches), Dewey was one of the shortest men to ever win a major party's nomination for president.[97] The sharp-tongued Alice Roosevelt Longworth memorably mocked the gang-busting governor, comparing Dewey to the "little man on top of a wedding cake."[98] Despite all of that baggage, Dewey had managed to do quite well for himself. He lost in 1944 to FDR but gave Roosevelt his closest race out of the four presidential elections he won. Four years later, Dewey nearly won the White House over a badly split Democratic Party—indeed, according to the *Chicago Daily Tribune*, he had defeated Truman.

Instead, after his second-consecutive loss, Dewey was effectively finished as a candidate. In 1955, two years after leaving the governor's mansion, he joined Ballantine, Bushby, Palmer & Wood as lead partner.[99] Much like how Mudge had been stuck in the sludge in the years leading up to Nixon's arrival, Ballantine Bushby's fortunes had been in decline in the decade or so prior to Dewey coming aboard. In 1946, leading partners George Cleary, Leo Gottlieb, Henry Friendly, and Melvin Steen left to form their own firm and took several important clients with them, including Pan American Airlines, Federated Department Stores (now Macy's), and estate work for several prominent families, including the Guggenheims.[100] Today, the firm of Cleary Gottlieb Steen & Hamilton is one of the largest firms in the world.[101]

Ballantine Bushby suffered two big blows in 1954. Top litigator John Marshall Harlan II, who handled some of the firm's most important clients, including the DuPont family, left the firm after being appointed to the Supreme Court by Eisenhower.[102] Worse, one of the firm's biggest clients, the Bank of the Manhattan Company (Mudge's former client) had just merged with Chase (another former Mudge client), and it looked like Milbank Tweed would get all of the work from the newly merged entity.[103]

Like Mudge, Ballantine Bushby was in desperate need of new blood at the top, and the firm looked to Dewey to turn around its sagging fortunes and lead it back to glory. Dewey immediately paid dividends, bringing in $10 million in business and working out a deal with Milbank to split Chase's legal work between the two of them. Now known as Dewey Ballantine Bushby Palmer & Wood, the firm gained many new clients, including Eli Lilly and Company, the State of New York, Schenley Industries, Continental Oil, the Japanese Trade Council, and the government of Turkey.[104] The firm even opened new offices in Paris and Brussels and grew from 105 lawyers in 1958 to 186 lawyers in 1973. When Dewey died in 1971, his firm was the second largest on Wall Street.[105]

"The senior partner of Dewey, Ballantine was a working lawyer and administrator," Richard Norton Smith wrote in his biography of Dewey.[106] "Dewey kept his promise about devoting himself exclusively to the work at hand. He refused to join outside boards or serve as an at-large delegate to a

1966 state constitutional convention. Those seeking a political entrée to Washington were politely ushered from his office."

Of course, that's not to say that Dewey took himself out of the political arena completely. Far from it. Dewey still exercised considerable behind-the-scenes power within the Republican Party and would remain one of the most influential brokers in the party until his death in 1971. He didn't hesitate to show off his muscle, either. It was Dewey that not only helped convince Eisenhower to run for president in 1952, but also swung the convention over to the general and away from the other guy vying for the GOP nomination: conservative isolationist and longtime Dewey rival Senator Robert Taft of Ohio. It was Dewey who bore the brunt of the conservative anger and outrage after his maneuvering denied Taft his last opportunity at the presidential nomination he had so cherished. "We followed you before and you took us down the path to defeat!" US Senator Everett Dirksen said angrily from the stage at the 1952 GOP National Convention while staring down and shaking his finger at Dewey.[107] It was Dewey who promoted Nixon as a VP choice, although he had also tried, unsuccessfully, to get Nixon to resign as Ike's running mate after the fund scandal.

When looking at that illustrious list, it was clear that Nixon was, really, the only choice for Mudge. Perhaps because he was nearly thirty years older than Nixon, Bobst was not only a close friend to the former vice president but also a confidant—Nixon's daughters even referred to Bobst as "Uncle Elmer." Bobst knew that, based on their conversations, the ex–vice president was ready, willing, and able to make a deal. After all, Bobst had been one of the first people Nixon had spoken to after he made the decision to leave California, and for Bobst, it was vindication. "Elmer Bobst, had been urging me to come to New York for a long time," Nixon said.[108] "He, as a matter of fact, urged me to come to New York in 1961."

"TAKING THE VEIL."

While Davis, Willkie, and Dewey had carved out successful careers in Washington, the common denominator was that they were all presidential losers who never came close to the White House again. At first, that didn't worry Nixon. After all, he certainly seemed as if he was finished with politics and talked as if he was ready to assume a Dewey-like "power behind the curtain" role. Even if he wasn't finished with politics, Wall Street would not have been the most obvious place for him to build a new power base from which he could run for president again. Tom Evans was fond of noting that Wall Street had served as a veritable breeding ground for presidents and presidential nominees.

> Nixon was a knowledgeable student of political history and may have been aware of the fact that six presidential candidates had emerged during the prior hundred years from law firms which occupied the tiny twenty-acre plot around Wall Street, and that two Wall Street lawyers had become President of the United States. In fact, in America's second century, no state, no home of Presidents, no base within the United States had provided more fertile ground for the growth of presidential aspirants than Wall Street. [109]

At closer inspection, however, it became clear that Wall Street wasn't quite the springboard to the White House that it appeared to be. For one thing, the two presidents in American history who had worked as lawyers on Wall Street that Evans had referred to weren't quite relevant to Nixon's situation. Grover Cleveland, who joined the firm that is known today as Davis Polk & Wardwell during the years between his two nonconsecutive terms in the White House,[110] had the advantage of having already been president during his years on Wall Street and was coming off a loss in one of the narrowest presidential elections in American history (in 1888, Cleveland had actually beaten Benjamin Harrison in the popular vote, only to lose in the Electoral College). The other (Franklin Delano Roosevelt) had long since left Wall Street by the time he won the White House (Roosevelt had been an associate at Carter Ledyard & Milburn from 1907 to 1911 before embarking on his political career—he was governor of New York when he was elected president of the United States in 1932).[111] In fact, until 1968, the only Wall Street lawyer who was actually a Wall Street lawyer when he ran for president and had not been a prior occupant of the White House was Davis. That wasn't quite the precedent Nixon was looking for.

In fact, over the years, Wall Street law firms have distinguished themselves as landing spots for politicians after they lost an election (or two).[112] As such, it seemed as if Nixon, by moving to Wall Street, was tacitly giving up on his political career. He certainly talked the talk, telling his new law partners that he was finished running for office. The metaphor he was fond of using was that he was "taking the veil"; in other words, he was giving up his most basic desires and pleasures in order to pursue an aesthetic lifestyle as a Wall Street lawyer. Nixon recalled:

> At that point, I had no illusions about my political future. I, of course, had lost in California, after losing for the Presidency, and I'd moved to New York, away from my political base in California. Rockefeller, of course, had New York, so nobody gave me a chance in the media—and frankly this was one of those occasions when I agreed with the media. I didn't have any chance. So consequently, when I went with the firm I felt that I was taking the veil politically—that was what I thought at the beginning. As far as they were concerned, they made it clear that they would welcome my, making speeches on occasion, which I did.[113]

John Sears, a lawyer Nixon helped recruit to the firm in 1965 who later served as executive director of the Nixon for President Committee from 1967 to 1968, got to know Nixon very well during his years with the firm. To Sears, Nixon's vow to "take the veil" seemed sincere. "I think, at the time he lost the 1962 gubernatorial race, that he really did think his political career was over," said Sears.[114] "His move to New York was, partly, to make his wife happy, but also to demonstrate that he was, indeed, through with politics. Of course, what happened was that he really couldn't keep away."

His new partners seemed convinced, and even if they weren't, they knew they could benefit from having Nixon's name on the masthead. Rose stated that, at no point, did the firm ask Nixon to promise not to seek office again. "No such commitment, to my mind, was made," said Rose.[115] "The attraction to us included, in large measure, the contacts that Nixon obviously had at that time in the business world and the prospects of his attracting substantial business." Rose also noted that he and his partners had been "hopeful" that Nixon would take a part in the day-to-day operations of the firm and saw him as "an appellate lawyer who would be very helpful in servicing existing clients of the firm as well as those that would be attracted to it by his association."[116]

Rose and his partners were satisfied with Nixon's vow to put the firm first that they responded in kind. After pounding out some of the finer details of his joining the firm in Nixon's suite at the Waldorf Towers on May 2, 1963, the two sides officially united with Nixon getting top billing as the new public partner. The partners agreed that Mudge's name would go second and the other partners would draw their names out of a hat to see where they fell on the masthead.[117] Milton Rose won the drawing, with Bob Guthrie's name coming out next. John Alexander's name would come at the end.

Nixon officially joined the firm in August 1963. However, before his name could go on the masthead, he had one piece of housekeeping to take care of. Under New York state bar regulations, Nixon could not practice law in the state until he was admitted to the state bar, which meant that he would serve as a consultant for Mudge for six months in order to fulfill the bar association's state residency requirement.

Nixon would also have to fill out an application form for admission, which was far less demanding than taking a bar exam. This was, undoubtedly, good news for a man who claimed to have bad memories of taking, and passing, the bar exam in California shortly after graduating from Duke Law. He liked to talk about how he had barely passed that exam and even used it as a moment of levity during what was, arguably, the worst day of his political career. "We think sometimes when things happen that don't go the right way," Nixon said during his resignation speech from the White House in 1974. "We think that when you don't pass the bar exam the first time—I happened to, but I was just lucky; I mean, my writing was so poor the bar examiner said, 'We have just got to let the guy through.'"[118]

If that's really what happened, then his writing skills improved tremendously in the twenty-five years since he took the California bar exam. Or maybe it helped that the essay portion of his New York bar application consisted of a question that was the equivalent of a meatball thrown straight down the middle of the strike zone for Babe Ruth: "What do you believe the principles underlying the form of government of the United States to be?"

It's a question that young, unsophisticated law school grads might struggle with, but for Nixon, it was not only his chance to show off his level of experience, it was an opportunity for him to articulate his ideals and principles in a nonelectoral setting.

> The principles underlying the Government of the United States are decentralization of power, separation of power and maintaining a balance between freedom and order.
>
> Above all else, the framers of the Constitution were fearful of the concentration of power in either individuals or government. The genius of their solution in this respect is that they were able to maintain a very definite but delicate balance between the Federal Government and the State Government on the one hand and between the executive, legislative and judicial branches of the Federal Government on the other hand.

Nixon also spoke at length about the role of the federal government and articulated his belief that "the American ideal is that private or individual enterprise should be allowed and encouraged to undertake all functions which it is capable to perform." Nixon further argued that "only when private enterprise cannot or will not do what needs to be done should government step in."[119]

He also foreshadowed a major theme of his 1968 campaign by talking about the need for order and how unrestrained freedom could result in lawlessness and chaos. Indeed, all he was missing was a reference to the "silent majority" and his bar admission essay could have doubled as his stump speech. Meanwhile, his criticism of extremism is illuminating, considering his experience with the far-right wing in California, as well as the looming specter of Barry Goldwater as the 1964 GOP front runner for president.

> Yet the genius of the founding fathers is further demonstrated by the fact that while freedom for the individual was their primary objective, they recognized that uncontrolled freedom for some would lead to anarchy, which would destroy freedom for all. Maintaining the delicate balance between freedom and order is, in my view, the greatest achievement of the American Constitutional system. Inability to maintain that balance is the basic reason for the failure of regimes in Latin America, Africa and Asia, which have tried to copy our system. They invariably go to one extreme or the other—too much emphasis

> on the freedom of men to do anything they please or too much emphasis on controlling the excesses of freedom. Each of these approaches leads inevitably to dictatorship, either of the right or of the left, a tragedy, which America will be able to avoid by continued dedication to the fundamental principles of our Constitution.[120]

Given his public profile, perhaps it was inevitable that his essay would get leaked to his arch-nemesis: the press. Fortunately for him, the press coverage for his personal manifesto was quite positive. The *Chicago Tribune*[121] and the *New York Times* contained articles praising his essay—all containing a quote from Lowell Wadmond, chairman of the New York State Bar Association's committee on character and fitness, calling Nixon's essay "the finest essay I've seen in 28 years on the committee."[122]

With that ringing endorsement, Nixon's admission to the bar was a formality. After fulfilling the residency requirement, Nixon was formally admitted to the bar in December 1963. Nixon, Mudge, Rose, Guthrie & Alexander was officially born on January 1, 1964.

NOTES

1. Thomas Evans, "The Education of Richard Nixon: The Wilderness Years on Wall Street," unpublished manuscript, 6–9.
2. Evans, "The Education of Richard Nixon," 9
3. Evans, "The Education of Richard Nixon."
4. Dwight Chapin, "Oral History," interview with Timothy Naftali, Richard Nixon Presidential Library and Museum, April 2, 2007, http://www.nixonlibrary.gov/virtuallibrary/documents/histories/chapin-2007-04-02.pdf.
5. Jules Witcover, *The Resurrection of Richard Nixon* (New York: G. P. Putnam's Sons, 1970), 40–41.
6. John A. Farrell, *Richard Nixon: A Life* (New York: Doubleday, 2017), 313.
7. Will Swift, *Pat and Dick: The Nixons, An Intimate Portrait of a Marriage* (New York: Threshold Editions, 2014), 175.
8. Richard Nixon, *RN: The Memoirs of Richard Nixon* (New York: Simon and Schuster, 2013).
9. Roscoe Drummond, "Pat Nixon Made the Decision to Move, Get Out of Political Fire," *Los Angeles Times*, May 16, 1963.
10. Stephen Ambrose, *Nixon: Volume 2, The Triumph of a Politician, 1962–1972* (New York: Simon & Schuster, 1989), 21–22.
11. Kenneth Reich, "Ex-Senator Kuchel Dies; Last of the State's GOP Progressives," *Los Angeles Times*, November 23, 1994, accessed on February 2, 2016, http://articles.latimes.com/1994-11-23/news/mn-696_1_progressive-republican/.
12. "Frank Gannon's Interview with Richard Nixon, Part 1," University of Georgia, September 7, 1983, accessed March 29, 2017, http://www.libs.uga.edu/media/collections/nixon/ohms/sept7part1.html.
13. Nixon, *RN*.
14. Mark David, "Rock It Like a Rockefeller," *Variety*, February 27, 2008, accessed on February 3, 2016, http://variety.com/2008/dirt/real-estalker/rock-it-like-a-rockefeller-1201227746/.
15. Ambrose, *Nixon: Volume 2*, 16.

16. Karal Ann Marling, *As Seen on TV: The Visual Culture of Everyday Life in the 1950s*, (Cambridge, MA: Harvard University Press, 1994), 243–50, 271–76.

17. Paul Hoffman, *Lions in the Street: The Inside Story of the Great Wall Street Law Firms* (New York: Saturday Review Press, 1973), 105–6.

18. Marling, *As Seen on TV*.

19. "Nixon vs. Khrushchev—The 1959 Kitchen Debate," Association for Diplomatic Studies & Training, accessed January 15, 2016, http://adst.org/2015/07/nixon-vs-khrushchev-the-1959-kitchen-debate/.

20. "Nixon vs. Khrushchev."

21. Hoffman, *Lions in the Street*, 106. Also: Thomas Evans, "Nixon Mudge," unpublished manuscript, 1994, 123.

22. Jonathan Aitken, *Nixon: A Life* (Washington, DC: Regnery History, 1993), 364.

23. Tom Braden, "Nixon and Pepsi-Cola," *Boca Raton News*, November 23, 1972.

24. Braden, "Nixon and Pepsi-Cola."

25. Witcover, *The Resurrection of Richard Nixon*, 35.

26. Witcover, *The Resurrection of Richard Nixon*.

27. David Stout, "William P. Rogers, Who Served as Nixon's Secretary of State, Is Dead at 87," *New York Times*, January 4, 2001, accessed on February 24, 2016, http://www.nytimes.com/2001/01/04/us/william-p-rogers-who-served-as-nixon-s-secretary-of-state-is-dead-at-87.html?pagewanted=all.

28. Richard Nixon, interview by Tom Evans, March 15, 1983, transcript.

29. Nixon, interview by Evans.

30. "Attorney Earl Adams, Architect of GOP Campaigns, Dies," *Los Angeles Times*, April 2, 1986, accessed on February 27, 2016, http://articles.latimes.com/1986-04-02/news/mn-2362_1_attorney-earl-adams.

31. Richard Norton Smith, *Thomas E. Dewey and His Times* (New York: Simon & Schuster, 1982), 626.

32. Nixon, interview by Evans.

33. Nixon, interview by Evans.

34. Nixon, interview by Evans.

35. Richard Nixon, Letter to Cliff Folger, March 18, 1961, Pre-Presidential Papers, Richard Nixon Presidential Library and Museum.

36. "Richard Nixon Goes to Work with Law Firm," *Deseret News*, March 14, 1961, accessed on February 27, 2017, https://news.google.com/newspapers?nid=336&dat=19610314&id=D5sJAAAAIBAJ&sjid=dkkDAAAAIBAJ&pg=6993,2572067&hl=en.

37. Richard Nixon, Letter from Frank Rackley, February 6, 1961, Pre-Presidential papers, Richard Nixon Presidential Library and Museum.

38. Richard Nixon, Letter from Frank Rackley, March 27, 1961, Pre-Presidential papers, Richard Nixon Presidential Library and Museum.

39. Richard Nixon, Letter from Walter Annenberg, May 29, 1961, Pre-Presidential papers, Richard Nixon Presidential Library and Museum.

40. Richard Nixon, Letter to Robert Abplanalp, August 21, 1961, Pre-Presidential papers, Richard Nixon Presidential Library and Museum.

41. Richard Nixon, Letter from Wm. J. De Martini, May 18, 1961, Pre-Presidential papers, Richard Nixon Presidential Library and Museum.

42. Conrad Black, *Richard M. Nixon: A Life in Full* (New York: PublicAffairs, 2007), 326.

43. Richard Nixon, Letter from W. Alton Jones, January 23, 1961, and March 24, 1961, Pre-Presidential papers, Richard Nixon Presidential Library and Museum.

44. Robert Lenzner, "Remember the Admirable Al Gordon," *Forbes*, May 27, 2009, accessed on February 27, 2017, http://www.forbes.com/2009/05/27/kidder-peabody-harvard-personal-finance-investing-ideas-al-gordon.html.

45. "Cleopatra," Turner Classic Movies, accessed on February 27, 2017, http://www.tcm.com/this-month/article/102757|102758/Cleopatra.html. *Cleopatra* held the record for most expensive movie (unadjusted for inflation) for fifteen years until *Superman* surpassed it in 1978. When adjusted for inflation, *Cleopatra* is still one of the twenty-five most expensive movies of all time.

46. Richard Nixon, Letter to Otto Koegel, August 18, 1961, Pre-Presidential papers, Richard Nixon Presidential Library and Museum.

47. Janet Leaf, "'Cleopatra' at Half-Way Point," *Sunday Gazette-Mail*, January 7, 1962.

48. Elizabeth Chambliss, "The Shoe Still Fits," *Legal Affairs*, September–October 2005, accessed on February 27, 2017, http://www.legalaffairs.org/issues/September-October-2005/toa_sepoct05.msp. Also: William Henderson and Rachel Zahorsky, "The Pedigree Problem: Are Law School Ties Choking the Profession?" *ABA Journal*, July 1, 2012, accessed on February 27, 2017, http://www.abajournal.com/magazine/article/the_pedigree_problem_are_law_school_ties_choking_the_profession.

49. Evan Thomas, *Being Nixon: A Man Divided* (New York: Random House, 2015).

50. Thomas, *Being Nixon*.

51. Gerald Strober and Deborah H. Strober, *Nixon: An Oral History of His Presidency* (New York: HarperCollins Publishers, 1994), 47.

52. Evan Thomas, "Why Nixon Hated Georgetown," *Politico*, June 4, 2015.

53. Matt Shinners, "How to Become a Law Firm Partner," American Bar Association, June 7, 2012, accessed June 11, 2017, https://apps.americanbar.org/litigation/committees/youngadvocate/email/spring2012/spring2012-0612-how-become-law-firm-partner.html.

54. "The System's History," *Cravath, Swaine & Moore*, accessed on January 15, 2016, https://www.cravath.com/systemshistory/.

55. Lincoln Caplan, *Skadden: Power, Money, and the Rise of a Legal Empire* (New York: Farrar Straus Giroux, 1993), 16.

56. Caplan, *Skadden*, 16. Also: "The System's History," *Cravath, Swaine & Moore*.

57. Casey Sullivan, "Has Big Law Associate Bonus Season Already Started?" *Bloomberg BNA*, October 16, 2015, accessed on February 27, 2017, https://bol.bna.com/has-big-law-associate-bonus-season-already-started.

58. Robert Taylor Swaine, *The Cravath Firm and Its Predecessors, 1819–1947* (New York: Ad Press, 1946–48), accessed on January 15, 2016, http://www.houseofrussell.com/legalhistory/alh/docs/rtswayne.html.

59. Caplan, *Skadden*, 17–18.

60. Marvine Howe, "Henry Stern, Jr., 80, Ex-Insurance Chief Of New York State," *The New York Times*, July 21, 1993, accessed on February 27, 2017, http://www.nytimes.com/1993/07/21/obituaries/henry-stern-jr-80-ex-insurance-chief-of-new-york-state.html?_r=0.

61. Evans, "Nixon Mudge," 26–28.

62. Jim Burnett, "Mount Who? How Did This Famous Park Get Its Name?" *National Parks Traveler*, accessed on January 16, 2016, http://www.nationalparkstraveler.com/2009/06/mount-who-how-did-famous-park-get-its-name.

63. Evans, "Nixon Mudge," 34–35.

64. 1930 Martindale's American Law Directory 1272, 1784 (1868–1930).

65. US Senate Committee on Banking and Currency, *The Pecora Investigation: Stock Exchange Practices and the Causes of the 1929 Wall Street Crash* (New York: Cosimo Reports, 2010), 189.

66. US Senate Committee on Banking and Currency, *The Pecora Investigation*.

67. Evans, "Nixon Mudge," 71.

68. Evans, "Nixon Mudge," 71–72. Also "Albert Wiggin Retires as Head of Chase Bank," *Chicago Daily Tribune*, December 22, 1932, accessed on February 27, 2017, http://archives.chicagotribune.com/1932/12/22/page/21/article/albert-wiggin-retires-as-head-of-chase-bank.

69. Evans, "Nixon Mudge," 72.

70. Evans, "Nixon Mudge," 75.

71. Evans, "Nixon Mudge," 111.

72. Randolph Guthrie, interview by Tom Evans, part 1, March 3, 1981, transcript.

73. Aitken, *Nixon*, 363.

74. Evans, "Nixon Mudge," 112-13.

75. Victor Li, "Have We Reached the End of the Partnership Model?" *ABA Journal*, August 1, 2015, accessed on February 27, 2017, http://www.abajournal.com/magazine/article/have_we_reached_the_end_of_the_partnership_model.

76. Evans, "Nixon Mudge," 112–14.

77. Leonard Garment, *Crazy Rhythm: From Brooklyn and Jazz to Nixon's White House, Watergate and Beyond* (Cambridge, MA: Da Capo Press, 1997), 59–61.
78. Garment, *Crazy Rhythm*, 61.
79. Garment, *Crazy Rhythm*.
80. Garment, *Crazy Rhythm*.
81. Hoffman, *Lions in the Street*, 106–7.
82. Victor Li, "Help Not Wanted," *The American Lawyer*, May 2013.
83. Wolfgang Saxton, "John Brosnan: Former Head of State U. and Regents Unit," *New York Times*, April 15, 1982, accessed February 27, 2017, http://www.nytimes.com/1982/04/15/obituaries/john-brosnan-former-head-of-state-u-and-regents-unit.html.
84. Evans, "Nixon Mudge," 114–15.
85. Evans, "Nixon Mudge," 115.
86. Evans, "Nixon Mudge," 119.
87. "Our History," Simpson Thacher & Bartlett, accessed on January 16, 2016, http://www.stblaw.com/about-us/our-history.
88. "Firm History," Hughes Hubbard & Reed, accessed on January 16, 2016, http://www.hugheshubbard.com/aboutus/Pages/FirmHistory.aspx.
89. "History: Davis Polk & Wardwell," accessed on January 16, 2016, https://www.davispolk.com/history/.
90. Davis didn't actually argue the Brown case. He, instead, argued one of the companion cases, *Briggs v. Elliott*, which originated from South Carolina. Then-governor James F. Byrnes (a former Supreme Court justice) had personally hired Davis to argue the case on behalf of the state. Perhaps unsurprisingly, this case is not listed on the Davis Polk website.
91. Julie Triedman, "The Am Law 100, the Early Numbers: Davis Polk Posts Record-High Revenue, PPP," *The American Lawyer*, February 13, 2015, accessed on January 16, 2016, http://www.americanlawyer.com/id=1202717880587/The-Am-Law-100-the-Early-Numbers-Davis-Polk-Posts-RecordHigh-Revenue-PPP?slreturn=20151119140124. Also: "Davis Polk & Wardwell Firm Profile," *The American Lawyer*, accessed on January 16, 2016, http://www.americanlawyer.com/law-firm-profiles-result?firmname=Davis+Polk+%26+Wardwell.
92. Li, "Golden Parachute."
93. Thomas Schatz, *Boom & Bust: American Cinema in the 1940s* (Berkeley, CA: University of California Press, 1997), 39.
94. "Thomas E. Dewey," *Dewey Defeats Truman: The Single Most Famous Newspaper Error . . . Ever*, accessed January 16, 2016, http://www.deweydefeatstruman.com/Deweybio.htm.
95. Smith, *Thomas E. Dewey and His Times* , 18.
96. Tim Jones, "Dewey Defeats Truman," *Chicago Tribune*, accessed on January 16, 2016, http://www.chicagotribune.com/news/nationworld/politics/chi-chicagodays-deweydefeats-story-story.html.
97. "The Measure of a President," *New York Times*, October 6, 2008, accessed on January 16, 2016, http://www.nytimes.com/interactive/2008/10/06/opinion/06opchart.html?_r=0. This article listed Dewey's height as 5′8″. Richard Norton Smith also referred to him as 5′8 ″. Contrast that with Dan Stap, "Mustache Man," *Milwaukee Journal* (November 28, 1982). That article listed his height at 5′6 ″. Either way, he's one of the shortest men to run for president in the modern era.
98. Stacy Cordery, *Alice: Alice Roosevelt Longworth, From White House Princess to Washington Power Broker* (New York: Penguin Books, 2007), 424. Alice Longworth Roosevelt didn't originate the insult, but given her high profile in Washington, once it was attributed to her, it caught on like wildfire.
99. "Then and Now: A Dewey Timeline," *Reuters*, accessed on January 16, 2016, http://www.reuters.com/article/us-dewey-timeline-idUSBRE84B00V20120512.
100. "Dewey Ballantine LLP History," Funding Universe, accessed on January 16, 2016, http://www.fundinguniverse.com/company-histories/dewey-ballantine-llp-history/. Also: "Dewey Ballantine LLP Firm History," Dewey Ballantine, accessed on January 16, 2016, http://web.archive.org/web/20030828143512/http://www.deweyballantine.com/history/history_fr.htm.

101. "Cleary Gottlieb Steen & Hamilton," *The American Lawyer*, accessed on January 16, 2016, http://www.americanlawyer.com/law-firm-profiles-result?firmname=Cleary+Gottlieb+Steen+%26+Hamilton.
102. "Dewey Ballantine LLP History," *Funding Universe*.
103. Smith, *Thomas E. Dewey and His Times* , 620.
104. Smith, *Thomas E. Dewey and His Times* , 621.
105. "Dewey Ballantine LLP History," *Funding Universe*.
106. Smith, *Thomas E. Dewey and His Times* .
107. Smith, *Thomas E. Dewey and His Times* , 592–93.
108. Nixon, interview by Evans.
109. Evans, "Nixon Mudge," 2–3.
110. "History," Davis Polk & Wardwell, accessed on January 16, 2016, http://www.davispolk.com/firm/history/.
111. "Carter Ledyard Alumnus Franklin Roosevelt Is Featured in PBS's The Roosevelts: An Intimate History ," Carter Ledyard & Milburn, accessed on January 16, 2016, http://www.clm.com/newsitem.cfm?ID=2602.
112. Victor Li, "Golden Parachute," *The American Lawyer*, October 2012.
113. Nixon, interview by Evans.
114. John Sears, interview by Victor Li, February 16, 2016.
115. Milton Rose, interview by Tom Evans, January 27, 1981, transcript.
116. Rose, interview by Tom Evans, January 27, 1981.
117. Evans, "Nixon Mudge," 119.
118. "Richard M. Nixon: White House Farewell," The History Place: Great Speeches Collection, accessed February 13, 2016, http://www.historyplace.com/speeches/nixon-farewell.htm.
119. Richard Nixon, New York Bar Admission Essay, November 15, 1963, Pre-Presidential papers, Richard Nixon Presidential Library and Museum.
120. Nixon, New York Bar Admission Essay.
121. "Nixon Essay on U.S. Hailed," *Chicago Tribune*, December 8, 1963, accessed on February 13, 2016, http://archives.chicagotribune.com/1963/12/08/page/1/article/nixons-essay-on-u-s-hailed.
122. "Nixon Essay on U.S. Hailed."

Chapter Three

"The Fast Track."

Before moving to New York to embark on his new career as a Wall Street lawyer, Richard Nixon did what a lot of people in his situation would do. He took a vacation.

"Before beginning my new job, I was determined to keep a longstanding promise to Pat and the girls," Nixon said.[1] Starting on June 12, 1963, the Nixons took off on a six-week trip to Europe and the Middle East. For Nixon, the trip was a more of a working vacation and allowed him to indulge in foreign policy.

As vice president, he had traveled extensively and had proven to be a quick study when it came to conducting international diplomacy. He devoured and retained volumes of information he received from the State Department and other sources about the countries on his itinerary, and he diligently prepared for every single meeting abroad—skills that would serve him well as a Wall Street lawyer. In 1953, he hit the road on a grueling seventy-day trip, during which time he visited nineteen countries, including several areas in Asia where the Cold War had actually turned hot.[2] In fact, a major part of Nixon's trip was to reassure leaders in South Vietnam, South Korea, and Taiwan that the United States was committed to helping them while trying to dissuade them from escalating their military options against their Communist counterparts. "The 1953 trip had a tremendously important effect on my thinking and on my career," Nixon recounted.[3] "It was an undisputed success in that it accomplished its stated objectives and more. But further, it established my foreign policy experience and expertise in what was to become the most critical and controversial part of the world."

Other trips soon followed as Ike dispatched his vice president all around the globe. In 1958, he survived hostile anti-American demonstrators in Lima, Peru, and a pipe-wielding mob in Caracas, Venezuela. Ambrose noted that

Nixon's courageous conduct "caused even some of his bitterest enemies to give him some grudging respect."[4] The following year, he made his highly publicized trip to the Soviet Union (the "Kitchen Debate"), where he showed the public that he wouldn't let Communist leaders push him around.

During his 1963 trip abroad, he took the time to meet with a number of world leaders, including French president Charles de Gaulle, Spanish dictator Francisco Franco, and Egyptian president Gamal Abdel Nasser. The visit with Nasser was more than just a courtesy call. According to several press reports, Nixon did a little early work for his new law firm, offering to represent Nasser with his legal needs for a cool $2 million retainer.[5] While there is no record as to whether or not Nasser ever took him up on his offer, and Nixon's legal papers do not include any client files relating to Nasser, Nixon certainly did what he could to curry favor with the Egyptian leader in public. During his visit to Egypt, Nixon held a press conference and praised Nasser for his policies. "I was very much impressed by President Nasser's strong personality, wisdom and immense knowledge," Nixon said.[6] "Judging by the conversation we had this morning, President Nasser was not only very knowledgeable in his country's own affairs and problems, but also and equally, in all the issues of the Arab world, Africa, Asia, Eastern and Western Europe, and the world at large."

The Nixons also took a trip to the Berlin Wall, where the former VP was able to expound on his favorite topic: communism. After describing the Wall as "a very ugly eyesore,"[7] Nixon turned to the issue of East Berlin and expressed concern for those trapped behind the concrete monstrosity. "The people want freedom and would certainly have it if they had their choice," he said.[8] "Budapest is a free city compared to this." Nixon said the United States ought to use its power to seek German reunification, as well as extending freedom throughout Eastern Europe.[9] In Vienna, he expressed support for a proposed nuclear test ban treaty between the United States and the Soviet Union, but warned: "We must be under no illusions that this indicates any change in [Soviet leader Nikita Khrushchev's] basic objective, which is to impose Communism on the Western world."[10] Nixon was in Paris when the treaty was signed in mid July, but he took time out of his schedule to announce his support for it and urged Republican senators to ratify it.[11]

Nixon also found the time to play politics, saying that the Republican Party would do more for people stuck behind the Iron Curtain than Democrats, all the while insisting he would not be a future candidate for anything. Instead, he reiterated what was becoming his go-to line about how he would be "limited to making speeches, writing articles and supporting candidates."[12]

It was understandable why Nixon would choose to travel the world. For one thing, he and his family got a warm reception. "From our welcome abroad, no one would have guessed that I had lost two elections in the past three years and that my prospects for any political comeback seemed extremely remote," said Nixon.[13] "Everywhere we went we were received as if I were still Vice President." For Nixon's still-bruised ego, being treated as if he were still an important official helped buoy his spirits and give him hope for the future. In Paris, for instance, de Gaulle threw him a lavish lunch in his honor at the Élysée Palace and even spoke with Nixon as if he knew he were speaking to a future US president. The two engaged in high-level discussions about whether or not the United States might share nuclear secrets with France in exchange for support for the test ban treaty, as well as general discussions about NATO, China, and the Soviet Union. At lunch, de Gaulle even proposed a warm toast to his guest of honor, noting Nixon's recent setbacks but predicting his eventual comeback "in an even higher capacity."[14] Coming from a man he had long admired and been in awe of, de Gaulle's words meant the world to Nixon—even though, to Nixon, they may have seemed like pure fantasy at the time.

Another reason for the trip was to help establish himself as the foremost foreign policy expert in the country. Phase one of his strategy had taken place in April 1963, approximately a month before he announced his move to New York, when Nixon traveled to the East Coast to deliver a high-profile speech on foreign affairs at the annual meeting of the American Society of Newspaper Editors in Washington, D.C. Nixon prepared diligently and even pulled a virtual all-nighter in his hotel suite at the Madison Hotel doing research and working on his speech. "After a few hours' sleep, he got up again at seven and went until noon, working it over and over," recalled John Whitaker, Nixon's aide that helped him with the speech.[15]

According to Witcover, Nixon's aides were somewhat confused as to why their boss was taking this speech so seriously. After all, Nixon had addressed the ASNE many times before. Nixon, however, believed that this could be his last chance to deliver an important foreign policy speech because, as a nonpolitician, he was in danger of being forgotten about. "It may be the last time I'm ever asked to give a speech to such a group," Nixon said.[16] "I have a number of things I want to say."

Nixon hoped that what he would say would be so well received that he wouldn't need to beg for an invitation back. "It was Nixon's view that what a man said always received more attention and was likely to have more real influence if he spoke as one who might be a future Presidential candidate," wrote Witcover.[17] Plus, even if the White House were longer a possibility, there were other top jobs in Washington that Nixon could aim for, and if he could reinforce his reputation as the GOP's leading mind on foreign relations, then he could easily be a future secretary of state to a Republican president.

With that in mind, Nixon decided to play the greatest hits when he hit the stage at the ASNE conference. He employed one of his favorite rhetorical devices when he said that he was not criticizing the Kennedy Administration for being soft on communism or for looking weak on Cuba, even when it was clear he was doing exactly that. "Nor do I charge that this Administration is trying to appease Khrushchev," Nixon said.[18] Nixon also refused to take the Kennedy Administration to task for botching the Bay of Pigs invasion or for the Cuban Missile Crisis (or, as Nixon called it, "snatching defeat from the jaws of victory"). He was, especially, uninterested in criticizing the president for allowing having "given the Soviets squatters' rights in our backyard."[19] Once he was finished not-criticizing the Kennedys for the sorry state of affairs in the world, Nixon provided some constructive comments. In particular, he argued that the United States needed to strengthen its alliances and provide aid to countries struggling against communism so that America could win over the hearts and minds of people around the world. "I say it is time for us proudly to declare that our ideas are for export," Nixon said.[20] "We need not apologize for taking this position." In the end, Nixon declared that there was no substitute for victory and that anything short of that was the equivalent of surrender. "Nothing less than a free Russia, a free China, a free Eastern Europe and a free Cuba."[21]

Nixon also took time to emphasize that he was out of politics and even referenced his infamous "last press conference" a couple of times. At one point, he even tried humor. Referencing Harry Truman's famous quote about how "if you can't take the heat, then get out of the kitchen," Nixon half-jokingly said that his 1962 meltdown proved that politics was too hot for him.[22] In that vein, he tried to deflect speculation about his presidential aspirations, saying that ideological opposites Barry Goldwater and Nelson Rockefeller could make for an excellent GOP ticket in 1964. "If Jack and Lyndon could get together," he pointed out. "Barry and Nelson can."[23]

Several of the newspapermen in attendance weren't buying it. John Averill of the *LA Times*, for instance, observed that "while he denied in response to one question that he has any plans to seek public office in the future, several of his listeners were heard to remark that he sounded for all the world like a man still seeking the Presidency."[24]

"I WILL NOT AGAIN BE A CANDIDATE FOR ANYTHING."

Turns out, it wasn't just those newsmen or de Gaulle who saw Nixon as a future presidential candidate. The specter of another White House run loomed over him like an angel that was stuck on Earth until it earned its wings, and many journalists, politicians, and even Nixon's new partners and colleagues at the firm doubted that he had truly given up on his dream of becoming president.

Nixon understood that he had a delicate balancing act to pull off. He had to keep his name alive as a potential candidate because, as he noted, his words carried greater weight and drew more attention if people thought he might run for president again. However, he couldn't look like he was actively considering a run while he still had the stink from 1960 and 1962 on him. For one thing, the optics made more sense for him to be out of the political game. Being finished as a candidate, only to be pulled back into the game due to the popular demands of the voters, as well as his own party, was a far more compelling story than being the guy who didn't know when to quit. By denying that he was a candidate, he could also avoid some of the press scrutiny that would come with running for president. Plus, he needed time—not just to wait out a probable Kennedy reelection and Democratic landslide in 1964, but to figure out how to reestablish himself as a top contender and to get the voters who had abandoned him in 1960 and 1962 to come back to the fold. His chosen path, focusing on foreign policy while launching a successful career on Wall Street, would need time to implement.

This balancing act also applied to his new job at the firm. He felt he owed it to his partners to put the firm first and dedicate himself to building up Nixon Mudge. On the other hand, Nixon was savvy enough to know that the possibility that he could run for president again would be very useful in bringing in clients—just like it had been at Adams Duque.

At first, Nixon tried using humor to deflect all of the speculation. In the months before he announced his move to New York, he had appeared on the popular television show *The Jack Paar Program*, where he had exchanged jokes with the host and demonstrated his piano-playing chops by performing one of his own compositions. The show, which was taped in February and aired in March, had been one of his first major public appearances since losing the gubernatorial race, and Nixon, as was his wont, had prepared diligently for what was supposed to be a light-hearted, easygoing affair. He had written to several of his political friends who had appeared on Paar's show to ask them what he should expect when he sat down with the former *Tonight Show* host. He had even tested out some attack lines he was planning on using to criticize Kennedy and his Cuba policy.[25] The appearance went off without a hitch, and Nixon had even earned some genuine laughs as he prepared to play the piano concerto he had composed (it was more like a piano piece accompanied by strings than an actual concerto). "You asked a moment ago whether I had any future political plans to run for anything," Nixon said with a smile.[26] Nixon then compared himself to Truman, another prominent piano-playing politician. "If last November didn't finish it, this will because believe me, the Republicans don't want another piano player in the White House!"

He also tried the more straightforward approach. The moment word leaked out that he was considering moving to New York, many reporters and politicians immediately wondered whether Nixon would be so bold as to waltz into New York and try to steal Rockefeller's base from under his nose. In the run-up to his joining Mudge, he repeatedly denied that his potential move to New York was a political maneuver. He even gave an exclusive interview to the *New York Times* in early May 1963 saying that while he would "from time to time speak out on politics," he emphasized that he was "not coming to New York for any political reason whatsoever."[27] Later that month, when he released a statement saying that he was joining Mudge, reporters parsed his every word, zeroing in on his statement about how he would "engage in matters relating to the Washington and Paris offices of the firm" as a sign that he would continue to remain active in politics and foreign policy.[28] CBS News anchor Walter Cronkite, regarded as "the most trusted man in America," even reported that Nixon was coming to New York to "establish a base for another try at the Presidency."[29]

Nixon tried his best to quell such talk. A couple of weeks after announcing his arrival in New York, Nixon gave an extensive interview to Roscoe Drummond. While many politicians might have been cagey or equivocal, Nixon was surprisingly frank and resolute about his political future. He didn't include any of the usual phrases that someone who wanted to leave his options open would use, like "being finished for the foreseeable future" or seeing "no set of circumstances that might change his mind." He didn't even do what he had done on the golf course in Baltusrol Golf Club when he responded to John Alexander's question about whether he was truly finished with politics with: "John, if you knew anything about politics, you would know that a politician does not change his base."

Instead, Nixon couldn't have been clearer about his future prospects. "I will not again be a candidate for anything," he told Drummond.[30] "Under no circumstances whatever. That is categorical." He emphatically ruled out entering New York politics, stating that he moved to New York for personal and legal reasons. He made clear that he would continue on as a thought leader and party elder rather than be an active candidate for any office. And if that wasn't good enough for all the doubters, Nixon summoned his skills as a lawyer and tried to prove his case as if he were arguing before a jury. "Let's look at the facts," Nixon said.[31] "I have no staff. I am not answering any political mail. I am only making an occasional speech, writing an occasional magazine article. I have no political base. Anyone who thinks I could be a candidate for anything in any year is just off his rocker."

"MY GOD! CANDLES IN THE MIDDLE OF THE DAY!"

While he was traveling the globe, preparations were being made for the Nixon family's arrival in New York. The twelve-room apartment at 810 Fifth

Avenue was being redecorated while Rose Mary Woods, Nixon's longtime secretary, set up his new office at the firm's headquarters on 20 Broad Street. Woods was also going to make the move to Nixon Mudge so that she could continue serving as Nixon's secretary.

The corner office has long symbolized power, influence, and importance in corporate America, and Nixon Mudge was no different. Each of the four leaders of the firm (Nixon, Rose, Guthrie, and Alexander) had a corner office that was larger and nicer than everyone else's.[32] Nixon's office, however, stood out. Part museum, part awe-inspiring conversation starter, Nixon's office was a monument to his political life. Strewn about the walls and tables were various mementos and tchotchkes from his long, distinguished political career that reminded visitors that this was no ordinary lawyer. On a long table located behind Nixon's desk were framed, inscribed photographs of world leaders and famous figures such as Queen Elizabeth II, Jawaharlal Nehru, and the shah of Iran. Next to his desk was the chair he had sat in during Cabinet meetings in the White House. His old boss loomed large, as Nixon also kept on display a pen set from Eisenhower, a landscape painted by Eisenhower, and various other photos and souvenirs from his time as vice president, including the gavel he used to preside over the Senate.

His many trips abroad were also represented, as he displayed various pieces of Asian art that he had collected on his travels. He also found space to show off the many awards, honors, and keys to the city that he had received throughout his career. One of his more prominent mementos was a framed golf scorecard documenting a hole-in-one he had made while playing in a foursome with Hollywood actor Randolph Scott, Congressman Don Jackson (R-CA), and Bebe Rebozo. Another table contained pictures of his family, including a framed picture of his mother that was among his prized possessions. When he became president, only the golf card and his mother's photo would make the trek from his law office to the Oval Office.[33] He had planned for all of this stuff to be in his Presidential Library one day. For now, the corner office at 20 Broad Street would have to do.

Outside of Nixon's not-quite-presidential library were several desks. Woods sat at the main desk where she answered Nixon's phone, took dictation, and served as her boss's gatekeeper. When Patrick Buchanan joined the firm in January 1966 to work for Nixon as a speechwriter and researcher, he sat at the second desk. The third desk was seldom used and reserved for "Miss Ryan," who would come in periodically and help answer phones or perform clerical duties. Miss Ryan was better known as Pat Nixon, who used her maiden name to avoid drawing attention to herself when she answered the phones.[34] When Dwight Chapin came to the firm in April 1967 to serve as Nixon's personal aide and body man, he shared the space outside Nixon's office with Buchanan and Woods.[35]

"The office looked right for Nixon," Garment said.[36] "Its size was spacious but not excessive. The furniture was comfortable but formal enough to discourage lounging around." Garment noted that the office was somewhat intimidating but was definitely awe inspiring. "It was easy to picture him conducting properly impressed guests, as he did with me, around the personal museum of his public and private life."[37]

As Nixon soon learned, having a nice office only went so far. Like the many exotic locales he visited on his travels abroad, Wall Street was very much a foreign country to him. He realized, almost immediately, that he faced a steep learning curve.

"Somehow, his years at the highest levels of government had not prepared him for the world that he now encountered in the law," said Tom Evans.[38] While he had demonstrated a marked ability to generate business and sign up clients during his short stint at Adams Duque, Wall Street was a different animal. Part of it was due to Nixon's change in circumstances. During his Adams Duque tenure, Nixon had stood out from the pack due to his political accomplishments, as well as his status as the probable governor-in-waiting. On Wall Street, he was one of many former politicians, and he wasn't even the most accomplished one at that—not with Thomas Dewey practicing law in the same neighborhood.

The other part came down to Wall Street culture. As Nixon himself said, he was mainly joining the firm to help drum up business, but one of his other roles would be to recruit the best and brightest law students and young lawyers.[39] For someone who had been known to distrust the elite and wealthy, he would have to learn how to win their favor and, more importantly, their business. The ultimate Orthogonian would have to learn how to schmooze with the Franklins.

Nixon threw himself into his new role. As was typical for him, he worked hard and put in long hours. If he weren't on the road, he would usually arrive at the office by 7 a.m. and stay until 6 p.m.[40] Work isn't limited to the office, and during Nixon's tenure on Wall Street, a lot of business got done at various social and dining clubs. He joined The Links, an exclusive men's club located on E. 62nd Street in Manhattan that became a go-to setting for business dinners with potential clients. He also joined the Metropolitan Club on E. 60th Street and India House, a fancy Wall Street restaurant and dining club. The Recess was another natural landing spot for him—the downtown club was a short distance from his office and was a popular hangout for prominent Republican politicians like Dewey and Herbert Brownell Jr., Eisenhower's former attorney general who was senior partner at Wall Street firm Lord, Day & Lord.[41] Nixon lunched there approximately twice a week and even had his own table at a prime location in the club—at a corner where two windows met, giving him a nice view of the East River. Not that he was there to take in the scenery. He was usually in the club to talk turkey with clients, law partners, or political advisors. "I don't think I ever thought of him as being a lawyer," Karl Brandon, the manager of Recess, recalled after Nixon became president.[42] "He was a lawyer, but to us he was the Vice President."

Nixon's lack of experience with the Wall Street lifestyle betrayed him during his first meeting with his new law partners at the firm's office on 20 Broad Street. "The meeting was with the four senior partners [including himself]," Nixon recalled.[43] "They had it in the conference room. I remember they had lunch. I particularly remember they had candles, lighted candles for lunch, which to me was quite impressive. My God! Candles in the middle of the day!"

His reception at the firm had been relatively warm. Most of his partners were pleased at the news that the firm had landed its high-profile public partner a la Dewey or Willkie and were excited at the possibilities he brought with him. "I was certainly very interested in meeting him," Milton Rose recalled.[44] "And I was impressed with his bearing and his determination to, at that point, practice law for the indefinite future." Donald Zoeller, an associate who became chairman of the firm in 1995, said he thought Nixon was a great fit. "It was good for the firm and good for him," Zoeller said.[45] "I thought he would help us attract a lot of important clients."

On the other hand, there were some who hated Nixon and everything he stood for. "There was a lot of opposition, lawyers who said, 'He's a loser, what do we need him for?'" Garment recalled.[46] "Democrats within the firm just didn't like him." To them, he was Satan incarnate—a sneering, shifty, and dishonest man who represented the worst excesses of partisan politics. According to Garment, some of them even put their money where their mouths were and quit the firm in protest.[47] Garment, however, agreed with the Nixon proponents at the firm that saw their newest recruit as a net positive for the firm. "But so far as I was concerned, it was something that this law firm had to do in order to grow up and become a big law firm," Garment said.[48] "[We had to] have a political name partner."

Nixon knew he was going to need help dealing with Wall Street businessmen and soliciting them for business. He had taken a liking to Randolph Guthrie during the recruitment process and relied on his new law partner to help him navigate the tricky world of corporate law and Wall Street.[49] Guthrie was a Harvard Law alum, but he was far from the kind of northeastern elite that Nixon was so suspicious of. Guthrie was a southerner and came from a military background, graduating from the prestigious Citadel in South Carolina before enrolling at Harvard. "He could be courtly in manner, or a good ol' boy, as the occasion demanded," Evans noted.[50] Garment recalled that Guthrie's "manner was good-old-boy small-town southern insurance executive, not *Harvard Law Review* editor, as was the fact."[51]

Guthrie had joined Rushmore, Bisbee & Stern in 1931 after graduating from law school. Prior to joining as an associate, he had worked at the firm during the summer after his second year, making $25 a week. As an associate, he had joined the corporate department at the firm but then decided to try his hand at litigation. The firm's main client, at that time, was Chase Bank, and Guthrie handled, by his estimation, several hundred trials for them. "I was handling, really, small litigation," Guthrie recalled.[52] "That was what I wanted to do because that was the one place where you could get some real experience in court."

Guthrie soon transferred back into corporate because he recognized that he was better suited for that world. "His professional passions were pursuing clients, charging large fees and rebuilding the firm into a leading national institution," Garment said.[53] Despite being an outsider to New York, Guthrie was utterly at home at Wall Street and loved the process of wooing and landing clients. "A stocky man of medium height, he had a perennial weight problem which bespoke good living" was how Evans described him.[54] With a cigarette in one hand and, at night, a glass of Scotch or a martini in the other, the cherubic-faced Guthrie embodied the "boy's club" ethos of Wall Street.[55] He even addressed everybody as "boy"—it didn't matter if you were an associate or partner, white or black, male or female, the salutation was the same.[56] Today, it would probably get him in trouble with human resources, but back then, no one thought anything of it. "Boy we're going to be the biggest and best goddamn law firm in America, make the most goddamn money, drink the most goddamn martinis [and] have the most goddamn fun!"[57] "He did have fun," Evans noted.[58] Garment later recalled Richard Nixon saying that Guthrie was more like Lyndon Johnson than Lyndon Johnson.[59]

Like Johnson, Guthrie recognized a power vacuum when he saw one and stepped up, at a young age, into a position of leadership and influence. After a string of ineffective or ineffectual senior partners, Guthrie took hold of the firm in 1954 as he and Alexander become coheads and negotiated the merger with Baldwin & Todd.

Guthrie was well connected, too. He served as chairman of the board for Studebaker-Packard Corporation from 1963 to 1971, and he was also US counsel for Daimler Benz.[60] When Guthrie took over Studebaker in June 1963, the automotive manufacturers had been in decline for years and were considering the possibility that it would stop producing cars. One of the first things he did as chairman was analyze the company and the automotive industry to determine whether it was worth it for Studebaker to stay in. He quickly determined that it wasn't and accelerated efforts to wind down, informing his board members during an August 1963 meeting that they had to start assuming Studebaker would leave the car business unless a miracle happened. Production had already been cut significantly, and the reason why

Studebaker hadn't halted or suspended production completely was because the lawyer in Guthrie worried about lawsuits from car dealers.[61]

A few months later, Guthrie and the board went ahead and closed its headquarters in South Bend, Indiana, while moving operations to Canada.[62] "We were being bled to death in South Bend," Guthrie said.[63] One of the trickier feats that Guthrie pulled off following Studebaker's US exodus was to negotiate the termination of a longstanding distribution agreement between Studebaker and his longtime clients at Daimler Benz. After several months of difficult, and sometimes ill-tempered, negotiations, which required Guthrie to straddle the line between zealously representing Studebaker and maintaining the confidentiality of his prior attorney-client relationship with Daimler Benz, both parties reached a deal and Guthrie was free to move onto the next step of his plan.[64] That step came to fruition in 1967, as a three-way merger between Studebaker, Wagner Electric, and Worthington Corporation created Studebaker-Worthington, a diversified company specializing in automotive components, construction equipment, and valves. Guthrie became chairman of the combined company, staying in that role until 1971.

Guthrie took an immediate liking to Nixon and recognized that he could be a great tool for the firm. "I was his tutor, really," Guthrie said.[65] "I went to the Far East with him. I was teaching him the business. He really didn't know anything about the law."

Guthrie aside, Nixon didn't bond with too many of his other partners. According to Witcover, Nixon found Rose and Alexander "narrow and boring" and usually lined up with Guthrie whenever there was a disagreement relating to firm management. Witcover also reported that Nixon rarely socialized with his law partners and preferred spending time at home in order to catch up on his reading. He also cut down on his golf, avoiding country clubs like Baltusrol where he and his partners had first forged their alliance because he often ran into colleagues that he didn't care for.[66] John Sears agreed, saying that Nixon seemed isolated at the firm. "I don't think he had much to do with the other partners," said Sears.[67] "Obviously, there were firm functions where everyone was together. Otherwise, I didn't get the feeling that they all went out in the evenings or that their families meshed."

On the other hand, Nixon's partners had no problem calling on him when they needed someone with his political connections. Alexander, for instance, had a brother in Florida who was dealing with emotional and mental trauma as a result of his World War I service and was seeking admission to a Veterans Administration hospital. Nixon sent a letter to his friend, Florida senator George Smathers, asking him to look into the matter. Smathers responded within two weeks, telling Nixon that he had spoken to officials at the regional VA office in St. Petersburg and they had determined that Alexander's brother had not established that his condition was related to his service. Despite that, Smathers assured Nixon that the St. Petersburg VA office would follow up with Alexander's brother to see if he could be admitted regardless of service connection.[68] Nixon also helped out Guthrie, writing reference letters for his son.

For his part, Rose downplayed any conflict and maintained that the four senior partners occasionally socialized outside of the office, holding dinner parties and spending weekends together at their respective weekend homes. When it came time for firm matters, however, Rose admitted that he rarely spoke to Nixon. "He was pretty much consumed with litigation matters in the firm," said Rose.[69] "It was Len Garment who had the close association with him."

At first sight, Leonard Garment and Richard Nixon made for a truly odd couple. Garment, a corporate litigator, was a longtime Democrat who had voted for JFK in 1960. In fact, a year before he met Nixon, Garment had even held a fundraiser at his Brooklyn home for Robert Kennedy.[70] His parents had been working-class Jewish immigrants—his father had come from Lithuania while his mother had been born in Poland—and they lived in a three-bedroom tenement apartment in the Brownsville section of Brooklyn. He had stayed within the borough for both undergrad and law school, having earned his bachelor's degree from Brooklyn College and his JD from Brooklyn Law School.[71]

Unlike Nixon, Garment had been an indifferent student and had sought a career away from law and politics. A talented clarinet and saxophone player, Garment had pursued a career as a jazz musician and had played in Henry Jerome's band as well as Woody Herman's. While in Jerome's band, he had played with another musician who was destined to play a very public role in D.C.: saxophone player and future chairman of the Federal Reserve, Alan Greenspan.

Knowing that he would never be as good as Louis Armstrong and Charlie Parker, whom he referred to as "black Mozarts," Garment went back to school in 1945.[72] A year later, he found his way to Brooklyn Law School where he did well, but not well enough to earn a transfer to Columbia Law School. "Brooklyn Law School was not on Paul Cravath's list of select law schools, nor on the lists of very many Wall Street hiring partners," Evans said.[73] However, Joesph Kline, Mudge's hiring partner, saw something in Garment and offered him a job with a starting salary of $60 a week.

In 1949, Garment officially joined the Wall Street world, and in doing so, helped break new ground. "I was one of a handful of Jews in my generation who squeezed through the keyhole of the tightly closed Gentile fraternity of Wall Street lawyers," Garment said.[74] He became a partner within eight years, which was almost unheard of in those days (Guthrie had to wait twelve years, for instance) and was named head of the litigation department in 1965.

Perhaps it wasn't surprising that Nixon, the Wall Street outsider, would be drawn to a fellow outlier. "Len Garment and Richard Nixon came to Wall

Street after abandoning other careers," Evans observed.[75] "They were outsiders who achieved success the hard way. Unlike many of their peers, they had suffered rejection at the hands of the very Wall Street establishment which now embraced them. And they met as partners in a firm which had itself known peaks and valleys of esteem rare among its kind—perhaps the only place that they could have met and worked closely together."

Garment, who eventually became White House counsel under President Nixon, remembered being excited with all the possibilities that having Nixon as a law partner might bring. In more than a decade of service to the firm, Garment had handled a number of high-profile litigation matters successfully, including a trademark infringement case against Colgate that stopped the toothpaste giants from running a multimillion dollar ad campaign.[76] In another case, he pulled off a nifty bit of lawyering as he defended a Midwestern grain company on charges that it had misappropriated grain that was owned by the government by arguing that his client actually owned it. Then, in a related civil case, he turned around and argued that his client had limited responsibilities when it came to the grain because it was actually government property. "I will never forget the look on the face of the government's attorney when the judge agreed with us," Garment said.[77] "Ah, the majesty of the law."

Maybe it's no surprise that Garment found himself drawn to politics. While he enjoyed being head of litigation at the firm and mentoring generations of young lawyers, he admitted that he had grown bored of corporate litigation and was desperate for a change of pace. "Most of my small-scale ambitions had been achieved, and I had that bleak midlife feeling that I was doing what I would be doing for the rest of my life," Garment said.[78] "I couldn't have cared less that Richard Nixon was the political Antichrist of eastern liberalism. He was also an opening to a different life and the possibility of salvation."

Despite, or maybe because of, his excitement at Nixon joining the firm, it took Garment months before he worked up enough courage to speak with the former vice president. It was after the weekly partnership lunch in late autumn 1963 when Garment finally spoke, one on one, with Nixon. The firm partners had gathered with Nixon (who was not yet, officially, a partner) in the firm's conference room for a catered, candle-lit meal. Nixon no longer seemed surprised to see candles in the middle of the day. Instead, as Garment recalled, he was more stunned by another firm tradition. "The partners sat down to a small self-administered treat," Garment said. "A crisp, new twenty-dollar bill passed to each diner as a reward for showing up and attending to his professional well-being. I remember Nixon's surprised reaction to this weird little custom of the inscrutable East."

After the meal, Garment went to Nixon's office where he asked Rose Mary Woods if he could speak with him. Garment was immediately admitted into Nixon's unofficial vice presidential library where he got his first up close and personal look at his firm's soon-to-be public partner. After taking in the portraits, pictures, and various other souvenirs and mementos all designed to reinforce his sense of inferiority, Garment sat down and gushed about how excited he was to have Nixon at the firm. "I told him about the high hopes I held for him and the firm and described the boredom and depression I had been feeling about my work," Garment said.[79] He also had a confession to make. "I told him I was a birthright Democrat," Garment admitted, revealing his vote for Jack Kennedy in 1960, as well as the fundraiser for Bobby two years later in his home.[80]

Luckily for Garment, Nixon didn't hold a grudge. Garment recalled that Nixon shrugged off his confession and said that he welcomed the opportunity to work with people with different political views than his own. In fact, Garment and Nixon seemed to hit it off immediately—helped in no small part by the fact that both men recognized that he could be useful to the other. Later on, Garment remembered that it seemed as if both Woods and Nixon had been expecting him, and that he believed Nixon had always planned on becoming his friend, just like Garment had planned on ingratiating himself with his firm's new lead partner.[81] Garment, obviously, was looking for a change of pace and knew that Nixon, as a powerful man with lots of important connections, could give him a more exciting practice. Nixon, meanwhile, needed help adapting to life on Wall Street, and Garment, like Guthrie, had seamlessly navigated the corporate world to become a highly respected lawyer and member of the firm. Garment also sensed that Nixon was already planning his political future and knew that having a Democrat on board would be useful if and when he decided to mount his comeback. "He knew that this contrast would be a political asset in his return to public life," Garment said.[82] "It would give him, in addition to his 99 percent name and face recognition, the capacity to surprise."

"HE WAS SMILING . . ."

While he may have had some growing pains at work, when it came to living in New York, Nixon and his family settled in almost immediately. Indeed, the Nixons had taken to their new surroundings with such ease and joy that it seemed as if DC and LA had been temporary stops in their long odyssey toward their spiritual home in Manhattan. For Pat and the girls, it had been, more or less, love at first sight when it came to New York. The three enjoyed exploring the city and all that it had to offer, and Pat, in particular, relished her increased anonymity—something that she hadn't experienced since before 1952. Tricia and Julie enrolled at the exclusive all-girl Chapin School located on the Upper East Side that boasted the likes of Jacqueline Kennedy,

Anna Roosevelt Halsted (daughter of FDR and Eleanor Roosevelt), and several members of the Rockefeller family as alumni. The two Nixon daughters were also presented as debutantes. Tricia debuted in 1964 with future husband, Edward Cox, as her escort,[83] and two years later, Julie did the same, with future husband David Eisenhower (Ike's grandson) on her arm.[84]

For Nixon, on the other hand, he might have expected some major growing pains, if not outright discomfort living in the de facto capital of the Eastern Establishment. Instead, he seemed happy and comfortable in the Big Apple.

Certainly, money helped make Nixon's landing in New York a soft one. For the first time in his life, he was a rich man. With his law firm salary and book royalties, he easily cleared $200,000 in annual income.[85] Nixon soon discovered that, for a man of means, New York City is one of the best cities in the world to live in. With his money, connections, and access to power, New York became his personal playground and, for the first time in his life, Nixon could actually indulge a bit. Of course, for him, indulging meant going to the theater or to classical music concerts. According to the *New York Times*, Nixon and his family particularly enjoyed *How to Succeed in Business without Really Trying*, as well as *Jennie*, starring renowned Broadway star Mary Martin.[86] Sometimes he and fellow music lover Garment would get together for informal jam sessions where Nixon would tickle the ivories and Garment would play his clarinet.[87] He'd also treat his inner sports fan, attending baseball and football games at Yankee Stadium. He even started getting into hockey, watching New York Rangers games at Madison Square Garden.[88]

Moving East had also given Nixon the opportunity to broaden his palette. A notoriously bad eater who, in his younger years, was known to consume Milky Way candy bars as breakfast, Nixon's tastes hadn't really progressed much from there. He was known to eat cottage cheese with ketchup, while plain old spaghetti with meat sauce was another staple of his diet.[89] Once in New York, however, he started eating better and healthier, taking advantage of the many great restaurants in the city. Several journalists observed that Nixon seemed to have put on weight but that the extra pounds had been good to him as they had smoothed out some of his features and given him a more rounded face. Theodore White, who covered the 1960 and 1964 presidential elections in depth, observed that while Nixon's face had filled out, some of his other features were every bit as sharp and conspicuous than ever. "The jaw jutted out, the nose was more pronounced, the bush thick hair of his earlier campaigns was slowly receding to a widow's peak, its curly wave more conspicuous," White found.[90] "The lines on his face from nose to chin, the cheek folds themselves, were deeper, more furrowed; yet the more mature man seemed more attractive, less harsh than the man of 1960."

White also found Nixon to be more relaxed—he was even jovial, at times—than the candidate he had previous encountered in 1960. "Once, I remember seeing him strolling solitary on Fifth Avenue on a cold December day," White wrote in *The Making of the President, 1968*.[91] "He had no topcoat, only a light suit jacket, and the habitual frown, I noticed, was gone from his face; he was smiling as if amused by some inner conversation."

Nixon had embraced New York City, and the city had embraced him right back. Upon their arrival, the Nixons had found themselves besieged with social calls and invitations to the point that they rarely had a quiet night at home during their first few months in Manhattan.[92] Once the novelty of that wore off, however, the Nixons found themselves turning down invitations left and right. Instead, they seemed content to spend most of their evenings inside their Fifth Avenue home. Decorated modestly, the apartment was refurnished in French provincial style with pastel yellows and golds predominating the twelve rooms.[93] There was a clear Asian flavor as well, as Nixon proudly displayed Chinese paintings he had received from Madame Chiang Kai-shek in the hallway, while the living room contained numerous Oriental-style jardinières and vases. And if there were any doubt that this was the home of, perhaps, the preeminent Republican in the country, there were many, many miniature elephants on display, varying by size and material. According to White, of all the Republican homes he had been in over the years, only William Scranton's home in Pennsylvania contained more.[94]

The Nixons had put in $50,000 to renovate the apartment, and Pat went to work, furnishing the living room with light draperies and understated upholstery.[95] She had also taken one of the servants' quarters and converted it into a walk-in closet for the master bedroom,[96] while another one of the servants' quarters was converted into a storage room for Nixon's papers. As for the Nixons' live-in servants, Fina and Manolo Sanchez, they were given a large room adjacent to the kitchen.

Once his social calendar cleared up, Nixon spent most of his time in his den. A voracious reader, Nixon hadn't been able to do much leisurely reading since entering politics. Now that he was no longer in office, he hoped to remedy that and spent most of his evenings reading biographies, histories, and various other nonfiction books. According to Witcover, Nixon's primary areas of fascination during this time were books about Theodore Roosevelt, Woodrow Wilson, and Winston Churchill. He admired Roosevelt because he was a born leader and a man of action who was bold, dynamic, and inspirational. Wilson, meanwhile, had an enviable intellect that even his fiercest critics had to respect and even admire. As for Churchill, Nixon had always been a fan of the venerable prime minister.[97] Reading between the lines, it was easy to see why Nixon was drawn to these three. Roosevelt was the ideal—the man of great charisma that could do what Nixon could not: inspire the masses and capture their imagination. Wilson was the blueprint—a man who had gotten ahead with his intelligence and brilliance. As for Churchill, he embodied both archetypes and also served as an inspiration to Nixon, given how he had bounced back after more than one bitter electoral setback.

"IN PERSON, HE WAS TOTALLY CHARMING AND MESMERIZING."

Nixon's law partners had hoped that having the former VP and presidential nominee in tow would give them a leg up in recruiting the best and brightest law students around the country. In that respect, Nixon proved to be a magnet for law students—some of whom would never have considered Nixon Mudge otherwise.

"Even though it was unusual for a senior partner to engage in [on campus interviews], Nixon committed himself to go to Harvard, Yale, Columbia and Michigan in the fall of 1965," Evans noted.[98]

Many law students signed up for interviews just so they could speak to Nixon. Harvard law grad John Milem, a Nixon Mudge associate who joined in 1966, recalled having almost zero interest in working in New York City but took an on-campus interview with Nixon Mudge, in part, because he wanted the opportunity to speak with Nixon. Milem remembered that Nixon had done most of the talking and, while the usually garrulous Guthrie was involved in the conversation, he ended up speaking about half as much as Nixon. "[B]asically the conversation went in the direction of efforts to convince me that I needed to try myself on 'the fast track'—Mr. Nixon kept using that expression," said Milem, who had his eyes on practicing law in the Pacific Northwest, where he was from.[99] "He said that I could always go back to Seattle from New York if I disliked New York, but if I went to Seattle first, then I'd probably never have that opportunity—and I just owed it to myself to do it." Nixon's hard sell worked, as Milem stayed with the firm until 1975, when he became chief financial officer of SEDCO, a Dallas-based oilfield services company.[100]

Richard Berenson Stone, a Harvard alum for both undergrad and law school who went on to a forty-plus-year career as a law professor at Columbia Law School, had more personal reasons to desire an audience with Nixon. Stone's father was Saul Stone, a prominent Louisiana lawyer and one of the top Republicans in a state that was still dominated by Democrats. The elder Stone ran Wisdom & Stone alongside his partner, future US Court of Appeals judge for the Fifth Circuit John Minor Wisdom, and both attorneys had become power players in the state GOP (such as it was in the 1950s) by backing Eisenhower during the contentious 1952 GOP convention. Despite his overwhelming personal popularity, Eisenhower had faced an uphill climb for the presidential nomination, as the party machinery seemed poised to give the nod to Robert Taft. According to Stone, Wisdom and his father had led the effort in Louisiana to elect Eisenhower delegates to the national convention, and they received national attention after Taft's lieutenants had tried to block them and all of the other Eisenhower delegates throughout the South from being seated at the convention. After public pressure, as well as some internal maneuvering, the Ike delegates were seated and helped swing a closely divided convention to the popular ex-general.

For Stone, those days held a special place in his heart. "My first job was handing out fliers for the Republican National Committee," Stone recalled.[101] "Wisdom gave me $1.50 for my work." As such, he was determined to meet the man who had stood on stage with Ike at that 1952 convention, beaming with pride and ambition as he raised his future boss's hand in the air as if he were a referee declaring the winner of a boxing match. "I was there to meet Nixon," said Stone, who wasn't really interested in joining Nixon Mudge.[102] "I was driven by the idea that you take the accolade you earn, and Mudge was a good firm but not in the same league as Cravath, Davis Polk or Sullivan & Cromwell in terms of ability to attract top students from Harvard Law School."

Stone recalled that he met Nixon and Guthrie inside a hotel room in Cambridge in 1965. Nixon took an immediate liking to him and seemed as if he really wanted Stone to join the firm. Whether Nixon's interest was genuine or if he were looking to strengthen his ties to Stone's father and law partner, both of who continued to hold great sway over the Louisiana GOP, was a question that Stone pondered even as his interview was going on.

Nevertheless, Stone remembered that Nixon used every bit of charm at his disposal to get him to sign on the dotted line. "In person, he was totally charismatic and mesmerizing," said Stone.[103] "No matter what people say about his TV personality, he's the ultimate proof that you don't get that far in life without having some degree of likeability." According to Stone, when he went to New York for a follow-up interview, Nixon accosted him in the hall and not only remembered him but made it clear he hoped Stone would come aboard. "We ended up in his office and spent an entire hour there," Stone said.[104] "He wanted me to work for him personally, and mentioned that I might handle some non-legal matters and some international affairs. I took it to mean that he was going to run again." Stone ultimately passed on the offer and joined Davis Polk. He soon found himself in Washington, D.C., where he did end up working for Nixon—in the US Solicitor General's Office.

Not all law students were swayed by the Nixon charm. Peter Rousselot, who graduated from Harvard Law in 1965, recalled being put off by the former vice president during his job interview with the firm. "Nixon and the two other partners interviewed me in Cambridge, and invited me to come to New York for further interviews, which I did," Rousselot recalled.[105] "During my follow-up visit to New York, Nixon interviewed me again, and he personally offered me a job with his firm at that time, promising that I would get to work with him at least part of the time." Rousselot remembered being struck by Nixon's intelligence, as well as his tendency to monopolize a conversation to the detriment of his partners. "[He] delighted in 'putting down' his fellow partners, showing off that he could run rings around them," said Rousselot, a future Democratic Committee Chairman of Arlington, Virginia, who turned down Nixon Mudge to join Hogan & Hartson. "This was evident and off-putting, even to a lowly law student like me."

Perhaps Nixon's most important recruit from the law school ranks was John Sears. A Syracuse native who earned his undergrad degree from the University of Notre Dame and his JD from Georgetown University, Sears wanted to return to Syracuse to practice law, but he was "waylaid" after receiving an offer to clerk with the New York State Court of Appeals. After serving as clerk from 1963 to 1965, he felt he needed to stay in New York City in order to take care of his growing family, which now included two young children. "I couldn't afford to go home," Sears recalled.[106] "So I wrote letters to the 20 largest firms and I got ten interviews. I thought I would go to Dewey Ballantine, but then Nixon Mudge called me."

Sears admitted that he only kept his appointment with Nixon Mudge because it was easier than canceling it. Sears, a lifelong Republican, was also interested in meeting the former vice president. "I had followed his career, of course," Sears recalled.[107] "I wasn't old enough to vote in 1960, otherwise I would have voted for him." During his interview, Sears spoke with both Nixon and Garment. "I noticed he was more nervous than I was," recalled Sears.[108] "That was my first impression of him. I thought it was very strange." Ultimately, Sears said that the firm offered him a bit more money that he would have made at Dewey Ballantine, so he signed up with Nixon Mudge. Sears would go on to play an important role in the 1968 campaign for Nixon before managing Ronald Reagan's 1976 presidential campaign.

While Nixon made his mark as a recruiter for the firm, where he truly excelled was as a rainmaker. With a little help from his corporate friends, Nixon proved he was every bit as good at bringing in business as his partners had hoped he would be. And with each bit of success, his partners began to accept, more and more, that what was good for Nixon was good for the firm. By the time 1968 rolled around, the firm was all in when it came to its public partner's political fortunes. For better or worse . . .

NOTES

1. Richard Nixon, *RN: The Memoirs of Richard Nixon* (New York: Simon & Schuster, 2013).
2. Stephen Ambrose, *Nixon: Volume 2: The Triumph of a Politician, 1962–1972* (New York: Simon & Schuster, 1989), 320.
3. Nixon, *RN*.

4. Ambrose, *Nixon: Volume 2*, 463.
5. Jon Frappier, "Invisible Power Brokers: The Nixon-Mitchell Law Firm," *North American Congress on Latin America* 7, no. 9 (November 1973).
6. Drew Pearson and Jack Anderson, "Nixon Called Nasser Wise, Strong," *Washington Post*, October 28, 1968.
7. "Nixon Visits Wall: Calls It an 'Ugly Eyesore,'" *Chicago Tribune*, July 24, 1963.
8. Ralph Bennington, "Nixons Land at Frankfurt after Look behind Wall," *Stars and Stripes*, June 26, 1963, accessed February 14, 2016, http://www.stripes.com/news/nixons-land-at-frankfurt-after-look-behind-wall-1.17111.
9. Jules Witcover, *The Resurrection of Richard Nixon* (New York: G. P. Putnam's Sons, 1970), 23.
10. Witcover, *The Resurrection of Richard Nixon*.
11. Witcover, *The Resurrection of Richard Nixon*.
12. Bennington, "Nixons Land at Frankfurt."
13. Nixon, *RN*.
14. Roger Morris, "Nixon Goes to Europe," *New York Times*, April 16, 2009, accessed February 14, 2016, http://100days.blogs.nytimes.com/2009/04/16/nixon-goes-to-europe-part-ii/?_r=0.
15. Witcover, *The Resurrection of Richard Nixon*, 43–44.
16. Witcover, *The Resurrection of Richard Nixon*, 44.
17. Witcover, *The Resurrection of Richard Nixon*.
18. Ambrose, *Nixon: Volume 2*, 19.
19. Ambrose, *Nixon: Volume 2*, 19–20.
20. David Schmitz, *Richard Nixon and the Vietnam War: The End of the American Century* (Lanham, MD: Rowman & Littlefield Publishers, 2014), 11.
21. Ambrose, *Nixon: Volume 2*, 20.
22. Ambrose, *Nixon: Volume 2*, 19.
23. Ambrose, *Nixon: Volume 2*, 20.
24. Witcover, *The Resurrection of Richard Nixon*, 48.
25. Ambrose, *Nixon: Volume 2*, 18.
26. Roboci Heyni, "Richard Nixon on 'The Jack Paar Program' (March 8, 1963)," YouTube video, 2:47, posted July 4, 2015, https://www.youtube.com/watch?v=PctLLLVqMrM.
27. "Nixon Says He May Move to New York," *Los Angeles Times*, May 2, 1963.
28. Ambrose, *Nixon: Volume 2*, 22.
29. Ambrose, *Nixon: Volume 2*, 22.
30. Roscoe Drummond, "Will Never Run Again, Nixon Insists," *Boston Globe*, May 14, 1963.
31. Drummond, "Will Never Run Again, Nixon Insists."
32. Thomas Evans, "Nixon Mudge," (unpublished manuscript, 1994), 121.
33. Rose Mary Woods, interview by Tom Evans, February 27, 1988, transcript. And Aitken, 26–27.
34. Jonathan Aitken, *Nixon: A Life* (Washington, DC: Regnery History, 1993), 63.
35. Dwight Chapin, interview by Victor Li, May 9, 2016.
36. Leonard Garment, *Crazy Rhythm: From Brooklyn and Jazz to Nixon's White House, Watergate and Beyond* (Cambridge, MA: Da Capo Press, 1997), 66.
37. Garment, *Crazy Rhythm*.
38. Evans, "Nixon Mudge," 122.
39. Richard Nixon, interview by Tom Evans, March 15, 1983, transcript.
40. Ambrose, *Nixon: Volume 2*, 24.
41. Eric Pace, "Herbert Brownell, 92, Eisenhower Attorney General, Dies," *New York Times*, May 2, 1996, accessed March 21, 2017, http://www.nytimes.com/1996/05/02/us/herbert-brownell-92-eisenhower-attorney-general-dies.html?pagewanted=all. Also Evans, "Nixon Mudge," 121–22.
42. Witcover, *The Resurrection of Richard Nixon*, 50–51.
43. Evans, "Nixon Mudge," 122.
44. Milton Rose, interview by Tom Evans, November 15, 1989, transcript.

45. Donald Zoeller, interview by Victor Li, February 1, 2016.

46. Jeffrey Frank, "When Leonard Garment Met Richard Nixon," *New Yorker*, July 18, 2013, accessed February 14, 2016, http://www.newyorker.com/news/news-desk/when-leonard-garment-met-richard-nixon.

47. Garment, *Crazy Rhythm*, 65.

48. Garment, *Crazy Rhythm*.

49. Evans, "Nixon Mudge," 122.

50. Evans, "Nixon Mudge."

51. Garment, *Crazy Rhythm*, 60–61.

52. Randolph Guthrie, interview by Tom Evans, March 3, 1981, transcript.

53. Garment, *Crazy Rhythm*, 60.

54. Evans, "Nixon Mudge," 123.

55. Evans, "Nixon Mudge," 122–23.

56. Garment, *Crazy Rhythm*, 61.

57. Garment, *Crazy Rhythm*, 61.

58. Evans, "Nixon Mudge," 123.

59. Garment, *Crazy Rhythm*, 61.

60. Patrick Foster, *Studebaker: The Complete History* (Minneapolis: Motorbooks, 2008), 123.

61. Donald Critchlow, *Studebaker: The Life and Death of an American Corporation* (Bloomington, IN: Indiana Unversity Press, 1996).

62. Robert Ebert, *Champion of the Lark: Harold E. Churchill and the Presidency of Studebaker-Packard, 1956–1961* (Jefferson, NC: McFarland & Co., Inc., 2013), 146.

63. Robert Langworth, *Studebaker 1946–1966: The Classic Postwar Years* (Osceola, WI: Motorbooks International Publishers & Wholesalers, 1979, 1993), 146.

64. Thomas Bonsall, *More Than They Promised: The Studebaker Story* (Stanford, CA: Stanford University Press, 2000), 372–90.

65. Evans, "Nixon Mudge," 123.

66. Witcover, *The Resurrection of Richard Nixon*, 50–51.

67. John Sears, interview by Victor Li, February 16, 2016.

68. Richard Nixon, Letter from George Smathers, October 1, 1963, Pre-Presidential Papers, Richard Nixon Presidential Library and Museum.

69. Milton Rose, interview by Tom Evans, supra.

70. Garment, *Crazy Rhythm*, 69.

71. Eric Lightblau, "Leonard Garment, Lawyer and Nixon Adviser during Watergate, Dies at 89," *New York Times*, July 15, 2013, accessed on March 21, 2017, http://www.nytimes.com/2013/07/16/us/politics/leonard-garment-nixon-lawyer-and-watergate-figure-dies-at-89.html?_r=0.

72. Garment, *Crazy Rhythm*, 38–44.

73. Evans, "Nixon Mudge," 94.

74. Garment, *Crazy Rhythm*, 46.

75. Evans, "Nixon Mudge," 96.

76. Garment, *Crazy Rhythm*, 62–65.

77. Garment, *Crazy Rhythm*, 62–63.

78. Garment, *Crazy Rhythm*, 64–65.

79. Garment, *Crazy Rhythm*, 66–68.

80. Garment, *Crazy Rhythm*.

81. Garment, *Crazy Rhythm*.

82. Garment, *Crazy Rhythm*, 128.

83. "The Marriage of Tricia Nixon and Edward Finch Cox," *The Nixon Foundation*, June 12, 2014, accessed June 30, 2016, https://www.nixonfoundation.org/2014/06/welcome-marriage-tricia-nixon-edward-finch-cox/.

84. "Throwing a Ball," *New York Social Diary*, December 29, 2016, accessed June 30, 2016, http://www.newyorksocialdiary.com/social-diary/2016/throwing-a-ball.

85. Theodore White, *The Making of the President, 1968* (New York: Atheneum Publishers, 1969), 47.

86. Peter Kihss, "Nixon, Happy as New Yorker, Says Job Is Law, Not Politics," *New York Times*, December 29, 1963.
87. White, *The Making of the President*, 45–46.
88. Kihiss, "Nixon, Happy as a New Yorker."
89. White, *The Making of the President*, 44–45.
90. White, *The Making of the President.*
91. White, *The Making of the President*, 44.
92. Ambrose, *Nixon: Volume 2*, 26.
93. Witcover, *The Resurrection of Richard Nixon*, 52.
94. White, *The Making of the President*, 43.
95. White, *The Making of the President*, 43. Also Ambrose, *Nixon: Volume 2*, 26–27.
96. Witcover, *The Resurrection of Richard Nixon*, 52.
97. Witcover, *The Resurrection of Richard Nixon*, 52–53.
98. Evans, "Nixon Mudge," 24.
99. John Milem, interview by Tom Evans, December 1, 1987.
100. "John Milem Obituary," *The Columbian*, accessed on March 22, 2017, http://obits.columbian.com/obituaries/columbian/obituary.aspx?pid=162415934#sthash.q7VbOTeR.dpuf.
101. Richard Stone, interview by Victor Li, May 24, 2016.
102. Stone, interview by Victor Li.
103. Stone, interview by Victor Li.
104. Stone, interview by Victor Li.
105. "A Job Offer from Nixon Draws a 'Thanks, but No Thanks' Response," *Arlington Sun Gazette*, June 7, 2010.
106. Sears, interview by Li.
107. Sears, interview by Li.
108. Sears, interview by Li.

Chapter Four

"I Have Never Asked Anybody for Business."

During his first meeting with Nixon, Garment recalled that his senior partner was pretty clear about his vision for the firm. "He thought that what was right for him would also be good for the firm," Garment said.[1]

The latter part of that statement came true almost immediately as Nixon proved to be every bit the client magnet he had promised to be. Business boomed at Nixon Mudge almost from the moment he joined. According to an accounting report prepared by Arthur Young & Company, the firm collected $2.6 million in fees in 1963 (Nixon joined in August 1963 and became partner in January 1964). That number shot up to nearly $3.5 million the following year before creeping up toward $3.8 million in 1965.[2] The $2.6 million in fees from 1963 translates to over $20.5 million in 2017 dollars based on the CPI Inflation Calculator from the US Bureau of Labor Statistics. Likewise, the $3.5 million in fees from 1964 is roughly equivalent to $27.5 million in 2017, while the following year's $3.8 million becomes nearly $29.3 million.

A lot of work came into the firm during that time, as Price Waterhouse & Co. found when it conducted a survey of various law firms in the country. In 1963, firm partners billed an average of 857 hours each, a decrease from 1962, when partners billed 929 hours each. In 1964, however, average partner billable hours shot up to 1,119 hours in 1964 before hitting 1,251 the following year. The firm's associates were, likewise, busy, seeing their average hours shoot up during that three-year span from approximately 1,500 hours a year to over 1,700.[3]

As a result of this increase in business, Nixon's partners at the firm saw their bank accounts swell. According to a Price Waterhouse & Co. study, average operating income per partner increased from $46,150 in 1963 to

$68,110 in 1964.[4] The study, which compared Nixon Mudge to a group of forty-nine large firms in the United States, ranked Nixon's firm forty-second in 1963 when it came to average operating income per partner. A year later, they were up to twenty-sixth. After 1965, the average operating income per partner increased further, going up to $73,500.[5] The $73,500 in 1965 translates to over $565,000 in 2017 dollars based on the CPI Inflation Calculator from the US Bureau of Labor Statistics.

Nixon's arrival also led to an expansion at the firm. In 1963, the same year Nixon came aboard, the firm acquired Dorr, Hand & Whittaker, a smaller firm on Wall Street that specialized in railroad law.[6] With Nixon in tow, the firm anticipated an uptick in government-related work. As such, the following year, Nixon Mudge acquired a two-partner maritime law firm in Washington, D.C., named Becker & Greenwald.[7] The main office, at 20 Broad Street in Manhattan, also expanded considerably, as the firm hired so many additional lawyers and employees that it went from three floors in 1962 to five by the start of 1967.[8]

Nixon was hardly the only rainmaker at the firm, but he quickly established himself as one of the biggest. Almost immediately after his arrival, several of the firm's existing clients like Bobst's Warner-Lambert and Studebaker started sending most of its work to Nixon Mudge.[9]

Nixon also proved highly adept at bringing in new clients. "For the young lawyers that wonder how business is gotten—it isn't done always directly," Nixon said.[10] "It's a matter of fact the most effective way is indirectly." For instance, he recounted that he would often go to dinner parties, meetings, and other social events with prospective clients, and he would never bring up business or legal representation. "As time goes on, when they need representation, or when they want to change their representation, they will think of you," Nixon said.[11] "In all the time I was with either Adams Duque or [Nixon Mudge], I have never asked anybody for business, never. And I think that's the most effective way to do it."

In private, Nixon was far less charitable. "I never realized how easy it is to make money," he said.[12] "I just got twenty-five thousand dollars for telling a bunch of stupid jerks something they could have learned from the newspapers." As one partner explained to Hoffman, corporate executives have "an almost childlike enthusiasm for celebrities," and Nixon was one of the biggest.[13] Some of them simply wanted to be able to brag: "You remember my lawyer, Dick Nixon, don't you?"

Oftentimes, he didn't have to do anything except trade on his own reputation and status as a political giant. His big name made him a highly attractive candidate for corporate boards, and he received a slew of offers from various companies. These directorships generated regular revenue for the firm as Nixon received a monthly salary for his services that he signed over to Nixon Mudge. Additionally, these directorships guaranteed Nixon Mudge business because the firm had a policy that its partners could only accept directorships with companies they performed legal services for in an attorney-client context. In fact, in early 1965, Nixon turned down a directorship offered by City Title Insurance Company, a New York–based company, because the firm didn't expect much legal work to emerge from the relationship. Despite that realization, the firm had actually let Nixon have the final say over whether or not to join them. A big reason why his partners were willing to let him deviate from firm policy was because joining the board, which consisted of prominent Democrats and Republicans and whose chairman was a former chair of the New York State Republican Party, would have been a good political move for Nixon.[14] Instead, he decided to adhere to firm policy and turned down the invitation.

One invitation he decided to accept came from Investors Diversified Services (IDS). In December 1964, Nixon became a director for four major mutual funds owned and operated by IDS: Investors Mutual, Inc.; Investor Stock Funds, Inc.; Investors Variable Payment Fund, Inc.; and Investors Selective Fund, Inc. The four IDS directorships gave his firm an approximate $1,333.33 per month in directors' fees.[15] IDS vice president George MacKinnon, who had served in the navy with Nixon, had helped put the deal together after reasoning that Nixon's name and reputation would go over well with IDS's base of Midwestern middle-class clients.[16] In addition to attending board meetings, Nixon also called upon the firm to advise IDS when it faced litigation.

Shortly after joining the IDS boards, Nixon was officially announced as a board member for the Harsco Corporation, a metal and construction company based in Harrisburg, Pennsylvania, as well as the Mutual Life Insurance Company of New York (MONY). Harsco paid him $500 a month, and Nixon made an important friend in Richard Buck, Harsco's finance committee chair. Like many of Nixon's clients, Buck would prove to be a major contributor to his 1968 campaign.[17]

Meanwhile, Pepsi wasn't the only client Nixon brought with him to his new firm. He also brought in a few clients from his Adams Duque days. One such client was Jessop Steel, whose president, Frank Rackley, had maintained his close personal and professional relationship with Nixon. Their relationship was such that Rackley even counseled Nixon about his move to New York, bringing up a litany of reasons to go for it, including New York's status as an international crossroads and intellectual mecca. In an April 1963 letter, Rackley also brought up familial considerations, asking Nixon if he preferred his daughters to marry a respectable New York professional or "a movie actor in the State of California." Rackley ended his letter with a pep talk, comparing Nixon to Winston Churchill and Abraham Lincoln and pointing out that they had also had their professional setbacks but had come back strong to reach the pinnacle of power. "Fortunately, such reverses as you have experienced happened at a very fine time in your life," Rackley wrote.[18] "And I say to all: 'Watch Nixon when he beats the drum!'"

Rackley was one of the first to come aboard, and Nixon made sure to send him a warm thank-you letter in June 1963.[19] Over the next few years, Rackley relied on Nixon for professional advice ranging from how to deal with a steelworkers' strike in 1965 and whether to merge with competitors Wheeling Steel Company.[20] Rackley, in turn, provided some political intel for Nixon—a task well suited for the Pennsylvania-based steel man. After all, the Keystone State was William Scranton's territory, and the moderate Republican governor loomed large as a potential presidential candidate in 1968. And even if he didn't throw his hat into the ring, Nixon knew that Scranton could be a complication. Following a 1965 meeting with the governor, Rackley called Nixon and said that he believed Scranton was "obviously" going to run.[21]

Other clients followed Nixon from Adams Duque to Nixon Mudge. Jack Dreyfus chose to keep Nixon on his $1,000 monthly retainer, while Richfield Oil and Precision Valve Corporation each continued paying Nixon his $10,000 annual retainer. Another Adams Duque client, Cliff Folger, did the same, giving Nixon $10,000 per year to represent Virginia Industries, Inc., as well as prior clients Folger, Nolan, Fleming and Company. "Your letter with the check enclosed just arrived and I can't tell you how much I appreciated not only the very generous retainer but, particularly, the warm words which accompanied it," Nixon wrote in an August 1963 letter to Folger.[22] "As I have often said, you are the best tonic I have found in my political career!"

When it came to bringing in new clients, Nixon proved to be a highly effective rainmaker for his firm. Eugene McGovern, a Long Island–based businessman and executive who had served with Nixon in the navy, signed with the firm shortly after Nixon moved to New York, and placed him on a $10,000 annual retainer beginning July 1, 1963. Nixon, as he did with Folger, sent a warm thank-you letter to McGovern. "After you left the office yesterday I discussed with my associates the terms of the retainer which you had suggested and they are delighted, as I am, to have you as one of my first clients in my New York firm," Nixon wrote in a letter dated June 4, 1963.[23]

Other clients soon followed. In September 1963, Constantin Diamantis, a wealthy Greek shipping magnate, hired Nixon Mudge to represent his interests in the United States for an annual $5,000 retainer.[24] Like with many of Nixon's other clients, Diamantis also saw fit to weigh in on political matters, commending Nixon for staying loyal to Barry Goldwater in 1964 and sending Nixon $2,000 to spend at his discretion for the Republican Party during the 1964 campaign. "No single act on the part of any individual during the recent campaign touched me as deeply as your sending not only your retainer fee for the year, for which I am enclosing a receipted statement, but also a contribution to be used for the Republican Party," Nixon wrote on November

13, 1964, ten days after Election Day.[25] "You were more than generous and I am most grateful for your continued loyal friendship and support."

In late 1963 to early 1964, Nixon signed up banknote manufacturers Thomas De La Rue, Inc., as a client. Francis "Frank" Sorg, chairman of the board for De La Rue, had met Nixon on the golf course of the Bel Aire Country Club shortly after Nixon had lost the 1962 gubernatorial contest. The two became frequent golfing buddies and stayed in touch after Nixon left for New York. In 1963, Sorg was looking for ways to expand De La Rue's business and hoped to get into the stock certificate printing business, as well as make deals with American Express and Chase Bank to print their traveler's checks. His old golfing buddy was the first name on his mind. "I thought: 'My God! This guy is perfect!'" Sorg said.[26] "He had visited over fifty countries throughout the world. And De La Rue is very much of an international company. And he knows [Chase chairman] George Champion, and might be helpful with his background and his influence with American Express."

Sorg put Nixon on retainer, and also gave him a seat on the De La Rue board. He recalled that when he sat down with Nixon and Bob Guthrie to hammer out the details, it was Guthrie that did most of the talking. The De La Rue board had a vast international reach and numerous connections to large financial institutions and wealthy, powerful individuals, and Sorg recalled that Nixon seemed desperate to be on it.

"Well," Guthrie said. "You know, Frank, Dick here was Vice President of the United States and he's a very prestigious man. To have somebody like that on your board will be a big feather in your cap." According to Sorg, when Guthrie made his point, Nixon furrowed his brow a bit and seemed upset, as if he was concerned about getting priced out of his seat on the board.

"Well, that's very true, Bob," Sorg replied. "But at the other hand, De La Rue is in over fifty countries throughout the world and is the eminent company of its kind. We're over 150 years old—a very prestigious worldwide firm." Sorg then took a pregnant pause in order to ratchet up the tension before he finally showed his cards. "And it's going to be an honor to your firm to have your senior partner on that board." At this point, Nixon broke into a grin as Sorg and Guthrie agreed on a $10,000 yearly retainer. "I was prepared to pay a $50,000 retainer," Sorg said.[27] "But you know what I got? I got the man who, four years later, was the President of the United States, for $10,000."

According to Sorg, Nixon was hired, solely, to be a "salesman" for the firm and not for his legal prowess. "As far as I knew, Richard Nixon did no legal work at all," said Sorg.[28] "With us, he was not going to be a lawyer, he was going to be a salesman. And, in fact, in a couple of meetings that he had with George Champion, we programmed him, [told him] what to say and how to say it, and so forth."

Ultimately, Sorg noted that Nixon's involvement petered out once Sorg left the De La Rue board. The two stayed in touch, however, and Sorg even saw fit to offer political advice and insight. In 1964, he told Nixon that he couldn't win the presidency and suggested that he remove himself as a prospective candidate at the GOP National Convention that year and throw his support to Scranton. "You run the serious risk right now of losing your prestige unless you do something which has the qualities of humility, sincerity and statesmanship," Sorg wrote to Nixon.[29] "You must forever remove the charge of personal ambition against yourself—a charge which has already deeply damaged Nelson Rockefeller." Instead, Sorg advised that if Nixon backed Scranton, not only could the Pennsylvania governor win, but he would owe the former vice president, big time. "Upon becoming President, [Scranton] should appoint you as Secretary of State," Sorg wrote in his letter.[30] "In this capacity, with your knowledge of world problems and affairs; your personal acquaintanceship with and understanding of the leaders of the world; your ability to win people on an intimate, personal basis; with your toughness; with your sincere concern for the world's future in right or wrong hands, you would accomplish so much more for mankind and yourself than as a possible (and I think probable) loser at the convention, or as a possible (and once again I think probable) loser in the election."

In May 1964, Nixon and Guthrie signed up Japanese general trading conglomerate Mitsui & Company. Nixon may have bragged that he never had to ask anyone for business, but he and Guthrie had to spend months selling Mitsui officials on the need to hire general counsel. As Guthrie noted in a May 22, 1964, letter to Nixon, the idea of a general counsel was an alien concept to the Japanese. Additionally, in a culture that was obsessed with honor, Guthrie noted that some Mitsui officials were worried that its current crop of attorneys would feel disgraced if the company hired new attorneys. Nixon and Guthrie had impressed upon the company's president, Tatsuzo Mizukami, the need for a large, complex international organization like Mitsui to have general outside counsel to handle a vast array of its affairs, including taxation, intellectual property, litigation, contracts, and governmental relations. Nixon had even written a letter to Mizukami detailing all of the benefits that a general counsel relationship with his firm would include, including the ability to handle complex joint ventures with the United States and/or Europe. Nixon also noted that he, personally, could leverage his relations with foreign heads and officials to help with certain projects that Mitsui was currently undertaking, including a Korean fertilizer project and a Turkish communications project.[31] "As you know, I have had for many years, both as a government official and in my private capacity, a great interest in Japan and in the Orient generally," Nixon wrote.[32] "Continued economic progress in this area is vitally important to the cause of freedom throughout the world."

Of course, there were limits to Nixon's powers. Shipping magnate Daniel Ludwig called on Nixon for a very important task that few, if any, lawyers practicing on Wall Street at the time could perform. A longtime friend of Nixon's, Ludwig was one of the wealthiest men in America, but he kept such a low profile that few people knew about him until 1982, when he topped Forbes' inaugural list of the wealthiest Americans.[33] In 1964, Ludwig's company, National Bulk Carriers, submitted a joint proposal with another company to develop phosphate in the Kingdom of Jordan. In order for the deal to go through, it needed the personal approval of King Hussein. That was as obvious a job for Nixon as there ever was, and the former vice president performed it with aplomb, dashing off a four-page letter in July 1964 that contained a lot of substance and more than a little flattery.[34] Nixon emphasized that the government of Jordan would retain majority control of the proposed venture, and that this went against the usual modus operandi for either company. Nixon also pointed out that the king and some of his advisers had come to the conclusion, on their own, that foreign investments and assistance were necessary to help the phosphate industry in Jordan reach its full potential. "I am convinced, based on my study of many projects of this type all over the world during the years I was in Washington, that the best interests of your Government will be served by allowing the American companies to participate in ownership to some degree," Nixon wrote.[35] And to prove that Nixon wasn't all about business, he wrapped up his letter with a personal touch. "As I am sure you understand, I have a major responsibility in matters of this type to serve the best interests of my clients," Nixon wrote.[36] "But I want to assure you I have, at the same time, an even deeper interest in seeing that your country continues to prosper under your leadership."

It's unclear whether Nixon's letter ever made it to its intended target. Nixon and his colleagues at the firm seemed convinced that the trusted intermediary they had given the letter to must have failed to deliver it to the king because, otherwise, King Hussein surely would have responded. Instead, Nixon and his fellow attorneys at Nixon Mudge and at National Bulk Carriers wondered if they were being used as pawns. "I might mention that Dr. Nuseibeh [the intermediary entrusted with delivering Nixon's letter to the king], who was economic adviser to the Palace in Jordan has been replaced," Nixon Mudge partner Gregory Brownell wrote to Nixon.[37] "As part of the Palace intrigues, Dr. Nuseibeh's brother, a lawyer in Jerusalem, had been retained by our competitors, International Minerals & Chemical Corporation."

Sometimes, it wasn't Nixon's political connections that were needed but his political skills. Patrick Frawley Jr., a longtime entrepreneur who had previously run Paper Mate, had become president of Eversharp Inc., the parent company to Schick Safety Razor Co., in 1958.[38] Frawley had once been fairly apolitical, but that changed after the Cuban Revolution in 1959 when Communists seized Frawley's Schick plant in Cuba and nationalized it.[39] Frawley became an outspoken conservative who didn't hesitate to dip into his considerable fortune to promote right-wing groups and politicians. To that end, Frawley had become friends with Nixon during the latter's vice presidency, and as his friend, Frawley was outraged when ABC ran its "Political Obituary of Richard Nixon" following his "last press conference." Frawley had even tried to cancel a $3 million advertising contract between Schick and ABC.[40]

In January 1965, Nixon and Frawley closed a deal to have Nixon Mudge represent Eversharp. In a letter to Frawley, Nixon summed up the terms of the representation. The New York office, he pointed out, was teeming with expertise in any number of fields including litigation, corporate law, antitrust law, and taxation. The Washington office, meanwhile, had expertise in dealing with federal regulators and legislators. Meanwhile, for an international company like Eversharp, Nixon noted that the firm's Paris-based office was more than capable of handling matters throughout Europe and North Africa. Finally, there was the ace in the hole: himself. "On any matters, of course, where you think my counsel will be helpful I will also make my services available," Nixon wrote to Frawley.[41] "Particularly with regard to problems that arise in Washington and abroad, I have found that the special experience that I have acquired during my years of government service can often be helpful to our clients in supplementing the technical legal counsel which our offices there will be able to provide."

Frawley put Nixon Mudge on a $25,000 annual retainer and called on them for help on a variety of matters. Frawley turned to Nixon's corporate and litigation experts in the New York office for help in defending several lawsuits, including a 1965 shareholders' derivative case involving DWG Cigar Corporation and Pepsi. A stockholder of DWG Cigar Corporation was trying to stop a proposed merger between DWG and one of Pepsi's bottling plants, and sued Eversharp after it tried to sell some of its shares in the cigar company. The case was ultimately rendered moot after the proposed merger was abandoned.[42]

Nixon's help also came in handy in the political arena. For an outspoken figure like Frawley, who had donated tons of money to ultraconservative political groups, controversy was never far away. In March 1965, *Newsweek* ran a story identifying Frawley as an "ardent backer of the John Birch Society." Frawley felt as if his reputation could be damaged by being associated with the Birchers and wanted *Newsweek* to give him more favorable coverage.

Frawley enlisted his attorney, Herbert Sturdy of Gibson, Dunn & Crutcher, to deal with *Newsweek*. The two agreed not to threaten *Newsweek* with a lawsuit or to even demand a retraction. Instead, they hoped to get *Newsweek*'s right-leaning editor, Frederick Beebe, to play ball. Beebe, however, stuck to his guns and stood by the report, while asking Frawley for additional details about his alleged ties to the Birchers. Frawley let the matter drop, but Sturdy reached out to Nixon, knowing that more allegations were coming down the pipes.[43]

Sure enough, in September 1965, Frawley found himself at the center of another firestorm when famed talk show host David Susskind linked him to certain far-right groups and individuals that were alleged to be anti-Semitic. "Patrick Frawley is the money superior underwriting all of the far right, crank, anti-Semitic, anti-liberal movements in this country," Susskind said during a radio show broadcast on WNBC in New York City.[44]

Susskind had been repeating allegations contained in a 1964 book titled *Danger on the Right* that sought to expose the money men behind radical right-wing groups and figures. According to the book, Frawley had been a longtime friend and patron of Dr. Fred Schwarz, the founder of extreme right-wing group the Christian Anti-Communist Crusade (CACC). In 1961, the CACC held a three-hour rally at the Hollywood Bowl, and it was Frawley, through his companies, Schick and Technicolor, that had paid for the event to be aired live on thirty-three stations on the West Coast.[45] The book also claimed that Frawley had ties to Dan Smoot, a conservative radio host and writer who had partnered with Texas oil baron (and Nixon friend) H. L. Hunt.

Nixon, who understood what it was like to tangle with the John Birch Society, called on Tom Evans to draft a detailed memorandum analyzing *Danger on the Right* and whether or not there were any grounds for pursuing a defamation suit against Susskind or WNBC. Focusing heavily on the anti-Semitic allegations levied by Susskind about Frawley, Evans found that there was no indication that the right-wing figures linked to the Eversharp president had engaged in anti-Semitism over the years. Sure, some of their followers may have held such views (Smoot, for instance, once had a meeting where two guys dressed up like Nazi stormtroopers showed up), but Evans concluded that it was unfair to impute their views to those of their leaders.

Evans also drafted a letter for Frawley to sign that was addressed to Susskind and implored him to retract his statements.

> Over the years, Mr. Susskind, you have professed to be a believer in political fair play. You have frequently spoken against personal accusations through distortion and innuendo. How can you possibly justify linking me with anti-Semitism? I am not an anti-Semite. I have never supported an anti-Semitic movement or broadcast. Nowhere in *Danger on the Right*—the single source on which you based your charge—is there a statement or suggestion that I underwrite or support anti-Semitic movements. But how does one go about disproving such an unfair and odious accusation? Am I supposed to sue you,

> and the broadcast media which carried your statements, for libel? Am I to spend years in legal proceedings presenting all of my personal and business relationships, and asking a jury to evaluate my thoughts and feelings? Certainly, you know how hopeless it is to try and undo the damage of a libel by a lawsuit.[46]

The letter also defended Frawley's views, emphasizing his belief in the importance of individual freedom and the virtues of American capitalism and constitutionalism. He also rejected racism and bigotry, saying that he did not believe in a system of government where any group had limited participation in the American way of life due to race, religion, economy, or politics. But mostly, he wanted to reiterate that he saw communism as a clear threat and that he believed, very strongly, that he had a duty to help groups dedicated to fighting it. "Because I view Communism as more than a theoretical danger, I have done everything that I could to acquaint my fellow citizens with the methods which communism is using, as revealed by the writings and practices of communist leaders, to destroy our free society," the letter said.[47]

One thing the draft of the letter omitted was any mention of Nixon or his firm. In fact, based on his available legal papers, it does not appear as if Nixon made any public defense of his client. Obviously, Nixon knew how controversial and radioactive some of these groups were (particularly the Birchers), and the last thing he needed was to be associated with them in any way—even if by proxy. That, of course, is purely conjecture since Nixon's available legal papers do not explicitly state one way or another whether he should keep quiet about his involvement in defending Frawley over his political ties.

"THE DRAGON LADY."

On other politically sensitive matters, however, the records are clear that he chose to maintain a low profile. One such instance involved Trần Lệ Xuân. Xuân was a glamorous, striking, and diminutive Vietnamese woman who was better known as Madame Nhu—although her outspoken and controversial nature caused friends and foes to bestow many other nicknames on her. "Dragon Lady" was a favorite for many in the media, as were comparisons to Lucrezia Borgia or Marie Antoinette. As the wife of Ngô Đình Nhu, who in turn, was the brother and chief adviser to South Vietnam's President Ngô Đình Diệm, Madame Nhu functioned as the official hostess and de facto First Lady of South Vietnam due to Diệm's bachelordom.[48]

When it came to running South Vietnam, Diệm, Nhu, and his wife functioned as an unofficial triumvirate. Diệm was, ostensibly, the senior partner by virtue of his office; however, he was publicly seen as weak—more than living up to the assessment by General J. Lawton Collins, the US special representative in South Vietnam under Eisenhower, of him as a "small, shy, diffident man with almost no personal magnetism."[49] His brother, meanwhile, enjoyed operating behind the scenes—a quality that made sense given the fact that his portfolio included control over the secret police and other intelligence-gathering agencies in South Vietnam.[50] That made the outspoken and attention-loving Madame Nhu the public face of the First Family, as well as the lightning rod for critics of the government. In fact, the popular image of the First Family in the media was of her calling the shots as her cowed husband and brother-in-law bowed to her demands.

Just how powerful she was remains a question for historians. What isn't a question, however, is that she had both power and influence and wasn't afraid to use them. She had been the one to convince a reluctant Diệm to crush his opposition shortly after assuming the presidency in 1955. While Diệm had empowered her, she wasn't solely reliant on her brother-in-law. For instance, after winning a seat in the National Assembly in 1956, Madame Nhu immediately set about pushing through her own domestic agenda, notably a package of "morality laws" that included banning abortions and contraception, forbidding divorce and adultery, outlawing boxing matches, beauty pageants, animal fights, and even bras with underwires, and shutting down brothels and opium dens, among other things.[51] She even went as far as to try to ban "The Twist," condemning the dance for its lack of safety.[52] The laws didn't sit well with the general public, who saw the flamboyant and sexually provocative Madame Nhu as a hypocrite, given her preference for wearing tight, low-cut dresses and robes, as well as near-constant rumors of her infidelity. South Vietnamese broke Madame Nhu's laws at their own peril, and Madame Nhu was ruthless with, and unsympathetic to, transgressors—even if they were her own family. When her sister, who had been embroiled in an extramarital affair and was seeking a divorce from her husband, caught wind of the new laws, she slashed her wrists but survived. An unmoved Madame Nhu reportedly told her sister that she was upset that she "didn't succeed at death."[53]

As the Vietnam War heated up, Madame Nhu assumed an even higher profile. She was seen as the driving force behind a growing crackdown on dissidents and suppression of the press, particularly foreign reporters. *Newsweek* journalist François Sully, who had once written that Madame Nhu was "conceited, and obsessed with a drive for power that far surpasses that of even her husband," and that she was, without question, "the most detested personality in South Vietnam," was expelled from the country after writing that the enemy seemed to have more enthusiasm and drive than the South Vietnamese.[54] David Halberstam, who replaced Sully in South Vietnam for *Newsweek*, also raised her ire. At one point, Madame Nhu said that she hoped to barbeque Halberstam and would be happy to provide the lighter fluid and matches.[55]

Her authoritarian nature and sharp tongue caused friction with South Vietnam's allies, particularly the United States, which pressured the First Family to ease up on its crackdowns and introduce more democratic reforms. True to her nature, Madame Nhu had an opinion about this, too. "If we open the window, not only the sunlight, but many bad things fly in also," she said.[56] When Madame Nhu helped spearhead a persecution of various Buddhist monks, accusing them of helping Communists, her bloodthirsty zeal shocked and angered Washington, D.C. She encouraged the army to gun down as many Buddhists as possible, and chastised one particular monk, who burned himself to death in order to avoid being taken by the death squads, for using foreign gasoline instead of domestic. She even called one particular massacre "the happiest day of my life."[57]

Finally, in late 1963, the United States gave up on the Diệm regime and sanctioned a coup against him. In November 1963, Madame Nhu was in the United States on a charm offensive to try to convince the United States to escalate its military involvement in Vietnam. Among other things, she denigrated President Kennedy and accused his inner circle of being Communist sympathizers. She was in Beverly Hills when her husband and brother-in-law were overthrown and killed, and she immediately pointed the finger at the Kennedy Administration, saying, "Whoever has the Americans as allies does not need any enemies."[58] Forbidden to return to South Vietnam, she went into exile, living in Rome where she continued to speak out against the United States—particularly anyone who was part of the Kennedy Administration during the coup against her brother-in-law.

One American political figure that retained her respect was Nixon, who she maintained a correspondence with. In January 1964, Madame Nhu sent a long letter to Nixon, requesting his advice on several legal matters. She had been offered a contract by a French publisher for her memoirs but was unsure about some of the proposed terms. She also asked Nixon to sue the *Arizona Journal* on her behalf over an October 1963 article that she found to be slanderous. She also asked for his advice concerning a potential lawsuit over fees and expenses from hotels she stayed in before the coup in South Vietnam that the new government refused to cover. Finally, she closed by encouraging him to run for president in 1964. "I hear in the Press that you do not intend to run for the Presidency again next year," wrote Madame Nhu.[59] "I think that you should, on the contrary, do it and that you will have great chance with a woman running as vice-president." To prove that she still held a grudge against the Kennedy Administration, she suggested that Nixon avoid picking his 1960 running mate, Henry Cabot Lodge, who had gone to work for JFK, serving as ambassador to South Vietnam when the coup against Diệm happened. "To such a point that his hands too are now stained with the blood of the Vietnamese patriots," she wrote about Lodge.[60] "To have him with you will not bring luck to you, and will prevent you from attacking your opponents on their most sensitive mistake which is a crime in the Vietnamese affair."

Nixon chose not to respond directly. Two months after receiving her letter, he sent it to Garment, along with a note pointing out that it involved "legal as well as political problems."[61] Garment then typed up a response to Madame Nhu that was fairly noncommittal and passive. After explaining that Nixon was indisposed due to his travels abroad and apologizing for the delay in getting back to her, Garment noted that he had no knowledge of the unflattering article in question while emphasizing the difficulties in successfully suing a media outlet for libel. As for the literary contract, Garment pointed out that he had read that she had signed a deal with a publisher, so he assumed she no longer needed guidance on that issue. He also referred all legal questions to William Landis, managing partner of the Paris office of Nixon Mudge, but made sure to send a separate letter to Landis, cautioning him that "we would have to consider all factors carefully before agreeing to handle any matters which would, in effect, commit the firm to a full-scale representation of Mme. Nhu."[62]

Undeterred, a couple of months later, a public relations representative for Madame Nhu was putting together a speaking tour of the United States and sent a letter to Nixon asking if he might be interested in being her American attorney. "At the moment, she is deeply in debt so that I doubt if she could pay any attorney's fees," John Graham of Société Graham wrote in May 1964, "but it is possible that the resulting publicity for representing her might be of value." Nixon responded via Landis stating that it would not be in her interest to retain Nixon Mudge for a variety of reasons. Instead, Nixon recommended that she should retain a firm that "specializes in representing celebrities who make such tours as the one she is contemplating."[63] Additionally, he stated that his "inevitable involvement through the press and otherwise in the political situation in the United States would hamper rather than help her."[64]

Indeed, Nixon seemed to want nothing to do with Madame Nhu's legal needs. After the previous letter in which Nixon declined to represent her during her speaking tour, Graham called Landis at least twice to ask him to ask Nixon to recommend someone who might be willing to represent her. Nixon waited a couple of weeks and finally answered Landis after reading in the newspapers that Nhu had hired Robert Morris, a noted anti-Communist attorney. "I would think that his selection for this assignment was probably as good a one as she could have made," Nixon said to Landis.[65] "Under the circumstances, I do not believe we should make any recommendations on our part."

"FLYING TIGER"

Another politically tricky situation for Nixon came from William Pawley. Born in 1896 in South Carolina, Pawley grew up in Cuba, where his father was a wealthy businessman. After a short career in real estate, Pawley made his reputation in the aviation industry, getting his start in 1927 working for the Curtiss-Wright Corporation. The next year, he returned to Cuba to serve as president of the newly formed Curtiss-Wright subsidiary, Nacional Cubana de Aviacion Curtiss. He held the job until the company was sold to Pan American Airways in 1932, whereupon he decided to head to China. While in China, he served as president of China National Aviation Corporation and established a good relationship with Chiang Kai-shek's government.[66]

He also became friends with Claire Lee Chennault, a retired major general with the US Army Air Corps. After leaving the army, Chennault moved to China in 1937 in order to help train Chinese pilots. During that time, he had come up with an idea of using volunteer American fighter pilots to help the Chinese fight off Japanese invaders. As one of the biggest airplane manufacturers in China, as well as a politically connected American, Pawley was a natural partner for Chennault. The two began planning the creation of the Flying Tigers, a group of volunteer American fighter pilots that would serve under the command of China. Known for their distinctive shark-faced design on the noses of their planes, the Flying Tigers solidified their reputation as a fearsome and effective fighting unit with their tenacious defense of Burma. The Tigers were disbanded after only seven months when Chennault redeployed many of his pilots to defend China. Despite the brevity of their run, the Tigers certainly made their mark. They were officially credited with destroying 297 enemy planes and only losing fourteen pilots.[67]

Pawley's postwar career held even more intrigue. In 1945, President Truman appointed Pawley as ambassador to Peru. Three years later, Truman gave him another ambassadorship, this time to Brazil.[68] Despite his relationship with Truman, Pawley was a conservative who found himself gravitating toward the Republican Party. He also had strong ties with several right-wing Latin American leaders, including Fulgencio Batista in Cuba and Rafael Trujillo in the Dominican Republic.

Pawley's move toward the GOP became official once his good friend, Eisenhower, decided to run for president in 1952. During the Eisenhower years, Pawley found himself involved in even more international intrigue. As relations between Batista and Eisenhower disintegrated amid the backdrop of the Cuban Revolution, Pawley was dispatched in early 1958 by the White House to try to get Batista to give up power peacefully so that an anti-Castro, anti-Batista, pro-US provisional government could take over. Batista refused and was ultimately overthrown by Castro and his forces the following year.[69]

Once Castro was in power, Pawley devoted himself to ridding Cuba of its newest dictator. "Find me one man, just one man who can go it alone and get Castro," he told a reporter in Miami shortly after Castro assumed power in Cuba.[70] "I'll pay anything—almost anything." He pressured Eisenhower to give military and financial support for anti-Castro Cubans living in the United States and had even drawn up a list of prominent Cuban exiles that could run the country once Castro was deposed.[71]

As a prominent and wealthy individual, Pawley found himself as one of the main advisors for plotters looking to get rid of Castro. Among some of the things he considered were a plot to devalue Cuban currency by issuing counterfeit bonds (a plot that another one of Nixon's clients eventually carried out) and getting Trujillo to invade Cuba. While he didn't have much use for some of the CIA's more infamous plots (like giving Castro an exploding cigar or poisoning his food), Pawley's determination to topple Castro by any means necessary became a cause for concern in Washington, D.C.[72] Indeed, after Kennedy became president, he essentially froze Pawley out of the White House. According to Pawley, the two had a tense meeting in May 1961, a month after the failed Bay of Pigs invasion, where the president summarily shut down all of Pawley's arguments for another invasion of Cuba and shooed him away from the Oval Office.[73]

The meeting was especially bitter for Pawley given everything he had done to try to get Nixon elected in 1960 instead of Kennedy. Pawley and then–vice president Nixon had become close friends during the Eisenhower Administration, as Nixon had taken a strong interest in Cuba.[74] In fact, it was Nixon who had intervened during planning sessions for the Bay of Pigs requesting that Pawley be kept informed.[75] Pawley formally endorsed Nixon for the presidency in 1960, campaigning hard for the Nixon-Lodge ticket in his home state of Florida. After Nixon lost, Pawley kept in touch and supported his friend for the governorship in 1962. Knowing that he was losing momentum as a result of Kennedy's popularity after the resolution of the Cuban Missile Crisis, Pawley wrote a last-minute letter to eight newspapers in California encouraging voters to back Nixon. "Richard Nixon would not have made the tremendous error of judgment of the Bay of Pigs, nor this second blunder of stopping short of removing the communist controlled government of Fidel Castro from Cuba," Pawley wrote.[76] "Every disturbed American who places his Nation above partisan politics can, in good conscience, vote for this great American."

Like many of Nixon's other friends, he also sent letters, over the years, encouraging Nixon not to give up on politics. "Do not bow out, Dick," he wrote in a letter dated November 12, 1962—less than a week after the gubernatorial election.[77] "You are a young man and it is hard to say at this time where the future may take you."

In fact, Pawley was highly sensitive to the possibility that Nixon didn't appreciate his advice or friendship and would call Nixon's office to complain. In a June 1964 call to Rose Mary Woods that was, ostensibly, about what Nixon planned on doing at the 1964 Republican National Convention, Pawley took time near the end to whine about Nixon not calling or visiting him during a recent trip to Florida. "I decided what Dick feels is that I am only a political friend—not a real friend," said Pawley.[78] "None of this has changed my feeling for [him]—I like him—I am his friend but he needs to watch treating his friends this way. Just from talking with other people I know this is a real stumbling block for him."

Nevertheless, Pawley sent work to Nixon Mudge. Hoping to take advantage of the ongoing sugar boom, Pawley had purchased Florida-based Talisman Sugar Company in 1964. The boom hadn't extended to Talisman, which saw its crop nearly destroyed in December 1962 due to cold weather. As a result, the company went broke, declaring bankruptcy and going into receivership with $8 million in debts. Pawley put plenty of his own skin in the game, investing nearly $4 million of his own money and taking out a $7.5 million loan to try to bring down Talisman's debts. He also expanded the company's planting capabilities, purchasing an additional eleven thousand acres of land.[79]

Soon after Pawley opened up his wallet, Talisman was hit with even more adversity, this time in the form of the federal government. A month after he bought those eleven thousand acres, the government froze sugarcane acreage usage, causing Pawley's new field to sit barren. "If it wasn't for my business background, I would have already lost my shirt," Pawley said at the time.[80]

That wasn't Pawley's only problem. The Sugar Act of 1948 established production quotas for domestic sugar companies, and whenever those companies fell short of their numbers, the US Department of Agriculture would purchase the rest from foreign companies. Florida- and Louisiana-based companies, however, consistently met or even exceeded their quotas, and Pawley was convinced that a modification of the existing quotas, as well as increasing the amount of usable acreage, would help Talisman become successful.[81]

In 1965, Pawley embarked on an intense lobbying campaign to get the sugar and acreage quotas modified. Accustomed to having access to the highest echelons of power, Pawley went right to the top, writing to President Johnson and several powerful senators and representatives. He even enlisted Elliott Roosevelt, the mayor of Miami Beach and son of FDR, to write a letter to the White House on his behalf. "Mr. William D. Pawley, who, the President will recall, played a vital role in assisting my father through the establishment of the 'Flying Tigers' and later served with distinction as our Ambassador to Brazil, made a tremendous investment in the cane sugar industry in Florida," Roosevelt wrote in September 1965, emphasizing the extreme hardships and inequities Talisman faced as a result of the quotas.[82]

He also retained Nixon Mudge to represent Talisman, albeit he made sure not to openly engage the firm's public partner. Understanding that "lobbying" can have negative connotations, he hired Arthur Becker, Nixon Mudge's Washington, D.C., managing partner, to work on his behalf. Once Becker signed on, he handled tasks ranging from meeting with Department of Agriculture officials to representing the company in allocation hearings in New Orleans to exploring government and private loans for Talisman, among many other things. Even though Becker was in charge, he made sure to keep Nixon in the loop and even routed the bill for his services to his firm's public partner rather than send it directly to Pawley. "I think that it would be advisable for you to transit the bill or take it up directly with Pawley," Becker wrote to Nixon in November 1965 after drawing up an invoice for $13,651.83.[83]

Another thing that Becker did was officially register as a lobbyist—much to the chagrin of both Pawley and Nixon. Under federal law, lobbyists must register with Congress, but Pawley had hired Becker and Nixon Mudge for legal representation and not, expressly, for lobbying purposes. When *Congressional Quarterly* announced the move in late August 1965, it contained several sentences where Becker spoke about what he hoped to accomplish for Talisman, as well as emphasizing that Nixon was not involved. At the end of the article, Becker specifically said that he was hired to lobby for Talisman and get them an increased allotment.[84]

Becker's candor did not seem to go over well in the New York office. One of Nixon's colleagues printed out the article and sent it to Rose Mary Woods with a handwritten note saying: "Personally, I don't see why Becker had to go into the detail at the end of the story." Meanwhile, Nixon handwrote the phrase *might come up* and *lobbying* on it.[85] Pawley was also upset. "I was terribly disappointed that Arthur registered as a lobbyist," Pawley wrote to Nixon in October 1965, "because I did not want your firm involved in any way in this sugar problem, as I have seen it is an extremely controversial problem and too many undesirables have been acting as lobbyists for quite some years." Instead, Pawley noted that had he wanted someone to formally lobby for Talisman, he would have hired someone like Tommy Corcoran, Clark Clifford, or Paul Porter—men who had connections and access to the Johnson White House.[86]

"I am as interested, Dick, in your political future as it is possible for one, of your friends to be, and the last thing that I wanted was for Richard Nixon's name to appear as lobbying for anyone in connection with sugar quota," he wrote to Nixon in October 1965.[87]

Ultimately, Pawley's efforts did not pay off the way he had hoped. The Sugar Act extension was passed by the House and Senate in October 1965 and signed by President Johnson the following month. The extension did raise the overall quota for domestic companies, but according to Pawley, what Talisman really needed was the acreage increase, which did not happen. "Unfortunately, none of the conferees considering the House and Senate versions of the Act will be willing to put up a fight for Talisman," he wrote, resignedly, to Nixon shortly after the bill passed both the House and Senate but before it went to a conference committee to resolve differences between the two passed bills. Despite the setback, Pawley stuck it out for another eight years where he faced even more headaches relating to Talisman, including a protracted and high-profile labor battle. Finally, in 1973, Pawley sold the controlling interest in the company to banker Edward Ball, the man who handled DuPont's holdings.[88]

"PRESIDENT OF THE DE FACTO GOVERNMENT OF CUBA."

Another prominent Cuban figure presented a different type of headache for Nixon.

Mario Garcia Kohly was born in Cuba in 1899 to a prominent, politically well-connected family. His father, also named Mario Garcia Kohly, had been Cuba's ambassador to Spain and, at one point, was in line to become Cuba's secretary of state before the overthrow of Gerardo Machado.[89] The younger Kohly became an international investment banker and did business with several major US corporations. Like many wealthy, politically connected Cubans, Kohly did very well under the Batista regime, only to lose everything and become a target once Castro took over.

Kohly was imprisoned in Cuba but managed to escape to America, where he became one of the leading anti-Castro figures in the country. Kohly became president of a group called the Cuban Government in Exile and considered himself to be the de facto president of Cuba. Kohly worked tirelessly to recruit followers, as well as finance plots designed to overthrow Castro. Kohly soon got on the radar of the CIA and agreed to accept the agency's help, according to intelligence officer Robert Morrow, who claimed to be Kohly's contact.[90]

According to both Morrow and journalist Anthony Summers, Kohly was soon introduced to Nixon. Summers claimed Kohly also had close ties to Nixon confidant Bebe Rebozo, himself a Cuban American, and that Nixon introduced Kohly to then-CIA chief Allen Dulles. Nixon, evidently, took a shine to Kohly, calling him a "red hot prospect to lead the Cubans" despite the views of many in the CIA that Kohly was too conservative and would not be able to get moderates in Cuba to follow him.[91]

Unlike many anti-Castro plots, which centered around killing the man or invading the island nation, Kohly's aim was to destabilize and disrupt the

Cuban economy.[92] Kohly carried out the aforementioned plan to produce counterfeit Cuban pesos and flood the market with them, thereby causing inflation and fomenting unrest among the people in the hope that it would provide the impetus for another revolution—this time with himself replacing Castro. Kohly's use of economic warfare drew him to Nixon, who agreed that it was the most effective path toward getting rid of Castro.[93]

On the other hand, counterfeiting foreign currency is illegal and, in 1963, Kohly was arrested along with a co-conspirator, American William Grosh. Kohly's defense was that he was engaged in a counter-revolution against the Castro government and was justified in doing whatever was necessary to bring about regime change in Cuba. More specifically, Kohly alleged that the government had approved of his venture and even claimed that then–vice president Nixon had signed off on his plot during a round of golf at Burning Tree Country Club in Bethesda, Maryland. In early 1964, Kohly's defense attorney, Marshall Diggs, sent numerous letters to Nixon desperately trying to schedule a face-to-face meeting between his client and the former vice president in New York.

"I have asked Mr. Mario Kohly to see you in New York sometime and maybe he will get there tomorrow," Diggs wrote in January 1964. "No," Nixon handwrote in the margins.

"Yesterday when I was in New York I found out that you were in North Carolina and I was sorry to have missed you," Diggs wrote the following month. "Mr. Kohly expects to be back in New York on Thursday and I would be very grateful if you can see him that afternoon." "No," Nixon wrote, once again, in the margins.

Even worse for Nixon was that Diggs seemed to have the subtlety of an undercover operative asking his subjects to speak slowly and clearly into his lapel or from whatever happened to be protruding from underneath his shirt. Diggs wrote detailed letters recounting Nixon's supposed history with Kohly in the hope that the former VP would confirm Kohly's allegations. In one letter, for instance, Diggs wrote: "You remember meeting him at the Club and that you had some mutual friends both in Miami and Chicago. He is from Havana and you were kind enough to arrange the meetings which we had with the C.I.A. in July 1960." In another letter, Diggs went about it again, writing: "You may remember meeting Mr. Kohly, my client, out at Burning Tree . . . "[94] Nixon didn't take the bait.

In the end, Kohly was convicted of counterfeiting. In December 1964, Nixon Mudge associate Robert Thornton informed his firm's lead partner that Kohly did, indeed, invoke Nixon's name during his trial, claiming to have had contact with the then–vice president in 1960, as well as others in the government. Thornton also told Nixon that "it might be possible to get a reduction or suspension of the sentence if some knowledgeable person would be willing to go to bat for Kohly" and that a letter to the presiding judge "might be of invaluable assistance."[95] Nixon did write a letter to the court, but he claimed he had no knowledge of meeting Kohly at Burning Tree. Nevertheless, Nixon requested leniency for Kohly, preferably in the form of a suspended sentence.[96]

According to Summers, however, Nixon had actually taken on an active role in advising Kohly during his criminal trial—even though his firm had no official role in representing the self-proclaimed de facto Cuban president. In an interview, Thornton told Summers that Nixon had advised Kohly to jump bail and that "everything would be all right" if he could go into hiding for a bit and hold up the court proceedings. Kohly did jump bail and, immediately after it happened, Thornton sent Nixon a note telling him that even though Kohly was a fugitive from justice, "I don't think his flight should necessarily prejudice us against him, since it seems clear that he got a raw deal."[97]

Kohly was picked up soon afterward and sent to prison.[98] Nixon Mudge continued to keep an eye on the Kohly case over the years. In 1965, Thornton mailed a letter to the Parole Board on behalf of Grosh asking for his release. Thornton made clear that, while the firm had not been involved in defending either Grosh or Kohly during the criminal or appellate proceedings, they had been invited to review the record and had come to the conclusion that Grosh deserved to be paroled. However, Thornton's letter was, primarily, about Kohly:

> Mario Kohly was an acknowledged leader of a major segment of the Cuban refugee movement in the United States, and maintained, not without a certain justification, that he was the head of a de facto government in exile. Kohly was unquestionably, in connection with his activities as an exile leader, in contact with officials of the U.S. government, to whom he disclosed a plan for the counterfeiting of Cuban currency in connection with efforts to overthrow the Castro government.[99]

Thornton did not mention Nixon's name—especially in connection to his assertion that Kohly was "unquestionably" in contact with governmental officials. However, in a 1966 letter to Kohly's wife, he offered the firm's services in applying for a reduction in Kohly's prison sentence and made clear that the firm, and its public partner, remained committed to her husband. "As I have already informed you, Mr. Nixon has authorized me to offer my services in this matter without charge to Mr. Kohly," Thornton wrote.[100]

As with the Frawley case, Nixon let one of his associates take the lead on a potentially controversial matter while keeping his involvement at a minimum—at least as far as what the public saw. Summers would claim that Nixon had a good reason for not wanting his name in bright lights when it came to Mario Kohly. According to Kohly's son, Mario Jr., when the senior Kohly had met with Nixon at the golf course (Kohly Jr. maintained it was the Burning Tree Club), Kohly had actually pitched Nixon on a plan that in-

volved a violent overthrow of the Castro regime involving an army of three hundred to four hundred guerrilla soldiers in the Escambray Mountains in Cuba. Kohly Jr. would claim that the plot centered around the assumption that Cuban revolutionary leaders Fidel and Raul Castro, as well as Che Guevara, would be executed. "Part of Washington went along with this—the Nixon part," Kohly Jr. told Summers.[101] "Many in the CIA were against it."

"EL JEFE"

On the other hand, there was one high-profile, politically charged matter where Nixon was happy to be out in front. This one involved another deposed leader in Central America.

Much like how Pawley had met with Batista in a last-ditch effort to stave off revolution, Pawley had traveled to the Dominican Republic in November 1960 with a similar mission. This time, it was his task to try to convince his longtime friend, dictator Rafael Trujillo, to put an end to his near three-decade reign.

As with Batista, the power had clearly gone to Trujillo's head. The Dominican strongman, who had been in office since 1930 after winning a presidential election in which his vote total was greater than the number of eligible voters in the country he sought to rule,[102] was known for demonstrating his clout in outrageous ways. During his first inauguration in 1931, he had worn a sash that said *Dios y Trujillo* (God and Trujillo). From that, he coined the new state slogan for the Dominican Republic: *Dios en el cielo y Trujillo en la República Dominicana* (God in Heaven, Trujillo in the Dominican Republic). Eventually, the phrases were reversed to put Trujillo before God: *Trujillo en la República Dominicana y Dios en el cielo.*

As the de facto God of his country, he could pretty much do whatever he wanted. He made his son, Rafael Jr. (known as "Ramfis"), a major in the Dominican army at the age of three,[103] campaigned for a Nobel Prize for literature for his wife, and gave himself multiple titles, including "Genius of Peace" and "Undefeated Generalissimo of the Dominican Armies."[104]

"El Jefe," as he was also known, was as brutal as he was outlandish, and regularly had political opponents jailed, tortured, and killed. On some occasions, he even did his best impression of a James Bond villain and threw his enemies into shark-infested waters.[105]

Perhaps his most infamous moment came in 1937, when he massacred tens of thousands of Haitians living in the Dominican Republic near the border with Haiti. The "Protector of All Workers" justified his actions by accusing the Haitians of stealing from Dominicans and believed that his response was perfectly proportional to the situation at hand:

> For some months, I have traveled and traversed the border in every sense of the word. I have seen, investigated, and inquired about the needs of the population. To the Dominicans who were complaining of the depredations by Haitians living among them, thefts of cattle, provisions, fruits, etc., and were thus prevented from enjoying in peace the products of their labor, I have responded, "I will fix this." And we have already begun to remedy the situation. Three hundred Haitians are now dead in Bánica. This remedy will continue.[106]

As with Batista, the United States feared that Trujillo's brutality would pave the way for a Communist insurgency. Trujillo had given up the presidency in 1952 to his brother, Hector; however, he continued to wield near-absolute power behind the scenes. In fact, he would force Hector to resign the presidency in 1960 in favor of Vice President Joaquín Balaguer.[107] Eisenhower dispatched Pawley to impress upon Trujillo the need to step down and allow democracy to take hold in the country. In return, Pawley promised Trujillo he could live out his years in comfort in the United States. Pawley recalled that Trujillo didn't take very kindly to the suggestion. "You can come in here with the Marines, and you can come in here with the Army, and you can come in here with the Navy or even the atomic bomb, but I'll never go out of here unless I go out on a stretcher," Trujillo told Pawley.[108] Pawley made another trip during the early days of the Kennedy Administration, this time in an unofficial capacity, where he, Bebe Rebozo, and Senator George Smathers made one last appeal to Trujillo to step aside for the good of the country and region, only to run into a brick wall.

"I don't know what you talking about," Trujillo told his incredulous guests.[109] "I am just a citizen in this country. I don't have any public office. We have a president, an executive, a legislature and a supreme court—just like your country. I really don't know what you are talking about."

Ultimately, Trujillo's earlier vow to hold onto power until he was carried out on a stretcher came true—only it didn't take the combined might of the US Armed Forces and an atomic bomb to make it happen. On May 30, 1961, Trujillo's car was ambushed by several gunmen as the "First Teacher, First Doctor, First Journalist of the Republic" was executed, gangland style, as he was being chauffeured home. The assassins wielded American-style M1 carbines, leading to the obvious conclusion that the CIA had Trujillo killed. That theory, however, didn't hold much water—especially coming on the heels of the Bay of Pigs debacle. The last thing the Kennedy Administration wanted was to take out an anti-Communist leader like Trujillo and leave a power vacuum for a Dominican Castro to fill. Indeed, declassified CIA documents indicated that the agency wasn't directly involved but almost certainly had foreknowledge of it and had provided the guns used by the assassins.[110]

With most long-term dictators, the safe assumption is that they probably have a veritable fortune squirreled away in a country with secretive banking laws like Switzerland or the Cayman Islands. Trujillo was no different, as he was rumored to have a personal wealth of nearly $500 million, with over $180 million stashed away in a Swiss bank account.[111] The sheer enormity of such a fortune guaranteed that it would serve as a battleground for the various Trujillo heirs who all wanted a piece of the late strongman's estate.

What made this battle even more complicated came down to the other dictatorial cliché that Trujillo had more than lived up to. "The Lover of Dominican Women" had not been one of his extravagant titles, but it probably should have been. Trujillo had many, many mistresses and girlfriends, and as a result, he had many, many illegitimate children (it's never been definitely proven how many he had). Given the reputed size of his fortune, it was inevitable that Trujillo's death would trigger a veritable battle royale for his riches.

In July 1964, the *LA Times* reported that a group of six illegitimate children had hired Nixon and his firm to represent them as they tried to recoup their portion of the estate. Nixon's clients were based in Miami and had named the Miami Beach First National Bank as their trustees. Nixon got the publicity, but how much work he actually did on the case is in dispute. For instance, Raymond Steckel, an associate in the Paris office of Nixon Mudge, recalled that the case belonged to Guthrie, who had a relationship with the chairman of the Miami bank. "I have no recollection of Nixon working on the case," said Steckel.[112] In fact, a December 1965 message from Rose Mary Woods to Nixon seemed to confirm this, as Woods relayed a message from John Davis Lodge, former ambassador to Spain, urgently requesting briefing materials for an expert Lodge wanted to weigh in on the matter. "I explained that this was not your case—that this material would have to come from Mr. Guthrie since this was his case—NOT YOURS [original emphasis]," Woods wrote to Nixon.[113]

The firm, on behalf of the Miami-based children, filed a criminal complaint in Geneva, accusing Trujillo's son, Radames, of misappropriating his late father's millions. Radames, who was living in exile in France at the time, was accused of stealing $150 million from his dad's coffers and was extradited to Switzerland in November 1964 to face the charges.[114] The Miami heirs claimed that, because of Radames's theft, there was less than $6 million left in the account. Ultimately, Nixon Mudge reached a settlement with Radames (the terms were not disclosed), and he was released from Swiss custody.[115]

However, there were other fish for the Miami heirs to fry. At one point, the lawyers looked at whether or not to file a case in Santo Domingo, and Steckel recalled flying into the Dominican Republic capital to explore that possibility further. The post-Trujillo years were highly unstable, with multiple revolutions and coup d'états taking place before the United States forcibly intervened in 1965. It was during one of these revolutionary periods when Steckel says he flew down to the country. "I could still hear guns going off in the background," he recalled.[116] "It was exciting but also scary." He met with the newly appointed Minister of Justice and asked to copy some files relevant to the Trujillo matter. "I show up, me in my little lawyer suit, and here's this rather burly fellow in his early 40s wearing a short sleeve white shirt," Steckel said.[117] "He asked me to sit down and then started explaining why I couldn't actually copy the files. Before I could say anything, he pulled open his right desk drawer and pulled out a .45 and put it on his desk. He didn't say another word." Ultimately, Steckel says he was allowed to look at the files and copy what he could by hand. "So, when the Miami bank suggested filing an action in Santo Domingo, I told them that, based on what little I knew about civil law in the Dominican Republic, pursuing this claim in middle of a revolution didn't strike me as a very useful thing!"[118]

Instead, Nixon Mudge turned its attention to Spain. The firm went after a group of Trujillo heirs living in Madrid, including the biggest fish of them all: Ramfis Trujillo. The eldest son and heir apparent to his father, Ramfis parlayed his lifelong career in the Dominican military to succeed his assassinated father as leader of the Dominican Republic in 1961. However, before he could bestow upon himself an outlandish title like "Defender of the Dominicans," he found himself out of power and forced into exile. He ultimately settled in Spain, where lived an extravagant lifestyle under the protection of that country's strongman, Generalissimo Francisco Franco. The *St. Petersburg Times* reported that Ramfis had about $60 million stashed away in his account in Spain, and mentioned that Nixon was working on trying to get some of it for his clients.[119]

On May 5, 1965, Nixon took a well-publicized trip to Geneva to meet with Swiss Department of Justice officials.[120] According to an internal firm memo, the trip was necessary because Nixon Mudge lawyers believed that, unlike with Radames Trujillo, the Swiss courts had been dragging their feet when it came to adjudicating the complaint against the Madrid heirs.[121] "The present inaction, on a complaint filed with impressive supporting fact, by an American bank and American citizens (or residents) might lead to wonder if the Swiss laws on secrecy in the banks are not construed to provide a safe haven for embezzlers and receivers of stolen goods," the internal memo stated.[122] The memo also noted that it was vital to have the threat of an "actively prosecuted" criminal case against the Madrid heirs to provide the kind of leverage necessary to get the Miami heirs their fair piece of the estate.[123]

To that end, a few days after the Geneva meeting, Charles Celier, European counsel at Nixon Mudge's Paris office, and John Davis Lodge met with Spanish officials to put pressure on them to extradite the Madrid heirs to Switzerland. According to a letter from Lodge to Nixon, the Spanish authorities were sympathetic but stated, outright, that "the basis for intervention did not seem entirely clear."[124]

Spain's stance only hardened in the year that followed. In a letter dated April 2, 1966, Spain's undersecretary of foreign affairs, Don Pedro Cortina, told John Davis Lodge that "there was no possibility on the part of Spanish administrative authorities in a matter strictly of a private order." Cortina said that the only way Spain would get involved would be if it received an extradition order from Switzerland, and that had not happened. Additionally, Cortina stated that Spain had an interest in maintaining its neutrality in this issue because of the Madrid heirs' status as refugees. "The desire that the Spanish authorities should intervene in the matter for the purpose of reaching a friendly settlement with the object of avoiding the publicity which repeatedly had taken place in the world press, was not at any time, considered appropriate for the Spanish government," Cortina said.[125]

The result was somewhat ironic for Nixon. An internal firm memo had emphasized that "there is strictly nothing political about this case" and that it was "strictly a family feud." Of course, things weren't that simple. After all, Trujillo may have been a bloodthirsty, megalomaniacal despot, but from the point of view of many American officials, he was "our" bloodthirsty, megalomaniacal despot. He had been an important counterweight to Castro in the Caribbean, and a friend to American businessmen like Pawley who had gotten rich by doing business in the Dominican Republic. Without him, the Dominican Republic could be the next domino to fall, and the last thing the White House wanted was another Castro in its backyard.[126] "If Castro is going to support revolution in the Dominican Republican, it is time for us to go to the source of the problem," Nixon told House Minority Leader Gerald Ford in 1965.[127] "I am not calling for war on Castro. I am saying he should be warned and this cannot be a one way street."

As for Nixon, it made sense why he would want his name in the papers in relation to the Dominican Republic and Trujillo. It reaffirmed his anti-Communist credentials and reminded voters of his foreign policy knowledge. Most importantly, his representation of Trujillo's offspring sent a signal that he remained interested in the fate of the Dominican Republic as well as the American businessmen and women who were heavily invested there, like Pawley had been. Indeed, for Pawley, there weren't many things that concerned him more than Cuba and the Dominican Republic. He even wrote a letter to Eisenhower in June 1965 encouraging the general and other Republicans to support President Johnson and his intervention into the Dominican Civil War to prevent another Communist takeover in Latin America. "As long as Castro is permitted to maintain a communist state in the Western Hemisphere, we are going to be tremendously handicapped in anything that we try to do, economically or in any other way, to help the countries of this hemisphere," Pawley wrote, hoping that Johnson would be emboldened by what happened in the Dominican Republic and unleash the Cubans and Americans willing to do the same thing in Cuba.[128]

Pepsi's Kendall went even further. With plants in Cuba and the Dominican Republic, Kendall had long been concerned about the region and had gone so far as to send Lyndon Johnson a letter heaping praise on the president for acting boldly and decisively by sending the military into the Dominican Republic in order to prevent another Cuba. Kendall even tried to forge an unofficial alliance between Johnson and Nixon, bringing up Nixon's solid and outspoken support for the intervention. "After listening to Nixon discuss both the Vietnam and Dominican Republic situations, it occurred to me that since there is a such a problem of selling your policies to certain segments of the American population, as well as some of our friends abroad, you might want to consider using him as a spokesman in this country and abroad to help sell your policies," Kendall wrote.[129]

In fact, Nixon was not only supporting the Johnson Administration, he was using the Dominican intervention as a wedge to drive between liberals and the Administration. In speeches, he would alternately commend Johnson and Vice President Hubert Humphrey for taking swift, decisive, and necessary action while criticizing their liberal base for opposing the move. "History will be kinder" to Vice President Humphrey than his fellow liberals, Nixon said mischievously during a speech before the forty-sixth US Junior Chamber of Commerce Convention in 1966.[130]

But for Pawley and others like him, who were desperately concerned about the fate of Latin America, Nixon's words were music to their ears. And like many of Nixon's clients and business friends, they did not forget Nixon when it came time for the 1968 campaign.

NOTES

1. Leonard Garment, *Crazy Rhythm: From Brooklyn and Jazz to Nixon's White House, Watergate and Beyond* (Cambridge, MA: Da Capo Press, 1997), 69.
2. Richard Nixon, "Nixon, Mudge, Rose, Guthrie & Alexander. Financial Statements and Information for Year Ending 1964 with Report of Certified Public Accountants," Arthur Young & Company, Pre-Presidential Papers, Richard Nixon Presidential Library and Museum. Also for Year Ending 1965.
3. Richard Nixon, "Nixon, Mudge, Rose, Guthrie & Alexander: Law Firm Statistical Survey, 1964," Price Waterhouse & Co., Pre-Presidential Papers, Richard Nixon Presidential Library and Museum. Also for 1965.
4. The $46,150 in 1963 translates to over $365,000 in 2017 dollars based on the CPI Inflation Calculator from the US Bureau of Labor Statistics. The $68,110 in 1964 is roughly equivalent to $533,800 in 2017.
5. Richard Nixon, "Nixon, Mudge, Rose, Guthrie & Alexander: Law Firm Statistical Survey, 1965," Price Waterhouse & Co. The $73,500 in 1965 translates to over $565,000 in 2017 dollars based on the CPI Inflation Calculator from the US Bureau of Labor Statistics.
6. Paul Hoffman, "Mudge Rose Guthrie & Alexander: The Firm to See?" *New York Magazine*, April 26, 1971.
7. Thomas Evans, "Nixon Mudge" (unpublished manuscript, 1994), 156.

8. Evans, "Nixon Mudge."
9. Evans, "Nixon Mudge."
10. Richard Nixon, interview by Tom Evans, March 15, 1983, transcript.
11. Nixon, interview by Evans.
12. Paul Hoffman, *Lions in the Street: The Inside Story of the Great Wall Street Law Firms* (New York: Saturday Review Press, 1973), 110.
13. Hoffman, *Lions in the Street.*
14. Richard Nixon, Memo from Joseph Kline, "Re: Directorship on City Title Insurance Company," February 4, 1965, Pre-Presidential Papers, Richard Nixon Presidential Library and Museum.
15. Richard Nixon, Memo to Vincent Andrews, Inc., March 3, 1967, Pre-Presidential Papers, Richard Nixon Presidential Library and Museum.
16. Jon Frappier, "Invisible Power Brokers: The Nixon-Mitchell Law Firm," *North American Congress on Latin America* 7, no. 9 (November 1973), 8.
17. Frappier, Invisible Power Brokers," 8.
18. Richard Nixon, Memo to Andrews.
19. Richard Nixon, Letter to Frank Rackley, June 3, 1963, Pre-Presidential Papers, Richard Nixon Presidential Library and Museum.
20. Wheeling Steel ultimately merged with Pittsburgh Steel Company in 1968 to form Wheeling-Pittsburgh Steel. This company went bankrupt twice (in 1991 and again in 2000) and was eventually folded into other organizations that also went broke.
21. Richard Nixon, "Frank Rackley to RMW on Telephone," January 9, 1964, Pre-Presidential Papers, Richard Nixon Presidential Library and Museum.
22. Richard Nixon, Letter to J. Clifford Folger, August 16, 1963, Pre-Presidential Papers, Richard Nixon Presidential Library and Museum.
23. Richard Nixon, Letter to Eugene McGovern, June 4, 1963, Pre-Presidential Papers, Richard Nixon Presidential Library and Museum.
24. Richard Nixon, "Mr. Constantin Diamantis, Annual Retainer, November 1, 1964 to October 31, 1965," Pre-Presidential Papers, Richard Nixon Presidential Library and Museum.
25. Richard Nixon, Letter to Constantin Diamantis, November 13, 1964, Pre-Presidential Papers, Richard Nixon Presidential Library and Museum.
26. Frank Sorg, interview by Tom Evans, December 6, 1989, transcript.
27. Sorg, interview by Evans.
28. Sorg, interview by Evans.
29. Richard Nixon, Letter from Francis Sorg, June 16, 1964, Pre-Presidential Papers, Richard Nixon Presidential Library and Museum.
30. Nixon, Letter from Sorg.
31. Richard Nixon, Letter to Tatsuzo Mizukami, May 5, 1964, Pre-Presidential Papers, Richard Nixon Presidential Library and Museum.
32. Nixon, Letter to Mizukami.
33. "Forbes's Hunt for Richest 400," *New York Times*, September 11, 1982, accessed March 22, 2017, http://www.nytimes.com/1982/09/11/business/forbes-s-hunt-for-richest-400.html.
34. Richard Nixon, Letter to King Hussein I, July 24, 1964, Pre-Presidential Papers, Richard Nixon Presidential Library and Museum.
35. Nixon, Letter to King Hussein.
36. Nixon, Letter to King Hussein.
37. Richard Nixon, Memo from Gregory Brownell, "National Bulk Carriers, Inc.—Jordan," January 4, 1965, Pre-Presidential Papers, Richard Nixon Presidential Library and Museum.
38. "Schick and Patrick Frawley," Quixotic Joust, accessed March 22, 2017, http://quixoticjoust.blogspot.com/2011/09/schick-and-patrick-frawley.html.
39. Robert McG. Thomas Jr., "Patrick Frawley Jr., 75, Ex-Owner of Schick," *New York Times*, November 9, 1988, accessed March 22, 2017, http://www.nytimes.com/1998/11/09/business/patrick-frawley-jr-75-ex-owner-of-schick.html.
40. Thomas Jr., "Patrick Frawley Jr.".
41. Richard Nixon, Letter to Patrick Frawley, January 28, 1965, Pre-Presidential Papers, Richard Nixon Presidential Library and Museum.

42. Richard Nixon, Letter to Touche, Ross, Bailey & Smart from Nixon, Mudge, Rose, Guthrie, Alexander & Mitchell, March 3, 1967, Pre-Presidential Papers, Richard Nixon Presidential Library and Museum.
43. Richard Nixon, Letter from Herbert Sturdy, October 6, 1965, Pre-Presidential Papers, Richard Nixon Presidential Library and Museum.
44. Richard Nixon, "Transcript of Radio Broadcast, WNBC, September 8, 1965," Pre-Presidential Papers, Richard Nixon Presidential Library and Museum.
45. Richard Nixon, Memo from Tom Evans to Leonard Garment, "Danger on the Right," October 19, 1965, Pre-Presidential Papers, Richard Nixon Presidential Library and Museum.
46. Richard Nixon, Draft letter for Patrick Frawley, October 18, 1965, Pre-Presidential Papers, Richard Nixon Presidential Library and Museum.
47. Nixon, Draft letter for Frawley.
48. Joseph R. Gregory, "Madame Nhu, Vietnam War Lightning Rod, Dies," *New York Times*, April 26, 2011, accessed March 22, 2017, http://www.nytimes.com/2011/04/27/world/asia/27nhu.html.
49. Robert D. Schulzinger, *A Time for War: The United States and Vietnam, 1941–1975* (New York: Oxford University Press, 1997), 83.
50. "Ngô Đình Nhu," Wikipedia, accessed March 22, 2017, https://en.wikipedia.org/wiki/Ng%C3%B4_%C4%90%C3%ACnh_Nhu.
51. Katie Baker, "Searching for Madame Nhu," *Daily Beast*, September 24, 2013, accessed March 22, 2017, http://www.thedailybeast.com/witw/articles/2013/09/24/finding-the-dragon-lady-in-search-of-vietnam-s-infamous-madame-nhu.html.
52. Robert Templer, "Madame Nhu Obituary," *The Guardian*, April 26, 2011, accessed March 22, 2017, https://www.theguardian.com/world/2011/apr/26/madame-nhu-obituary.
53. Templer, "Madame Nhu Obituary."
54. David Halberstam, *The Making of a Quagmire: America and Vietnam during the Kennedy Era* (Lanham, MD: Rowman & Littlefield, 2008), 3.
55. Halberstam, *The Making of a Quagmire*.
56. Baker, "Searching for Madame Nhu."
57. Baker, "Searching for Madame Nhu."
58. Baker, "Searching for Madame Nhu."
59. Richard Nixon, Letter from Madame Nhu, January 16, 1964, Pre-Presidential Papers, Richard Nixon Presidential Library and Museum.
60. Nixon, Letter from Madame Nhu.
61. Richard Nixon, Memo to Leonard Garment, March 13, 1964, Pre-Presidential Papers, Richard Nixon Presidential Library and Museum.
62. Richard Nixon, Letter to Leonard Garment to William Landis, March 30, 1964, Pre-Presidential Papers, Richard Nixon Presidential Library and Museum.
63. Richard Nixon, Letter to William Landis, June 1, 1964, Pre-Presidential Papers, Richard Nixon Presidential Library and Museum.
64. Nixon, Letter to William Landis.
65. Richard Nixon, Letter to John Larson, July 9, 1964, Pre-Presidential Papers, Richard Nixon Presidential Library and Museum.
66. Anthony Carrozza, *William D. Pawley: The Extraordinary Life of the Adventurer, Entrepreneur and Diplomat Who Co-Founded the Flying Tigers* (Washington, DC: Potomac Books, 2012), 3–18.
67. Carrozza, *William D. Pawley*, 95–108.
68. Carrozza, *William D. Pawley*, at 125–38.
69. "The National Security Archive," George Washington University, accessed March 22, 2017, http://nsarchive.gwu.edu/NSAEBB/NSAEBB355/.
70. Carrozza, *William D. Pawley*, 229.
71. Carrozza, *William D. Pawley*, at 244.
72. Carrozza, *William D. Pawley*, at 237.
73. Carrozza, *William D. Pawley*, at 246–47.
74. Carrozza, *William D. Pawley*, at 220.
75. The National Security Archive.

76. Carrozza, *William D. Pawley*, 312.
77. Richard Nixon, Letter from William Pawley, November 12, 1962, Pre-Presidential Papers, Richard Nixon Presidential Library and Museum.
78. Richard Nixon, Transcript of Phone Call from William Pawley to Rose Mary Woods, June 30, 1964, Pre-Presidential Papers, Richard Nixon Presidential Library and Museum.
79. Carrozza, *William D. Pawley*, 295–96.
80. Richard Nixon, Copy of Letter from Pawley to President Lyndon Johnson, September 3, 1965, Pre-Presidential Papers, Richard Nixon Presidential Library and Museum.
81. Nixon, Copy of Letter from Pawley to President Lyndon Johnson.
82. Richard Nixon, Copy of Letter from Elliott Roosevelt to W. Marvin Watson, Special Assistant to President Johnson, September 3, 1965, Pre-Presidential Papers, Richard Nixon Presidential Library and Museum.
83. Richard Nixon, Letter from Arthur Becker, November 29, 1965, Pre-Presidential Papers, Richard Nixon Presidential Library and Museum.
84. Richard Nixon, "Congressional Quarterly Weekly Report—No. 35, August 27, 1965," Pre-Presidential Papers, Richard Nixon Presidential Library and Museum.
85. Richard Nixon, Memo from Rose Mary Woods to Richard Nixon, Pre-Presidential Papers, Richard Nixon Presidential Library and Museum.
86. Nixon, Memo from Rose Mary Woods to Richard Nixon.
87. Richard Nixon, Letter from William Pawley, October 21, 1965, Pre-Presidential Papers, Richard Nixon Presidential Library and Museum.
88. Carrozza, *William D. Pawley*, 304–7.
89. "The Morrow-Kohly-Nixon Connection," Kennedy Assassination Homepage, accessed March 22, 2017, http://mcadams.posc.mu.edu/morrow2.htm.
90. Robert Morrow, *First Hand Knowledge: How I Participated in the CIA-Mafia Murder of President Kennedy* (New York: S.P.I. Books, 1992), 303.
91. Anthony Summers, *The Arrogance of Power: The Secret World of Richard Nixon* (New York: Viking, 2000), 186–87.
92. Summers and Robert Morrow maintain that Kohly's original aim was to utilize guerrilla warfare and that he had recruited a force of approximately three hundred to four hundred soldiers within Cuba.
93. Summers, *The Arrogance of Power*, 186–87.
94. Richard Nixon, Letters from Marshall Diggs, January 20, 1964, February 4, 1964, and October 15, 1964, Pre-Presidential Papers, Richard Nixon Presidential Library and Museum.
95. Richard Nixon, Memo from Robert Thornton to Richard Nixon, December 10, 1964, Pre-Presidential Papers, Richard Nixon Presidential Library and Museum.
96. Fred Graham, "Cuban Says U.S. Knew of Counterfeiting Plan," *New York Times*, June 10, 1965.
97. Richard Nixon, Memo from Robert Thornton to Richard Nixon, October 27, 1964, Pre-Presidential Papers, Richard Nixon Presidential Library and Museum.
98. Summers, *The Arrogance of Power*, 187.
99. Richard Nixon, Application for Parole of William Grosh, October 18, 1965, Pre-Presidential Papers, Richard Nixon Presidential Library and Museum.
100. Richard Nixon, Letter to Margarita Kohly, April 21, 1966, Pre-Presidential Papers, Richard Nixon Presidential Library and Museum.
101. Summers, *The Arrogance of Power*, 187.
102. Rogelio Saenz PhD, and Aurelia Lorena Murga. *Latino Issues: A Reference Handbook: A Reference Handbook* (Santa Barbara, CA: ABC-CLIO, 2011), 109.
103. "Dominican Military Chief Was a Major at Age 3; His Father Made Trujillo Jr. a Teen-Age General He Drew Criticism in U.S. over Lavish Entertaining," *New York Times*, June 2, 1961, accessed March 24, 2017, http://query.nytimes.com/gst/abstract.html?res=9C03E6DF1239EE32A25751C0A9609C946091D6CF.
104. Carlos Alberto Montaner, *Trujillo: The Most Insane Dictator*, Real Clear Politics, March 18, 2006, accessed March 24, 2017, http://www.realclearpolitics.com/articles/2006/03/trujillo_the_most_insane_dicta.html.

105. Tim Mansel, "I Shot the Cruelest Dictator in the Americas," BBC, May 28, 2011, accessed March 24, 2017, http://www.bbc.com/news/world-latin-america-13560512.
106. Richard Lee Turtis, "A World Destroyed, A Nation Imposed: The 1937 Haitian Massacre in the Dominican Republic," *Hispanic American Historical Review* (August 2002): 613.
107. Robert D. Crassweller, *Trujillo: The Life and Times of a Caribbean Dictator* (New York: The MacMillan Co., 1966), 375.
108. Carrozza, *William D. Pawley*, 284–86.
109. Alex von Tunzelmann, *Red Heat: Conspiracy, Murder and the Cold War in the Caribbean* (London, Simon & Schuster, 2011).
110. "Intelligence—Report on CIA Assassination Plots (1)," Ford Library Museum, accessed on March 24, 2017, https://www.fordlibrarymuseum.gov/library/document/0005/7324009.pdf.
111. von Tunzelmann, *Red Heat*.Also R.T. Naylor, *Hot Money and the Politics of Debt* (Montreal & Kingston: McGill Queen's University Press, 2004), 237.
112. Raymond Steckel, interview by Victor Li, November 2, 2016.
113. Richard Nixon, Memo from Rose Mary Woods, December 9, 1965, Pre-Presidential Papers, Richard Nixon Presidential Library and Museum.
114. "Trujillo's Son Now in Switzerland," *New York Times*, November 25, 1964, accessed March 24, 2017, http://www.nytimes.com/1964/11/25/trujillos-son-now-in-switzerland.html?_r=0.
115. Richard Nixon, Memo for Nixon, May 4, 1965, Pre-Presidential Papers, Richard Nixon Presidential Library and Museum.
116. Steckel, interview by Li.
117. Steckel, interview by Li.
118. Steckel, interview by Li.
119. Lloyd Shearer, "The Vanishing Playboys," *St. Petersburg Times*, August 15, 1965.
120. "Nixon Confers in Geneva on Trujillo Estate Suits," *New York Times*, May 5, 1965.
121. Nixon, Memo for Nixon, May 4, 1965.
122. Nixon, Memo for Nixon, May 4, 1965.
123. Nixon, Memo for Nixon, May 4, 1965.
124. Richard Nixon, Memo from John Davis Lodge to Richard Nixon, May 9, 1965, Pre-Presidential Papers, Richard Nixon Presidential Library and Museum.
125. Richard Nixon, Letter from Don Pedro Cortina to John Davis Lodge, April 2, 1966, Pre-Presidential Papers, Richard Nixon Presidential Library and Museum.
126. Carrozza, *William D. Pawley*, 289.
127. Richard Nixon, Transcript of his side of phone conversation with Gerald Ford, May 3, 1965, Pre-Presidential Papers, Richard Nixon Presidential Library and Museum.
128. Richard Nixon, Copy of William Pawley letter to Dwight D. Eisenhower, June 4, 1965, Pre-Presidential Papers, Richard Nixon Presidential Library and Museum.
129. Richard Nixon, Copy of Donald Kendall letter to Lyndon B. Johnson, May 4, 1965, Pre-Presidential Papers, Richard Nixon Presidential Library and Museum.
130. Jules Witcover, *The Resurrection of Richard Nixon* (New York: G. P. Putnam's Sons, 1970), 135.

Chapter Five

"There But for the Grace of God Go I."

Throughout history, the best rivalries are often born out of friendship. Caesar and Pompey. Adams and Jefferson. Kennedy and Nixon.

Kennedy and Nixon weren't the type of friends who vacationed together or had dinner at each other's houses every weekend or so. Instead, their friendship was forged from their early days in Washington, when each man represented the brightest hopes of not only their political parties but also their entire generation. It seemed their destinies were irrevocably intertwined since the moment they both arrived in Washington, D.C., in January 1947 as newly elected members of the US House of Representatives. Because both men would eventually be defined by their differences, it may seem hard to believe that, once upon a time, John F. Kennedy and Richard M. Nixon were distinguished more by what they had in common. They both served in the navy during World War II, seeing time in the South Pacific. They were both seen as Cold Warriors during their early years in Congress. They were both assigned to the Education and Labor Committee where they would play opposing but leading roles in contentious debate over the passage of the Taft-Hartley Act.

Most importantly, Kennedy and Nixon were seen as rising stars within their respective parties. Given how quickly each young man climbed up the ladder of power in D.C., it is obvious that their paths would cross sooner rather than later.

An illustration of their exalted status came early in their tenures as representatives. As a result of Taft-Hartley, both men had, seemingly, increased their public profiles overnight as Nixon helped draft and pass the act while Kennedy helped lead the charge against it. On April 22, 1947, the Chamber of Commerce in McKeesport, Pennsylvania, sponsored a debate about the bill, which had passed the House the previous week and was being considered by the Senate. Each side was invited to send a young, appealing representative that it considered to have a bright future and would best articulate its views about the proposed law. Kennedy and Nixon were the two obvious choices.[1]

The two had a spirited but civil debate at the Penn-McKee Hotel that, in retrospect, was a clear dress rehearsal for what was to come thirteen years later. Like the more celebrated 1960 debates, the two men were fairly evenly matched and showed respect for one another on stage. Nixon, as he would when he was seeking to succeed Eisenhower, focused more on trying to win the argument and engaged in a combative and didactic defense of Taft-Hartley. "Nixon was tense, making his points in a pile-driving way," the *Pittsburgh Post Gazette* editorial board recalled in 1976.[2] "He had an eagerness to get in there and fight to the last comma." Despite that, the consensus was that he had acquitted himself well—especially considering the fact that he was arguing in favor of a bill that organized labor saw as a step above enslavement while deep in the heart of Pittsburgh, a labor union stronghold.

Kennedy, on the other hand, understood then, as he did when he became the Democratic nominee for president, that winning the debate was secondary to winning the room. The suave, relaxed, and confident man easily charmed the audience despite taking a more conciliatory approach toward Taft-Hartley and even praising parts of it before expressing his overall opposition to the bill. "While Nixon debated, Kennedy simply ignored his opponent, carefully making sure that the businessmen in the room understood his justified concern that the Republican's get-tough approach to labor might create more trouble, not less," wrote Chris Matthews.[3]

Despite their divergent styles, both men came out of the event with their reputations intact. The debate moderator even singled Nixon out for praise, saying that the Republican was "going to go places."[4] The media, however, had a different take. In another bit of foreshadowing, when the *McKeesport Daily News* ran a story about the debate the following morning, they put a picture of a tanned, handsome, smiling Kennedy next to a shifty-eyed, pointy-chinned, five-o-clock-shadow-wearing Nixon.[5]

Once the very first Kennedy-Nixon debate was in the books, the two men boarded a train and made the overnight trip back to D.C. "It was a night train because we had to get back for a vote the next day," Nixon recalled in his memoirs.[6] "And so we drew as to who got the upper berth and who got the lower berth, and I won, one of the few times I did against him." Ultimately, neither man got much sleep as they spent most of the trip talking about their lives and how they saw the world.

The two men maintained their friendship, even as they moved up the D.C. food chain. Nixon was the first to go for higher office, winning the nomination for Senate in 1950. One day during the campaign, Kennedy stopped by Nixon's Capitol Hill office and handed a surprised Nixon a check from his father for $1,000. The older Kennedy may have been a loyal Democrat, but the former ambassador to the United Kingdom represented the conservative wing of the party and was a strong anti-Communist. He distrusted liberals like Helen Gahagan Douglas and, like many California voters who had bought into Nixon's "Pink Lady" gibe, came to see the former Hollywood star as a Communist. At least that's what he told Tip O'Neill years later when he seemed to regret his decision to boost the man who would, eventually, seek to deny his son the presidency.[7]

"Dick, I know you're in for a pretty rough campaign and my father wanted to help out," Kennedy said after he handed over the check.[8] Kennedy noted that he could not endorse Nixon; however, he made his personal loyalties clear. Neither he nor his father would shed any tears over the prospect of Nixon ending Douglas's political career and sending her back into the arms of Hollywood. "Isn't this something?" Nixon later said to aide Pat Hillings about Kennedy's gesture.[9]

Kennedy became a senator two years after Nixon, unseating Massachusetts Republican (and Nixon's 1960 running mate) Henry Cabot Lodge. Nixon, however, was on to bigger and better things, winning the vice presidency the same night Kennedy pulled off his triumph. Despite missing each other in the Senate, the two would still be in each other's orbit. Kennedy's Senate office happened to be located across the hall from the president of the Senate's office, and between Nixon's status as GOP presidential nominee-in-waiting and Kennedy's youth and charisma, the corridor between their two offices soon became a popular spot for reporters and cameramen.

They weren't the only ones. Nixon would often come by to see how Kennedy was doing, and the two developed a friendly relationship. After Kennedy underwent life-threatening back surgery in 1954, Nixon, reportedly, broke down in front of Secret Service guards and cried for his friend. "Poor, brave Jack is going to die. Oh God, don't let him die."[10]

Kennedy lived, but it took him nearly two years before he could resume his work in the Senate. Democrats had a mere one-seat majority at the time, and with Kennedy's absence, Republicans could have used his unavailability to retake control of the Senate. However, Nixon, as presiding officer of the Senate, made it clear that he wouldn't allow it.[11] This gesture prompted Jacqueline Kennedy to write Nixon, telling him that "there's no man my husband admires more."[12] The sentiment seemed genuine. As he was gearing up to run for president in 1960, Kennedy reportedly told friends that, if he didn't win the Democratic nomination, he would vote for Nixon. Joe Kennedy went a step further. In early 1960, Nixon and the senior Kennedy bumped into one another on an airplane, and Kennedy explicitly told Nixon that, if his son didn't win the Democratic nomination, he'd support the vice president.[13]

The elder Kennedy's hedge made sense. After all, while Nixon had long been the presumptive nominee for the GOP, Kennedy's ascension was anything but certain. No Catholic had ever won the presidency, and the only other to win a major party's nomination, Democrat Al Smith in 1928, had lost in a landslide. Anti-Catholic animus had especially hurt Smith in the Democratic Solid South, as Smith only carried six of the eleven former Confederate states in what was, at the time, the worst performance by a Democrat since Reconstruction. Kennedy faced many of the same attacks that Smith had, including one that questioned whether a Catholic president would take his orders from the Vatican. Kennedy tried to put those fears to bed in a famous speech to the Greater Houston Ministerial Association on September 12, 1960. "I am not the Catholic candidate for president," Kennedy said.[14] "I am the Democratic Party's candidate for president who also happens to be a Catholic. I do not speak for my Church on public matters—and the Church does not speak for me."

Even without the religion issue, Kennedy was still facing an uphill battle for the nomination. Kennedy's star turn in the House during his first year had become a distant memory by 1960, as a combination of poor health and indifference in both the House and Senate had seemed to confirm his status as just another pretty face. Largely regarded as a lightweight dilettante with almost no legislative accomplishments to speak of, Kennedy had never been widely respected by his peers in the House or Senate. Sam Rayburn, the powerful Speaker of the House, had called him "lazy." Lyndon Johnson, the powerful Senate Majority Leader, had called him "pathetic as a Congressman and Senator" and "a weak and indecisive politician."[15] Even his best friend in the Senate, George Smathers of Florida, struggled to identify any of Kennedy's legislative accomplishments, conceding that "while he did, from time to time, make some brilliant speech about something or other . . . he was not what you would call a really effective Senator."[16]

Nixon was another who had underestimated Kennedy. He had consistently believed that someone or something would stop JFK, be it Lyndon Johnson winning the nomination at the convention, Hubert Humphrey beating Kennedy in the primaries, or a health scare or scandal torpedoing his campaign. Plus, Nixon saw Kennedy the same way Johnson, Rayburn, and the others did. "We just didn't think he was a heavyweight," said Hillings.[17] "Also, we just didn't think he would work that hard."

Hillings also said that they had underestimated Kennedy as a campaigner. Having, seemingly, gotten over his health problems, Kennedy was no longer the gaunt, sickly, rail-thin man-child who looked like he would have trouble staying upright on a windy day. Fueled by cortisone shots, Kennedy's body and face had filled out and, by the time he ran for president, he looked more like a matinee idol than a politician. On the stump, Kennedy was charming, likeable, and exuded charisma—three qualities that were rarely used to describe Nixon. Aided by his father's deep pockets and his brother's well-disciplined campaign operation, perhaps the bigger surprise was that so few people saw JFK coming. "Kennedy's got no chance," Nixon said during the run-up to the campaign.[18] "I'm running against Johnson."

"THE GENTLEMAN FROM VIRGINIA IS IN THE LEAD."

If familiarity breeds contempt, then Kennedy and Nixon were always destined to become foes.

For one thing, there wasn't a ton of daylight between the two when it came to political ideology. Despite his enduring image as a liberal icon, Kennedy had actually carved out a fairly moderate-to-conservative voting record in the House and Senate.[19] When coupled with Johnson's reputation as a conservative southerner, one could argue that the GOP ticket of Nixon and his fellow moderate Lodge was, on the whole, to the left of the Democratic ticket. On some issues, like national defense and Cuba, Kennedy had actually run to the right of Nixon, hammering the Eisenhower Administration (and Nixon, by proxy) of falling behind the USSR in the arms race and not doing enough to rein in Batista in Cuba. "Today Cuba is lost for freedom," Kennedy said during the second debate with Nixon.[20] The former VP and ardent Cold Warrior, who had risen through the ranks, in part, because of his anti-Communist credentials, would later ruefully remark that "Kennedy conveyed the image—to 60 million people—that he was tougher on Castro and Communism than I was."[21]

Commentator Eric Sevareid put his finger on another common trait between the two. "They are both 'cool cats,' we are told, men devoid of deep passions or strong convictions, sharp, ambitious, opportunistic, with no commitments except to personal advancement," he observed.[22] "They are junior executives on the make, political status seekers, end products of the Age of Public Relations . . . The Processed Politician has finally arrived."

They weren't exactly two peas in a pod, however. For one thing, Nixon had several clear advantages over Kennedy, especially when it came to experience and competence. However, Kennedy had several things going for him that Nixon couldn't hope to match, including natural charisma, an upbeat, hopeful message, and an almost limitless family fortune. Most importantly, Kennedy was able to run as the "change candidate" and attack the status quo that Nixon, as vice president, was forced to defend.

Nixon didn't help his cause by acting as a micromanager who ignored his advisors. He also made some boneheaded mistakes, including an inexplicable pledge to campaign in all fifty states (causing him to waste valuable time traveling to remote, noncompetitive states like Alaska while Kennedy was able to shore up support in battleground states). Nixon also disregarded the value of television to his peril, refusing makeup or rest prior to his first televised debate with Kennedy. "[Nixon] wants, as always, to hold all the reins in his own hot lil' paws," aide James Bassett told his wife.[23] "Ergo: he was to make all the decisions, most of which ought to be handled by somebody with delegated authority."

In the end, Nixon lost the popular vote to Kennedy by less than two-tenths of a percentage point and lost four states by less than a percentage point. There had been widespread allegations of voter fraud in Illinois (where Nixon had carried 92 of the state's 101 counties, only to lose the state because of a massive defeat in the city of Chicago—the home of Mayor Daley's imposing Democratic machine) and Texas (home of JFK's running mate, Lyndon Johnson—a man widely believed to have won a Senate race in 1948 by engaging in rampant voter fraud). If Nixon had won those two states, then he would have won the Electoral College. He could have instituted a constitutional crisis by challenging the results of the election, and according to Nixon, Eisenhower had encouraged him to do just that. Nixon, ultimately, chose not to formally challenge the results, although he didn't do much to discourage his allies or groups affiliated with his campaign from pushing for recounts in a host of states, including Illinois and Texas.[24]

Publicly, he played the part of the classy loser. He met face to face with Kennedy in Key Biscayne, Florida, the week after the election and congratulated the president-elect. Nixon's grace and good humor extended to what was, undoubtedly, an awkward and difficult situation in January 1961 when he was required, under the Twelfth Amendment, to preside over a joint session of Congress in his capacity as president of the Senate in order to certify the Electoral College results. Sitting in the big chair, he had a front row seat to Kennedy's ascension to the job Nixon had so coveted. However, instead of going into "mean Droopy" mode, Nixon handled the situation deftly and with good humor. Voting alphabetically by state, Alabama cast its electoral votes for Senator Harry F. Byrd of Virginia, a man who had neither sought nor run for the office of the presidency during the just-completed campaign, as a protest against the pro–civil rights ideologies of both Nixon and Kennedy. "The gentleman from Virginia is in the lead," Nixon said, drawing laughter from the audience. After Kennedy was officially certified as the winner of the race, Nixon seized the moment and delivered a pseudo-concession speech that conferred even more legitimacy on the new president while reinforcing the foundation of the American democratic system.

> This is the first time in one hundred years that a candidate for the presidency announced the result of an election in which he was defeated. I do not think we could have a more striking and eloquent example of the stability of our constitutional system and of the proud tradition of the American people of developing, respecting and honoring institutions of self-government. In our campaigns, no matter how hard fought they may be, no matter how close the election may turn out to be, those who lose accept the verdict and support

> those who win. It is in that spirit that I now declare that John F. Kennedy has been elected President of the United States.[25]

Nixon's speech resulted in a standing ovation and even inspired Sam Rayburn, the powerful Speaker of the House who had long despised him, to shake his hand.[26]

Nixon's words were even more poignant when one considers whom he was referring to as the previous presidential nominee to announce the winner of the election in which he ran and lost. In 1860, John Breckinridge was vice president when he lost in a four-way election to Abraham Lincoln. A Kentucky Democrat who was pro-slavery and believed in a state's right to secede, Breckinridge grudgingly certified Lincoln's election in February 1861. "It was evidently an exceedingly unpleasant duty to Mr. B," the *Salem Register* reported.[27] By the end of the year, Breckinridge had enlisted in the Confederate Army and had been condemned as a traitor on the floor of the US Senate.

Despite Nixon's grace in defeat, it was obvious that whatever friendship had existed between he and Kennedy was gone. Following their meeting in Florida after Election Day that was widely portrayed in the media as the vanquished vice president paying his respects to the man who had bested him, the president-elect had expressed hope that he and Nixon could "resume our relationship, which had been somewhat interrupted by the campaign."[28]

That wasn't going to happen. Nixon, for one thing, still had presidential aspirations and had decided to take up the mantle as leader of the loyal opposition, which would require him to speak out against Kennedy and Democrats as much as possible. Kennedy, despite telling Nixon that he had hoped to resume their friendship, had seemingly done a 180 on him. "If I've done nothing for this country, I've saved them from Dick Nixon," Kennedy told a friend shortly after the race.[29]

Nixon was, similarly, peeved. "He left 1960 with a sore mistrust of the Kennedys, a swollen sense of grievance, and a consuming resolve to never be outdone by a rival's dirty tricks," John Farrell wrote.[30] Nixon's grievances weren't limited to JFK and his family, however. He blamed a lot of people for his defeat, particularly the press for lionizing the inexperienced and unaccomplished Kennedy. "In Kennedy, they saw someone they would like to be," Nixon said about the press.[31] "He was a 'Stevenson with balls,' and . . . attracted the people who wanted a young courageous man in the presidency."

Despite their differences, Nixon and Kennedy managed to have a few moments of warmth during the intervening years. In the aftermath of the disastrous Bay of Pigs invasion in 1961, a humiliated Kennedy had summoned Nixon to the White House to vent his frustration, but also to ask his "loyal opposition" leader for advice. Taking pity on him, Nixon suggested several courses of action, including a full-scale invasion of Cuba, and promised to back him should he go that route.[32] Nixon even tried to cheer up the devastated Kennedy, suggesting that he go up to the residence and have a drink with his wife. "I just saw a crushed man today," Nixon would later say.[33] "He needs our help." Kennedy, for his part, recommended to Nixon that he write his memoirs and may have even planted the seed of the 1962 California gubernatorial race into his head, telling Nixon that the incumbent, Pat Brown, was concerned about Nixon's poll numbers and the prospect of facing off against the former vice president.[34]

Of course, Kennedy never forgot what team he played for and stood front and center among the queue of politicians waiting to dance on Nixon's political grave, calling Brown after his victory and praising him for a job well done.

"I will tell you this," Kennedy told Brown.[35] "You reduced him to the nut house."

"But you gave me instructions and I follow your orders," replied Brown.

"I understand," Kennedy chuckled. "God, that last farewell speech of his."

"Wasn't that terrible?" Brown agreed. "I don't see how he can ever recover."

The last time Kennedy and Nixon would speak was during Nixon's pre–New York world tour in 1963. The former vice president was in a hotel in Rome when he received a phone call from Kennedy. The president was also in town, having arrived from West Germany, days after he had just delivered his famous "*Ich bin ein Berliner*" speech. The two had what Nixon described as a nice, friendly chat.[36]

"WAS IT ONE OF THE NUTS?"

The next time they would be in the same city, it would be under far more tragic circumstances.

As covered earlier, Nixon had no shortage of clients from the moment he hit Wall Street. However, his biggest and most public client was the one that helped pave the way for him to hit Wall Street in the first place. As promised, Pepsi had transferred its business to Nixon Mudge, and Nixon immediately went to work representing the cola giant's interests throughout the world.

In one of his first major appearances for Pepsi, Nixon found himself in Dallas for a Pepsi bottlers' convention on November 21, 1963. He had received a rude reminder of his diminished public status as he showed up in a city that was focused more on the president's arrival the following day. In fact, Nixon wasn't even the big cheese in his own entourage. The bodyguards stationed at Nixon's hotel in downtown Dallas were there to protect Oscar-winning actress Joan Crawford, a member of the Pepsi board of directors and the widow of former Pepsi chairman Alfred Steele.[37]

Despite the city's fixation on Kennedy's imminent arrival, Dallas wasn't necessarily happy about the president coming to town. For one thing, Kennedy was highly unpopular in Dallas, as well as in Texas as a whole, and he was looking at an uphill battle to keep the state in his vote column in 1964. The Lone Star State was still a Democratic stronghold, but the party's grip on power had been slipping for several years as voters had begun gravitating toward the Republicans. Eisenhower had won the state in both 1952 and 1956, and after the formerly all-powerful Senate Majority Leader Lyndon Johnson was elected vice president, it was a Republican, John Tower, that had won his former seat. Indeed, Nixon had actually won Dallas in 1960—garnering an impressive 62 percent of the vote there before narrowly losing the state.[38]

In the years since the 1960 race, Kennedy seemed to have lost even more ground in the state. Most voters in Dallas, and Texas in general, distrusted the rich, preppy Kennedy and cared little about his New Frontier. Many were openly hostile to Kennedy's embrace of civil rights and believed his administration wasn't doing enough to fight communism. "The general opinion of the grassroots thinking in this country is that you and your administration are weak sisters," Ted Dealey, owner of the *Dallas Morning News*, told the president at the White House in 1961.[39] "If we stand firm, there will be no war. The Russians will back down. We need a man on horseback to lead this nation, and many people in Texas and the South-West think that you are riding Caroline's tricycle." A month before Kennedy's trip to Dallas, his UN ambassador, Adlai Stevenson, found out just how angry many in the city were, having been hit by a placard and spit on during a protest. There were a number of demonstrations planned for the president's visit, and Dealey himself had run a full-page ad paid for by three local businessmen in the *Dallas Morning News* on the morning of November 22, 1963, criticizing the president and accusing him of being soft on communism—mere hours before Kennedy would be gunned down at the plaza that was named after Dealey's father.[40] Stevenson had advised Kennedy against going to Dallas, and the president had seemed ambivalent about even making the trip. However, he felt an obligation to be there. Between jump-starting his reelection campaign and mediating a feud between the state's two most powerful Democrats not named Johnson—conservative governor John Connally and liberal senator Ralph Yarborough—Kennedy felt he had no choice but to pay a visit to a state he had barely won in 1960 and would, most likely, need in 1964. Otherwise, Kennedy had no desire to be in "nut country," as he described Dallas to his wife on the morning of his last day on Earth.[41]

Nixon, meanwhile, was already looking ahead to 1964 and was in attack mode. Sensing that there was trouble within the Democratic ranks, Nixon stirred the pot by acknowledging rumors that Johnson could be dropped from the ticket. "But we must remember that President Kennedy and his advisers are practical politicians," Nixon said during a press conference in Dallas on November 21, the day before Kennedy's scheduled arrival in the city.[42] "I believe that, if they think the race is a shoo-in, they will keep Lyndon. Otherwise, I think they'll choose someone who can help the Democratic ticket." Nixon couldn't resist taking a slight dig at Johnson, pointing out that the Texas man had originally been chosen for his ability to deliver the South to the Democrats. "Now he is becoming a liability in the South, just as he is in the North," Nixon said about the former Senate Majority Leader.[43]

As for Kennedy, Nixon was no less critical, saying that the president had failed to deliver on his promises and had accomplished very little despite having a comfortable legislative majority. "President Kennedy's stock is considerably lower today than it was in Texas in 1960 when I ran against him," Nixon pointed out during his press conference.[44] Among the reasons he listed for his erstwhile rival's decline in popularity were persistent unemployment and the fact that Castro was still in power in Cuba.

Despite that, Nixon urged Dallas to give the president and First Lady a courteous reception. "Over-enthusiastic opponents really harm their own cause and help their opponents by showing discourtesy," Nixon said.[45] "On the other hand, peaceful picketing is in the American tradition."

It was only after Nixon left Dallas and returned to New York that he realized that his words had not come true. He had flown out on the morning of November 22, 1963, having concluded his business for Pepsi, and was in a taxicab leaving New York's Idlewild Airport (which would soon be renamed in honor of JFK) when he heard the news that Kennedy had been shot. According to Nixon, the cab was stopped at a traffic light when a random man ran over and said he heard a rumor that Kennedy had been shot and asked the cab driver if he had a radio. Nixon dismissed the man as "one of the nuts" and thought nothing of it until he got home and his doorman told him that Kennedy had been killed. Nixon recalled that he rushed up to his apartment and immediately called FBI director J. Edgar Hoover to find out more about it.

"What happened?" Nixon asked. "Was it one of the nuts?"

"No," Hoover replied.[46] "It was an anti-Communist." Nearly fifteen years later, it was reported that the anti-Communist in question, Lee Harvey Oswald, had originally planned on assassinating Nixon after learning from the *Dallas Morning News* that he was in town, only to be talked out of it by his wife.[47]

Nixon was shocked by the death of his longtime rival. However, in his memoirs and in interviews with reporters after the assassination, he claimed he never reflected on his own mortality—nor did he reflect on the simple twist of fate that had landed Kennedy in the White House after one of the closest elections in American history and Nixon in New York. "I never felt the 'there but for the grace of God go I' reaction to Kennedy's death that many people seemed to imagine I would," Nixon wrote in his memoirs.[48] "I did not think of Kennedy and myself as interchangeable. I did not think that if I had won in 1960, it would have been I rather than he riding through Dealey Plaza in Dallas at that time, at that day."

A Nixon aide had a different take. Stephen Hess, who was at Nixon's Fifth Avenue apartment that afternoon to speak with Nixon about a possible book project, recalled that Nixon seemed highly shaken about what had happened. "He told me how he had heard it, and I did feel there was a degree of 'there but for the grace of God go I' there," said Hess.[49] Nixon then showed Hess the *Dallas Morning News* articles covering his press conference and asking the city to give the Kennedys a warm reception. "He tried to make the point that he had tried to prevent it," Hess recalled.[50] "It was his way of saying 'Look, I didn't fuel this thing.'"

Of course, Nixon only focused on the few sentences he had uttered encouraging Dallas to treat the Kennedys warmly without focusing on all of the stuff he had said leading up to it, including Kennedy's lack of accomplishments, being weak on Cuba, possibly dumping Johnson, and whatnot. Others did not forget about his comments, and Pepsi received letters from outraged customers vowing never to drink their products again. While it's unclear how many letters they actually received, Pepsi's public relations officials saw fit to write up a form letter that they used to respond to the outraged writers:

> Mr. Nixon's statements regarding Pepsi-Cola Company were made in closed business meetings. They had nothing to do with the American political scene. It was this part of the trip—his meetings with bottlers and other executives—that was underwritten by Pepsi-Cola. His business advice is already being widely followed by the company.
>
> It was inevitable that a national figure of Mr. Nixon's stature would attract members of the press. It was equally inevitable that the press discussions would center around political questions, especially in light of Mr. Kennedy's impending arrival the next day.
>
> Mr. Nixon was interviewed as a former Vice President of the United States and a key member of the Republican Party. He was not representing Pepsi-Cola Company, but giving his views as a knowledgeable American citizen. His views, as you know, have been widely sought after in the press, the radio and on television. His comments as an American are widely respected around the world.
>
> His ideas and thoughts about the upcoming Presidential campaigns were, in the American tradition, objective statements. He was exercising the same right of freedom of expression that you or I use when we discuss politics, and when we go into the voting booth on Election Day.
>
> Mr. Nixon's statements were sought after as a politician, not as a lawyer representing this company or that. And, incidentally, his firm represents some

> of the finest and most respected business organizations in the country, in addition to Pepsi-Cola Company. The political statements that he made were based upon the best possible news and information being circulated on the political scene at that time.
>
> We, naturally hope that you will reconsider your decision about not purchasing Pepsi-Cola in the future. We also hope that you will consider the aforementioned facts concerning the Dallas, Texas interview.[51]

Later that evening, Nixon composed a note to Jackie Kennedy, expressing his condolences and offering his thoughts and prayers. "While the hand of fate made Jack and me political opponents I always cherished the fact that we were personal friends from the time we came to the Congress together in 1947," he wrote. When she responded a few weeks later, she also made reference to the intertwined destinies of her late husband and the man he clashed with for the presidency.

> You two young men, colleagues in Congress, adversaries in 1960—and now look what has happened. Whoever thought such a hideous thing could happen in this country? I know how you must feel, so long on the path, so closely missing the greatest prize. And now for you, all the questions come up again, and you must commit all you and your family's hopes and efforts again. Just one thing I would say to you: If it does not work out as you have hoped for so long, please be consoled by what you already have, your life and your family.[52]

ASIAN AFFAIRS

The assassination of Kennedy prompted an outpouring of grief throughout the United States, as well as around the world. The last thing people wanted was to think about partisan politics, and Nixon understood the new reality he was facing. In fact, with the 1964 presidential primaries looming, both parties had agreed to a thirty-day moratorium on politics and campaigning.[53]

By the time spring rolled around, however, it was back to business. Starting in March, Nixon undertook a three-week tour of Asia that was designed to promote Pepsi's interests throughout the region. As would become custom during his time at the firm, his trip abroad would also include a political element, as Nixon would meet with dignitaries and diplomats while weighing in on foreign policy matters.[54] For instance, during the first real stop on the tour, a seven-hour stay in Beirut, Nixon gave a press conference, took a tour of the local Pepsi plant while phalanxed by television and newspaper reporters, attended a reception at the home of a Pepsi bottler that was attended by various government officials and dignitaries (and also covered by local media), and filmed a video with the Pepsi bottler to be played on television. He also found time to call on Lebanon president Fouad Chehab.[55]

Once Nixon finished up his activities in a particular city, he immediately jumped back on the plane and flew to his next destination, where he would do many of the same things he had done in Beirut on behalf of Pepsi. Nixon would be briefed before each stop on his tour, and would adjust his remarks or itinerary based on which city he was going to and what Pepsi was hoping to accomplish there.[56] In Japan, for instance, Nixon met with Prime Minister Hayato Ikeda in Tokyo before heading to Hiroshima to dedicate a $1 million Pepsi bottling plant there.[57] During his stay in Karachi, he posed for a lot of pictures, including a promotional shot with local bottlers standing next to a giant replica of a Pepsi bottle.[58] On the other hand, Nixon got the opposite reception in Bangkok, as Pepsi bottlers there kept his visit low profile as they were concerned that business would suffer if it looked like the company was trying to exploit the former vice president's visit for commercial purposes.[59]

Meanwhile, Pepsi made sure to hold a reception at each airport Nixon arrived at or departed from so that government and business officials could speak with Nixon, as well as welcome him to their country or see him off to his next destination. Of course, Pepsi was served at each of these receptions.[60] Nixon noted in his papers that the only time there was not an airport reception or press conference for him was in Saigon, which he attributed to the ongoing war in Vietnam.[61]

There was also no reception in Taipei's airport, but that was because Pepsi didn't have any operations in Taiwan—something Nixon was there to help rectify. At that point, Taiwan (known formally as the "Republic of China") was still recognized by most of the Western world as the legitimate government of China despite having been driven off the mainland by Mao Tse-tung and the Communists in 1949. Relations between the United States and Taiwan's ruling Kuomintang (KMT) Party had long been complicated and marked by mutual suspicion and distrust. However, the United States had demonstrated a strong commitment to protecting Taiwan, starting in 1950, when President Truman sent the US Navy's 7th Fleet into the Taiwan Strait to prevent an invasion from Mao's People's Republic of China. In the ensuing decade, the United States formalized its obligation to defend Taiwan from a PRC attack with the Sino-American Mutual Defense Treaty in 1955.

Self-defense, however, wasn't enough for Generalissimo Chiang Kai-shek. Still smarting over losing the civil war and control of Mainland China to Mao, Chiang dreamed of retaking his former homeland, and even had secret plans drawn up for an ambitious (and some would say quixotic) invasion. Chiang knew he would need international support for such plans—especially from the United States. As such, it made sense for him to roll out the welcome mat for Nixon—a potential future president or secretary of state. It helped that the two had a warm relationship that dated back to Nixon's tenure as vice president. Nixon had gone to Taiwan during his initial foreign tour in 1953 and had hit it off with both Chiang and his wife. Indeed,

Madame Chiang had showered the Nixons with gifts and art, some of which were on display in Nixon's Fifth Avenue apartment.

Chiang also considered Nixon to be a true ally to his cause. Nixon had long proven his anti-Communist bona fides, as well as his commitment to the ROC. After all, Nixon had launched his political career by going after Alger Hiss, and he had demonstrated his fealty with the China Lobby in the United States by pointing the finger at Dean Acheson, Truman's secretary of state, for "losing China."[62] If anyone could be persuaded to support an invasion of the PRC, it would surely be Nixon—the ultimate Cold Warrior.

As a result, Chiang and his subordinates were in an accommodating mood when Nixon and Don Kendall arrived in Taipei. Pepsi had identified Taiwan as one of its best potential markets in Asia, and the company was determined to get access to its market. "The weather is unbearably hot, the local cola products are horrible, and the per capita income in Taiwan is rising at the highest rate in Asia—10 percent last year," Nixon observed.[63] Nixon and Kendall put forth a full-court press, requesting multiple times that the KMT grant Pepsi a franchise in Taiwan. Nixon noted in a memorandum that he brought up the Pepsi franchise during a luncheon with Vice President Chen Cheng, during a private conference with Premier Yen Chia-kan, and at dinner with Chiang and Madame Chiang.[64] Chiang ultimately agreed and opened up Taiwan to Pepsi shortly after Nixon's visit.

That didn't mean that Pepsi's trials and tribulations in Taiwan were over. In a 1965 memo to Kendall, Nixon pointed out that there were still a number of obstacles to overcome before Pepsi could start operating in Taiwan. For instance, Pepsi had to secure an import license for syrup and other necessary ingredients. Nixon, however, wasn't concerned about getting the license, noting that the procedure was fairly routine. The big problem, as Nixon saw it, related to Pepsi's intellectual property—particularly its trademarks. There was no problem trademarking the word *Pepsi*. However, Taiwan's Central Bureau of Standards rejected *Pepsi-Cola* after finding that the word *cola* infringed on Coca-Cola's trademark.

Pepsi had appealed the Bureau's decision to Taiwan's Executive Yuan (the executive branch of the ROC), but Nixon counseled Kendall not to press for a decision immediately, citing the possibility that the government would simply defer to the Bureau's findings. Pepsi's Taiwan attorney, Joseph Twanmoh, advised Nixon that the premier tended to accept the decision of lower courts unless he received guidance from a higher authority. Nixon advised that they wait until he had a chance to provide such guidance to high-ranking government officials, namely Premier Yen and Chang Chun, secretary general to the president, Chiang's "closest and most influential adviser."[65] Nixon even went as far as to say that, even though Pepsi had secured an agreement with Coca-Cola permitting Pepsi to use *cola*, it would not be persuasive to ROC authorities. "The Taiwanese are very sensitive on the point that a private agreement cannot change the law of the Republic of Taiwan," said Nixon in his memo to Kendall.[66] "What will be more effective is reference to the fact that the term 'cola' is widely used in the United States by a number of so-called cola drinks and that the term is no longer considered to be a trademark which is special property of Coca-Cola alone."

Their efforts finally paid off in June 1967, when the Executive Yuan ruled in favor of Pepsi. "After a two-year trying struggle, the battle is, at last, won," Twanmoh wrote to Kendall.[67] "And much of it is due to Mr. Richard Nixon's effort and support."

"TOKYO OFFICE."

In advance of his visit to Japan, Nixon hit upon an idea that could have transformed the legal industry and turned Nixon Mudge from a rising Wall Street force into an international powerhouse.

With Nixon Mudge lawyers frequently traveling to Asia to do work for Japanese companies like Mitsui, as well as American companies with significant Asian business like Pepsi, it made sense to have a firm office in Tokyo. That way, Nixon Mudge lawyers could better serve their Asian-centric clients and be available, locally, to give immediate advice rather than have their clients wait to hear from the firm's lawyers in New York, D.C., or Paris.

In November 1963, Nixon received a letter from Henry Kearns, owner of consulting firm Kearns International, with the subject heading of "Tokyo Office."[68] Kearns noted that he had been in conversation with Nixon about the possibility of opening a Nixon Mudge office in Toyko and was reporting back with his findings. According to Kearns, there were only a handful of American attorneys practicing in Japan and no major Western firms. The reason for this was a Japanese law passed in 1955 that made it more difficult for foreign lawyers to get licensed in Japan, and the only American attorneys that were permitted to practice law in the country had been grandfathered in under the old law.

If Americans wanted to practice in Japan without passing the country's bar exam and undergoing the admission process, which Kearns called "cumbersome," then they would have to enter into a joint venture with a Japanese firm.[69] In this structure, American lawyers could work in Japan, but if a case went to court, then they would not be able to appear on behalf of their clients. Instead, it would be up to the Japanese firm to try the case. Or, Kearns pointed out, a US law firm could open an office in Japan and then hire a bunch of Japanese-trained and -admitted lawyers. However, a joint venture would have a number of advantages over opening a Nixon Mudge office in Toyko and hiring a bunch of local attorneys. Partnering with an established Japanese firm would allow Nixon Mudge to go to work immediately while giving it time to learn about Japan, its market, and its legal industry. A joint venture would also give Nixon Mudge some security and protection from being labeled as a foreign invader, allowing them to serve their clients without worrying about the consequences of jumping into a new, unfamiliar environment and competing with well-known local firms.

Kearns noted that there was a strong need for American lawyers to practice in Japan—especially for a firm with Nixon Mudge's credentials. "In the experience of Mitsui, they have difficulties in the fields of convertibility, U.S. patent law, U.S. security measures and American defenses," Kearns said.[70] He also observed that Japanese firms "are not well-versed in current U.S. political and legal matters."

Nixon's papers do not include copies of his responses to Kearns's letters—if there were any. Nevertheless, Kearns frequently references conversations that he says the two had and it appears, at least from Kearns's telling, that Nixon was closely involved with the discussions for the proposed Tokyo office. "Attached is report from . . . Robert Story, who recently retired as Executive of the American Chamber of Commerce in Japan," Kearns wrote in December 1963.[71] "His judgment verifies our opinion that there is a great need and opportunity for a facility such as you can offer." Kearns also put in a considerable amount of legwork, speaking with leading Japanese businessmen and political figures, including several officials at Mitsui and a former Japanese ambassador to the United States to see if there was a demand for such a joint venture. "It is evident that, at the present time, a major company, such as Mitsui & Co., must engage the services of several attorneys in Japan, in the United States, and in Europe," Kearns wrote.[72] "There is not, at present, any legal facility that has substantial knowledge of the legal aspects of business in all three areas. The result is duplication of cost, great delay in formalizing arrangements, and in many cases, extremely costly errors."

Kearns even went so far as to speak with a number of Japanese lawyers and firms to see if they might be interested in a joint venture with Nixon Mudge, and told Nixon that he would send along a list of two or more firms to consider joining with. One response came from Kyozo Yuasa, head of Japanese patent firm Yuasa, Sakamoto, Kawai and Ikenaga. Yuasa had written to Kearns in February 1964 offering to meet with Nixon when the latter arrived in Tokyo. Yuasa admitted he didn't know much about Nixon Mudge, but went so far as to attach a list of his clients and write a summary of his firm's makeup to Kearns.

It's not clear whether that meeting ever took place. Nixon had forwarded his correspondence with Kearns to his partners, and one, John Frey, studied the proposal on behalf of the rest of the partnership. In Kearns's November 26, 1963, letter to Nixon where the former first talked about whether American lawyers could practice in Japan, Nixon had handwritten a question in the margins, wondering whether nonadmitted US attorneys in Japan could advise on US or other law. Frey agreed that this was the critical point as far as Nixon Mudge was concerned, and came to the conclusion that the answer was "no." "If non-admitted foreigners cannot function at all in Japan in the area of giving advice, the possibilities are severely limited," Frey wrote in a memo to Nixon dated March 12, 1964.[73] Frey added that it might be "impossible" to set up a branch office to advise on non-Japanese law unless the firm, somehow, was able to hire one of the American lawyers already practicing in Japan.

Frey's finding seemed to throw cold water on the proposal. Western firms wouldn't arrive in the Land of the Rising Sun until the 1970s, when Baker & McKenzie and Clifford Chance entered into joint ventures with Japanese firms. In 1976, Milbank Tweed became the first American firm allowed into Japan on its own.[74] The idea of a Mudge office in Japan would not become a reality until 1991.

"THIS HAS TO BE A FIGHT TO THE FINISH."

The Asian tour also served to further Nixon's political ambitions. In Beirut, he got the usual question about whether or not he would run for president. This time, rather than deflect the issue or categorically deny his interest in another White House run (the way he had when he first started at Nixon Mudge), Nixon sounded receptive, telling the reporters present that he would accept the nomination "if the party leaders ask me to run."[75] Nixon also spoke about Communist China, criticizing US senator J. William Fulbright (D-Ark.) for saying that the United States should "review" its policy toward the PRC in light of its recent split with the Soviet Union. "It would be disastrous to the cause of freedom for the U.S. to recognize Red China or accept its admission into the United Nations," Nixon stated during his visit to Hong Kong in what was, surely, music to Chiang Kai-shek's ears.[76]

"Everywhere I went, I heard about America's declining prestige, and I heard expressions of dismay that the world's strongest nation was showing so little positive leadership," Nixon said.[77] "Perhaps most disturbing of all, I saw for myself how dangerously different the reality of the situation in Vietnam was from the version of it being presented to the American people at home."

According to Nixon, the situation in Vietnam was the main area of concern for anti-Communist leaders in the region. Pakistan's president, Ayub Khan, warned Nixon that the suspected US involvement in the assassination of Diệm would have grave consequences, as many of the leaders in the region now distrusted the Americans and were leaning toward remaining neutral when it came to Vietnam. On the other hand, Thailand prime minister Thanom Kittikachorn brought up the domino theory and told Nixon that the

United States had to press on with the war against the Vietcong for fear of triggering Communist uprisings throughout Southeast Asia. [78] Chiang Kai-shek, Nixon recalled, was more blunt, telling him that "only bullets will really defeat [the North Vietnamese]." [79]

In his memorandum recapping his Asian trip for Pepsi, his entry for Saigon is conspicuously short. Other than noting the lack of the standard Pepsi-sponsored reception at the airport, the only other thing he put in his memo was that he attended a two-hour luncheon sponsored by a Pepsi bottler where he spoke about government regulation and its effect on Pepsi's pricing. [80] His memoirs provide more information about his 1964 trip to Vietnam. He noted many of the same themes he experienced in other parts of the region, including a sense from South Vietnamese leaders that the Kennedy/Johnson Administration didn't fully support them and wasn't doing everything to win the war. Nixon even recounted that a South Vietnamese military leader told him, outright, that the Vietcong were uncompromising enemies that could not be negotiated with. "This has to be a fight to the finish," he told Nixon. [81]

Nixon was also dismayed when he met with Ambassador Henry Cabot Lodge. Nixon had presented his former ticket mate with his findings, and also relayed the concerns of the various military and political leaders in South Vietnam and Southeast Asia that he had met with on his tour, only to be summarily dismissed by the ambassador. Instead, Nixon was shocked as Lodge diligently defended the Kennedy/Johnson approach of limited military engagement while focusing on economic outreach. "I wondered whether he felt it was his duty to defend the administration's policy regardless of his own feelings, or whether he had actually been converted by the academic theorists around Johnson who thought that the problem of communism in Southeast Asia could be solved by economic development," Nixon said. [82] Of course, their conversation may have been influenced by the fact that Lodge had been the surprise winner of the New Hampshire primary in March. Regardless of how he may have felt about his superiors in the White House, Lodge would have had to own his actions if he wanted to mount a credible run for the presidency—something that Lodge later admitted to Nixon he would have been willing to do had he won the Oregon primary the following month. [83]

If the trip did anything, it gave Nixon the ammunition he needed to go public with his views. "There's no substitute for victory in South Vietnam," Nixon said in Saigon, paraphrasing General Douglas MacArthur's famous statement about the Korean War.[84] In fact, Nixon called for an immediate escalation of American activities in Vietnam, including an expansion of the war into North Vietnam. According to Ambrose, this was a fairly extreme view for 1964, and that, while Nixon had always been in favor of escalating the war effort, he had not made his views public until then. Additionally, it allowed Nixon to reclaim one of his favorite attack lines—that the Democrats were soft on communism. During the 1960 campaign, Kennedy had co-opted the issue by attacking Nixon and Eisenhower for not doing enough about communism, forcing Nixon into uncharacteristically playing defense. Instead, Nixon's public pivot on Vietnam now left him to the right of even Barry Goldwater (a man who would become famous, or infamous, for his strident conservatism in 1964).[85]

Ultimately, Pepsi was more than willing to put up with the politicking because of the benefits it reaped by having Richard Nixon as its attorney. According to Evans, who worked on many of Pepsi's matters at Nixon Mudge, Pepsi-Cola Company nearly tripled in size during Nixon's tenure. This growth was fueled, in no small part, by the formation of PepsiCo in 1965, after Pepsi-Cola decided to get into the snack business by purchasing Frito-Lay. Along with some other acquisitions, as well as internal growth, Evans states that corporate sales increased from $184 million in 1964 to $456 million by the end of 1965.[86] "By and large, the legal work on these acquisitions was done by [Nixon Mudge]," Evans stated.[87] "In 1966, sales passed the half-billion dollar mark and Nixon Mudge handled a large Eurodollar financing—one of the first—for PepsiCo."

Like many of his other satisfied clients, Kendall became a valuable ally for Nixon once he finally decided to reenter the political arena as a contestant rather than a spectator. That day, once a distant possibility, was approaching quicker than anyone might have imagined. Nixon may have proven himself to be a good corporate lawyer and rainmaker for his firm. However, he longed to get back into the political game and was desperate to make one more run for the White House. The year 1964 would represent one of his rare missteps as he gave into his all-consuming desire to be president and made an ill-fated, half-hearted move for the doomed GOP nomination.

NOTES

1. "McKeesport: The First Great Debate," *Pittsburgh Post Gazette*, October 21, 1976.
2. "McKeesport: The First Great Debate."
3. Chris Matthews, *Kennedy & Nixon: The Rivalry That Shaped Postwar America* (New York: Simon & Schuster, 1996).
4. Matthews, *Kennedy & Nixon.*
5. Matthews, *Kennedy & Nixon.*
6. Richard Nixon, *RN: The Memoirs of Richard Nixon* (New York: Simon and Schuster, 2013).
7. Sally Denton, *The Pink Lady: The Many Lives of Helen Gahagan Douglas* (New York: Bloomsbury Press, 2009), 166.
8. Greg Mitchell, "When JFK Backed Nixon in His Notorious Race vs. Helen Gahagan Douglas," *The Nation*, November 19, 2013, accessed March 26, 2017, https://www.thenation.com/article/when-jfk-backed-nixon-his-notorious-race-vs-helen-gahagan-douglas/.
9. Mitchell, "When JFK Backed Nixon."
10. Matthews, *Kennedy & Nixon*, 17–18.

11. Matthews, *Kennedy & Nixon*.
12. Matthews, *Kennedy & Nixon*.
13. Matthews, *Kennedy & Nixon*, 128, 133.
14. "Transcript: JFK's Speech on His Religion," NPR, December 5, 2007, accessed March 26, 2017, http://www.npr.org/templates/story/story.php?storyId=16920600.
15. Robert Caro, *The Years of Lyndon Johnson: The Passage of Power* (New York: Alfred A. Knopf, 2012), 33.
16. Caro, *The Years of Lyndon Johnson*.
17. Matthews, *Kennedy & Nixon*, 126.
18. Matthews, *Kennedy & Nixon*, 127.
19. Ira Stoll, *JFK: Conservative* (Boston: Houghton Mifflin Harcourt, 2013), 36–37.
20. "October 7, 1960 Debate Transcript," Commission on Presidential Debates, accessed March 26, 2017, http://www.debates.org/index.php?page=october-7-1960-debate-transcript.
21. Nixon, *RN*.
22. Matthews, *Kennedy & Nixon*, 128.
23. John A. Farrell, *Richard Nixon: A Life* (New York: Doubleday, 2017), 281–82.
24. David Greenberg, "It's a Myth That Nixon Acquiesced in 1960," *Los Angeles Times*, November 10, 2000, accessed June 11, 2017, http://articles.latimes.com/2000/nov/10/local/me-49741.
25. Jonathan Aitken, *Nixon: A Life* (Washington, DC: Regnery History, 1993), 343.
26. Conrad Black, *Richard M. Nixon: A Life in Full* (New York: PublicAffairs, 2007), 423.
27. *Salem (MA) Register*, February 18, 1861.
28. Matthews, *Kennedy & Nixon*, 186.
29. Matthews, *Kennedy & Nixon*, 188.
30. Farrell, *Richard Nixon: A Life*, 298–99.
31. Farrell, *Richard Nixon: A Life*, 299.
32. Nixon, *RN*.
33. Matthews, *Kennedy & Nixon*, 199.
34. Nixon, *RN*.
35. David Coleman, "The Fourteenth Day: JFK and the Aftermath of the Cuban Missile Crisis," JFK14thDay.com, accessed January 9, 2016, http://jfk14thday.com/jfk-pat-brown-jerry-brown/.
36. Alan Peppard, "Kennedy Rival Nixon Left Dallas as JFK Arrived in November 1963," *Dallas Morning News*, November 2, 2013, accessed March 26, 2017, http://www.dallasnews.com/news/jfk50/explore/20131102-kennedy-rival-richard-nixon-left-dallas-as-jfk-arrived-in-november-1963.ece.
37. Peppard, "Kennedy Rival Nixon Left Dallas.
38. Peter Pringle, "'We're Heading into Nut Country': President Kennedy said This to an Aide as He Began his Fatal Visit to Texas Thirty Years Ago," *The Independent*, November 20, 1993, accessed March 26, 2017, http://www.independent.co.uk/life-style/were-heading-into-nut-country-president-kennedy-said-this-to-an-aide-as-he-began-his-fatal-visit-to-1505387.html.
39. Pringle, "'We're Heading into Nut Country.'"
40. Stephen Ambrose, *Nixon: Vol. 2: The Triumphs of a Politician 1962–1972* (New York: Simon and Schuster, 1989), 31. And "Welcome Mr. Kennedy to Dallas," Latin American Studies, accessed March 26, 2017, http://www.latinamericanstudies.org/mrkennedy.htm.
41. Pringle, "'We're Heading into Nut Country.'"
42. Jules Witcover, *The Resurrection of Richard Nixon* (New York: G. P. Putnam's Sons, 1970), 59.
43. Witcover, *The Resurrection of Richard Nixon*.
44. HelmerReenberg, "November 21, 1963—Richard M. Nixon in Dallas, Texas," YouTube video, 2:03, posted December 19, 2012, https://www.youtube.com/watch?v=UkeCQWk9ID8.
45. "Nixon, in Texas, Asks for Polite Kennedy Reception," *Dallas Morning News*, November 22, 1963.
46. Witcover, *The Resurrection of Richard Nixon*, 60.

47. "Wife Kept Lee Harvey Oswald from Shooting Richard Nixon," *Lodi News-Sentinel*, September 19, 1977.
48. Nixon, *RN*.
49. Witcover, *The Resurrection of Richard Nixon*, 61. Ambrose, *Nixon: Volume 2*, 32.
50. Witcover, *The Resurrection of Richard Nixon*; Ambrose, *Nixon: Volume 2*.
51. Richard Nixon, Copy of Letters from Robert Windt to Leo Juergens, December 12, 1963, Pre-Presidential Papers, Richard Nixon Presidential Library and Museum.
52. Nixon, *RN*.
53. "Goldwater Set to Reveal Plans at Home Friday," *The Bulletin*, December 31, 1963.
54. Ambrose, *Nixon: Volume 2*, 43.
55. Witcover, *The Resurrection of Richard Nixon*, 76.
56. Richard Nixon, "Memorandum Covering Pepsi-Cola Activities on Richard Nixon's Far Eastern Trip, March 22, 1964 to April 15, 1964," Pre-Presidential Papers, Richard Nixon Presidential Library and Museum.
57. Nixon, "Memorandum Covering Pepsi-Cola Activities."
58. Nixon, "Memorandum Covering Pepsi-Cola Activities."
59. Nixon, "Memorandum Covering Pepsi-Cola Activities."
60. Nixon, "Memorandum Covering Pepsi-Cola Activities."
61. Nixon, "Memorandum Covering Pepsi-Cola Activities."
62. Laura Tyson Li, *Madame Chiang Kai-Shek: China's Eternal First Lady* (New York: Grove Press, 2006), 357.
63. Richard Nixon, Memo from Nixon to Donald Kendall, September 2, 1965, Thomas Evans Collection.
64. Nixon, "Memorandum Covering Pepsi-Cola Activities."
65. Richard Nixon, Memo from Nixon to Donald Kendall, September 1, 1965, Thomas Evans Collection.
66. Nixon, Memo from Nixon to Donald Kendall.
67. Richard Nixon, Copy of Letter from Joseph Twanmoh to Harold Rome, July 3, 1967, Pre-Presidential Papers, Richard Nixon Presidential Library and Museum.
68. Richard Nixon, Henry Kearns letter to Richard Nixon, November 26, 1963, Pre-Presidential Papers, Richard Nixon Presidential Library and Museum.
69. Nixon, Henry Kearns letter to Richard Nixon, November 26, 1963.
70. Nixon, Henry Kearns letter to Richard Nixon, November 26, 1963.
71. Richard Nixon, Henry Kearns letter to Richard Nixon, December 5, 1963, Pre-Presidential Papers, Richard Nixon Presidential Library and Museum.
72. Nixon, Henry Kearns letter to Richard Nixon, December 5, 1963.
73. Richard Nixon, John Frey Memo to Nixon, March 12, 1964, Pre-Presidential Papers, Richard Nixon Presidential Library and Museum.
74. John O. Haley, "The New Regulatory Regime for Foreign Lawyers in Japan: An Escape from Freedom," *UCLA Pacific Basin Law Journal* 1–2 (1986), https://escholarship.org/uc/item/1xg8k8r8#page-8.
75. Ambrose, *Nixon: Volume 2*, 43.
76. Ambrose, *Nixon: Volume 2*, 44.
77. Nixon, *RN*.
78. Nixon, *RN*.
79. Nixon, *RN*.
80. Nixon, "Memorandum Covering Pepsi-Cola Activities on Richard Nixon's Far Eastern Trip, March 22, 1964 to April 15, 1964."
81. Nixon, *RN*.
82. Nixon, *RN*.
83. Nixon, *RN*.
84. Ambrose, *Nixon: Volume 2*, 43.
85. Ambrose, *Nixon: Volume 2*.
86. Thomas Evans, "The Education of Richard Nixon: The Wilderness Years on Wall Street." Unpublished manuscript, 98.
87. Evans, "The Education of Richard Nixon."

Chapter Six

"Mentally Dead in Two Years and Physically Dead in Four."

When Republicans gathered at the Cow Palace near San Francisco for the 1964 national convention, they experienced an unfamiliar feeling. Convention attendees would vote for the party's presidential and vice presidential nominees, and for the first time in twelve years, Richard Nixon's name would not be on either ballot.

And Nixon was fine with that—or so it seemed.

He had long known that 1964 wouldn't be his year. Prior to Dallas, the expectation had been that Kennedy would run for reelection, and the last thing Nixon wanted was to face him again. The two may have been on somewhat equal footing in 1960, but Kennedy now had the power of incumbency behind him. It's rare in American history for sitting presidents to lose their reelection bids, so Nixon was already starting from behind the eight ball. Throw in Kennedy's popularity, as well as Nixon's gubernatorial loss and subsequent public meltdown, and Nixon would have been hard-pressed to improve on his 1960 performance—let alone overtake a well-liked president.

Plus, Nixon had made a commitment to his law firm, and 1964 would represent the first full year of the firm in its "Nixon Mudge" incarnation. Throughout 1963, he had gone out of his way to deny his interest in the race, going so far as to point out his lack of campaign staff as well as his decision to give up his California base. As he had said to the press right after announcing his move to New York: " Anyone who thinks I could be a candidate for anything in any year is just off his rocker."

There was just one thing: Nixon still wanted to be president. Very badly. And as 1964 got underway, he began to indulge in his White House fantasy once again, proving that, when it came to his ultimate dream, his heart could be every bit as powerful as his head.

STEALTH CAMPAIGN

To be fair, Nixon had a compelling reason for reconsidering his plans for 1964. Dallas had changed everything, and taking on the untested Lyndon Johnson was a much more favorable prospect for a well-known Republican like Nixon. In the first Gallup poll after Kennedy's assassination, Nixon led the Republican field by two points over Barry Goldwater (29 percent to 27 percent) and had more than double the support of Nelson Rockefeller, the only declared candidate at the time (13 percent).[1]

Nevertheless, Johnson also had some strong advantages that Nixon was cognizant of. For one thing, the new president had emerged as a unifying figure for a country still in shock over his predecessor's death. He had, wisely, chosen to continue with Kennedy's presidency, keeping in place JFK's cabinet, initiatives, and policies, and thereby portraying himself as caretaker rather than usurper. He had also displayed the kind of uplifting and soaring rhetoric that his former boss had been known for, providing comfort and projecting stability for a still grieving populace. In his first address to Congress after becoming president, Johnson even eulogized Kennedy as the "greatest leader of our time" while using his new bully pulpit to commit to enacting Kennedy's agenda. Johnson named a long-stalled tax bill, as well as an even longer-stalled civil rights bill, as his two major priorities and promised that he would use his considerable mastery of the legislative process to get them both passed. "I urge you again, as I did in 1957 and again in 1960, to enact a civil rights law so that we can move forward to eliminate from this Nation every trace of discrimination and oppression that is based upon race or color," Johnson said.[2] "There could be no greater source of strength to this Nation both at home and abroad."

Johnson then put his money where his mouth had been. He closed a deal with influential Virginia senator Harry Byrd to get the tax bill through the Senate. Johnson knew that a southern-led filibuster was looming over civil rights, so he wanted to get the tax bill passed before debate started over what became the 1964 Civil Rights Act. In those days, filibusters actually took place on the floor of the Senate, and no other business would be conducted while it was going on. With the election looming, there would be overwhelming pressure to compromise on, or even shelve, the Civil Rights Act in order to get the tax cut passed.

It was no small feat, either. Byrd was one of the most hardcore fiscal conservatives in Washington, and he absolutely abhorred debt of any kind. Johnson had to get the federal budget below $100 billion before Byrd would even think about releasing the bill from the Senate Finance Committee he ruled with an iron fist. Johnson and his staff burned the midnight oil for weeks until they finally got the budget to $97.9 billion—complete with the certification that Byrd had demanded that there had been no accounting tricks or gimmicks used to cook the books. The tax bill ultimately passed the Senate on February 7, 1964—three days before the Civil Rights Act was passed by the House and sent to the Senate.[3]

Johnson's leadership in passing the Civil Rights Act stunned many of his former colleagues in the Senate—especially his fellow southerners. While he had, previously, shepherded a civil rights bill through the Senate in 1957, the bill had been watered down and weakened to the point where it had largely been symbolic. Robert Caro argued that the toothless bill only got through the Senate because powerful Southern Democrats, particularly Johnson's longtime mentor and patron Richard Russell of Georgia, wanted to bolster Johnson's presidential prospects in 1960.[4] The Civil Rights Act of 1964, however, had plenty of teeth. The proposed bill would outlaw discrimination in hotels, restaurants, stores, and other places open to the public and engaged in interstate commerce, desegregate public schools and facilities, and empower the attorney general to file lawsuits to enforce the act, among other things. Ultimately, the bill passed after a fifty-seven-day filibuster that was the longest in Senate history.

With his approval rating hovering around 75 percent for much of 1964, Johnson promised to be a difficult man to beat in the upcoming presidential election.[5] Indeed, he would have been a formidable foe even in the face of a unified GOP. Given that the Republicans were in the midst of a destructive civil war with the moderate-to-liberal wing of the party lining up behind Nelson Rockefeller and the conservatives backing Goldwater, Johnson's reelection was virtually assured. Whichever of those two declared candidates ended up winning the nomination was bound to antagonize a large chunk of the Republican Party.

Republicans sensed that an electoral disaster was in the offing. As a result, they ratcheted up the pressure on the one man they believed could unify the party and take on a popular, albeit untested, incumbent like Johnson. " At the present time the Goldwater forces have a significant advantage in Maryland because they have been working steadily for over a year," Baltimore County, Maryland, executive Spiro Agnew wrote Nixon in January 1964, noting the Goldwater/Rockefeller split among elected officials in his own county.[6] "I have taken the position that neither of these candidates represents the best interest of the Republican Party, and have found that many other Republicans favor a more moderate candidate but do not know which way to turn since one is not in the field." Agnew then closed by encouraging his future running mate to take the plunge, writing: "I believe you would be a candidate who could avoid the split in our Party and I urge you to make known, at the earliest moment, your intentions."

Other prominent Republican officials and private citizens encouraged Nixon to run again. Edwin Beaman, a prominent Indiana politician who had backed Nixon in 1960, sent a handwritten note in March pledging his allegiance to "Nixon for 1964" while citing Indiana polls putting his once and future standard-bearer in a strong second place behind Goldwater.[7] TV producer Cecil Barker sent Nixon a note on CBS Television Network stationary telling him that he was "in the starting blocks" and that all Nixon had to do was yell "go!"[8] Ohio lieutenant governor John W. Brown wrote Nixon in May, tipping him off that the entire state's delegation would be staying in the Drake Hotel in San Francisco during the GOP National Convention and encouraging Nixon to let him know if he needed help with anything before or after the Convention. "As you may recall, we operate under the 'favorite son' policy in Ohio," Brown wrote, essentially telling Nixon that the Ohio delegation would be up for grabs if the Convention deadlocked after the first few rounds of balloting.[9] "In this instance, the Governor, Jim Rhodes, being first choice and yours truly being the second." Brown tipped his hand even further, enclosing an article about Nixon's recent trip to Cincinnati where he criticized civil rights "extremists." The article, which ran in the *Columbus Dispatch* on February 13, 1964, posited whether Nixon could overtake Goldwater's popularity in the state and if his words might appeal to some of the Arizona senator's voters.

Some of his clients encouraged him to throw his hat back into the ring. George MacKinnon, general counsel and vice president of Investors, sent regular messages to New York briefing Nixon on political intelligence in the state of Minnesota—where Investors was based. "The widespread, generally expressed, voluntary opinion out here is that you would be a preferable candidate to Goldwater or Rockefeller," MacKinnon told Nixon.[10] "It is ten times the strength it was before Dallas." MacKinnon, however, understood Nixon's need to remain a neutral noncandidate and encouraged him to use that to his advantage. Arguing that the real trick with primary elections was to win the news cycle rather than the actual contest, Nixon could generate a raft of positive stories by simply surpassing expectations in states where he wouldn't actively campaign. "If you are running as a reluctant candidate up there and are constantly predicting that you won't do well because you aren't going to campaign, and you aren't going to spend any money and that yours is purely a true grass roots effort, you would be sowing the seeds for some favorable comment however you ran," MacKinnon wrote to Nixon, which prompted the "reluctant" candidate to scribble "right" in the margins.[11]

Frank Rackley of Jessop Steel went so far as to offer suggestions for speech topics. In a September letter to Nixon, he suggested that, rather than spend a fortune on foreign aid and dollar diplomacy, the former vice president could promote subsidies for domestic businesses. Rackley argued that exporting their surpluses to countries around the world was a more effective means of promoting the American way of life. Plus, the move would allow Nixon to assume the mantle of the common man. "Dick Nixon is the only man in the United States today, who can qualify as a candidate for the Presidency, not born a millionaire," Rackley said.[12] "No other potential Presidential candidate can make that statement."

Not all of his friends were behind him. Texas oil tycoon H. L. Hunt, one of the wealthiest men in the country, wrote Nixon and tore into him for 1960 and 1962. In one letter, Hunt even included a laundry list of grievances, including Nixon's decision to run as a moderate, his fight with the John Birch Society, and even the color of his shirt during the first debate with Kennedy. Hunt fervently believed that Republicans had to win in 1964 in order to stem the growth of communism and curb the powers of the federal government, and he called on Nixon to do whatever he could to make sure Goldwater won—even if it meant serving as his vice president or secretary of state. "You owe everything to America, to the Republican Party and all of the members of the Party," Hunt wrote in one letter to Nixon,[13] "and the Republican Party cannot save the nation unless it regains power."

Wealthy oil and pharmaceutical magnate J. D. Stetson Coleman was similarly critical. Telling Nixon that he "failed the country by losing to Kennedy," Coleman told Nixon to fall in line behind Goldwater and offer to be his vice president. "It would really take a truly BIG MAN to do this—and I believe you are just that," Coleman wrote.[14] "Behind Barry you could MAKE a two party system in the South. Then, even if he can't beat Johnson—it would make you for '68 [original emphasis]."

Even strangers were offering their unsolicited advice. John Clements ran a marketing research firm in Dallas and, starting in 1963, sent near-weekly messages and poll results trying to convince Nixon to get into the race. Casting himself as a modern-day Cassandra, Clements introduced himself by telling Nixon that he had tried to give him advice and warn him of potential errors during the 1960 and 1962 campaigns, only to be ignored by Nixon's advisers. "I wired you prior to the California disaster and again you looked upon me as nobody," Clements wrote.[15] "Nobody, yes, but if you had listened, the somebody who was a nobody would now be a somebody."

With 1964 on the horizon, Clements hoped Nixon would, this time, take his advice and go for the nomination. Citing numerous polls and studies his firm had conducted showing Nixon in strong shape heading into 1964, Clements begged Nixon to jump in the race. Based on his correspondence with Nixon, Clements had plenty of selfish motivations. For instance, in one letter, he helpfully included a proposed flowchart for what a Nixon '64 campaign might look like. Clements placed himself and his firm one rung below Nixon and Maurice Carlson, a Texas Republican and friend to Clements who would serve as national chairman.[16] Evidently, Clements's zeal was such that he paid for many Nixon-related expenses out of his own pocket, and at one point, he even solicited Nixon for $2,000 to help him stay afloat. Nixon curtly responded with a letter telling Clements that, since he was not a candidate, he could not raise money to give to him.[17]

Despite that bump in the road, Clements continued to send Nixon letters and even met with him in Dallas during Nixon's fateful trip to the city in November 1963. "Each and every day mail brings brighter and brighter Nixon reports," Clements wrote in a February 1964 letter that was typical of the style he used when corresponding with Nixon.[18] "Bandwagon days are drawing near and we are sharpening our procedures and systems to razor-like edges. This blade will be the best of steel." Nixon, for his part, kept Clements on the line, saying that he was interested in getting Clements's take on long-term trends beyond 1964.

Mainly, Nixon relied on his old comrades within the Republican Party for advice. "The political pot is certainly boiling," Nixon wrote to Walter Robertson, former assistant secretary of state for Far Eastern Affairs, in January 1964.[19] "I think there is particularly a need for new direction in foreign policy." Nixon then invited Robertson to weigh in on the political situation in 1964, pointing out that "[s]ince I have no research staff I have to depend on upon good friends like yourself to keep me posted on developments around the country."

Nixon also reached out to Charles Kersten, a former US Representative from Wisconsin and a good friend of Nixon's from his House days. Like Nixon, Kersten fell back on his law degree after suffering an electoral setback. In Kersten's case, he returned to the law firm of Kersten & McKinnon, a firm he had previously started with his brother-in-law, Arlo McKinnon, in 1931.[20] The Wisconsin Republican sent Nixon a letter in early December 1963 encouraging him to run, prompting Nixon to respond with a request for intel. "I would be most interested in getting your evaluation of the relative strength of the Republican candidates both in Wisconsin and nationally, and also how you estimate Johnson's appeal as a campaigner as compared with Kennedy's," Nixon wrote.[21]

Nixon's ears perked up some more when Louis Wyman, a freshman US Representative from New Hampshire, wrote to him in January 1964. Wyman was, ostensibly, writing to Nixon about the debate over the ratification of what would become the Twenty-Fifth Amendment to the Constitution, which governs the inability of the president to discharge his or her duties. However, it was Wyman's final sentence that prompted a detailed response from Nixon that laid out his strategy heading into the 1964 nominating process. "Are you going to try anything in New Hampshire?" he asked Nixon, offhandedly.[22] That one sentence prompted Nixon to respond with an entire paragraph about how precarious his political situation was. Calling the upcoming New Hampshire primary "a can of worms," Nixon said he would not actively campaign or make any trips to the state, but that he couldn't help it if people were to write in his name. "As far as you are concerned, my primary interest is that you do nothing which would jeopardize your own reelection," Nixon wrote.[23]

Wyman responded by giving Nixon some inside information. The New Hampshire congressman told Nixon in January 1964 that "most of the good delegates [in New Hampshire] are gone."[24] Wyman also expressed dissatisfaction with both Rockefeller and Goldwater, bringing up the former's divorce and subsequent remarriage and the latter's controversial views. "The more I see developments the more inclined I am to the view that a friend named Nixon will eventually be the Republican nominee," Wyman wrote.[25] "However, just how this can develop unless some delegates enter the picture before July is difficult to make out."

He didn't just rely on friends from afar. Nixon showed just how seriously he was looking at 1964 by calling a secret meeting in January at the Waldorf Astoria in New York with fifteen of his friends, colleagues, and former advisers, including his campaign managers from 1960 and 1962, respectively, Bob Finch and H. R. Haldeman. Also at the meeting were former Eisenhower secretary of the interior Fred Seaton, Nixon aide Stephen Hess, former Nixon campaign aide John Whitaker, businessman Bernard "Bunny" Lasker, and others.[26] Conspicuous by their absence were members of the GOP Eastern Establishment, including Dewey, Herbert Brownell, and others. Members of Nixon's law firm were also absent from the meeting, but perhaps that was to be expected. After all, Nixon had only, officially, been the senior partner at Nixon Mudge since December 1963. Between bringing in business, getting admitted to the bar, and traveling on behalf of clients like Pepsi, Nixon would have had almost no time to establish a political, much less a personal, base at the firm.

The consensus from Nixon's brain trust was that the Republican Party was hopelessly split going into the 1964 presidential election, and that Goldwater and Rockefeller would battle each other to a standstill at the Convention. As such, the obvious play for Nixon was to stay on the sidelines and not get actively involved with the nomination process. Instead, he would preach party unity and compromise—thereby making himself available should the Convention need to find a consensus nominee. By staying publicly neutral, he would also have the advantage of not alienating either Goldwater's passionate supporters or Rockefeller's more moderate backers.[27] "He was positioning himself in case lightning did strike," Hess said later.[28] "At the same time, he was deliberately keeping the door open as a way of giving more credence and play in the press to what he did say." After all, Nixon had long learned that the press gave more weight and coverage to someone if they thought he was a presidential candidate. "He knew it always made the difference in whether you were on page one or the back pages," Hess said.

Nixon's brain trust turned out to be partially correct. The Republican Party that gathered in San Francisco in July 1964 for its quadrennial display of unity and determination was on the verge of a civil war that had been brewing for decades. It just turned out that, as the opening gavel dropped at the Cow Palace, the winners had already been determined.

BARRY

It may be hard for anyone who has seen how the Republican Party has developed since the 1980s to realize that, once upon a time, not only were there a lot of moderate-to-liberal Republicans but also that they held sway over national party affairs for the better part of three decades. After Franklin D. Roosevelt's 1932 electoral destruction of the conservative incumbent Herbert Hoover, the Republicans spent the next several electoral cycles nominating moderates as their standard-bearers. In 1936, Alfred Landon was widely known as a moderate conservative who had once supported Teddy Roosevelt's Progressive Party. Landon had even supported parts of the New Deal and personally admired and respected FDR.[29] The 1940 nominee Wendell Willkie was a former Democrat who was an internationalist during a time when most top Republicans were devout isolationists. Thomas Dewey, who got the nod in 1944 and 1948, had amassed a moderate-to-liberal record as governor of New York by creating and expanding social programs, as well as signing antidiscrimination bills into law.[30] Finally, Eisenhower, the only Republican to win the presidency from 1932 to 1964, was so moderate he could have run as a Democrat had he wanted to. It seemed as if the national Republican Party had accepted their fate as the permanent minority party, and what differences existed between them and their Democratic counterparts were a matter of degrees, with the GOP advocating restraint rather than repudiation.[31]

Nevertheless, conservatives were feeling hopeful going into 1964—more hopeful than they had been in a long time. Barry Goldwater, the outspoken, combative, and ardently conservative two-term senator from Arizona, wasn't interested in being like the Democrats. In announcing his candidacy, he had promised to give voters a "choice, not an echo."[32] He had already laid out much of his ideology, authoring his influential and best-selling 1960 book *The Conscience of a Conservative*. In his political manifesto, Goldwater railed against big government and the welfare state, arguing that the private sector was better equipped to run social programs than the federal government. He also called for the abolition of the graduated income tax in favor of a flat tax and the elimination of farm subsidies. On foreign affairs, he called for total victory in the Cold War and argued that America had to defeat communism rather than be content to simply contain it.[33] In the years since his book, Goldwater cemented his conservative credentials, especially in the area of civil rights. While he, personally, supported civil rights, he was also an ardent believer in states' rights and even voted against the 1964 Civil Rights Act because he saw it as an unconstitutional encroachment on state sovereignty.[34] His opposition to the act made him an attractive candidate to southern states, some of which had already started gravitating toward the Republican Party.

In a vacuum, those views made him no different than any number of conservative Republicans or Democrats. What distinguished Goldwater was his mouth, which often reacted before his mind did. His "shoot-from-the-hip" mentality made him seem more extreme and dangerous than he really was. An offhand comment about possibly using low-yield atomic weapons in Vietnam made him look like a madman itching to press the button.[35] Another offhand comment, this time about possibly selling the popular Tennessee Valley Authority, brought him more bad press.[36] His argument that Social Security should be voluntary helped cost him the New Hampshire primary, which boasted a large bloc of senior voters.[37] Oftentimes, he was his own worst enemy. In one memorable gaffe, he even admitted to the *Saturday Evening Post* in 1963: "You know, I haven't got a really first-class brain."[38] Goldwater, like Nixon, blamed the media for misrepresenting him, even going so far as to note that if he had believed the things the press had written about him during the 1964 campaign, then he wouldn't have voted for himself, either.[39]

Despite that, Goldwater was the only GOP candidate heading into the convention with any sort of momentum. In fact, the convention should have really been a coronation. Energized by a wave of grassroots support, Goldwater had finished a strong second in New Hampshire despite scaring off those elderly voters with his Social Security views. He then reeled off a string of victories in states including Illinois, California, Florida, and Texas. Coming into the convention, Goldwater actually had enough delegates to win on the first ballot. In practice, however, his nomination was far from secure. For one thing, only a slight majority of his pledged delegates were actually bound by state law to vote for him. Additionally, politicians at the time doubted that those bound delegates were really obligated to vote for Goldwater, noting that the Convention rules allowed delegates to vote for whomever they wanted to regardless of state law.[40] In other words, Goldwater could easily lose out to any number of rivals—especially if his opponents coalesced around the right candidate.

In 1964, Goldwater's biggest opponent within the party was Nixon's longtime rival, Nelson Rockefeller. When it came to pursuing the presidency, Rockefeller had dithered in the past (and would dither in the future). However, in 1964, he was all-in and was widely regarded as the front runner as primary season started. His wealth, name recognition, and record as governor made him a formidable candidate, and his moderate-to-liberal views made him a more palatable alternative to those who worried about Goldwater's ideology. Rockefeller, himself, encouraged such discomfort, calling Goldwater dangerous and delusional. Months before Johnson would unveil the "daisy girl" attack ad where a girl plucks petals off a daisy while an unseen voice counts down to a nuclear detonation, Rockefeller's campaign mailed out pamphlets to voters on the eve of the crucial California primary asking: "Who do you want in the room with the H-bomb button?"[41]

Rockefeller, however, never really established a foothold in the primaries and could not overcome the wave of support for Goldwater. The Arizona senator, for his part, was looking past Rockefeller and ahead to what he believed was an inevitable showdown with Nixon. The proverbial elephant in a room full of elephants, Nixon's intentions had been speculated upon and guessed at ever since his move to New York. Almost every one of his public statements had been analyzed; almost every word he uttered had been carefully parsed—all to figure out whether or not he would run for president in 1964. Nixon, himself, had already starting moving away from the explicit, unequivocal denials he had issued when he first joined the firm. In January 1964, Nixon had even given an interview from his law office openly equivocating about his interest in the nomination. "I believe that any man who has become a public figure belongs to the public, and as long as they want to lead, to lead," Nixon said in response to a question that mentioned his two-point lead over Goldwater in the latest Gallup poll.[42] Nixon, as mentioned earlier, went even further during his Asian tour in early 1964, saying that he would run if the party wanted him to.

Goldwater had picked up on this and had started addressing the former vice president during his campaign stops. In the run-up to the Indiana primary, he had told the press that he saw his predecessor as the GOP nominee as his "last hurdle" before he could clinch the nomination. "I can't say exactly why I feel that," Goldwater said on April 20, two weeks before he won the Hoosier state's primary.[43] "I think he'll be in the convention pitching when the chips are down." Indeed, a poll released the same day Goldwater spoke about Nixon showed that Republican county chairmen rated the former vice president as the "most likely nominee."[44]

Nevertheless, Nixon's brain told him to forget about 1964. Eisenhower was aghast at the possibility of a Goldwater nomination and had reached out to several moderates, most notably Scranton, to convince them to make a last-minute play for the GOP nod. Nixon resisted entreaties to join Eisenhower's cause—or to be his candidate. Nixon observed that, if Goldwater lost the nomination at the convention as a result of some backroom maneuvering or procedural shenanigans, then "Goldwater people by the millions across the country would sit on their hands" come Election Day. The GOP nomination "would not be worth anything at all," Nixon said at a fundraiser in Long Island.[45]

On the other hand, the heart wants what the heart wants, and Nixon's heart wanted the presidency. In May, with Goldwater surging ahead, Nixon was concerned that there would be no deadlock at the Convention for him to take advantage of. As such, he decided to dip his toe into the water. He authorized a write-in campaign for the Nebraska primary, entrusting Seaton, a former newspaper publisher from Nebraska, to run what was, ostensibly, an unofficial, grassroots effort without authorization from Nixon. Of course, it was anything but that, as Seaton told Nixon he needed $50,000 to pull off a credible campaign. Because he was not a declared candidate and his strategy of being the unifier at the GOP Convention required him to stay, officially, neutral, Nixon's ability to raise money was limited. In the end, he only got about $20,000.[46] Nevertheless, he finished a surprisingly strong second when all the ballots were counted—a tremendous showing, given the fact that he wasn't, officially, running.

The result emboldened him to consider running an actual campaign in the Oregon primary, which took place three days after Nebraska. Under Oregon state law, the secretary of state had to put all declared candidates on the ballot, as well as any person who was perceived or recognized as running for president. Basically, absent an absolute statement of noninterest or a formal withdrawal, any person believed to be running for president would go on the ballot, and Nixon, as the previous nominee and man most likely to be a compromise candidate for a badly split GOP, certainly fit the bill. The situation would allow him to disclaim overt interest while staying on the ballot in order to see how things shook out.[47]

Nixon had been eyeing Oregon for months. Nate Crabtree, vice president of General Mills and a friend of Nixon's, had been a constant pen pal over the past couple of years, passing along intelligence and encouragement from the trenches. In March, Crabtree had commissioned a survey to see where Nixon stood among Republican voters in Oregon. The results, which Nixon received while he was in Japan on his Asia trip, contained some good news for the noncandidate. He was a distant third in the polls but was tied for first place when voters were asked which candidate they would support as their second choice. Nixon also seemed to have escaped, unscathed, from the Rockefeller/Goldwater fight as only 23 percent of those surveyed said they would never vote for Nixon, compared to 42 percent for both Goldwater and Rockefeller.[48]

Despite signaling to his wealthy friends and clients that he would make a push in Oregon, Nixon found it hard to raise money. J. Clifford Folger donated $21,000 while Gene McGovern and Bob Abplanalp chipped in with a combined $8,000. However, some of Nixon's friends, including Bobst, believed the former vice president had a better chance in 1968 and had decided to wait until then.[49]

Additionally, his impromptu staffers knew that Oregon could blow up in Nixon's face. Crabtree's public relations man, Len Nadasdy, had been active in the Young Republicans and knew many of the top Republicans in the state. He reported in March that none of the candidates for delegate he had spoken to were willing to vote for Nixon. His advice was for Nixon to give a press conference where he would stay on the ballot but encourage voters to support someone else. That way, he could maintain his neutrality without angering the Goldwater or Rockefeller voters. And if, by some chance, he won or did well without actively campaigning in the state, then it would fuel the perception that there was a groundswell of support for him. Nixon, however, decided not to follow Nadasdy's advice and decided to run a stealth campaign in Oregon. Nadasdy would later marvel how an intelligent and calculating politician like Nixon could eschew the smart play in favor of an amateurish secret plot with very little chance of success.[50]

Nixon would finish a distant fourth in Oregon behind Rockefeller, Henry Cabot Lodge, and Goldwater. While it wasn't the result he was hoping for, it did seem to slow Goldwater's momentum. If Rockefeller could pull off a victory in the California primary in June, then the convention would likely deadlock on the first ballot, giving Nixon the opening he needed. Unfortunately for Nixon, Goldwater would pull off a narrow win in Nixon's old home state that, essentially, finished off Rockefeller's campaign. Rockefeller, for his part, seemed to know how momentous Goldwater's win truly was, not just in 1964 but looking ahead. During the campaigning, Rockefeller's campaign manager had pressed his candidate to call the Eastern Establishment powers-that-be for help. "You're looking at it, buddy," Rockefeller quipped.[51] "I'm all that's left."

Nixon still had one play to run. If he wanted to force a deadlock at the Convention, then he'd have to do some maneuvering and get another Rockefeller-esque moderate into the fight while maintaining his public neutrality. During a June 7, 1964, press conference in Detroit, he said that it was best for him not to get involved in the ongoing fight. "I think the party wants to search for a new face, and I think the search should go forward," Nixon said.[52] However, he also made clear that he'd be there to pick up the pieces if needed. "If the party should decide on me as its candidate, Mr. Johnson would know he'd been in a fight," Nixon vowed.[53]

The next day, at the National Governor's Association annual meeting, which was being held in Cleveland, Nixon made his move. The Republican governors in attendance were in a state of panic and uproar as a result of the impending Goldwater coronation, and two leading moderate GOP governors, William Scranton of Pennsylvania and George Romney of Michigan, were debating throwing their hats into the ring to try to stop the conservative

Arizonan. Romney had loudly denounced Goldwater and his views, particularly on the Civil Rights Act, during a breakfast meeting of Republican governors and was trying to build up support for a run of his own. Meanwhile, Scranton thought he had an ace in the hole in the form of Eisenhower. The ex-president had called the Pennsylvania governor to his home in Gettysburg and had, seemingly, given him the green light to mount a last-minute bid to take on Goldwater at the Convention.[54]

Nixon needed at least one of them to mount an open challenge so that the party would look split at the Convention. That way, panicked Republicans would look to Nixon to ride in on his white horse and unify the party so that it could stand a chance against Johnson in the fall. By the time he got to Cleveland to meet with the GOP governors, however, he found that neither Romney nor Scranton seemed all that willing to take the plunge. Eisenhower had called Scranton with a change of heart and had decided that he would not get involved with any eleventh-hour intrigues with respect to Goldwater and the nomination. Without the support he had been counting on, Scranton then decided to climb back on the fence, declining to enter the race but taking the Nixonian position that he would serve if called upon.[55]

That left Romney. Nixon launched an intensive, all-out lobbying campaign designed to strong-arm the Michigan governor into publicly challenging Goldwater. The only problem was that, despite his outspoken opposition to Goldwater, Romney seemed genuinely torn about launching a presidential bid. For one thing, he had felt bound by a campaign promise he had made during his 1962 gubernatorial campaign to serve an entire four-year term as governor. He had even asked Nixon if he could, ethically, break his campaign promise provided enough governors got together and begged him to run, to which Nixon quickly said "yes." At one point, Nixon even cornered Romney inside the men's room of the hotel they were staying at to try to assuage some more of the Michigan man's concerns. By the end of his Cleveland visit, Nixon believed he had received a firm commitment from Romney to run, allowing him to leave for London on firm business. Instead, advance man John Whitaker told Nixon after he landed in London that Romney was out. "What do you mean he's not going to run?" a stunned Nixon asked Whitaker.[56] "He told me he was!"

It was obvious to Romney, Scranton, and plenty of others in Cleveland that Nixon was just looking for a stalking horse. At one point, he dropped the façade completely and made his ambitions crystal clear to everyone at the meeting. During a breakfast session, Nixon tried to orchestrate a spontaneous draft and show of support for someone (either Romney, Scranton, or someone else) to step up and agree to try to wrest the nomination from Goldwater's hands. Instead, the room fell into a stony silence while Nixon waited, in vain, for a volunteer. Several in the room, however, posited that what Nixon had really been after was for someone to ask him to make another run at the presidency and to save the GOP from itself. "After a moment or two, I realized what was happening," one governor told columnists Rowland Evans and Robert Novak.[57] "Nixon was waiting for us to ask him to run for President. It was unbelievable, just unbelievable."

Witcover reported that Nixon had even gone so far as to arrange for his supporters to draft a letter calling the former VP into action as the only person that could stop Goldwater.[58] At one point, when Nixon was furiously lobbying Scranton to run, the Pennsylvania Republican called Nixon on his bluff. "Dick, if you want to run for President, why don't you just go ahead and run?"[59] Nixon then promptly ended the conversation.

Without either a horse to back or the backing of his fellow party members, Nixon had little room to maneuver in public. He had to remain noncommittal during a press conference shortly after his unsuccessful breakfast meeting, telling reporters that there was interest from several governors in making it a contest while demurring on his own potential candidacy. However, he did, essentially, reveal himself as the final hurdle to the nomination, much as Goldwater foresaw. "Looking to the future of the party, it would be a tragedy if Sen. Goldwater's views, as previously stated, were not challenged and repudiated," Nixon said.[60]

The cat was now officially out of the bag. The Arizona senator shrugged off Nixon's words, telling the press: "I guess he doesn't know my views very well—I got most of them from him!"[61] Goldwater then compared Nixon to former Minnesota governor Harold Stassen, a once serious presidential candidate who had become a perennial candidate and an afterthought at every GOP convention after 1948.

Ultimately, Scranton would launch a last-minute bid for the nomination on the eve of the Convention. During his speech announcing his candidacy, he condemned Goldwater's views on the Civil Rights Act and warned that the Arizona senator would get trounced in a general election against Johnson. "The nation, and indeed the world, waits to see if another proud political banner, which is our own, will falter, grow limp and collapse in the dust," said Scranton to a roaring ovation while holding a rally to make his candidacy official.[62] "Has the Republican Party, a great many of our fellow citizens are asking, outlived its usefulness? Of course, the answer is no . . . Lincoln would cry out in pain if we sold out our principles. But he would laugh out with scorn if we threw away an election."

Scranton, however, never really got out of the box. Despite having the support of both Rockefeller and Henry Cabot Lodge, Scranton had a hard time picking up votes. Eisenhower had stuck with his pre-Convention stance of neutrality, so support was not forthcoming from the still-popular ex-president.[63] Senate Minority Leader Everett Dirksen, whose support for the Civil Rights Act had been instrumental in securing its passage in the Senate, also refused to get involved.[64] Even if those men had decided to act, it's doubtful that they could have stopped the inevitable. The Goldwater operation ran a sophisticated whip operation, making sure that any delegate that met with someone from the "Stop Goldwater" movement would also get a visit from the campaign in order to keep that delegate in the fold.[65] After a month of fruitless cat herding, Scranton bowed to the inevitable as it was clear to the anti-Goldwater forces that their efforts had come up short.

" THIS TIME, NO MIRACLE OCCURRED."

When Nixon arrived in San Francisco for the GOP National Convention, he knew he didn't stand much of a chance of being the party's presidential nominee. His only avenue to the nomination had been closed off as Romney had refused to contest the nomination and Scranton had tried and failed. Nixon would not get the divisive floor fight he needed in order to be seen as the consensus candidate.

And even if he had been hoping to launch some type of eleventh-hour bid for the nomination, he was severely outgunned. Operating, essentially, as a one-man outfit in contrast to the gigantic, well-oiled machine that was Goldwater's campaign, Nixon was fighting a modern war with medieval weapons.

In a sense, his isolation was understandable. As the GOP Convention hit, Nixon was still in his first full year as public partner at Nixon Mudge and hadn't yet figured out which of his fellow lawyers at the firm he could trust. He was still in the early stages of his friendship with Leonard Garment, and Garment had not yet been accepted into Nixon's inner circle and had little to no input into Nixon's political plans in 1964. Instead, Garment noted that Nixon veterans Finch, Haldeman, Ehrlichman, and a New York lawyer named Sherman Unger, who had been Nixon's advance man in 1960, were informally consulting with Nixon in 1964.[66] But when it came to formulating day-to-day strategy, especially when it came to pulling off his delicate balancing act by challenging Goldwater without alienating the presumptive nominee's supporters, Nixon was, largely, on his own.

Without a full-time political staff devoted to helping promote his cause, carry out his wishes, coordinate his schedule, interact with the media, and operate behind the scenes, Nixon was operating at a disadvantage compared to his Republican rivals. During the Cleveland meetings, for instance, having a full-time political staff might have helped with Nixon's goal of roping Romney into undertaking a last-minute challenge to Goldwater. With Nixon on his prearranged flight to London for firm business, his staffers could have kept up the pressure on Romney, either directly or through the press. Even if it such efforts had been unsuccessful, surely they would have been preferable to Witcover's account of what actually happened: Nixon finding out the bad news upon landing in London and feeling betrayed, yet powerless to do anything about it.[67]

Another area where having a full-time political staff might have made a difference had been at the Convention itself. Nixon had no hope of taking on Goldwater's machine by himself—especially with a makeshift political staff that wasn't entirely sure whether Nixon would, or could, make a last-minute play for the nomination. For instance, a few weeks before the event, Nixon had told Garment to "just go out there and get the feel of it."[68] Garment sensed that this was his informal induction into Nixon's political circle and hoped to please. But beyond any additional instructions beyond that vague directive, there was really nothing for him to do other than "hang out, look at the Republicans assembled en masse, sample the city's splendid food, and visit the suite of rooms rented at the Saint Francis Hotel for a small Nixon delegation that included Haldeman, Ehrlichman, Herb Klein."[69]

When the Convention got underway, Nixon's makeshift staff was holed up in their hotel suite when they noticed a sudden commotion on the floor. Rockefeller was getting booed and jeered at by the Goldwater forces, but the New York governor was grinning like a Cheshire cat. Garment noted that Rockefeller's only chance at derailing Goldwater's inexorable march toward the nomination was to bait the Arizona senator's rabid supporters into behaving in such a way that would scare the rest of the Convention (and voters watching on television) and, hopefully, force them to rethink who they wanted to be their standard-bearer. In his speech, Rockefeller spoke about how he had spent the last year traveling across the country warning against "the extremist threat" in a line that was intended to provoke a negative reaction from Goldwater supporters. The line did just that, as Rockefeller had, seemingly, brought out the crazy in Goldwater's followers. "In our suite at the Saint Francis, Haldeman jumped up and off went our little band, sprinting to waiting cars for a dash out to the Cow Palace to see whether a miracle might occur," Garment recalled, noting that, during the entire car ride, Haldeman followed the proceedings on a contraption Garment had never seen before: a portable television set.[70]

When they entered the convention center, they were dismayed to find that the Goldwater forces had the situation well in hand. "This time, no miracle occurred," Garment said.[71] "The Goldwater marshals, spread out among the delegates and linked by walkie-talkies to coordinators watching the melee on TV in vans outside the hall, kept tight control of the floor." Whatever opening that might have existed for Nixon to force his way through and steal the nomination was gone—crushed with brutal efficiency by a determined and well-organized opposition.

Once Nixon had accepted that Goldwater would be the nominee, he started looking ahead—to Election Day of 1964 and beyond. The Arizona senator was going to lose and lose badly, giving Johnson the chance to finally live up to his "Landslide Lyndon" sobriquet.[72] The only question would be whether Goldwater would drag down GOP candidates across the country along with him.

Nixon was okay with that. After all, the Republican Party would be devastated after losing in a landslide, and would, naturally, turn to one of the few unifying figures left in the party to pick up the pieces and run in 1968. Nixon was perfectly positioned to be that person, and the press knew it. The *LA Times* even ran a stunningly prescient column on July 14 (day two of the convention) positing this very theory. "At 51, identified with the GOP center, Nixon would be the likeliest man to weld together the dissident elements of right and left," the *Times* wrote.[73] "This he would accomplish by persuasion, by conferences, by speech-making, by traveling and by writing, without seeking interim public office as he did, regrettably, two years ago in California." The column then went on to speculate that Nixon could play an important role in the 1966 midterm elections.

The only thing left for Nixon to do was to ensure that he would have a part in Goldwater's coronation in San Francisco. He arranged to give his speech after Goldwater secured the nomination, in part, so that the 1960 standard-bearer could pass the torch to his successor. Nixon also wanted to show that he wasn't trying to steal the nomination from Goldwater, so waiting until after it was official meant that there would be no possibility of a spontaneous or planned maneuver from Nixon's supporters to put his name before the Convention.[74]

Once Goldwater had the nomination wrapped up, Nixon took the stage to deliver a rousing speech calling for the party to unify behind Goldwater and do whatever it took to elect him president. "Before this convention, we were Goldwater Republicans, Rockefeller Republicans, Scranton Republicans, Lodge Republicans, but now that this convention has met and made its decision, we are Republicans, period, working for Barry Goldwater for President of the United States," Nixon said from the stage, to a warm reception.[75] "T here are some who may say that they are going to sit it out or take a walk, or even go on a boat ride. I have an answer: In the words of Barry Goldwater in 1960, 'Let's grow up, Republicans, let's go to work—and we shall win in November!'"

As it turned out, neither the Goldwater Republicans nor the Rockefeller/Scranton/Lodge Republicans were in the mood to work together. Taking the stage after Nixon's stirring introduction, Goldwater seemingly ignored his predecessor's exhortations for unity and the need to put aside ideological differences for the greater good. "Anyone who joins us in all sincerity, we welcome," Goldwater said.[76] "Those who do not care for our cause, we do not expect to enter our ranks in any case." Goldwater then hit moderate Republicans with one of the more famous lines in American political history. "Extremism in the defense of liberty is no vice," Goldwater roared to a thunderous ovation.[77] "And let me remind you also, that moderation in the pursuit of justice is no virtue."

Watching from off stage, Nixon was aghast at Goldwater's divisive rhetoric. "I felt almost physically sick as I sat there on the platform," Nixon recalled.[78] "Not only did Goldwater fail to close the rifts in the party and heal its wounds; he opened new wounds and then rubbed salt in them." His refusal to extend an olive branch to the moderates in the party gave the likes of Rockefeller, Romney, and President Eisenhower an excuse to abandon ship, and Rockefeller and Romney would take advantage, refusing to endorse their party's standard-bearer or lift a finger to campaign for him.

Goldwater's confrontational speech also played right into the Democrats' hand. Johnson was able to portray Goldwater as dangerous and unstable—and the "daisy girl" ad was just the tip of the iceberg. Democrats turned Goldwater's campaign slogan, "In your heart, you know he's right," around on him, producing buttons and bumper stickers that read: "In your guts, you know he's nuts." Another popular parody was: "In your heart, you know he might" with a mushroom cloud in the background. Other Johnson ads played off Goldwater's image as an extremist, including the famous "Confessions of a Republican" ad, which featured a young man, identified as a Republican, who was concerned about Goldwater's ideology and seeming eagerness to confront the USSR. Playing off Goldwater's opposition to the 1964 Civil Rights Act, the ad also suggested that the Ku Klux Klan backed Goldwater.[79] Goldwater, for his part, did not help his public image with moderate and undecided voters by pulling no punches on the campaign trail. "What good is prosperity if you are a slave?" he asked a group of young girls at a campaign stop.[80] "What good is justice if you are a slave? . . . Without freedom you can't enjoy life."

Despite Nixon's disgust at Goldwater's rhetoric, he campaigned hard for his party's nominee. He, along with Rose Mary Woods, took a leave of absence from Nixon Mudge and maintained a grueling campaign schedule. He made over 150 appearances in thirty-six states—oftentimes on behalf of beleaguered Senate and House candidates who wanted to avoid being associated with the guy at the top of the ballot. "Time after time, the senatorial or congressional candidate on whose behalf I was to speak begged me to avoid associating his candidacy with Goldwater," Nixon said.[81] "It was a difficult tightrope to walk, but I usually found some way to praise the local candidates independently of expressing, as I did in every speech I gave, my personal support of Goldwater."

Nixon even had to play peacemaker. Shortly after the Convention, Nixon interceded with a furious Eisenhower and tried to convince his former boss to speak with Goldwater about toning down his harsh words. Eisenhower ultimately agreed, but Goldwater's subsequent face-to-face sitdown with the ex-president at his Gettysburg home went about as well as the famous battle did.

When Goldwater, Eisenhower, Scranton, and Nixon held a joint press conference in an attempted demonstration of party unity, the 1964 nominee started speaking off the cuff, which was always eventful. At one point, a reporter asked Goldwater about his policy toward Germany, and the Republican Party's standard-bearer actually had the temerity to say: "I think Germany originated the modern concept of peace through strength" while standing next to the war hero who helped bring about Nazi Germany's defeat.[82] An irate Eisenhower refused to help Goldwater, telling Nixon: "I thought that Goldwater was just stubborn. Now I'm convinced he's just plain dumb."[83]

The worst fears of Eisenhower, Nixon, and many other Republicans came true on Election Night when the GOP suffered an electoral wipeout of historic proportions. With 61 percent of the popular vote, Johnson set an all-time record that still hasn't been beaten (indeed, his percentage of the popular vote was higher than either Nixon in 1972 or Reagan in 1984—both of whom won forty-nine-state landslides). Goldwater only managed 52 electoral votes to Johnson's 486, but in a bit of foreshadowing, the Republican nominee did surprisingly well in the South, winning five states there. Democrats added two seats to their Senate majority, giving them a 68–32 edge. Republicans, meanwhile, lost thirty-eight seats in the House, giving Democrats a two-thirds majority in the House.

Nixon's hard work on behalf of what was always going to be a losing effort did not go unnoticed. His yeoman's work was, obviously, in preparation for 1968 when he'd have plenty of IOUs to cash in with Republicans around the country. Nevertheless, as Witcover observed, Nixon had honored himself and his party by fighting loyally for the Republican cause even under the worst circumstances imaginable. Most importantly, he had stuck by Goldwater and his conservative base even after other party luminaries cut bait. Goldwater, for his part, did not forget Nixon's help. Several months after his landslide loss, Goldwater spoke at a party meeting and introduced Nixon as "the man who worked harder than any one person for the ticket."[84] Goldwater even addressed the elephant in the room by telling Nixon: "I know you did it in the interest of the Republican Party and not for any selfish reasons, but if there ever comes a time I can turn those into selfish reasons, I am going to do all I can to see that it comes about."[85]

Turns out, there was a time for Nixon to develop "selfish reasons." With a power vacuum in the GOP and no obvious candidate to step into the void, all eyes, once again, turned to him. While it's clear that he had never, really, given up on his goal of being president, the 1964 campaign irrevocably reignited his desire to pursue the ultimate prize. "I had finally come to the realization that there was no other life for me but politics and public service," Nixon said.[86] "Even when my legal work was at its most interesting I never found it truly fulfilling."

And it was just as well. As he told several of his friends: "If all I have is my legal work, I would be mentally dead in two years and physically dead in four."[87]

NOTES

1. Jules Witcover, *The Resurrection of Richard Nixon* (New York: G. P. Putnam's Sons, 1970), 66–67.
2. "Lyndon B. Johnson, Address before a Joint Session of the Congress, November 27, 1963," The American Presidency Project, accessed March 26, 2017, http://www.presidency.ucsb.edu/ws/?pid=25988.
3. Robert Caro, *The Years of Lyndon Johnson: The Passage of Power* (New York: Alfred A. Knopf, 2012), 552–57.
4. Robert Caro, *Master of the Senate* (New York: Vintage Books, 2003), 853–54.
5. David Coleman, "LBJ's Presidential Approval Ratings," History in Pieces, accessed March 27, 2017, http://historyinpieces.com/research/lbj-presidential-approval-ratings.
6. Richard Nixon, Letter from Spiro T. Agnew, January 15, 1964, Pre-Presidential Papers, Richard Nixon Presidential Library and Museum.
7. Richard Nixon, Letter from Edwin Beaman, March 4, 1964, Pre-Presidential Papers, Richard Nixon Presidential Library and Museum.
8. Richard Nixon, Letter from Cecil Barker, May 15, 1964, Pre-Presidential Papers, Richard Nixon Presidential Library and Museum.
9. Richard Nixon, Letter from John Brown, May 22, 1964, Pre-Presidential Papers, Richard Nixon Presidential Library and Museum.
10. Richard Nixon, Letter from George MacKinnon, December 6, 1963, Pre-Presidential Papers, Richard Nixon Presidential Library and Museum.
11. Richard Nixon, Letter from George MacKinnon, January 27, 1964, Pre-Presidential Papers, Richard Nixon Presidential Library and Museum.
12. Richard Nixon, Letter from Frank Rackley, September 27, 1963, Pre-Presidential Papers, Richard Nixon Presidential Library and Museum.
13. Richard Nixon, Letter from H. L. Hunt, November 19, 1963, Pre-Presidential Papers, Richard Nixon Presidential Library and Museum.
14. Richard Nixon, Letter from J. D. Stetson Coleman, February 29, 1964 Pre-Presidential Papers, Richard Nixon Presidential Library and Museum.
15. Richard Nixon, Letter from John Clements, August 12, 1963, Pre-Presidential Papers, Richard Nixon Presidential Library and Museum.
16. Richard Nixon, Letter from John Clements, February 14, 1964, Pre-Presidential Papers, Richard Nixon Presidential Library and Museum.
17. Richard Nixon, Letter to John Clements, December 31, 1963, Pre-Presidential Papers, Richard Nixon Presidential Library and Museum.
18. Richard Nixon, Letter from John Clements, February 14, 1964, supra.
19. Richard Nixon, Letter to Walter Robertson, January 14, 1964, Pre-Presidential Papers, Richard Nixon Presidential Library and Museum.
20. Josh Karp and Tom Barry, "We Are Family: Relatives Who Play and Work Well Together," *Wisconsin Super Lawyers*, December 2007, accessed March 27, 2017, http://www.superlawyers.com/wisconsin/article/we-are-family/f2b3e6ff-2139-4e08-81b1-a11fc024de5c.html.
21. Richard Nixon, Letter to Charles Kersten, December 13, 1963, Pre-Presidential Papers, Richard Nixon Presidential Library and Museum.
22. Richard Nixon, Letter from Louis Wyman, January 19, 1964, Pre-Presidential Papers, Richard Nixon Presidential Library and Museum.
23. Richard Nixon, Letter to Louis Wyman, January 21, 1964, Pre-Presidential Papers, Richard Nixon Presidential Library and Museum.

24. Richard Nixon, Letter from Louis Wyman, January 23, 1964, Pre-Presidential Papers, Richard Nixon Presidential Library and Museum.
25. Nixon, Letter from Louis Wyman, January 23, 1964.
26. Witcover, *The Resurrection of Richard Nixon*, 66.
27. Witcover, *The Resurrection of Richard Nixon*, and Stephen Ambrose, *Nixon: Volume 2, The Triumph of a Politician, 1962–1972* (New York: Simon and Schuster, 1989), 38–39.
28. Witcover, *The Resurrection of Richard Nixon*, 69.
29. "Alf Landon, G.O.P. Stand-Bearer, Dies at 100," *New York Times*, October 13, 1987, accessed March 27, 2017, http://www.nytimes.com/learning/general/onthisday/bday/0909.html.
30. "Tom Dewey Sticks to His Albany Knitting," *Life*, March 20, 1944.
31. John Dickerson, "Never Goldwater: The Failed Attempt to Wrest the 1964 GOP Nomination from the Arizona Senator and the Birth of the Modern GOP," *Slate*, May 12, 2016, accessed March 27, 2017, http://www.slate.com/articles/news_and_politics/politics/2016/05/never_goldwater_the_failed_attempt_to_wrest_the_1964_gop_nomination_from.html.
32. "Race Entered by Goldwater," *Spokesman-Review*, January 4, 1964.
33. Lee Edwards, "Barry M. Goldwater: The Most Consequential Loser in American Politics," The Heritage Foundation, July 3, 2014, accessed March 27, 2017, http://www.heritage.org/research/reports/2014/07/barry-m-goldwater-the-most-consequential-loser-in-american-politics.
34. Bret Barnes, "Barry Goldwater, GOP Hero, Dies," *Washington Post*, May 30, 1998, accessed March 27, 2017, http://www.washingtonpost.com/wp-srv/politics/daily/may98/goldwater30.htm.
35. Barnes, "Barry Goldwater, GOP Hero, Dies."
36. "Barry Goldwater Is Dead at 89; Conservatives' Standard Bearer," *New York Times*, May 30, 1998, accessed March 27, 2017, http://www.nytimes.com/1998/05/30/us/barry-goldwater-is-dead-at-89-conservatives-standardbearer.html?pagewanted=all.
37. "Barry Goldwater Is Dead at 89."
38. Dickerson, "Never Goldwater."
39. Barnes, "Barry Goldwater, GOP Hero, Dies."
40. Larry Osius, "361 Delegates Firmly for Barry; 316 Others Favor Him," *Eugene Register-Guard*, June 18, 1964.
41. "The 1964 Republican Campaign," *PBS*, accessed March 27, 2017, http://www.pbs.org/wgbh/americanexperience/features/general-article/rockefellers-campaign/.
42. Witcover, *The Resurrection of Richard Nixon*, 69.
43. Osius, "361 Delegates Firmly for Barry."
44. Ambrose, *Nixon: Volume 2*, 45.
45. Ambrose, *Nixon: Volume 2*, 51.
46. Ambrose, *Nixon: Volume 2*, 46–47.
47. Rick Perlstein, *Before the Storm: Barry Goldwater and the Unmaking of American Consensus* (New York: Nation Books, 2001), 311.
48. Richard Nixon, "Copy of North Star Surveys, Inc., Report—Oregon 1964," March 1964, Pre-Presidential Papers, Richard Nixon Presidential Library and Museum.
49. Richard Nixon, Transcript of Conversation with Cliff Folger, June 2, 1964, Pre-Presidential Papers, Richard Nixon Presidential Library and Museum.
50. Perlstein, *Before the Storm*, 311.
51. Dickerson, "Never Goldwater."
52. Witcover, *The Resurrection of Richard Nixon*, 85.
53. Witcover, *The Resurrection of Richard Nixon*, 86.
54. Witcover, *The Resurrection of Richard Nixon*, 84–85.
55. Witcover, *The Resurrection of Richard Nixon*, 86–87.
56. Witcover, *The Resurrection of Richard Nixon*, 93.
57. Witcover, *The Resurrection of Richard Nixon*, 89.
58. Witcover, *The Resurrection of Richard Nixon*, 90–91.
59. Witcover, *The Resurrection of Richard Nixon*, 91.
60. Dickerson, "Never Goldwater."

61. Ambrose, *Nixon: Volume 2*, 51.
62. Dickerson, "Never Goldwater."
63. Ambrose, *Nixon: Volume 2*, 51.
64. Dickerson, "Never Goldwater."
65. Dickerson, "Never Goldwater."
66. Leonard Garment, *Crazy Rhythm: From Brooklyn and Jazz to Nixon's White House, Watergate and Beyond* (Cambridge, MA: Da Capo Press, 1997), 102–3.
67. Witcover, *The Resurrection of Richard Nixon*, 93.
68. Garment, *Crazy Rhythm*, 103.
69. Garment, *Crazy Rhythm*.
70. Garment, *Crazy Rhythm*, 104.
71. Garment, *Crazy Rhythm*.
72. During Johnson's successful 1948 election to the US Senate, he eeked out a close victory over Texas governor Coke Stevenson in the Democratic primary that included allegations of voter fraud from both sides. After some political and legal maneuvering, Johnson overcame a twenty-thousand-vote deficit to win by a mere eighty-seven votes. The result stood and Johnson earned the ironic nickname of "Landslide Lyndon." Robert Caro writes about the election, at length, in *Means of Ascent* (New York: Alfred A. Knopf, 1990).
73. Witcover, *The Resurrection of Richard Nixon*, 97.
74. Witcover, *The Resurrection of Richard Nixon*, 96.
75. Ambrose, *Nixon: Volume 2*, 53.
76. Ambrose, *Nixon: Volume 2*, 53.
77. Dickerson, "Never Goldwater."
78. Nixon, *RN*.
79. "Confessions of a Republican," Wikipedia, accessed March 27, 2017, https://en.wikipedia.org/wiki/Confessions_of_a_Republican.
80. Theodore White, *The Making of the President, 1964* (New York: Antheneum Publishers, 1965), 326–27.
81. Nixon, *RN*.
82. Nixon, *RN*.
83. Nixon, *RN*.
84. Rick Perlstein, *Nixonland: The Rise of a President and the Fracturing of America* (New York, Scribner, 2008), 65.
85. Perlstein, *Nixonland*.
86. Nixon, *RN*.
87. Nixon, *RN*.

Chapter Seven

"Why Are These Men for Nixon?"

When one thinks of a presidential candidate surrounded by a staff consisting of bright, young, well-educated, photogenic men who fervently believed in their candidate's cause and were willing to do, just about anything, to see that candidate in the Oval Office, Richard Nixon is probably not the first name to come to mind.

In fact, it was his longtime rival, John F. Kennedy, who had, seemingly, established the mold. Flanked by an impressive array of young, talented, and tireless advisors (many of whom were fellow Harvard alums) like Kenneth O'Donnell (aged thirty-six at the time of JFK's inauguration), Larry O'Brien (forty-three), Richard Donahue (thirty-three), Ralph Dungan (thirty-seven), David Powers (forty-eight), and others, who were close personal friends as well as longtime loyal aides, Kennedy's cadre of advisors served as the perfect poster children for the president's "New Frontier." Like a loyal band of knights faithfully serving their liege, Kennedy's staff very much lived up to the image of Camelot that would later be associated with JFK's brief presidency. Their detractors, of course, had some other names for this group of mostly Irish, mostly Massachusetts, natives, who had, mostly, been associated with Harvard in some way, and had no problems taking off the gloves if it meant protecting their leader. Some called them the Irish Republican Army. Others called them the Irish Mafia.[1]

In his seminal book *The Making of the President, 1960*, journalist Theodore White helped lionize Kennedy's youthful staff as a group of highly competent, well-organized, and easily adaptable soldiers who could overcome any obstacle. Some of Kennedy's young staffers even treated the older aides with contempt or pity, telling White that "the old-timers are afraid of us" and that they only kept some around "to make them feel like we're safe." One aide even told White that the younger aides who had served in World

War II had a distinct advantage over their older counterparts who had stayed home. "I think we learned something during the war about how to do things; we learned how to work in a way the generals didn't understand," the aide told White.[2] "They'd tell us what to do, but then we had to go out and organize the thing—cut the red tape, get the stuff there on time, no matter how, throw away the rule book."

While Nixon had plenty of young aides working for him in both 1960 and 1962, they didn't quite capture the imagination of the American public the same way. Perhaps it was because he lost those races—Americans don't usually embrace or remember people who come in second. As White put it, Nixon's staffers just seemed less inspirational. Kennedy's men were young, dashing, and single; vital gears in a well-oiled machine that worked and played hard together. Most of Nixon's main staffers during the 1960 campaign were older, married, and less telegenic when compared to their counterparts. When White described Nixon's campaign manager Bob Finch, he called him "handsome, pleasant of manner, incisive of mind, graceful of phrase and expression"—all qualities that made him a rarity on the Nixon staff. White then dropped the hammer: those qualities made Finch "classy enough" to "make the first team on the Kennedy side of the fence if he had wanted."[3]

Or maybe it was because, in both 1960 and 1962, Nixon seemed to keep his own counsel and didn't rely much on his aides. "Hell, Dick insisted on doing everything for himself, including sharpening the pencils," one of his 1960 strategists told *Newsday* in 1968.[4] White had observed that, in the closing days of the presidential campaign, Nixon had, in essence, erected a wall between himself and all but his closest circle of advisers.

> By the end of the campaign, disaffection from the candidate had become general. Nixon's top-level planners and volunteers were men of high talent, many of them absentees on leave from impressively important jobs in American enterprise; yet they could receive no hearing from their political chief, and their efforts to reach him degenerated into both the bizarre and humiliating as they tried to penetrate through his inner court to his attention.[5]

According to White, one staffer had even resorted to calling Nixon "the meanest man in the world." If Kennedy was Camelot, then Nixon seemed to represent Prince John from "Robin Hood"—the scheming, unlikeable man who was widely disliked within his own court and was always in the shadow of his more popular predecessor.

As he prepared for his political comeback, however, Nixon decided to take a page from his former rival's playbook. He recruited a number of young, accomplished, hard-working intellectuals to his team—the bulk of whom resided within the confines of the Nixon Mudge firm—and allowed them to grab, at least, a portion of a spotlight. This Wall Street–based staff may not have been romanticized the same way as Kennedy's knights of Camelot had been, but Nixon's aides helped their boss in ways that went beyond performing their required political and legal tasks. Their very existence allowed Nixon to dispel the notion that he couldn't win over young people, while his recruitment of so many new faces put distance between himself and his disastrous prior campaigns. "I've started out all-new for this campaign," Nixon told the *New York Times* in 1968 while emphasizing that his primary staff was, overall, younger than Kennedy's inner circle had been in 1960.[6] "I used the past year to go to school again." He even gushed that his young staffers were smart, courageous, and men of high character. "They're not for sale," Nixon bragged. "These are guys that money can't buy."

There was a reason why he once cited his lack of a political staff as evidence that he had no intention of being a candidate in 1964. He needed smart, talented people to do his legwork and help him plan out his comeback—but he couldn't rely on the same people that he had in 1960 and 1962 for risk of resurrecting the "loser label." Luckily, there were a bunch of people at 20 Broad Street that were ready, willing, and able to help him out.

"HUMAN TRAINS."

The 1964 Convention had served as Garment's informal induction into Nixon's political world—and after getting a taste of the pomp, circumstance, and chaos of the American political process, he wanted more. He recalled being "fascinated by every moment of [his] sudden plunge into politics" and was spellbound when he saw the Convention floor for the first time, likening the crowd noise he experienced from the Goldwaterites at the Cow Palace to the Polo Grounds after Bobby Thomson's famous "Shot Heard 'Round the World" home run in 1951.[7]

Nixon hadn't said anything about wanting to run again. Yet Garment realized, from the moment he had first met Nixon that another White House run was inevitable, and he was determined to demonstrate his strong interest in working for the future presidential campaign. "I think it was made clear that I was just very interested in his political future because it was clear to me from the start that he was planning to do what he could to have another run at the Presidency," Garment said.[8] "And what could be more attractive to a kind of a hungry personality like myself than to enter politics at the top by taking part in a Presidential campaign as a colleague of the candidate?"

Nixon, for his part, had decided to groom Garment for a larger role within his inner circle. Ehrlichman recalled that, at the Convention, despite Garment's lack of experience and name recognition within the Nixon camp, Nixon was already relying on Garment for advice. "There was a lot of interaction—a lot of Nixon asking Garment, 'what do you think of this?' or explaining to Garment what was happening in relation to Rockefeller, Knowland and the other players," Ehrlichman recalled.[9] "It was almost as if Garment was a sounding board for Nixon."

Garment decided to take it upon himself to recruit for Nixon's new political staff. The firm understood their famous public partner had far more demands on his time and needed a larger staff to deal with all of them. Answering his mail and phone were already Herculean tasks that were too much for Rose Mary Woods and Pat Nixon (in her alias as "Miss Ryan") to handle. He needed more full-time staffers to help with speechwriting, research, correspondence, travel, and logistics—and Nixon's partners approved it, knowing that he would be getting tons of media attention as he crisscrossed the globe and that his increased public profile would help the firm.[10]

Garment knew that there were plenty of other hungry personalities like himself at the firm that could help the cause. "I was good at introducing people to one another and getting them to work together in complicated enterprises—assembling human trains, tracks, and switches, even when I wasn't sure where I wanted to go," Garment said.[11]

One of the first people he signed up was fellow Mudge lawyer Tom Evans. Like Garment, Evans was a New York City native and was looking to do political work in addition to being a lawyer. Unlike Garment, Evans was a lifelong Republican who had campaigned, vigorously, for Nixon in 1960—even going so far as help lead the "New York Republicans for Nixon," an act Garment noted was especially brave considering the fact that the state was Rockefeller territory.[12] Evans also had the pedigree that Nixon and Garment both lacked, having earned his bachelor's degree from Williams College and his JD from Columbia Law School. He had also served in the Marines between his two degrees, earning a Silver Star and two Purple Hearts for his service in the Korean War.[13]

After graduating from law school in 1958, Evans went to work for Simpson, Thacher & Bartlett as a litigator. Evans recalled that he was disappointed that he was unable to participate in politics while working the long hours that were customary for any newly minted Wall Street attorney, and after four years at Simpson Thacher, he joined a New York State commission investigating corruption within the government.[14] After a few years with the commission, he had a chance meeting with Garment in 1965 at a Brooklyn Heights playground one weekend. While their kids played in the sandbox together, Garment invited Evans to join Nixon Mudge as a litigator.[15]

Garment threw Evans into the deep end, giving him an assignment immediately on behalf of Nixon's main client, Pepsi. Garment explained that Pepsi had been sued the previous Friday by eighty-eight of its distributors over Pepsi's decision to phase out its Patio Diet Cola line in favor of a new product, Diet Pepsi. He asked Evans to appear in court the following Monday, his first official day on the job, to oppose the distributors' request for an injunction to prevent Pepsi from taking away the popular Patio line from them. Evans was successful and, immediately upon arriving at the office from the courthouse, was taken to Nixon's corner office where he got to meet the firm's famous public partner.[16]

After taking in his public partner's impressive museum of an office and his various mementos, tchotchkes, and souvenirs from his glory days, Evans actually recalled being disappointed with his initial meeting with Nixon. "At this first meeting, I was somewhat let down," Evans said.[17] "Although Nixon was plainly making an effort to be pleasant and outgoing, he appeared distracted. His eyes would occasionally roll toward the ceiling or shift around the room." Evans also recalled being transfixed by the famous (or infamous) "Nixon nose," noting that it looked "more like a caricature than the real thing."[18] Despite that less-than-auspicious beginning (Garment made the excuse that Nixon was suffering from jet lag after one of his many trips), Evans immediately started handling political work for Nixon.

Other young recruits soon followed. John Sears was another one of Garment's men in the litigation department that Garment had earmarked for Nixon's political staff. Sears recalls that he wasn't very politically active at the time, and as mentioned earlier, he didn't have a burning desire to work at Nixon Mudge.[19] Despite that, Garment considered Sears to be an intellectual who demonstrated a "concrete genius for politics." Nixon agreed and immediately selected Sears to join his fledging staff.[20] Sears recalled that, at first, he didn't think much of their chances. As time went on, however, Sears began to feel more optimistic. "What we came to realize was that Johnson was very unpopular," he said.[21]

All politicians have to have good speechwriters, and on that front, Nixon took the lead in determining who would be the ones that would write his words for him. His first pick was Patrick Buchanan, a conservative editorial writer for the *St. Louis Globe-Democrat*. At the age of twenty-three, Buchanan had earned his master's degree from the Columbia University Graduate School of Journalism in 1962, whereupon he immediately went to work for the *Globe-Democrat*.[22] Buchanan had been a strong supporter of Goldwater during the 1964 race and had written numerous editorials in support of the GOP nominee. The *Globe-Democrat*, despite its name, had been a solidly Republican newspaper. Nevertheless, in a decision that rankled Buchanan, the newspaper refused to endorse Goldwater. Buchanan later claimed that there had been a secret deal between the paper's editorial staff and Lyndon Johnson.[23]

Buchanan underscored his conservative values when he authored a two-thousand-word essay for the paper titled "What Is the Future for Conservatism?" Lest there be any confusion, Buchanan thought the future was extremely bright. "No, no matter that the scribes of the left are now publishing their meticulously prepared elegies over conservatism, the movement was not repudiated and is by no means dead," Buchanan wrote.[24] "It was Mr. Goldwater who was repudiated and may well be politically dead."

Buchanan was determined to be involved in the next presidential election. With Goldwater vanquished, the young writer turned his attention to the man he believed had the inside track to the GOP nomination in 1968. In December 1965, Buchanan headed to Illinois to see Nixon speak and volunteer his services. "I wanted to meet Nixon to see if I might get aboard his 1968 campaign early, a campaign I saw as inevitable," Buchanan recalled.[25] "I was certain he was going to run, that his only serious rival was Romney, and that an alignment of the conservative movement with the Nixon Republicans could ensure his nomination."

According to Buchanan, Nixon didn't seem too interested and wanted to know what issues he had written about. Buchanan responded that he wrote on all issues and did three to four editorials a day. Nixon still seemed noncommittal, and even told Buchanan that 1968 depended on whether or not he could help the party gain congressional seats during the 1966 midterm elections. Buchanan believed he had blown his impromptu interview until he got a call from Nixon several days later asking him to come to New York.[26]

Nixon saw Buchanan as, potentially, his issues guy and tested him on a number of domestic and foreign matters. "He moved from subject to subject swiftly and pressed me on everything from the war to the conservative movement to civil rights," Buchanan stated.[27] "He was an exhausting interviewer." Nixon also inquired about Buchanan's ideology, asking: "You're not as conservative as Bill Buckley, are you?"[28]

Buchanan admired Buckley and had endorsed him when he split from the Republican Party to run for mayor of New York City in 1965 as the nominee of the newly formed Conservative Party. Buchanan, however, sensed that Nixon didn't want to hear a full-throated defense of the man whom many considered to be the intellectual founder of the modern-day conservative movement in American politics, so he gave a noncommittal answer.[29] Buchanan may have been a true believer, but he knew that Nixon had to maintain his image as the consensus candidate for the GOP and couldn't veer too much to the right. "There's no question about it, Nixon was not a conservative—as I was," Buchanan acknowledged.[30] "He was a 'small c' conservative about a lot of things: social, cultural issues. But he was also a progressive Republican in a lot of ways. You didn't get the sense he was upset with Social Security or the TVA at all. He accepted them as part of the culture of the country and, unlike Goldwater, who wanted to roll back the New Deal, Nixon was never going to do that."

One area where the two did see eye to eye was in the area of politics. "We did agree, enormously, when it came to building a new majority, how to conduct a campaign, what issues would cut right, and how to go after political adversaries," said Buchanan.[31] Ultimately, Buchanan recognized that there would be plenty of opportunities to try to make Nixon embrace his inner conservative—but he'd have to be on his staff if he had any hope of making Nixon more like Goldwater or Buckley.

Buchanan would have his work cut out for him, given that Nixon's other two speechwriters self-identified as moderates. William Safire had the most history with Nixon, having encountered the then–vice president in 1959 during the celebrated "Kitchen Debate" with Khrushchev. It was Safire, who was working in public relations at the time, who had helped steer Nixon and Khrushchev toward the model American kitchen where the two engaged in their extended colloquy about capitalism versus communism. According to Safire and others who were present, when the Soviet leader started with his critical rhetoric about capitalism and the American way of life, Nixon seemed uncomfortable and, at first, tried to appear gracious in the face of Khrushchev's aggressiveness. In doing so, Nixon became worried that he had looked weak and allowed Khrushchev to walk all over him.[32] "Khrushchev wiped the floor with him," Safire recalled.[33] "Because Nixon was trying to be Mr. Nice Guy, and he was getting clobbered."

The vice president needed to regroup and, according to Safire, he directed Nixon and Khrushchev over to the model kitchen that had been built by the company Safire worked for. Once there, Nixon got his bearings, and his "debate" performance improved considerably. Even better for Nixon, Safire and an AP photographer snapped several pictures of Nixon looking authoritative, including one of Nixon jabbing his finger at a surprised Khrushchev. The photos seemingly flipped the narrative around so that now it was the Soviet leader that was, seemingly, being bullied. "A few hours after the kitchen conference, at our ambassador's residence, I was introduced to Nixon, who showed his grasp of capitalism's priorities by commenting, 'We really put your kitchen on the map, didn't we?'" Safire recalled.[34]

After volunteering for Nixon's 1960 campaign, Safire opened his own PR firm and worked for Rockefeller's presidential campaign in 1964. "You'll like him," Nixon told Garment about Safire.[35] "He's with Rockefeller now, but he's smart and funny and important to us, so get to know him." Garment recalled that he did, indeed, like Safire and described him as "smart, feisty and funny" as well as a garish dresser that made him seem like the last person who would work for a Wall Street firm, let alone a potential Republican candidate for president.

Garment also observed that Safire had a sharp wit and seemed to have a natural talent for puns. With his clever turns of phrases and an avowed affection for abundant alliteration, Safire would distinguish himself from Buchanan, who was more of an issues man. In time, Safire would push the boundaries of political discourse, most notably in 1970 when he penned a speech for vice president Spiro Agnew in which the famously inarticulate politician described members of the media as "nattering nabobs of negativism" who have formed their own 4-H club: "the 'hopeless, hysterical hypochondriacs of history.'"[36]

A couple of years later, Nixon would recruit another moderate Republican to his staff. A lifelong Republican who had attended his first national convention at the age of eighteen in 1948, Ray Price had been an editor with the *New York Herald Tribune* when the paper went under in 1966. Sitting at home and working on writing a novel, Price got a call in early 1967 from Nixon to see if he would be willing to join his staff. Price had reservations—for one thing, he knew that joining a campaign would be a full-time commitment that would leave him with no time to do the things he wanted, like finish his novel. Also, Price admitted that he was unsure about Nixon as a candidate, noting that Nixon was "anathema to many of those in the New York world I inhabited, and at least mildly disliked by most."

Ultimately, Price agreed to meet with Nixon and hear him out. "He invited me to lunch," Price recalled.[37] "We talked for three hours about everything under the sun. I found myself, even though I had been writing about him for years, vastly more impressed than I expected him to be. He asked me to give him an answer in a week. I studied intensively for a week, decided he was my candidate, and I should do it, called him back on the seventh day." Price officially joined on March 1, 1967, reporting to Nixon's law firm office where he joined the others that had already come on board. He would, eventually, achieve fame as the man who wrote both of Nixon's inaugural addresses, as well as Nixon's resignation speech. And one month after Nixon left office, Price would write President Gerald Ford's speech pardoning his predecessor.

" I'M FOR AMERICAN BOYS EVERY TIME."

Nixon's new team, minus Price, made its debut toward the end of 1965. Nixon was already looking toward the 1966 midterm elections as his springboard to 1968. However, there were a couple of high-profile races in 1965 that gave Nixon and his Nixon Mudge–based staff a chance for a dress rehearsal.

In Virginia, A. Linwood Holton was the GOP nominee for governor in a state that hadn't elected a Republican chief executive since Reconstruction. Holton was a Harvard Law–educated lawyer who had been active in the Virginia GOP for years before he decided to take the plunge into electoral politics himself. A virtual unknown to most voters in the state, Holton was running an uphill race against the Democratic nominee, Mills Godwin Jr., who had been hand picked by Harry Byrd's dominant political machine. Nixon, who had carried Virginia in 1960, knew that the state could go for a

Republican, so he campaigned hard for Holton. During one day of the campaign, Nixon visited every major population center in the state,[38] exhorting Virginians to "lead the way to restoring two-party government throughout the nation."[39] Holton ended up losing the race but captured a better-than-expected 38 percent of the vote—setting himself up for a victorious gubernatorial campaign four years later. Holton and state GOP officials were ecstatic about the result and gave Nixon the lion's share of the credit.[40]

New Jersey, however, was a different story. Like Virginia, New Jersey held its gubernatorial election in 1965, and provided Nixon with a chance to prepare for 1966. The New Jersey race also featured a Republican facing an uphill struggle in his race. In this case, Republican state senator Wayne Dumont was a moderate who was widely disliked within his own ranks due to his support for a state income tax.[41] Dumont narrowly emerged from the GOP primary, earning the right to take on the popular incumbent, Democrat Richard Hughes. However, Dumont had very little in his war chest, having used up most of his campaign funds to secure his nomination. Without much of an advertising budget, Dumont would need to rely on press coverage to get his message across to the voters, and the best way to secure that kind of attention would be to take advantage of a divisive issue in order to stir up his base.[42]

That issue dropped in his lap, thanks to a college professor from Rutgers University named Eugene Genovese. Born in Brooklyn in 1930 to a working-class Italian American family, Genovese joined the Communist Party at the age of fifteen. Five years later, he was expelled from the party for, in his words, "having zigged when [he] was supposed to zag."[43] He received his bachelor's degree from Brooklyn College before joining the military. After only serving ten months, he was discharged from the army after his previous ties to communism came to light. He then went to Columbia University where he earned his PhD in history.

Despite the fact that he was no longer a card-carrying member of the Communist Party, Genovese continued to self-identify as Marxist and Socialist.[44] On April 23, 1965, exactly two weeks after Rutgers granted him tenure,[45] Genovese spoke at a "teach-in" and made a comment about the ongoing hostilities in Vietnam that got under Nixon's skin. "Those of you who know me know that I am a Marxist and a Socialist," Genovese told the group of protesting students.[46] "Therefore, unlike most of my distinguished colleagues here this morning, I do not fear or regret the impending Viet Cong victory in Vietnam. I welcome it."

Genovese's comments generated immediate controversy and breathed life into what had been a fairly boring gubernatorial election in New Jersey.[47] Genovese maintained that he had not advocated for American soldiers to be killed, nor was he necessarily rooting against his home country. "I did not in April, nor do I now, advocate the military defeat of American forces in

Vietnam," Genovese said in September 1965.[48] "What I proposed at that time was the withdrawal of American forces which were present only in an advisory capacity, under specific conditions to insure the neutrality of the area."

Despite an avalanche of criticism toward Genovese, he had the full support of the Rutgers Board of Governors, which refused to dismiss him and even conducted an internal investigation, finding that Genovese did not let his political views influence his teaching. When an outraged constituent sent a letter to Hughes demanding the governor intercede and use his influence to get Genovese fired, Hughes responded by defending the professor's right to free speech.[49] The governor made clear that he found Genovese's views repugnant, but he found no reason to overrule the university's decision to keep Genovese on, citing academic freedom.[50]

Sensing an opening, Dumont seized upon the professor's comments as the issue he needed to jump-start his campaign. Dumont insisted on Genovese's dismissal, and even tried to get the Rutgers Board of Governors to reopen its investigation. When it refused, Dumont went public with his demand for Genovese to be fired, and even attacked the university as a whole, calling its teach-ins "part and parcel of an organized conspiracy to undermine our position in Vietnam."[51] During an October debate between the candidates, Dumont went further, arguing: "It's an abuse of academic freedom to make such irresponsible, seditious statements."[52]

Dumont would eventually lose in a landslide, but not before nearly derailing Nixon's comeback before it even started. Dumont's anti-Communist rhetoric had, seemingly, been inspired by some of Nixon's greatest hits. As such, like a bee drawn to honey, Nixon couldn't resist weighing in on the controversy. Years later, one of Nixon's intimates hypothesized that Dumont deliberately drew in the ex-VP so that he could give Dumont's words a much-needed signal boost.[53]

Nixon, for his part, was happy to oblige. On October 24, Nixon arrived in Morristown, New Jersey, for a joint appearance with Dumont and tore into Genovese with the kind of fervor that he had once reserved for people like Alger Hiss. "I do not raise the question of Professor Genovese's right to be for segregation or integration, for free love or celibacy, for Communism or anarchy, or anything else—in peacetime," Nixon said, utilizing one of his favorite rhetorical devices—attacking someone by saying that you're not going to attack.[54] "But the United States is at war. Genovese is employed by a state university, and he used the state college as a forum to, in effect, give aid and comfort to the enemy. World War II was a big war and this is a little war. If anyone had welcomed a Nazi victory during World War II there would have been no question about what to do. . . . Leadership requires that the governor step in and put the security of the nation above the security of the individual." It didn't matter to Nixon that the United States had not declared war on North Vietnam the way it had against Japan in World War II. Nor did it matter to him that the professor had been expressing his personal beliefs. Instead, Nixon, as he often did, used the facts the way he saw them to deliver a message that drew the ire of many, but also resonated with many others.[55]

To wit: later that same day, Nixon delivered a similar speech at an American Legion meeting in Flemington, New Jersey. He got a rousing ovation and had the crowd eating out of the palm of his hand as he engaged them in an extended call-and-response. "Does an individual employed by the state have the right to use his position to give aid and comfort to the enemies of the United States in wartime?"

"No! No! No!" came the response from the raucous crowd of about five hundred American Legionnaires and their families.

"The choice is simple. When it comes between American boys defending freedom of speech and Professor Genovese's rights to use that freedom, I'm for American boys every time."[56]

The audience may have cheered him on, but the people in his immediate orbit were horrified. This was no "new Nixon" or "new, new Nixon." This was the vintage, Red-baiting Nixon that had engendered so much hostility and distrust from various corners of the country. The *New York Times* even called him out on it, publishing an editorial pointing out that Nixon was up to his old tricks. "As with the moth and the flame, Richard M. Nixon on the stump is drawn, inexorably, back to the dangerous and mostly irrelevant themes that helped him to early success in California but probably cost him the Presidency," the *Times* wrote.[57] "Here is the old Nixon in action."

Many of Nixon's law partners were also upset at their public partner's outburst, and some were concerned about the effect it might have on the firm's business.[58] However, Nixon's partners had long known that this was a possibility—especially when they had allowed him to staff up in preparation for 1966 and beyond. In the end, they adhered to their policy that what was good for Nixon was good for the firm.

Garment had also been disappointed with Nixon's outburst, but he had a more pragmatic reason. In his eyes, Nixon had taken the bait so easily that Garment worried that he was dealing with a loose cannon as a potential presidential candidate. Later on, he came to realize that Nixon was simply speaking to a constituency that was different than the one Garment was used to, and that Nixon was deliberately appealing to them because he knew he would need their votes and their support to run the kind of campaign he was planning to run in 1968.[59] As Perlstein points out, Nixon's success on Wall Street may have convinced some people that he had changed his ways in order to become a member of the Establishment (the ultimate Franklin, if you will), when, in reality, Nixon hadn't changed at all.[60] The Genovese incident helped remind Garment and the others as to whom they were dealing with.

Meanwhile, Nixon, as was his wont, projected different façades to different staffers. Safire, who had been with Nixon during the New Jersey trip, recalled that, after giving his speeches on behalf of Dumont, Nixon had been in high spirits during the trip back to New York. Safire would later say that he believed Nixon was genuinely insulted by Genovese's words and that his patriotism was 100 percent authentic.[61] Safire, however, had been disappointed with his boss's relapse into "Old Nixon" territory. "Oh I know you and the rest of the intellectuals won't like it, but somebody had to take 'em on," Nixon said.[62] "Imagine a professor teaching that line to kids!"

Buchanan agreed, noting that he saw no remorse or regret from Nixon for his Genovese comments. He agreed that Nixon's comments had caused a stir at the law firm, especially with liberals, but he found that Nixon had taken it all in stride. "He seemed defiant," Buchanan said.[63]

Witcover, however, reported that Nixon did seem remorseful in that he knew he had senselessly put his comeback in danger. Regarding the Genovese incident, Nixon later told an aide that "you don't change all the colors of a horse at age fifty," and privately resolved not to be so undisciplined again.[64]

In the meantime, he'd have to do damage control. His fledgling staff at Nixon Mudge got together to strategize the best way to put the Genovese controversy behind them. Garment and Safire started the ball rolling when they drafted a response to the *New York Times* editorial for Nixon to sign. In it, Nixon argued, in a convoluted way, that "by defending the system of government that guarantees freedom of speech to individuals" he was, by extension, actually protecting academic freedom.[65] Nixon went so far as to argue that "victory for the Vietcong, which Professor Genovese 'welcomes' would mean, ultimately, the destruction of freedom of speech for all men for all time, not only in Asia but in the United States as well."[66] Nixon's staff hoped that would be enough and that the issue would recede into the background.

It was not to be. The Genovese issue reared its ugly head, once again, in June 1966 when Nixon was due to deliver the commencement address at Rochester University in upstate New York. Nixon's appearance at the university had been over one year in the making, as university president W. Allen Wallis had reached out in April 1965 to offer Nixon the spot as the commencement speaker for 1966, as well as an honorary Doctor of Laws degree. At the time, it had hardly seemed like a controversial move. Wallis even referenced Nixon's prior visit during the 1964 presidential campaign, reminding him that he had been warmly received by the vast majority of the student body.[67]

That was before Genovese. With Nixon's impending arrival on campus, many faculty members and students were aghast that Nixon was to be honored and signed a petition demanding that the university withdraw its invitation.[68] A majority of professors also passed a resolution protesting Nixon's honorary degree.[69] Ultimately, Nixon and Wallis agreed to a face-saving measure where Nixon issued a statement saying that it was his policy not to accept honorary degrees, but that he would still speak at commencement. For Nixon, the speech was more important as he saw the opportunity to put the Genovese controversy to bed, once and for all. He had decided that the theme of his commencement address would be "academic freedom," and he called on Garment, Evans, Sears, and Safire to help him write it.

"In the course of working on that speech in his 20 Broad Street office—with its ivory elephants, souvenir gavels, and gifts from potentates met on his Vice-Presidential travels—we came across an idea for a contrapuntal line, like one of those that Ted Sorensen did so well for John Kennedy," Safire recalled.[70] "It didn't quite come off, so I started to move to the next paragraph, but Nixon knew what I was after, and he hung in there—for twenty minutes we worked on a single line. I was surprised; politicians I had known would not do that." Ultimately, they decided to invoke Woodrow Wilson. "[Wilson's] distinction between men of thought and men of action can no longer be made," the line read.[71] "The man of thought who will not act is ineffective; the man of action who will not think is dangerous."

That set the tone for the entire speech. Together with Garment, Sears, and Safire, Nixon crafted an address focused on broad themes like academic freedom, national security, and law and order that barely touched on the actual individual who had inspired it all in the first place. They had good reason to do this. After all, Nixon's main argument when it came to whether or not Genovese should be fired had been that there was a difference between Genovese the tenured professor and Genovese the state employee. Despite the fact that tenure is tenure, Nixon had argued that Genovese was acting as a state employee when he made his comments in question, and as a result, he could, and should, be fired. Evans had called a number of Nixon's friends in academia to see how much support Nixon could count on for his position on Genovese. "There was none," Evans recalled.[72]

Instead, after a brief, perfunctory defense of his views on Genovese, Nixon pivoted and started talking about academic freedom in general. "Academic freedom is no 'academic question'; it is one of the most powerful forces in human history," Nixon began his speech with the kind of soaring rhetoric that he was not necessarily known for.[73] "Princes, presidents, even generals tremble in its presence. Academic freedom is a free society's greatest single advantage in its competition with totalitarian societies." He waxed poetic about the how academic freedom and the First Amendment were inextricably intertwined. He emphasized the importance for individuals to consider all sides of the argument before being able to make a truly informed decision. He also noted how every society on earth that had ever suppressed academic freedom had suffered as a result. "The American scholar stands at the height of his power," Nixon said.[74] "His prestige and influence reach into every sector of our national life."

However, in a classic "I come to bury Caesar, not praise him" moment, Nixon then turned his speech into lengthy exposition about the dangers facing the United States, making the case that freedom could only be as strong as the armies protecting it. After building up the importance of academic freedom, Nixon argued that such a vital and fundamental freedom had to be protected, at all costs, against all threats—including those from within. Teachers, he maintained, were free to take whatever positions they saw fit. However, academic freedom was not a blank check—Nixon argued that teachers had to act with self-restraint. It was okay "to be against war, to be against this war, to be against the way this war is conducted, to be against the inequities of the draft," he stated. Academics, however, did not have "the right to root for the other side," Nixon declared.[75] In fact, he argued that academic freedom was less about benefitting academia and more about benefiting society as a whole. Simply put, there was a fine line between liberty and license, and it was the responsibility of those in academia not to traverse it.

Nixon also took the opportunity to test out some themes that he would use in 1968. Harkening back to one of the major themes of his bar application essay, Nixon warned of the dangers of unchecked freedom. "If we are to defend academic freedom from encroachment we must also defend it from its own excesses," Nixon said.[76] He went further, arguing that freedom and order were mutually exclusive. "The wisdom of our people to limit freedom so as to ensure freedom has kept our nation strong and given it direction," Nixon maintained.[77]

The consequences, Nixon warned, could be dire. He understood that the Genovese affair had touched such a nerve, but he wasn't entirely sure why. After all, as he had pointed out during his earlier attack on Genovese, if a professor had spoken out in favor of the Nazis or Japanese during World War II, then no one would have complained if that professor had been fired. Perhaps it was because the Vietnam War wasn't like other wars in American history. Make no mistake about it, Nixon warned the audience and, to wit, the voters nationwide, that the conflict in Vietnam was every bit as serious and precarious as any other war the United States had ever been involved with. "To those who would welcome victory for the enemy, I would respectfully suggest that they do not know the enemy," Nixon declared.[78] "I have seen what the enemy has done to freedom in the third of the world which communism now occupies. I am convinced that victory for the enemy in South Vietnam will mean not only the blotting out of freedom for fifteen million South Vietnamese but an immense escalation of the danger of World War III."

Nixon also used the opportunity to push the narrative that he had spoken out about this issue at considerable peril to his own interests because it was the right thing to do. "I could not take what would have been the much more expedient course of refusing to comment on an issue of such importance to the freedom and security of the nation," Nixon said.[79] Nixon conveniently left out the part about how he had only weighed in because he wanted to help a Republican win an election in New Jersey.

Nevertheless, the speech seemed to have served its purpose. Genovese had been forgotten about and Nixon had cast himself as a principled patriot whose only concern was reining in excess (and who couldn't get behind that?). Plus, his words seemed to have won over the Rochester audience. According to most press reports, he received a warm reception from the Rochester students and faculty that showed up and even elicited applause for several of his points.[80] His dexterity on the issue had also bought him a reprieve from liberals—indeed, some conservatives were mad at him for going as far as he did in his defense of academic freedom. Eisenhower even sent him a letter expressing skepticism about Nixon's assertion that people in academia have "special freedom." The general was especially critical about the idea that a professor had the right to advocate communism.[81] According to Garment, Nixon rather pointedly sent copies of Ike's letter to him and Safire.[82]

While Nixon was pleased to have put Genovese in the rearview mirror, he also believed that he had found a winning issue for 1968. Sure, Dumont had lost his race, but he was always going to lose. He had been a flawed candidate who wasn't well liked by his own party taking on a popular incumbent governor. Nixon couldn't be blamed for any of that. Plus, as Nixon observed, Dumont lost his race by approximately 365,000 votes—a little less than one-third the margin Johnson won by when he carried the state the previous year. Nixon wrote to Eisenhower a few days after the Jersey race, telling his old boss that he sensed that "an increasing number of people throughout the country are beginning to resent the arrogant tactics of the so-called intellectuals who are demonstrating against our Vietnam policy."[83]

The Genovese affair had given Nixon the green light to pursue a strategy accusing Democrats of being weak on Vietnam for refusing to do whatever it took to defeat the Communist forces abroad while allowing protesters and dissidents at home to undermine the war effort. "This was not a liberal country in 1965," Buchanan maintained.[84] "The Genovese incident didn't sink him at all. In fact, it helped him with conservatives. A lot of people agreed with him." Buchanan also pointed out that many of these people who were in agreement with Nixon were fed up with antiwar activists and flocked to both the Nixon and Wallace campaigns in 1968. "You had antiwar protesters doing things like burning ROTC buildings, fighting with cops, taking over deans' offices—those people were detested," Buchanan said.[85]

The affair also proved to Nixon that he could rely on his new team to help him out when he needed them. "By hard work and concerted effort, the team managed to develop a plus—or at least a break even—from a situation that could have been a disaster," Evans said.[86] Sears, meanwhile, recalls that Nixon seemed particularly happy with his contribution to the cause—mainly the line about how "freedom and order are mutually exclusive and the wisdom of the American people to limit freedom so as to ensure freedom has kept our nation strong and given it direction."[87] As a result, Sears found that Nixon began to rely on him more often—especially when it came to political matters. "It seemed like we helped him out of a tough spot," Sears says.[88] "After that, I started getting little notes from him—at first I thought someone was kidding me for a while, but then I spoke to Rose Mary Woods and confirmed they were authentic. He had something coming up and wondered if I had any thoughts that might be helpful." That something, as it turned out, was the Congress '66 group.

"A COMING TOGETHER OF THE MAN AND THE TIMES."

Nixon's young staff also served an important purpose when it came to campaign optics and public relations. The fact that Nixon had even received the support of these young, brilliant men in the first place was a small victory. After all, the former VP had never really commanded much affection from young voters—indeed, in 1960, Kennedy had beaten Nixon decisively among voters under the age of thirty as well as voters between the ages of thirty to forty-nine (Kennedy got 54 percent of both groups).[89]

"Especially after the 1960 campaign, Kennedy was never far from Nixon's thoughts," Evans noted.[90] "Whether competent or not, according to White's account, [Nixon's 1960 staff] did not have the hard-hitting youthful *appearance* of Kennedy's team. Nixon would not make that mistake again." Chapin was more blunt in his assessment: "This game is all about youth."[91]

Starting in 1967, stories began popping up about Nixon's new-look staff of young go-getters. Robert Semple Jr. wrote a piece for the *New York Times* that was published in October 1967 titled: "Core of Nixon Advisers and Experts Is Advancing His Cause for 1968." In the story, Semple identified a group of five primary aides, most of whom were in their thirties or early forties. There were the writers, Buchanan and Price. Evans, the lawyer, was there to concentrate "almost exclusively on politics" and to serve as a key liaison between the various groups backing Nixon for the presidency. Charles McWhorter, a lawyer and former Nixon administrative assistant who had gone on to be public affairs officer at AT&T, was the oldest at forty-five—but the lifelong bachelor, Greenwich Village resident, and jazz lover was hardly a fuddy-duddy, as the *Times* pointed out. Rounding out the list was Garment, the original jazz man, whose primary job was to find and recruit intellectuals and creative thinkers for the group that he refused to refer to as a "brain trust." "'Energy bank' would be better," Garment said to the *Times*.[92]

A few months later, in January 1968, *Newsday* ran a multipage spread highlighting Nixon's Nixon Mudge–based staff with the headline: "Why Are These Men for Nixon?" It was as if the reporter couldn't quite believe it, either. The story featured a large photograph that showed several Nixon Mudge lawyers and employees lined up in military formation as if they were waiting to receive their marching orders from Nixon, their commanding officer. Dressed in the typical Wall Street uniform of a dark business suit, white dress shirt, and dark neck tie, the men were all well educated and impressively coiffed while displaying a stern determination in their faces that signaled absolute commitment to their cause.

Perhaps what was even more surprising was that the lineup included several people that would have seemed like his natural enemies. Garment, a forty-three-year-old Democrat, stood at the head of the line, just in front of Price, the Yale-educated newspaper editor. Professor Martin Anderson, a thirty-one-year-old Massachusetts-born intellectual who had been one of the youngest professors ever to receive tenure at Columbia University, was next in line, followed by Chapin, the twenty-seven-year-old advertising executive who actually had the longest history with Nixon, having served on his 1962 campaign. After Chapin stood the twenty-nine-year-old Buchanan, another newspaper editor who boasted Ivy League credentials. At the end was Evans, the thirty-seven-year-old Columbia Law grad. An additional, smaller picture in the feature showed four aides who were based in D.C.: the twenty-seven-year-old Sears; the forty-one-year-old ex-US Representative from Kansas, Robert Ellsworth; the thirty-two--year-old best-selling author Richard Whalen; and the thirty-eight-year-old financier Drew Mason.

Boasting an average age of thirty-four, with none over the age of forty-three, these ten aides formed the backbone of Nixon's 1968 staff. In time, they would be supplemented with Nixon veterans such as H. R. Haldeman, John Ehrlichman, and Herb Klein, as well as newcomers such as John Mitchell. Until then, this core group was responsible for running Nixon's shadow campaign. In the coming years, they would handle just about everything for their boss, including keeping track of his busy schedule, briefing him on important issues, providing him with research and writing support for his speeches, and laying the foundation for his 1968 presidential campaign. In some cases, they even helped him with his legal work—after all, he still had clients to work for and a law firm to help run.

At first glance, they seemed to be true believers. Nick Thimmesch, who wrote the aforementioned feature for *Newsday*, observed that Nixon's staffers maintained that their boss had been greatly misunderstood and unfairly maligned over the years. Whalen, for instance, had been dismissive of Nixon before meeting him, even publishing a negative review of Nixon's memoirs, *Six Crises*, that described it as "prissy and self-contained." "As I got to know Nixon, however, the public stereotype gave way to a much different man in private," Whalen told Thimmesch.[93] "I am impressed with his willingness to listen and give direction." Anderson, meanwhile, revealed to Thimmesch that he had gotten a lot of grief among his academic brethren for his decision to work for Nixon. "Their antagonism is based on ignorance," Anderson said.[94] "Many intellectuals make judgments without knowledge of the facts. I feel he is the right man for our time. He isn't running a popularity contest." Price was similarly effusive in his praise, telling *Newsday* that he was surprised to learn that Nixon was a "warm, sensitive human being" and that "people don't hate him anymore." "When the nation has this complex of fears, people want a competent, capable man with experience like Nixon," Price said.[95]

Garment also sang Nixon's praises to Thimmesch. Instead of providing the answer that he would use in his book—namely that he was looking for a change of pace and was drawn to Nixon because he knew it was a good opportunity for him—Garment also played the "man of destiny" card. "Nearly all of my friends are Democrats, and so are the candidates I've voted for," Garment told *Newsday*.[96] "Yet I am sold on Nixon because I know him." Garment went on, saying that he got to know Nixon as a lawyer, and was impressed by how his law partner calmly weighed different arguments and listened to various viewpoints before making an informed decision—in stark contrast to the reputation he had attained as a result of previous campaigns. "People grow," Garment said.[97] "With Nixon, it may be a coming together of the man and the times as it was with Churchill and Truman. Nixon carries himself in a presidential way, even in his private life."

Other news outlets would soon publish similar stories. The *National Observer*, a former weekly paper owned and operated by Dow Jones & Company as a companion to the *Wall Street Journal*, took its turn shortly after the *Newsday* feature came out. "The new Nixon staffers come from varying backgrounds—some are newspapermen by training, some are businessmen, a few are professors, but the men who count the most are lawyers," the *National Observer* reported.[98] "A special breed of lawyers—Wall Street lawyers. These are men who wear dark suits with a vest, black British-made shoes, men who smoke pipes and sip Scotch."

In September, less than two months before Election Day, the *New York Times* would revisit this territory. Richard Reeves's story, titled "Nixon's Men Are Smart But No Swingers," was published on September 29, 1968—one day before Nixon's Democratic opponent, Vice President Hubert Humphrey, would start his last-minute comeback in the polls. As such, Reeves found that spirits were high within the Nixon campaign as Nixon, Mitchell, Garment, and others seemed focused on posterity. In fact, Garment would give the same line about Churchill to Reeves as he gave to Thimmesch, while others pushed the narrative of this latest "new Nixon" who had finally learned from his mistakes and no longer had to micromanage every little detail because he trusted his subordinates to get him to where he needed to go. The *Times* even compared Nixon, favorably, to his blood rival, reporting that Nixon had taken a page from JFK's playbook by giving his staffers a free hand while he served as a front man and figurehead for the campaign. "I'm astonished at how he uses staff now," Finch told the *Times*.[99] "He's not obsessed now with handling every detail himself. Speech-writing, for one thing, fell apart in 1960 because he insisted on writing every word himself."

In actuality, many of these staffers had learned, the hard way, that old habits died hard and they were simply toeing the company line about Nixon being a changed man. As Election Day approached, most of the Nixon Mudge–based staffers found themselves on the outside of Nixon's tightening inner circle. Nevertheless, it was a price that they were prepared to pay as Nixon's faithful staffers fervently believed in what he represented. To them, the country was headed down the wrong path, and Nixon promised a more conservative, orderly alternative. Sure, they were also in it for their own self-interest and because they wanted to be close to a powerful figure like Nixon in the hope that it would lead to more powerful and prestigious jobs down the line in a Nixon Administration. Nevertheless, as Price noted, he and his colleagues were mainly driven by a desire to reverse America's descent into socialism and lawlessness. "They were not moths attracted to the flame of the presidency," Price said.[100] "They were mostly people of independent stature, and uniformly people of high public purpose. They saw their loyalty to Richard Nixon as an extension of their concern for the country's welfare."

Reflecting back on those days, Garment would later say that he didn't really understand what Nixon's grand strategy for winning the GOP nomination in 1968 was. Ultimately, he came to realize that Nixon's biggest fear about 1968 was getting drawn into the fray too early and taking too much fire from the press that, surely, still had it out for him. "This time, Nixon must have said to himself over and over, there must be no screwup," Garment said.[101] In that sense, it made sense why his staff would be dominated with lawyers and legal professionals. After all, lawyers are, by nature and necessity, cautious and careful. Lawyers are also trained to fix problems, and as the Genovese incident demonstrated, Nixon's law firm–based staff could perform that task.

Of course, that was just one isolated incident. Nixon didn't know if he could rely on his fledgling staff for an entire campaign. Before he would entrust them with his presidential campaign, they had to prove that they were worthy of being part of the team. The year 1966 would give them that opportunity.

NOTES

1. Tom Deignan, "Irish Mafia Takes Another Hit with Death of JFK Aide Ralph Dungan," *Irish Central*, October 17, 2013, accessed March 27, 2017, http://www.irishcentral.com/opinion/others/irish-mafia-takes-another-hit-with-death-of-jfk-aide-ralph-dungan-228158071-238258461.html.

2. Theodore White, *The Making of the President, 1960* (New York: Harper Perennial Political Classics, 2009), 155–56.

3. White, *The Making of the President*, at 62–63.

4. Nick Thimmesch, "Why Are These Men for Nixon?" *Newsday*, January 27, 1968.

5. White, *Making of the President, 1960*, 313. Also Richard Reeves, "Nixon's Men Are Smart But No Swingers," *New York Times*, September 29, 1968.

6. Reeves, "Nixon's Men Are Smart But No Swingers."

7. Leonard Garment, *Crazy Rhythm: From Brooklyn and Jazz to Nixon's White House, Watergate and Beyond* (Cambridge, MA: Da Capo Press, 1997), 104.

8. Leonard Garment, interview by Timothy Naftali, April 6, 2007, Richard Nixon Oral History Project, Richard Nixon Presidential Library and Museum.

9. John Ehrlichman, interview by Tom Evans, January 28, 1988, transcript.

10. Thomas Evans, "Nixon Mudge" (unpublished manuscript, 1994), 144.

11. Garment, *Crazy Rhythm*, 99

12. Garment, *Crazy Rhythm*, 106.

13. Matt Schudel, "Thomas W. Evans, Early Backer of Nixon in 1968, Dies at 82," *Washington Post*, June 18, 2013, accessed March 27, 2017, https://www.washingtonpost.com/local/obituaries/thomas-w-evans-early-backer-of-nixon-in-1968-dies-at-82/2013/06/18/eb159646-d82e-11e2-a9f2-42ee3912ae0e_story.html.

14. Evans, "Nixon Mudge," 147–48.

15. Garment, *Crazy Rhythm*, 106.

16. Evans, "Nixon Mudge," 148.

17. Evans, "Nixon Mudge," 149–50.

18. Evans, "Nixon Mudge," 150

19. John Sears, interview by Victor Li, February 16, 2016.

20. Garment, *Crazy Rhythm*, 106.

21. Sears interview by Li.

22. Patrick Buchanan, *The Greatest Comeback: How Richard Nixon Rose from Defeat to Create the New Majority* (New York: Crown Forum, 2014), 24.

23. Henry Allen, "The Iron Fist of Pat Buchanan," *Washington Post*, February 17, 1992, accessed March 28, 2017, https://www.washingtonpost.com/archive/lifestyle/1992/02/17/the-iron-fist-of-pat-buchanan/832ad9b5-783d-425c-a792-b5fc5bc8e70a/.

24. Buchanan, *The Greatest Comeback*, 24.

25. Buchanan, *The Greatest Comeback*.

26. Buchanan, *The Greatest Comeback*, at 26–27.

27. Buchanan, *The Greatest Comeback*, at 27.

28. Buchanan, *The Greatest Comeback*.

29. Buchanan, *The Greatest Comeback*.

30. Patrick Buchanan, interview by Victor Li, June 21, 2017.

31. Buchanan, interview by Li.

32. "Nixon vs. Khrushchev—The 1959 Kitchen Debate," *Huffington Post*, accessed March 28, 2017, http://www.huffingtonpost.com/adst/nixon-vs-khrushchev--the_b_7857916.html.

33. William Safire, interview by Timothy Naftali, March 27, 2008, Richard Nixon Oral History Project, Richard Nixon Presidential Library and Museum.

34. William Safire, "The Cold War's Hot Kitchen," *New York Times*, July 23, 2009, accessed March 28, 2017, http://www.nytimes.com/2009/07/24/opinion/24safire.html.

35. Garment, *Crazy Rhythm*, 106.

36. Rick Perlstein, *Nixonland: The Rise of a President and the Fracturing of America* (New York: Scribner, 2008).

37. Raymond Price, *With Nixon* (New York: The Viking Press, 1977), 16–17.

38. Jules Witcover, *The Resurrection of Richard Nixon* (New York: G. P. Putnam's Sons, 1970), 116.

39. Jack Hunter, "Linwood Holton's Long Quest for the Governorship of Virginia and Its Impact on the Growth of the Republican Party," *University of Richmond*, June 1972, master's thesis, accessed March 28, 2017, http://scholarship.richmond.edu/cgi/viewcontent.cgi?article=1350&context=masters-theses.

40. Hunter, "Linwood Holton's Long Quest for the Governorship."

41. Ian Fisher, "Wayne Dumont, Jr., 77, Is Dead; Was Dean of New Jersey Senate," *New York Times*, March 21, 1992, accessed March 28, 2017, http://www.nytimes.com/1992/03/21/nyregion/wayne-dumont-jr-77-is-dead-was-dean-of-new-jersey-senate.html.

42. John Wefing, *The Life and Times of Richard J. Hughes: The Politics of Civility* (New Brunswick, NJ: Rivergate Books, 2009), 123.

43. Douglas Martin, "Eugene D. Genovese, Historian of the South, Dies at 82," *New York Times*, September 30, 2012, accessed March 28, 2017, http://www.nytimes.com/2012/09/30/us/eugene-d-genovese-historian-of-south-dies-at-82.html?_r=0.

44. Genovese became more and more conservative as the years progressed. By the 1990s, he even became an outspoken supporter of one Pat Buchanan, endorsing him for the presidency.

45. Dorothy Ansart and Judith Grier, "Inventory to the Records of the Office of Public Information on the Vietnam War Teach-Ins, 1965–1966," Rutgers University, accessed March 28, 2017, http://www2.scc.rutgers.edu/ead/uarchives/teachinsb.html.

46. Ansart and Grier, "Inventory to the Records of the Office of Public Information."

47. John Kolesar, "Case History of a Political Campaign Issue," *Tuscaloosa News*, September 2, 1965.

48. Kolesar, "Case History of a Political Campaign Issue."

49. Wefing, *The Life and Times of Richard J. Hughes*, 123–24.

50. Kolesar, "Case History of a Political Campaign Issue."

51. "Marxism and Vietnam Were Issues in 1965 N.J. Gubernatorial Race," *The Observer*, September 29, 2009, accessed March 28, 2017, http://observer.com/2009/09/marxism-and-vietnam-were-issues-in-1965-n-j-gubernatorial-race/.

52. "New Jersey: The Genovese Campaign," *Time*, October 22, 1965, accessed March 28, 2017, http://content.time.com/time/magazine/article/0,9171,941391,00.html.

53. Witcover, *The Resurrection of Richard Nixon*, 117.

54. Witcover, *The Resurrection of Richard Nixon*, 117.

55. Stephen Ambrose, *Nixon: Volume 2: The Triumph of a Politician, 1962–1972* (New York: Simon and Schuster, 1989), 73.

56. Ambrose, *Nixon: Volume 2*, 73–74.

57. Ambrose, *Nixon: Volume 2*, 74. Also "Mr. Nixon in New Jersey," *New York Times*, October 27, 1965.

58. Witcover, *The Resurrection of Richard Nixon*, 118.

59. Garment, *Crazy Rhythm*, 111.

60. Perlstein, *Nixonland*, 68.

61. Ambrose, *Nixon: Volume 2*, 74.

62. Ambrose, *Nixon: Volume 2*.

63. Buchanan, *The Greatest Comeback*, 49.

64. Witcover, *The Resurrection of Richard Nixon*, 118.

65. Perlstein, *Nixonland*, 68.

66. Ambrose, *Nixon: Volume 2*, 74.

67. Richard Nixon, Letter from W. Allen Wallis, April 28, 1965, Pre-Presidential Papers, Richard Nixon Presidential Library and Museum.

68. Evans, "Nixon Mudge," 153.

69. "Nixon Degree Protest," *New York Herald Tribune*, April 15, 1966.

70. Safire, 24–25.

71. Safire.

72. Evans, "Nixon Mudge," 153.

73. Richard Nixon, "Commencement Address by Richard M. Nixon," University of Rochester, June 5, 1966, Pre-Presidential Papers, Richard Nixon Presidential Library and Museum.

74. Nixon, "Commencement Address by Richard M. Nixon."
75. Nixon, "Commencement Address by Richard M. Nixon."
76. Nixon, "Commencement Address by Richard M. Nixon."
77. Nixon, "Commencement Address by Richard M. Nixon."
78. Nixon, "Commencement Address by Richard M. Nixon."
79. Nixon, "Commencement Address by Richard M. Nixon."
80. "Academic Rights Defined by Nixon: He Backs Opposing War, but Not Rooting for Foe," *New York Times*, June 5, 1966.
81. Ambrose, *Nixon: Volume 2*, 83.
82. Garment, *Crazy Rhythm*, 111–12.
83. Ambrose, *Nixon: Volume 2*, 74.
84. Buchanan, interview by Li.
85. Buchanan, interview by Li.
86. Evans, "Nixon Mudge," 154.
87. Richard Nixon, "Four Academic Freedoms," *College and University Journal* (Summer 1966): 4–9.
88. Sears, interview by Li.
89. "Election Polls—Vote by Groups, 1960–1964," Gallup, accessed March 28, 2017, http://www.gallup.com/poll/9454/election-polls-vote-groups-19601964.aspx.
90. Tom Evans, "The Education of Richard Nixon: The Wilderness Years on Wall Street," unpublished manuscript, 130.
91. Gabriel Sherman, *The Loudest Voice in the Room: How the Brilliant, Bombastic Roger Ailes Built FOX News—and Divided a Country* (New York: Random House, 2014), 35.
92. Robert Semple Jr. "Core of Nixon Advisers and Experts Is Advancing His Cause for 1968," *New York Times*, October 23, 1967.
93. Thimmesch, "Why Are These Men for Nixon?"
94. Thimmesch, "Why Are These Men for Nixon?"
95. Thimmesch, "Why Are These Men for Nixon?"
96. Thimmesch, "Why Are These Men for Nixon?"
97. Thimmesch, "Why Are These Men for Nixon?"
98. Quoted in Evans, "Education of Richard Nixon," 132–33.
99. Reeves, "Nixon's Men Are Smart But No Swingers."
100. Price, *With Nixon*, 31.
101. Garment, *Crazy Rhythm*, 100.

Chapter Eight

"A Chronic Campaigner"

When it came to what he thought about Richard Nixon, Lyndon Johnson wasn't like most Democrats.

The lanky Texan had long had a cordial, even friendly relationship with the man many Democrats considered to be the Antichrist. When Johnson suffered a serious heart attack in 1955, Nixon had paid him, what was supposed to be, a cursory visit in his hospital room to wish him a speedy recovery. Instead, the two ended up falling into a long conversation about their lives and their futures that was not unlike Nixon's overnight train trip with Kennedy after their Pittsburgh debate eight years earlier. Johnson thought that his career might be over, but he eventually recovered to make it back to work in time for the beginning of the 1956 congressional session. After the traditional chaplain's prayer to mark the opening of the session, Johnson rose from his seat in order to be recognized by the chair, as was his prerogative as majority leader. Nixon, in his role as president of the Senate, declined to recognize Johnson immediately. Instead, he launched into an impromptu statement expressing his joy at seeing the leader back in his rightful place in the Senate chamber. "The Chair knows that he expresses the heartfelt sentiments of all the members of this body when he says that we are most happy to see the senator from Texas back in his accustomed seat," Nixon said from the presiding officer's chair.[1] A grateful Johnson responded that he was thrilled to be back before the two then exited the chamber together. Nixon threw his arm around Johnson as photographers and Johnson's fellow senators lined up for face time with the most powerful man in the Senate.

Three years later, Johnson returned the favor when Vice President Nixon arrived home from his trip abroad that had included the riot in Caracas, Venezuela. Johnson was part of the official delegation that welcomed Nixon home once his plane touched down in D.C., and the majority leader threw his arm around the VP and gave him a warm hug.[2] When Nixon was briefly hospitalized during the 1960 presidential race, it was Johnson, not Kennedy, who visited Nixon at Walter Reed Hospital.[3]

Obviously, these two men were savvy political operators, and their public displays of affection for one another served an important purpose beyond maintaining whatever friendship existed between the two. Nixon and Johnson were two men with limitless ambitions, but those ambitions were constrained, somewhat, given their high-profile partisan roles, as vice president and majority leader, respectively. Both men wanted to be president, but their jobs forced them to put their party's interests first. As such, any campaign for the White House would be problematic, given the fact that they would be lightning rods for their opposition. An across-the-aisle friendship could help blunt those inevitable attacks while allowing both men to portray themselves as unifiers.

It wasn't a surprise that Johnson and Nixon would gravitate toward one another. For one thing, the two had a lot in common. Both had come from modest means and lacked the fancy academic credentials of many of their peers in D.C. Both men were suspicious of intellectuals and wealthy Eastern Establishment types and burned with resentment over how they were treated by the well-heeled section of society. Both men were politically precocious, rising rapidly through the ranks as young men and becoming national figures. On their way up the ladder of power, they had both claimed some very high-profile scalps. Nixon, obviously, had taken down Alger Hiss en route toward becoming a rising GOP star. Johnson, meanwhile, led the effort to defeat the renomination of Leland Olds as chair of the Federal Power Commission in 1949. The liberal Olds had angered some of Johnson's friends in the oil industry by enforcing the Natural Gas Act of 1938, and Johnson saw his chance to ingratiate himself with a powerful base of wealth and power, as well as quickly move up the senatorial totem pole. According to Robert Caro, Johnson organized a smear campaign against Olds, leaking information to the press that suggested Olds was a Communist sympathizer. As chairman of the subcommittee handling Olds's renomination, Johnson lined up numerous anti-Olds witnesses and even coached some of them on what to say. By the end of the hearing, Olds barely knew what had hit him. His renomination was easily defeated, and Johnson was widely credited for being the mastermind.[4]

Another thing Nixon and Johnson had in common was that they were both blessed with the ability to accumulate power and to create power bases where none had previously existed. As majority leader, Johnson had taken what had, historically, been a weak, ceremonial, and thankless job and turned it into, arguably, the most powerful position in Washington after the president. Nixon, meanwhile, had transformed the vice presidency, with Eisenhower's blessing, from a job whose only real requirement was that its occupant not die at the same time as the president into an influential perch that handled a number of important areas relating to foreign policy, national security, and domestic affairs. Finally, both men shared a distaste for the Kennedys—Nixon for losing in 1960 and Johnson for being sidelined by the White House while serving as vice president. "I never shared the intense dislike of Richard Nixon felt by many of my fellow Democrats," Johnson wrote in his memoirs.[5]

By the time 1966 rolled around, friendship had given way to politics. Under the terms of the Twenty-Second Amendment, Johnson was eligible to run for reelection in 1968, and the president knew whom his likely opponent would be. And that suited him just fine. After all, Johnson was coming off one of the largest electoral landslides in American history, and Nixon had already lost one presidential race (as well as a subsequent gubernatorial race in 1962). With the midterms looming, however, Johnson's honeymoon was over and he was starting to lose support among antiwar liberals. He and his advisors were concerned that those liberals could abandon him in 1968, and the best way to prevent that, in their mind, was to run against the one guy guaranteed to galvanize Democratic voters and unify them in favor of four more years of LBJ. "Johnson thought Nixon was the most vulnerable man in American politics," said Johnson aide Bill Moyers.[6] Short of a rematch with Goldwater, Nixon was the one Republican Johnson wanted to run against. And like any good chess master, Johnson was going to try his best to ensure he got what he wanted.

"THE CAMPAIGN BEGINS"

First, Johnson was going to sit back and see how Nixon handled the 1966 midterm elections. These elections were vitally important to Nixon if he wanted to mount a serious bid for the presidency in 1968. During the 1964 elections, as Johnson was on his way to securing a historic landslide, Democrats running throughout the country had reaped the benefits. Republicans lost two seats in the Senate, as well as thirty-six in the House, giving Democrats a two-thirds majority in both chambers.

While those numbers didn't give the GOP much reason to be optimistic, there were some promising signs for a party that was still picking itself up off the mat after the Goldwater fiasco. For one thing, even as Republicans were getting wiped out at the polls in 1964, they were making significant inroads into the historically Democratic Solid South. Not only had Goldwater won five states south of the Mason-Dixon line, but several House districts had voted for Republicans for the first time since Reconstruction, including five districts in Alabama, and one each in Mississippi, Georgia, and South Carolina. These results heartened Nixon and convinced him that the South could be competitive in 1968—foretelling his "Southern Strategy" and providing a base for GOP presidential candidates that they continue to rely on.

Plus, Nixon believed that the Democrats were vulnerable on a host of issues. Rising deficits, racial tension, and the growing unpopularity of the Vietnam War put Democrats on the defensive, and that suited Nixon well because he was always better on the attack. Throw in the fact that, historically, the party that holds the White House loses seats in a midterm election and Nixon felt optimistic—more optimistic than he'd ever been heading into an election cycle.[7] If Republicans did well in 1966 and picked up seats in both Houses, as well as captured governors' houses in several states, Nixon would get the credit. After all, with Dewey and Eisenhower retired, Goldwater in political exile, Romney and Rockefeller running for reelection, and new star Ronald Reagan pursuing the governorship of California that had eluded Nixon in 1962, Nixon would be the only Republican traveling the country and campaigning for multiple candidates.

A strong showing in 1966 was vital for Nixon's chances in 1968. In order to have a chance at the presidency, Nixon believed he needed a substantial increase in GOP elected officials throughout the country. "I had to run five percent ahead of the ticket in 1960 if I were to win," Nixon said.[8] "I did run five percent ahead, but I still lost by that minimal amount. So I realized that in 1968 we had to close that gap some, because after 1964 the party was down to the same level it was in 1958. So we had to increase the number of governors. We had to increase the number of senators, increase the number of congressmen."

Before 1966 even started, Nixon set the tone by publicly predicting big gains for the GOP in the midterm elections. In December 1965, during an appearance on a radio show sponsored by the Republican National Committee, he claimed that voters were getting frustrated with the Johnson Administration and that "a united Republican Party can win in 1966."[9] The following month, he upped the ante, forecasting that his party would gain forty to forty-five seats in the House—a conservative estimate in his mind, but one that was bold enough to shock most in the press corps.[10] He also tried to deflect speculation that he intended to use 1966 as a springboard to another White House run by refusing to talk about 1968.

With those lofty goals, Nixon convened the first meeting of the group that would soon be known as "Congress '66." On March 20, 1966, the would-be presidential candidate sat down with ten men at a table inside the venerable Metropolitan Club in Manhattan. Located at the corner of E. 60th Street and 5th Avenue, a few blocks from Nixon's apartment, the club had been one of the several that Nixon had joined soon after becoming a Wall Street lawyer. Looking very much like something one would see in a movie, the club was perfect for rich and powerful men to gather together and talk shop while sitting in comfy chairs and drinking scotch.

On this day, however, the group retired to one of the conference rooms instead of partaking of the plush armchairs. Perhaps they wanted some privacy—after all, they were there to discuss a very important matter. "The campaign begins," Evans recalled writing in his notebook. Later on, Evans reflected that the March 20, 1966, meeting was "the first time that I heard Nixon himself speak of running again for the Presidency."[11] Garment had invited Evans to the meeting, where they were joined by several of Nixon's closest friends and confidants. Evans, by this time, was already knee deep in Nixon's political activities, so his presence at the meeting, alongside Garment, made sense. A couple of months prior to the meeting at Metropolitan, Evans had met with Tom Charles Huston and Richard Allen of Young Americans for Freedom, a national youth conservative organization, to discuss setting up youth organizations for Nixon at various college campuses throughout the country.

Maurice Stans, who served as Nixon's 1962 finance chair, was stationed at the head of the table. With his gray hair, impeccable taste in suits, and expressive eyes that could either make him look impish, serious, or sleepy, Stans was one of the best and most well-respected accountants in the country—he was inducted into the Accounting Hall of Fame in 1960, fresh off five-plus years in the Eisenhower Administration in a variety of roles, including director of the Bureau of the Budget (now known as the Office of Management and Budget).[12] In fact, he and Evans had already been working together, unofficially, on behalf of Nixon for an extended period of time leading up to the meeting. Together, they had set up the Issues Research Council, a fundraising vehicle to help Nixon pay for his expanded personal staff.[13]

Nixon friend and former campaign manager Bob Finch was also present, although his participation would be limited. Finch was running for lieutenant governor of California, giving Nixon a race to concentrate on as he looked to elect Republican candidates throughout the country.[14] Besides Garment and Evans, there were several lawyers present at the Metropolitan Club. Pat Hillings, former Nixon congressional aide and his successor in the House, was there to brainstorm alongside Chapman Rose, a partner at Jones Day who had served in the Eisenhower Administration as Undersecretary of the Treasury and Charles Rhyne, a former classmate of Nixon's at Duke Law who had served as president of the American Bar Association. Three other Nixon intimates were there to help plan their friend's comeback: Charles McWhorter; Peter Flanigan, an investment banker with Dillon, Read & Company who had worked for Nixon in 1960; and Hobart Lewis, executive editor of *Reader's Digest*.[15]

Nixon wasted little time and got right to the point. He addressed the elephant in the room and evaluated his options for 1968. The way he saw it he had three choices: decline to run, announce his candidacy immediately, or continue to deny being an active candidate while building an organization that would allow him to campaign for various Republicans around the country in 1966 that could be converted into a presidential campaign committee once the midterms were over, if he chose to run.[16]

Option number 3 was always going to be the choice, but Evans noted that those present considered all of Nixon's options in depth before, finally, coming to the obvious conclusion. The group decided to expand its operations, fundraise more intensely, beef up Nixon's research and issues staff, and come up with a few issues that Nixon could run on in 1968 (Evans notes that the group didn't get very far on this last point, speaking generally about topics including cybernetics, movability of pension benefits, and an "unemployment census").[17]

The main consensus among those present at the Metropolitan Club that day was that the organization they were building should not focus on Nixon and his prospects in 1968. Instead, as Evans noted, the group decided that it "should proceed under the guise of Nixon's 1966 campaign effort on behalf of other candidates."[18] The committee named Stans chairman, with Flanigan treasurer and Evans secretary. The first order of business would be to expand the existing Issues Research Council by adding additional researchers, as well as a political director. Lewis recommended Albert Cole, his former colleague at *Reader's Digest*, to lead the fundraising efforts for the IRC.[19]

The group made several determinations as to how they would run things in 1966. For one thing, they decided to raise funds for Congress '66 from as few people as possible—presumably saving the rest of the donor pool for 1968. Stans and Flanigan would raise $100,000 to pay for the group's expenses, with $30,000 coming from Nixon friend and client Robert Abplanalp of Precision Valve.[20]

The group also decided to try to appeal to young voters, which meant that Evans would be busy for the next couple of years setting up youth organizations at various college campuses. Most importantly, the group discussed the need to accumulate data on potential Nixon supporters while collecting intelligence on those supporting others. "Names and commitments should be entered on card files and those involved should be dealt with as carefully as possible," Evans wrote in a memo summarizing the meeting.[21]

The Congress '66 committee met regularly throughout the year, with new members coming in to supplement the core group. The group had mentioned recruiting Texas politician George H. W. Bush into Congress '66 during its initial meeting in March. Bush, however, was coming off a loss in 1964 for US Senate and had turned his attention to a seat in the US House of Representatives as 1966 rolled around. Bush would win that 1966 race with the help of a highly successful media campaign—something that would have tremendous repercussions for Nixon in 1968.

Another name on the list of potential members was John Ehrlichman. The Seattle lawyer had worked on both the 1960 and 1962 campaigns for Nixon, and he had also been with Nixon in 1964 when he made an abortive effort for the presidential nomination. Ehrlichman, however, was reluctant to come back as he had some bad memories of his experiences with Nixon and decided to sit out the 1966 elections. In fact, his involvement in the 1968 elections was in question until he sat down with Nixon and demanded assurances from his once and future boss. According to Ehrlichman, he flew to New York and had a meeting with Nixon where he expressed concern about Nixon's drinking and how it seemed to affect him and his decision making.[22] Ehrlichman had seen Nixon's "last press conference" up close and wasn't about to hitch his wagon to a candidate that was just going to implode because he didn't know when to say when. Nixon, according to Ambrose, assured Ehrlichman that he would "keep himself in the best of condition in a campaign." That was enough to sway Ehrlichman, who ultimately came aboard for 1968.[23]

Robert Merriam was another name on the list, and he, like Ehrlichman, had needed some coaxing. Merriam had been Stans's assistant in the Eisenhower Administration, and had worked on Nixon's 1960 campaign. Merriam told Nixon during a 1965 meeting in Nixon's Fifth Avenue apartment that Nixon's unwillingness to listen to advice and his tendency to do everything himself had cost him in 1960, and Merriam wasn't willing to invest time and money into a candidate if that candidate was just going to close himself off from everyone else's input once again. It took a promise from Nixon that he had changed and that he had learned from his past mistakes for Merriam to agree to join Nixon's efforts in 1966.[24]

Another Nixon veteran, H. R. Haldeman, had a standing invitation to join. The future chief of staff, however, seemed to be keeping his distance—at least until he saw how things shook out after the 1966 midterms. "Still unable to attend—but expect to be able to get to meeting after Nov.—assuming you continue," was typical of the notes he sent.[25]

Others were more willing to come aboard without any reservations. Fred Seaton joined the group within a month of its formation. Ralph Cake, a prominent GOP official from Oregon who had served in the Republican National Committee, came aboard in May 1966, the same month that John Davis Lodge, the diplomat who had advised Nixon during the Trujillo heirs matter, joined.[26] Additionally, Nixon staffers Safire and Buchanan became fixtures at meetings, as did Pepsi's Donald Kendall.

Congress '66 meetings tended to focus on logistics and organizational strategy. During May 22, 1966, for instance, Stans spoke about reimbursable expenses while Safire, Cake, and Flanigan discussed setting up different mailing lists so that recipients could receive articles and statements from the campaign that could, in turn, be used to persuade and influence delegates.

Flanigan proposed one list for political figures, one for "opinion-makers" such as educators and newspaper editors, and finally, one for the "business elite."[27] Given that there were many lawyers involved, sometimes the meetings would cover legal issues, such as when was the most advantageous date for the group to, officially, file as a political committee and whether or not it was legal for corporations like Kendall's Pepsi to donate a private plane for Nixon's political staff to use at their discretion (ultimately, Nixon's friend, Bill Lear, an aviation and electronics pioneer who manufactured the Lear Jet, loaned one to Nixon).[28]

The jet issue underscored another ongoing topic of regular conversation at the Congress '66 meetings. The group had tried to get the Republican National Committee to pay for (or at least to reimburse) Nixon and his staffers to travel around the country to campaign for various Republican candidates. Ray Bliss, the RNC chair, however, refused to do so, citing a need to appear unbiased and impartial. Like many other Republican Party officials, Bliss easily guessed at Nixon's 1968 intentions and knew that 1966 was the dress rehearsal. Not wanting to appear to favor Nixon over any of the other prospective candidates, such as Romney or Rockefeller, Bliss regularly shot down requests from the Congress '66 group for help. During a May 11, 1966, meeting, for instance, Stans reported that he had met with Bliss and the RNC chair was okay with Nixon's friends and backers paying for his staffers to conduct research and perform administrative work, but he flatly refused to devote RNC resources to help Nixon procure his own plane.[29]

The group also set up an organizational structure that would serve as a minitemplate for the 1968 campaign. There would be a "detail man" whose job it would be to plan the itinerary. As the name implied, no detail would be too small, and Hillings made sure to mention that the "detail man" would even need to plan out when to get Nixon's suits pressed. For someone who had always been a little too hands on in previous campaigns, the group hoped to take a mind-numbing and logistics-heavy job away from Nixon, allowing him to focus on more important matters, as well as to relax and unwind between appearances. For this job, Hillings had one name in mind: John Davies, an old Nixon friend from California and telephone company executive. Davies joined the cause and would, eventually, be rewarded with a White House job where his meticulous nature was put to good use. Among the things he did was establish the White House Visitors Office.[30]

The next link in the chain was the advance man. A typical advance man arrives in a city a day or two before the rest of the campaign and makes sure the candidate's visit will go smoothly. For Nixon, that meant setting up meetings with local officials, as well as important people in the private sector. The advance man was also expected to brief Nixon as to the new faces in a particular city that he might not recognize, as well as to refresh his memory as to how he met or knew the faces that weren't new but not familiar either. Hillings stressed the importance of this position and noted that, because they didn't yet have one, simple but important tasks like calling local officials to see if they wanted to meet with Nixon when he was in town weren't being done.[31]

The group had several names in mind for the advance position, including Ehrlichman and John Whitaker. However, Ehrlichman was already ambivalent about signing up for another spin on the Nixon carousel, and Whitaker was being considered for the next link on the chain—the scheduler.[32] That left Nicholas Ruwe, a GOP operative who had worked on Nixon's 1960 campaign and had been an advance man in the past, particularly in 1964 when he helped coordinate logistics for Nixon's grueling national tour campaigning on behalf of Goldwater. Ruwe was well versed in political campaigns; in between his stints working for Nixon, he had worked on a pair of congressional campaigns in Texas in 1961, helping John Tower win Lyndon Johnson's former Senate seat while seeing John Goode lose in a squeaker in a race for House of Representatives. Ruwe also served on Charles Percy's unsuccessful campaign for governor of Illinois in 1964, two years before Percy would be elected to the Senate.[33]

As mentioned earlier, Whitaker was being considered for the next link on the chain: scheduling appointments and speaking engagements for Nixon. The group made a note that Nixon should ask Whitaker, personally, since the job would probably require him to "rearrange his personal life significantly" and "only a call from [Nixon] would seem appropriate."[34] Whitaker ultimately was able to take the job part time for the 1966 elections, quitting his job and becoming the full-time scheduler when Nixon announced his presidential run in 1968.[35]

Finally, the group wanted follow-up men who would stick around after Nixon left town to meet with local officials and others to listen to their concerns, ask about their requests, and do what they can to solidify their support for Nixon. The group decided that these follow-up men should be people of stature and importance and listed John Davis Lodge, Maurice Stans, Ralph Cake, Pat Hillings, or Charles McWhorter as examples of people that should be used for the task.[36]

Congress '66 meetings touched on other important issues that would come into play during the 1968 campaign. Several members of the group, in particular Kendall, were concerned about Nixon's image. Kendall argued during the May 22, 1968, meeting that the campaign would need a "concrete program" to "restructure" Nixon's entire persona.[37] The group members came up with several options. Seaton, the former newspaper man, pointed to several stories that had painted Nixon as being more relaxed ever since moving to New York and suggested playing up that image.[38] Lodge, the diplomat, proposed that Nixon burnish his foreign policy credentials and make a high-profile trip to Israel. Safire and others, however, shot this down as an obvious political ploy that would get called out by the press. Instead, Safire's idea was for Nixon to focus on Asia and prepare a position paper or article dealing with Red China.[39]

As for the man in question, Nixon rarely sat through the Congress '66 meetings. For one thing, he had his law practice to attend to, including a very important Supreme Court oral argument to prepare for. Instead, he would usually drop in for a few minutes—usually at the end of the meeting—to offer his input and to pump up the troops. "You're natural conspirators," Safire recalled Nixon telling the group with a wink after one meeting, to the great satisfaction of his men.[40]

Nixon did have time, however, to weigh in on political issues—especially to provide predictions and electoral forecasts. For instance, Nixon posited that Johnson was in a no-win situation when it came to the midterm elections and the economy. He figured Johnson could take some short-term measures to boost the economy and give his party an advantage as voters headed to the polls in November 1966. By doing this, however, Johnson then ran the risk that his temporary stimulus could wear off by the time the election got underway in 1968, plunging the country into recession and dooming his reelection bid. Nixon even foreshadowed the possibility of an "October Surprise," noting that Johnson, as commander in chief, could easily manipulate the war situation to try to engineer a favorable turn of events in order to secure his reelection.[41]

PICKING BATTLES

Nixon hit the campaign trail with the energy of a robot. He had long had a reputation as a tireless campaigner, and his opponents had always envied him for that.[42] During the last week of June 1966, for instance, he made appearances in Chicago, as well as Detroit, Flint, and Bay City, Michigan, before heading for the East Coast for stops in Roanoke, Virginia, and Washington, D.C. In July, he headed on one his usual foreign trips designed to enhance his stature, as well as open doors for his law firm clients. During that month alone, he went to Europe and Asia, stopping over in Dublin, London, Paris, Tel Aviv, Karachi, Bangkok, Saigon, Manila, Hong Kong, Tokyo, and Seoul.[43] In Saigon, for instance, he undertook a heavily publicized fact-finding mission about the ongoing war that turned into a partisan political attack. After performing his patented rhetorical trick where he claimed he wasn't going to attack Democrats or Johnson over Vietnam, Nixon then did the exact thing he promised he wouldn't do: blaming Democrats for the worsening morass in Vietnam and accusing them of lacking the will to win. Nixon claimed that Americans needed "unity of purpose" if they wished to snatch victory from the jaws of defeat. The only way to do that, he argued, was to elect Republicans in the midterm elections.[44]

Nixon was hoping to triangulate his position on Vietnam when he ran in 1968. Obviously, he was sensitive to the notion that governments, during wartime, shouldn't be criticized, so he tried to couch his attack on the Johnson Administration's war policy as simply advocating a more hawkish position. He called for a substantial increase in troop levels, from less than three hundred thousand to over five hundred thousand. He also called for more frequent bombing attacks of North Vietnam. The *New York Times*, however, called him out for his actions, pointing out that he was doing exactly what he had said he wouldn't: criticize the Johnson Administration. "A commitment to endless escalation in pursuit of military victory on the Asian mainland would be a commitment to disaster," the *Times* editors wrote.[45]

Despite that commitment to total victory, when it came to the 1966 campaign, Nixon decided to pick his battles. He decided to focus on races in districts that had, historically, been Republican but had been swept up in the Democratic tidal wave in 1964. Most of these seats were always going to swing back, but Nixon wanted to make sure he was seen as the reason why these districts came home to the GOP.[46]

During the course of the year, Nixon ended up campaigning for 105 candidates in thirty-five states. One of those candidates was a young Republican from Michigan named Donald Riegle Jr. Riegle was studying for a doctorate in business and government relations from Harvard Business School. Toward the end of 1965, he and several other members of Harvard's Young Republicans Club were invited to a reception sponsored by Nixon Mudge. A month later, Riegle and several other students joined Nixon, Evans, and some others at his apartment for dinner, cigars, and brandy. Riegle told Nixon that he was being courted to run for the US House of Representatives but that he and, in particular, his wife, were undecided about it. Nixon's ears perked up and told Riegle that he couldn't turn down the opportunity to run for Congress. He even demanded to speak with Riegle's wife, who was living in Michigan, over the phone. After rousing her from her sleep, Nixon gave her the hard sell, telling her that if they didn't pursue this opportunity, then they would regret it for the rest of their lives. No matter what they did in life, be it academics or business, they would always wonder what might have been, Nixon argued. Much like he did for John Milem, the young lawyer who was torn between going home to the Pacific Northwest or working on Wall Street, Nixon turned on the charm and applied the pressure.[47]

"He encouraged me to run and said he would come out to campaign for me in Flint, and that he might also be able to introduce me to President Eisenhower," Riegle recalled.[48]

Nixon got his way, and Riegle returned to his Flint, Michigan, home district to run for Congress against Democratic incumbent John Mackie. Nixon rewarded Riegle by appearing at a fundraising breakfast on his behalf early in the campaign. By appearing so early in the campaign season, Nixon risked breaking a personal rule not to interfere with a contested Republican primary. The then-unknown Riegle would, eventually, draw a primary challenge, albeit one that he would easily beat back (Riegle won over two-thirds of the vote in the April primary).[49]

When Nixon returned to Flint in the summer of 1966, Riegle was front and center as Nixon talked him up to reporters and predicted that he would win. In fact, Michigan epitomized Nixon's 1966 strategy. Johnson had won the state handily in 1964, picking up 67 percent of the vote. His coattails had helped elect five freshman Democrats to the House. All five had picked up previously Republican-held seats—three had even knocked off long-time Republican incumbents. However, they had all run behind Johnson and, in some cases, had won close races. "The Five Fluke Freshman," as they were later dubbed, seemed ripe for defeat, and Nixon campaigned hard in Michigan on behalf of Riegle and his fellow GOP candidates. Ultimately, those efforts paid off as all five of the "fluke freshman" were beaten by Republicans—including Riegle, who won his race by a 54 to 46 percent margin.[50] Riegle would eventually carve out a long career in Washington, including an eighteen-year career in the Senate; however, things would turn out much differently than either he or Nixon had originally intended. In 1973, the Michigan man jumped to the Democratic Party after several policy disagreements with the Nixon Administration.[51]

Nixon's Michigan success also underlined another part of his strategy: looking the part as the one Republican candidate capable of winning in 1968. By coming to Michigan, which was George Romney's turf, Nixon burnished his credentials as a party unifier while picking up valuable IOUs in an important state that would, otherwise, be closed off to him in 1968—assuming Romney ran for president (and most people saw that as a fait accompli). Indeed, the media seemed to delight in pitting Romney against Nixon and peppered the latter with questions about a potential 1968 contest against the popular governor. "The obsession of the moment about the two names you mentioned is somewhat naïve," Nixon responded to one reporter in Michigan who asked whether he would run against Romney in 1968 for the presidential nomination. Nixon then followed up by sticking with the script and downplaying his 1968 chances, saying: "The 1966 election will furnish the stable [of candidates in 1968]."

Another state that Nixon believed had been an anomaly in 1964 was Oklahoma. The state had been a reliable Democratic state during the FDR era but had swung over to the GOP in 1952 and 1956 when Eisenhower ran. Four years later, Nixon won the state handily, taking nearly 60 percent of the vote.

The state swung back to the Democrats in 1964, as Goldwater lost the state to Johnson by a 56 to 44 percent margin. Meanwhile, Republicans had captured the governor's mansion in 1962 with Henry Bellmon becoming the state's first Republican governor since 1907. Bellmon, who would go on to serve as national chairman of Nixon's 1968 campaign, was stepping down, and Nixon came to Oklahoma to campaign for Bellmon's would-be successor, Dewey Bartlett.

Once again, Nixon had chosen his spot wisely. Bartlett would end up winning his race easily, garnering nearly 56 percent of the vote. Nixon was also heartened by the hero's welcome he received among state Republicans when he arrived in Tulsa. They all seemed to know that this was just a dress rehearsal for 1968, and many Oklahoma Republicans made it clear that they were on board. "Tulsa has been, is and will be again a Nixon city," Tulsa County GOP chairman Bert McElroy said during a $25-a-plate fundraiser that Nixon attended.[52] "This is the kind of man we should have at the helm," US Representative Page Belcher said while introducing Nixon at the fundraiser.[53] "America faces a storm and I only regret we don't have this man at the helm." Witcover reported that, after Belcher finished his introduction, the crowd of 850 rose and gave Nixon a long, thunderous ovation—the kind usually reserved for the moment an actual, declared candidate clinches the presidential nomination.[54] During the obligatory handshake line after the speeches ended, several attendees told him "you must run," to which Nixon simply smiled in response.[55]

Nixon also took the opportunity to set the stage for what would become the Southern Strategy. Multiple journalists observed that Nixon had campaigned in all eleven of the original Confederate states and seemed to be creating a base of power in the South. "The South provides a base of more than adequate dimensions for a serious bid," observed *New York Times* reporter David Broder.[56]

The reporters following Nixon on the campaign trail emphasized that he, unlike Goldwater, expressed his support for the 1964 Civil Rights Act and the 1965 Voting Rights Act. He also condemned segregation, in general, telling southern audiences: "I am opposed to any segregation plank in a Republican platform. I would fight it in the national Republican platform and speak against it in any state I appear in."[57]

Despite his open support of civil rights, Nixon threw in enough qualifiers (or, some would say, "dog whistles") such as endorsements of "states rights" and criticisms of federal overreach to satisfy all but the most die-hard segregationists. Mostly, southern Republicans felt like they could take Nixon seriously but not literally—trusting him that he was only saying he was pro–civil rights because he had to. "[Romney] really means it," one Atlanta Republican told Witcover.[58] "Dick Nixon comes down South and talks hard on civil rights, but you know he *has* to say what he does, for the Northern press."

Plus, as Ambrose observed, Nixon surrounded himself with young, bona fide conservatives like Buchanan who knew how to connect with, and inspire trust from, southerners.

Buchanan and Nixon had coordinated a strategy of publicly repudiating race-baiting, segregationist politicians like George Wallace of Alabama, George Mahoney of Maryland, and Lester Maddox of Georgia, all Democrats, and tying the national Democratic Party to these longtime Dixiecrats (Wallace would run as an independent in 1968 for president). "I have yet to find a Republican candidate anywhere who is campaigning on the white backlash," Nixon said to Broder, during a campaign stop in California.[59] "It's time for the national Democratic leadership and the Johnson administration to make it clear whether it is going into the South as the party of Maddox, Mahoney and Wallace."

Instead, Nixon spent most of his time appealing to southern conservatives' sense of patriotism and desire for law and order. In particular, his calls for total victory in Vietnam resonated with southern conservatives.[60] For instance, during a $50-per-plate fundraiser in Birmingham, Alabama, Nixon got, arguably, an even more rousing ovation than he did in Tulsa. Witcover compared the treatment Nixon received from the Alabama faithful to the hero's reception Goldwater got at the 1964 GOP National Convention in San Francisco.[61] "These Democrats who want peace at any price; let's call them the appeasement Democrats for lack of a better term," Nixon said to rapturous applause.[62] "If you have conservative friends who are looking where to go, tell them to come to the Republican Party because the Republican Party is the party of conservatives. The Democrat Party on the national level hasn't been conservative for thirty years and never will be, so get out of it and join the Republican Party!"

Of course, race played a part in Nixon's Southern Strategy. The Republican Party was, clearly, trying to appeal to disaffected white voters throughout the South. Taking their cues from Nixon, they just weren't going to be blatant about it. "From now on, the Republicans are never going to get more than 10 to 20 percent of the Negro vote and they don't need any more than that . . . but Republicans would be shortsighted if they weakened enforcement of the Voting Rights Act," said Kevin Phillips, Nixon's political strategist in 1968.[63] "The more Negroes who register as Democrats in the South, the sooner the Negrophobe whites will quit the Democrats and become Republicans. That's where the votes are. Without that prodding from the blacks, the whites will backslide into their old comfortable arrangement with the local Democrats."

"IT'S OVER THE WALL WE GO!"

For many of his newer aides, especially the ones based at Nixon Mudge, the 1966 campaign was their first real opportunity to get to know Nixon on a deeper level. What many of them discovered was that Nixon was a profoundly complicated and contradictory man who was every bit as brilliant as he was self-destructive. Capable of great warmth one moment and cold indifference the next, Nixon revealed the cynical side of politics to many of his inexperienced charges.

"Whatever I say in here, don't you believe a word of it," Nixon told Sears as they entered a Mormon Cathedral in Salt Lake City.[64] "I can say things that if someone else said them, they would be lies, but when I say them, nobody believes them, anyway." Nixon's liberal definition of the truth and the ease with which he deployed it on the campaign trail also led him to make the following assessment about Garment: "You'll never make it in politics, Len. You just don't know how to lie."[65]

On the other hand, Sears maintained that Nixon seemed to care about what others thought of him—especially his staffers. "He was always worried that I'd think he was doing something stupid or that I'd have a different view of his actions," Sears said.[66] That sense of worry carried over to other parts, according to Sears. At one point, during the 1968 campaign, Nixon was looking over some ads shot by the TV advertising group. "God, I hope the Russians don't see any of that; they'll think I'm an idiot," Nixon said.[67]

Garment noted that it was during his travels with Nixon in 1966 that he first began to see what Nixon might do if he were to become president. During a trip to Miami where Nixon would speak to his fellow directors at Investors Diversified Services, the two men joined Elmer Bobst at his mansion for drinks. As Nixon and Garment were being whisked to their evening quarters inside a brand new real estate development in Miami, Nixon suddenly had a change of heart. Always worried that his face and image might be used for publicity purposes without his consent, Nixon sensed he was being set up by the developers. Instead, Nixon and Garment went back to Bobst's mansion, only to find that the gates were locked. The two men stared at a high wall that surrounded the Bobst compound before Nixon proposed the only logical solution for two middle-aged men. "Come on Garment, it's over the wall we go!"[68]

The two men eventually made it inside and crashed in Bobst's pool house. As with some other, similar moments in Nixon's history, the two men talked for most of the evening, and Nixon laid bare his overriding desire to be president. "He told me his consuming interest was foreign policy," Garment recalled.[69] "He talked about world affairs at length and said he felt his life had to be dedicated to great foreign policy purposes." With that, Garment finally realized why Nixon seemed so insistent on remaining in politics, even though he seemed so ill suited for it and even though it had caused him such heartbreak in the past. Money, status, and even his accomplishments as a lawyer would never be enough for him. He would do anything to be president—if for no other reason than to set America's foreign policy. "Anything except see a shrink," Nixon said.[70]

Garment recalled that, the following morning, he and Bobst spoke at length about Nixon's presidential ambitions. Bobst was convinced that, based on his discussions with his longtime friend, Nixon would open up Mainland China to the West, and despite his public statements to the contrary, he would withdraw from Vietnam.

Garment also found that his newfound intimacy with Nixon proved to be short-lived. On the flight home, Garment on was the aisle seat, eating and reading a book while Nixon sat inside, furiously scribbling away on his yellow pad. The two men barely exchanged a word. "There were no questions, no more summer-camp confessions," said Garment.[71]

"JESUS, DID HE HIT US!"

One thing that his aides noted about Nixon during the 1966 campaign swing was that he seemed to be, genuinely, having a good time. At home on the campaign stump in a way he would never be on Wall Street or in a courtroom, Nixon relished being back in the spotlight and seemed energized by his new, young staff.

For instance, he loved having Safire or Buchanan come up with attack lines for him to use on stage. "Any Republican who believes LBJ is a conservative would believe Richard Burton married Elizabeth Taylor for her money," was one of Nixon's favorites. Another one was: "Johnson's War on Poverty has become the War on Prosperity." Nixon had some of his own jokes, too. For instance, he dusted off his old standby about being a dropout from the Electoral College ("I failed debate," he often added). He also had a line about how Democrats had given Republicans so many issues to run on that he felt like a "mosquito in a nudist camp."[72]

When he got down to the meat-and-potatoes portion of his stump speech, he usually spent most of his time attacking President Johnson. This was a concerted strategy on Nixon's part. During the early fall of 1966, Nixon had convened a meeting in New York of GOP heavyweights including Eisenhower and Dewey, and suggested that Republican candidates throughout the country run against Johnson rather than their named opponents. Nixon's speechwriters even came up with some biting, albeit wordy attack lines that candidates could use. One of them went: "All the way with LBJ means a five-year war in Asia, a spiraling increase in the cost of living, crime growing six times as fast as the population." "It is time to call a truce in Johnson's War against Poverty and to declare war on Johnson's inflation," was another.

It was a sound strategy, considering Johnson's declining approval ratings,[73] as well as the fact that he seemed vulnerable on a host of issues, both foreign and domestic.[74] Nixon had another, more selfish reason for poking the bear. Nixon was hoping to elevate himself beyond the GOP field and make himself into Johnson's equal, albeit from the other side of the aisle.[75] The best way to accomplish this would be to have Johnson address Nixon directly, as if Nixon were the leader of the opposition, and worthy of such respect and recognition. "Nixon was known too much for being on the attack, so it was important that Johnson hit him first," Sears said.[76]

Nixon finally got what he was looking for in October 1966. With less than a month before the election, Johnson flew to Manila to meet with South Vietnamese officials and other US allies. Sensing an "October Surprise," Nixon publicly called out Johnson, wondering whether the president was embarking on a "quest for peace or a quest for votes."[77]

On October 25, 1966, Johnson issued a joint communiqué with the prime ministers of Australia, New Zealand, Thailand, South Korea, the Philippines, and South Vietnam emphasizing their commitment to victory in Vietnam, as well as the preservation of a free and independent South Vietnam. South Vietnam, for its part, reaffirmed its commitment to democratic reforms, as well as programs to modernize its economy. "The Government of the Republic of Vietnam declares that the Vietnamese people, having suffered the ravages of war for more than two decades, were second to none in their desire for peace," the communiqué stated.[78] "It welcomes any initiative that will lead to an end to hostilities, preserve the independence of South Vietnam and protect the right to choose their own way of life."

However, the communiqué also contained a couple of provisions that caught Nixon's eye. In the case that North Vietnam decided to cease hostilities and withdraw back behind its border, then the signatories all committed to withdrawing their troops from Vietnam within six months. The communiqué also committed its signatories to limited warfare that was proportional to whatever aggressive actions the Communist forces undertook.[79]

To Nixon, these provisions proved that the Johnson Administration lacked the wherewithal to do whatever was necessary to win the war in Vietnam. Even though he had privately told aides that he didn't think the United States could win the war militarily,[80] for political reasons, he publicly clung to the notion that, of course, the US armed forces could win if only the White House weren't holding them back. The communiqué gave him all the ammunition he needed to call Johnson out for being a defeatist. He tasked Buchanan and Safire with writing up a critique of the Manila communiqué that could be printed in newspapers throughout the country.

Thinking that it would get more attention from the press, Safire proposed that they write Nixon's critique in the form of a letter to the president. Nixon and Buchanan, however, refused after finding such an approach to be too gimmicky. Instead, Safire and Buchanan met up at the Nixon Mudge office to draft a more formal statement that threatened to run longer than the actual communiqué it was critiquing. "There was excitement in the 20 Broad Street office, secretaries Rose Woods, Shelley Scarney and Ann Volz were typing portions of the manuscript, and I was going from one to another with changes, and Buchanan was telling the reporters who came up to the law offices early that we would be ready in plenty of time," Safire recalled.[81]

Among the arguments they made were that the withdrawal offer, as well as the six-month deadline, essentially gave the North Vietnamese a blueprint for conquering the South. All they had to do was pretend to withdraw and then wait six months before marching into an unprotected Saigon. "President Johnson states clearly that if North Vietnam withdraws its forces back across its border and the violence, thus, subsides, we shall withdraw all American forces out of Vietnam, most of them ten thousand miles back to the United States," Nixon's statement read.[82] "The effect of this mutual withdrawal would be to leave the fate of South Vietnam to the Vietcong and the South Vietnamese Army." The statement also addressed Johnson's commitment to limited war, accusing the White House of "surrendering a decisive military advantage" and allowing the Communist forces to dictate the nature and intensity of the war. "I know of no successful military effort that ever keyed its own intensity simply to match that of the aggressor—thus deliberately surrendering to the aggressors the initiative for major offenses," Nixon's statement said.[83] Finally, the statement ended with a personal touch, as Nixon claimed that "in my travels across the country in recent months, I have encountered an odd sense of helplessness on the part of many thoughtful Americans in the field of foreign policy" and that part of the problem was "a confusion of goals and a lack of answers to legitimate questions." He concluded the statement with a fairly innocuous call for the president to sit down with leaders of both parties to propose a "clear, practical, bi-partisan foreign policy that will end the war and provide the basis for a lasting peace."[84]

The statement was released on November 3, 1966, five days before Election Day. Safire had some connections at the *New York Times*—one of the editors, Harrison Salisbury, had been a reporter covering Nixon's visit to Moscow during the infamous "Kitchen Debate." According to Safire, after he steered Nixon and Khrushchev over to the model kitchen where they would have their argument, he grabbed Salisbury so that the reporter could write about it. Seven years later, Safire called on Salisbury again, this time to request that the *Times* run Nixon's entire statement, verbatim. Salisbury agreed, to Safire's surprise. "Now, was [Salisbury] doing me a favor to return the favor for letting him in the kitchen," Safire wondered.[85] "Who knows, but at any rate, he not only did a story on it, but he ran the text."

Running the entire statement verbatim was something that was usually reserved for presidential addresses.[86] The following day, the *New York Times* printed Nixon's entire statement, and published a front-page story summarizing Nixon's arguments against the Manila communiqué. The fact that the *Times* had given Nixon such treatment was a pretty big deal. "It is rare for the full text of anything, including presidential speeches, to run in the *New York Times*," Garment said.[87] "When the paper does run a full statement, particularly by a private person, the message to political professionals is 'This is very important.'"

The statement worked like a charm. Whether it was Nixon's relentless attacks throughout the campaign season, the content of Nixon's critique of the Manila communiqué, or the fact that the *New York Times* was covering Nixon as if he were shadow president, Johnson had decided that enough was enough. "Don't they know it's all a lot of politics?" he raged to aide Bill Moyers, apoplectic that the *Times* had been taken in by Nixon's ploy.[88] Much like when Nixon blew up at the gaggle of reporters on hand at the Beverly Hilton, Johnson was in a foul mood and spoiling for a fight when he stepped to the podium inside the East Room of the White House. He was also in physical pain, as his doctors had recommended that he have some minor surgery to remove a throat polyp and fix a hernia[89] —moves that would prevent him from engaging in any last-minute campaigning during the 1966 election.

After a single, solitary reference to Nixon as a "chronic campaigner" early on in the half-hour-plus press conference, Johnson didn't mention Nixon again until close to the end. When a reporter finally asked Johnson to respond to Nixon's critique of the Manila communiqué, the president did so with relish, launching into an extended soliloquy about his would-be replacement.

"I do not want to get into a debate on a foreign policy meeting in Manila with a chronic campaigner like Mr. Nixon," Johnson said contemptuously while the reporters in the room laughed.[90] "It is his problem to find fault with his country and with his government during a period of October every two years. If you will look back over his record, you will find that to be true." Johnson continued to deride Nixon while bringing up his various electoral failures over the years, including 1960, when Eisenhower had flippantly responded to a question from a reporter about what major decisions Nixon had helped him make by saying: "If you give me a week, I might think of one."[91] "Since then, he has made a temporary stand in California, and you saw what action the people took out there," Johnson said, utilizing the slow, solemn style of speaking that he had adopted ever since assuming the presidency.[92] "Then he crossed the country to New York. Then he went back to

San Francisco, hoping that he would be in the wings if Goldwater stumbled. But Goldwater didn't stumble. Now he is out talking about a conference that, obviously, he is not well-prepared on or informed about."

Johnson's "presidential voice" began to falter as he engaged in a spirited defense of the Manila communiqué. Speaking louder and faster, as well as throwing out sarcastic barbs, Johnson sounded aggrieved and bemoaned what he saw as the politicization of the Vietnam War. "Why would we want to stay there if there was no aggression, if there was no infiltration and the violence ceased?" he asked rhetorically.[93] "We wouldn't want to stay there as tourists." Johnson lashed out against Nixon and other "politicians" who got mixed up in the process and muddied the waters. "When the aggression, infiltration and violence ceases, not a nation there wants to keep occupying troops in South Vietnam," Johnson said.[94] "Mr. Nixon doesn't serve his country well by trying to leave that kind of impression in the hope that he can pick up a precinct or two, or a ward or two."

Those in attendance were shocked by Johnson's performance. Lady Bird Johnson shook her head disapprovingly while frantically trying to catch her husband's eye in order to tell to stop.[95] Johnson's aides were also surprised. Jack Valenti, Johnson's longtime assistant, later told Safire that he didn't know what had gotten into his boss and that he had never seen him like that in public.[96] "It was so obvious that Nixon had gotten his goat and that he was just playing into Nixon's hands," he said.

The assembled press were also stunned by what they had witnessed. "It was, in the memory of veteran reporters, the most brutal verbal bludgeoning ever administered from the White House by Johnson, or any other President, for that matter, to a leader of the opposition party," Witcover reported.[97] Witcover argued that Johnson's attack, effectively, elevated Nixon to *the* leader of the opposition—all the more impressive considering Nixon was a private citizen. "Intentionally or not, the President's words immediately swung the national spotlight on Nixon at a time he was climaxing one of the greatest personal efforts in behalf of other candidates ever launched by a political leader not, himself, running for public office," Witcover said.[98]

Interestingly, Witcover left open the possibility that Johnson could have done this intentionally. After all, Johnson was as savvy a political operator as there was in D.C., and he must have known what the consequences of his actions would be. Moyers later claimed that the "chronic campaigner" bit had been planned and that Johnson was trying to ensure that his 1968 reelection campaign would be opposite the former vice president. Another Johnson aide, Joseph Califano, confirmed that the hit had been premeditated. "When Johnson thought he was going to run, he thought he would run against Richard Nixon, which is why he deliberately and calculatingly attacked him at the press conference as being very political," Califano recalled.[99] "He thought Nixon would run and we thought Nixon would be the easiest candidate to beat." Safire later wrote that Johnson's attack was actually a savvy move. "The growing dovecote in the Democratic Party might defect to a Rockefeller or a Romney, or throw away its vote to a splinter party or stay home, but Nixon—characterized as that 'chronic campaigner,' remembered as a Herblock cartoon—could frighten them back into LBJ's arms," Safire said.[100]

It didn't matter to Nixon what Johnson's intentions were. After Buchanan gleefully called Nixon to tell him that Johnson "hit us . . . Jesus did he hit us,"[101] Nixon implemented the next phase of his plan. Provoking an attack from an opponent and then playing the wounded party card for sympathy points had long been one of Nixon's favorite maneuvers, and he used it, one more time, to twist the dagger into President Johnson some more. "I was shocked that President Johnson saw fit to respond to the serious questions which I related about American policy in Asia with a personal assault upon me," Nixon said from New Hampshire.[102] "But the President's temper or the fact that I was its target is not the issue. The issue is larger than either Lyndon Johnson or Richard Nixon."

He had his stature, now, as the de facto leader of the Republican Party and the head of the loyal opposition. When Election Day came about, his stature only increased as positive results for the GOP came pouring in. Republicans won forty-seven seats in the House, three Senate seats, eight governorships, and 540 state legislative seats. Those numbers were fairly consistent with Nixon's predictions (forty House seats, three Senate seats, six governorships, and seven hundred state legislative seats). The party made significant inroads in Dixie as Republicans won eight House seats, one Senate seat, and two governorships in states south of the Mason-Dixon Line (including Maryland, where a man by the name of Spiro Agnew won the governor's mansion).[103] When the *New York Times* calculated Nixon's success rate in terms of how many of the candidates he campaigned for actually won their races, the paper found that Nixon had batted a remarkable .686 (Nixon campaigned for eighty-six candidates and fifty-nine won). In contrast, Robert Kennedy, who was another figure that loomed large in 1968, had only hit .391.[104]

For his part, Nixon couldn't have been happier. After fielding a seemingly never-ending stream of congratulatory phone calls from party luminaries like Rockefeller (who was easily reelected in New York, while his brother, Winthrop, was elected governor of Arkansas) and Romney, as well as newly elected stars like Reagan (who defeated Pat Brown in California) and Charles Percy (who won a Senate seat in Illinois), Nixon giddily went out on the town to celebrate with Davies and Ruwe. "This is too great a night to go home!" he exclaimed as he tried to hail a cab outside the Drake Hotel in Manhattan.[105] After a night of revelry and merriment, or at least what passed for both as far as Nixon was concerned, the triumphant and resurgent Republican leader finally got home at approximately 2:30 a.m. He immediately called Sears to get an update on some late election returns. "We've beaten the hell out of them," Nixon said to Sears.[106] "And we're going to kill them in '68!"

As Safire noted, "The band of loyalists at the Drake didn't feel like such minor-league conspirators anymore . . . Dick could go all the way."[107] But before Nixon could venture back to the big leagues of presidential politics, he had to prove himself in the lawyer's equivalent of the major leagues—the Supreme Court.

NOTES

1. Robert Caro, *Master of the Senate* (New York: Vintage Books, 2003), 655.
2. David Stokes, "RN and LBJ—An Overlooked Relationship," The Nixon Foundation, May 13, 2011, accessed March 28, 2017, http://www.nixonlegacy.org/the-new-nixon/2011/05/rn-and-lbj-an-overlooked-relationship.
3. Stokes, "RN and LBJ."
4. Caro, *Master of the Senate*, 232–303.
5. Quoted in: Nancy Gibbs and Michael Duffy, *The Presidents Club: Inside the World's Most Exclusive Fraternity* (New York: Simon & Schuster Paperbacks, 2012).
6. Gibbs and Duffy, *The Presidents Club*; also Stephen Ambrose, *Nixon: Volume 2, The Triumph of a Politician, 1962–1972* (New York: Simon and Schuster, 1989), 97.
7. Ambrose, *Nixon: Volume 2*, 80.
8. "Frank Gannon's Interview with Richard Nixon, Part 2," University of Georgia, September 7, 1983, accessed March 29, 2017, http://www.libs.uga.edu/media/collections/nixon/ohms/sept7part2.html.
9. "Nixon Sees GOP Victory in 1966," *Schenectady Gazette* , December 27, 1965.
10. Ambrose, *Nixon: Volume 2*, 81.
11. Thomas Evans, "Nixon Mudge," unpublished manuscript, 1994, 167.
12. "Maurice H. Stans," Accounting Hall of Fame, The Ohio State University Fisher College of Business, accessed September 1, 2017, https://fisher.osu.edu/academic-departments/amis/accounting-hall-fame/membership-hall/maurice-h.-stans.
13. Thomas Evans, "The Education of Richard Nixon: The Wilderness Years on Wall Street," unpublished manuscript, 107.
14. Rowland Evans and Robert Novak, "Kuchel Stays Potent Force Even out of Governor's Race," *Lawrence Journal-World*, September 28, 1965.
15. Evans, "Education of Richard Nixon," 107.
16. Evans, "Education of Richard Nixon."
17. Tom Evans, Memorandum of March 20, 1966, Meeting, Tom Evans Collection.
18. Evans, "Education of Richard Nixon," 108.
19. Evans, "Education of Richard Nixon."
20. Jonathan Aitken, *Nixon: A Life* (Washington, DC: Regnery History, 1993), 323.
21. Evans, Memorandum of March 20, 1966 Meeting.
22. John Ehrlichman, *Witness to Power: The Nixon Years* (New York: Simon Schuster, 1982), 37.
23. Ambrose, *Nixon: Volume 2*, 84–85.
24. Ambrose, *Nixon: Volume 2*, 66.
25. Ambrose, *Nixon: Volume 2*.
26. Evans, "Education of Richard Nixon," 109.
27. Tom Evans, Memorandum of May 22, 1966 Meeting, Tom Evans Collection.
28. Evans, Memorandum of May 22, 1966 Meeting.
29. Tom Evans, Memorandum of May 11, 1966 Meeting, Tom Evans Collection.
30. "Pat Makes White House 'Live' for Tourists," *Pittsburgh Press*, September 3, 1970.
31. Evans, May 22, 1966 Memo.
32. Evans, May 22, 1966 Memo.

33. Alfonso Naravez, "L. Nicholas Ruwe, Ex-Ambassador, 56; Assisted Presidents," *New York Times*, May 4, 1990, accessed March 29, 2017, http://www.nytimes.com/1990/05/04/obituaries/l-nicholas-ruwe-ex-ambassador-56-assisted-presidents.html.
34. Evans, May 22, 1966 Memo.
35. John Whitaker, exit interview by Susan Yowell, May 4, 1963, accessed April 16, 2017, https://nixonlibrary.gov/virtuallibrary/documents/exitinterviews/whitaker-exit.pdf
36. Evans, May 22, 1966 Memo.
37. Evans, May 22, 1966 Memo.
38. Evans, May 11, 1966 Memo.
39. Evans, May 11, 1966 Memo.
40. William Safire, *Before the Fall: An Inside View of the Pre-Watergate White House* (Garden City, NY: Doubleday & Company, Inc., 1975), 27.
41. Tom Evans, Memorandum of April 24, 1966 Meeting, Tom Evans Collection.
42. Ambrose, *Nixon: Volume 2*, 85.
43. Ambrose, *Nixon: Volume 2*.
44. Ambrose, *Nixon: Volume 2*.
45. Ambrose, *Nixon: Volume 2*, 85–86.
46. Ambrose, *Nixon: Volume 2*, 80–81.
47. Evans, "Nixon Mudge," 127.
48. Jeffrey Frank, *Ike and Dick: Portrait of a Strange Political Marriage* (New York: Simon & Schuster Paperbacks, 2013), 272–73.
49. "MI District 7—R Primary," Our Campaigns, accessed March 29, 2017, http://www.ourcampaigns.com/RaceDetail.html?RaceID=758664.
50. "MI District 7," Our Campaigns, accessed March 29, 2017, http://www.ourcampaigns.com/RaceDetail.html?RaceID=150341.
51. "He's a Democrat: Riegle Switches Parties," *Argus-Press*, February 27, 1973.
52. Jules Witcover, *The Resurrection of Richard Nixon* (New York: G. P. Putnam's Sons, 1970), 143.
53. Witcover, *The Resurrection of Richard Nixon*
54. Witcover, *The Resurrection of Richard Nixon*
55. Witcover, *The Resurrection of Richard Nixon*
56. Ambrose, *Nixon: Volume 2*, 88–89.
57. Ambrose, *Nixon: Volume 2*.
58. Witcover, *The Resurrection of Richard Nixon*, 130.
59. Patrick Buchanan, *The Greatest Comeback: How Richard Nixon Rose from Defeat to Create the New Majority* (New York: Crown Forum, 2014), 73.
60. Ambrose, *Nixon: Volume 2*, 89–90.
61. Witcover, *The Resurrection of Richard Nixon*, 146.
62. Witcover, *The Resurrection of Richard Nixon*.
63. James Boyd, "Nixon's Southern Strategy, 'It's All in the Charts,'" *New York Times*, May 17, 1970.
64. John Sears, "The Nation: With Nixon: 'Politics Is Great—Except for People,'" *Los Angeles Times*, April 24, 1994, accessed March 29, 2017, http://articles.latimes.com/1994-04-24/opinion/op-49925_1_great-people.
65. Leonard Garment, *Crazy Rhythm: From Brooklyn and Jazz to Nixon's White House, Watergate and Beyond* (Cambridge, MA: Da Capo Press, 1997), 115.
66. John Sears, interview by Victor Li, February 16, 2016.
67. Sears, "The Nation: With Nixon."
68. Garment, *Crazy Rhythm*, 84–85.
69. Garment, *Crazy Rhythm*, at 85.
70. Garment, *Crazy Rhythm*.
71. Garment, *Crazy Rhythm*, at 85–86.
72. Ambrose, *Nixon: Volume 2*, 86–87.
73. Coleman, supra.
74. Ambrose, *Nixon: Volume 2*, 90.
75. Gibbs and Duffy, *The Presidents Club*.

76. Sears, interview by Li.
77. Buchanan, *The Greatest Comeback*, 81.
78. "Manila Summit Conference, Joint Communique," VietnamWar.govt.nz, accessed March 29, 2017, http://www.vietnamwar.govt.nz/sites/default/files/documents/manila-summit-communique.pdf.
79. "Manila Summit Conference, Joint Communique."
80. Gibbs and Duffy, *The Presidents Club*.
81. Safire, *Before the Fall*, 36–37.
82. Buchanan, *The Greatest Comeback*, 84–85. Also "An Appraisal of Manila," Issuu.com/RichardNixonFoundation, accessed March 29, 2017, http://issuu.com/richardnixonfoundation/docs/an_appraisal_of_manila?e=7983691/12996707.
83. Buchanan, *The Greatest Comeback*.
84. Buchanan, *The Greatest Comeback*.
85. Safire, oral history.
86. Buchanan, *The Greatest Comeback*, 86. Also Gibbs and Duffy, *The Presidents Club*.
87. Garment, *Crazy Rhythm*, 114.
88. Ambrose, *Nixon: Volume 2*, 94.
89. Aldo Beckman, "LBJ Surgery Is Scheduled Wednesday," *Chicago Tribune*, November 14, 1966.
90. The LBJ Library, "The President's News Conference, 11/4/66," YouTube video, 33:25, posted March 20, 2013, https://www.youtube.com/watch?v=sZeDR6j7YZ4.
91. David Graham, "If You Give Me a Week, I Might Think of One," *The Atlantic*, May 20, 2016, accessed March 29, 2017, https://www.theatlantic.com/notes/2016/05/if-you-give-me-a-week-i-might-think-of-one/484556/.
92. Robert Caro, *The Years of Lyndon Johnson: The Passage of Power* (New York: Alfred A. Knopf, 2012), 433.
93. The LBJ Library, "The President's News Conference, 11/4/66," YouTube video.
94. The LBJ Library, "The President's News Conference."
95. Gibbs and Duffy, *The Presidents Club*.
96. Safire, *Before the Fall*, 38.
97. Witcover, *The Resurrection of Richard Nixon*, 165.
98. Witcover, *The Resurrection of Richard Nixon*, 165.
99. Joseph Califano, interview by Timothy Naftali, April 3, 2007, Richard Nixon Oral History Project, Richard Nixon Presidential Library and Museum.
100. Safire, *Before the Fall*, 39.
101. Gibbs and Duffy, *The Presidents Club*.
102. "The Manila Communique: Nixon's Comeback," The Richard Nixon Foundation, May 20, 2015, accessed March 29, 2017, http://www.nixonlegacy.org/the-new-nixon/2015/05/the-manila-communique-nixons-comeback.
103. Witcover, *The Resurrection of Richard Nixon*, 169.
104. Witcover, *The Resurrection of Richard Nixon*, 170.
105. Witcover, *The Resurrection of Richard Nixon*.
106. Witcover, *The Resurrection of Richard Nixon*.
107. Safire, *Before the Fall*, 41.

Chapter Nine

"I Always Knew I Wouldn't Be Permitted to Win a Big Appeal against the Press."

Approximately two months before Richard Nixon would be elected vice president for the first time, three prisoners staged a daring jailbreak from a federal penitentiary in Lewisburg, Pennsylvania. On September 10, 1952, the three inmates sawed through their cell bars and, using a rope made of several towels tied together, lowered themselves out of their second-floor cell into the prison yard, where they had stashed a makeshift ladder fashioned out of various pieces of pipe they had collected during their time behind bars. On the lam, they stole a car and made it as far as Whitemarsh Township, located a few miles outside Philadelphia, before they decided they needed a place to hide from the manhunt that was underway. In the early morning hours of September 11, 1952, they broke into the home of James and Elizabeth Hill and held the Hills and their five children hostage for nineteen hours before absconding with some clothes and the Hills' car. During that time, the fugitives actually treated the Hill family politely and courteously and, ultimately, left them unharmed. The escaped prisoners even managed to get along well with the Hill children and, in the words of Elizabeth Hill, were "perfect gentlemen."[1] As far as home invasion burglaries and hostage situations went, what the Hills experienced was hardly the crime of the century.

But it was a good story. It even had a Hollywood-style ending as, a few weeks after the Hills' home invasion, law enforcement caught up to the three fugitives in Manhattan, where two of the three were killed in a shootout with police. The Hills became an overnight media sensation as their ordeal was splashed across the front pages of newspapers throughout the country. Reporters published, virtually, every detail about the Hills they could get their hands on, including what their house looked like, where their children went to school, and what kind of car they owned. The scrutiny lasted for months after the home invasion took place and took a heavy toll on the Hills. Ultimately, the Hills relocated to Connecticut whereupon the media attention started to die down.

The harsh glare of the spotlight that the Hills loathed would soon return with a vengeance. In 1954, author Joseph Hayes wrote *The Desperate Hours*, a best-selling home-invasion hostage novel that contained some obvious similarities with what the Hills had experienced. Hayes, for his part, claimed that he had been wrestling with a story like this for a while—well before the Hill incident had occurred. He also claimed that when he sat down and wrote *The Desperate Hours*, he had been inspired by his clippings file, which contained a number of hostage-style home-invasion news stories from the last few years, including the Hill case. Nevertheless there were a number of clear similarities between his story and the Hill incident. For instance, in both versions there were three escaped cons who chose a house at random to hide out in—in the case of *The Desperate Hours*, fate drew them to a house owned by "the Hilliards."[2] On the other hand, Hayes, admittedly, took significant artistic license with the story in order to make it marketable. His version included violence, profanity, and even a threatened sexual assault by one of the home invaders to the family's teenaged daughter. Hayes also created a new ending, in which the Hilliards bravely fight back against their captors and reclaim their freedom and home.

Almost immediately after the novel came out, both Broadway and Hollywood came calling. The following year, *The Desperate Hours* was adapted into a Broadway play starring a young up-and-coming actor named Paul Newman, as well as a major Hollywood film starring Academy Award winners Humphrey Bogart and Frederic March.[3]

Even though Hayes had made it clear that *The Desperate Hours* was not meant to be an accurate portrayal of what the Hills had gone through, the novel, play, and movie were, obviously, meant to remind readers and viewers about the now-famous 1952 home invasion. It certainly brought a flood of unwanted memories for the Hill family. James Hill found himself constantly denying that *The Desperate Hours* bore anything other than a superficial resemblance to what he and his family had experienced, while Elizabeth Hill became severely depressed.[4]

Their anguish was compounded when *Life* magazine got involved. Then the most popular magazine in the country, *Life* published a feature on the Broadway production in its February 28, 1955, edition (coincidentally, this issue also featured a positive story about then–vice president Nixon's goodwill trip to Latin and Central America). Unlike Hayes, who had gone to great lengths to distinguish his work of (mostly) fiction from what had happened inside the Hills' home, *Life* played up the connection between the play and the actual event it was, partially, based on. Calling it a "True Crime Story," *Life* maintained that the play "re-enacted" the actual crime, and editors even went so far as to remove several references in the story that made clear that the play was, mostly, fiction. Additionally, *Life* had decided to take the nontraditional tack and have actors from the play perform scenes from *The Desperate Hours* at the Hills' former home, thereby strengthening the connection between the two.

> Three years ago Americans all over the country read about the desperate ordeal of the James Hill family, who were held prisoners in their home outside Philadelphia by three escaped convicts. Later they read about it in Joseph Hayes's novel, *The Desperate Hours*, inspired by the family's experience. Now they can see the story re-enacted in Hayes's Broadway play based on the book.[5]

The Hills, who had subscribed to *Life*, were outraged when they saw the story.

"We couldn't understand how [*Life*] could do that just for the sake of some free publicity," Hill said.[6] "We certainly couldn't understand how *Life* could publish an article such as this without first checking the newspapers or at least picking up a telephone to find out whether this was the truth or how we felt about it. It was just like we didn't exist, like we were dirt, like they didn't care."

Hill wanted to sue *Life* and called up his old friend, Bob Guthrie. Wall Street firms rarely take individual tort cases, but Guthrie made an exception as a favor to his friend. Guthrie then assigned the case to Garment, then a thirty-one-year-old associate and rising star in the litigation department. After an attempt to get *Life* to issue a retraction went nowhere, Garment filed suit.[7] In response, *Life*'s parent company, Time, Inc., retained longtime outside counsel Cravath, Swaine & Moore—the venerated Wall Street firm that liked to brag that it had never lost a libel or privacy case.[8]

In this case, libel wasn't applicable. After all, in order to prove libel or defamation, the Hills would have had to show that *Life* had published a false statement that was damaging to the Hills' reputation. *Life*'s story may not have been entirely accurate, but it certainly didn't portray the Hills in a negative light. If anything, the story, along with the novel, play, and movie, painted the Hills positively—as heroes who finally had enough and bravely fought back against their would-be tormentors.

Instead, Garment filed suit under a New York State privacy law that prohibited the use of someone's identity or name for commercial or trade purposes.[9] As Samantha Barbas, professor at the University of Buffalo School of Law pointed out, in the years leading up to the Hills' lawsuit, courts throughout the country had been running into the problem of how to balance privacy statutes, like the one in New York, with the First Amendment rights of the media.[10] The Hills' lawsuit addressed that divide, head on, as Garment filed a complaint that accused *Life* of running a false, fictional story that rendered it outside the realm of First Amendment protection.[11] "The *Life* magazine article of February 28, 1955, was intended to, and actually did convey the impression that the plaintiffs Hill and their children were the family . . . depicted in the novel, play and motion picture *The Desperate Hours*," the complaint stated.[12]

As the trial date approached, Garment realized that convincing a judge and jury that the Hills were actually hurt by the *Life* article was easier said than done. After all, an easy counterargument to make against the Hills that had nothing to do with First Amendment law or the intersection between privacy and newsworthiness was that the Hills should have been able to just suck it up and deal with it. Garment realized that he had to get the jury angry at *Life* and its actions, and the best way to do this would be to demonstrate how arrogant and indifferent *Life* had been toward the Hills and their well-being. "So, we readily conceded at the trial that *Life* had not set out, deliberately, to harm the Hills," Garment said.[13] "Who the Hills were, how they might feel about being drawn back into the public eye and identified as victims of the kind of ordeal portrayed in *The Desperate Hours*—these questions were the furthest thing from *Life*'s editorial mind."

In short, Garment and his trial assistant, Donald Zoeller, had bet their case on "the theme of ice-cold institutional indifference"—and it worked.[14] According to Garment, *Life*'s own witnesses helped undermine the magazine's case. One fact-checker admitted on the stand that she had not checked one fairly important and relevant fact—namely whether the play had been intended as a factual reenactment of the Hill home invasion. Instead, she testified that her editor had, merely, told her that it was a reenactment and that she accepted his edict and moved on.[15] Garment recalled that another important witness, editor Tom Prideaux, was almost flippant on the stand, telling the jury that he never bothered to ask Hayes whether or not his story was based on what happened to the Hills. "Prideaux said authors are not necessarily the best judge of what inspires them," Garment recalled.[16] Garment also believed that Prideaux, essentially, handed the case to him and the Hills, testifying that since there was a connection between the play and the real-life event, it was his obligation to point it out to the reader.[17]

Garment also put forth extensive medical and psychiatric evidence detailing Elizabeth Hill's extreme depression, including the revelation that she received regular electroshock treatments (she would commit suicide in 1971). "The doctors testified that she was and would remain a psychological tinderbox," Garment said.[18] "*Life*, calling no expert to refute this testimony, attributed Mrs. Hill's symptoms to menopause and malingering."

In the end, it seemed as if the jury disliked *Life* every bit as much as Garment and Zoeller had hoped. Needing only five hours of deliberation to hand down a verdict in favor of the Hills, the jury hit Time, Inc., with a $175,000 judgment. According to Garment, it was the largest verdict ever handed down in an invasion of privacy case.[19]

The verdict sent shockwaves throughout the publishing industry. "Traditionally, newsmen have assumed that stories about a legitimate news event, presented in legitimate fashion, do not constitute invasion of privacy," *Newsweek* wrote after the jury handed down its verdict.[20] Time, Inc., in particular, was upset by the decision and its potential implications for the entire publishing industry, and vowed that it would spare no expense to get it wiped off the books.[21] In 1963, the appellate court upheld the verdict but deemed the damage award excessive and ordered a new trial, just on damages. After a reduced award was handed down to James Hill and then affirmed on appeal (Garment had settled Elizabeth Hill's claim), Time, Inc., appealed to the Supreme Court. In 1965, the high court agreed to hear the case and set oral arguments for April 27, 1966.

Since Garment had served as lead attorney on the case ever since it was assigned to him, he would have been the one to deliver the oral argument before the Supreme Court. Even though he had never argued a case before the Supreme Court, he was, probably, the best lawyer to handle the important oral argument because he knew the case backward and forward after trying it twice and arguing multiple appeals. Most lawyers would kill for a chance to argue before the Supreme Court, and Garment was sitting on a winning lottery ticket.

Garment, however, had another idea.

"UNPRECEDENTED SOLICITUDE FOR INDIVIDUALS."

Garment knew that having a Supreme Court argument under his belt could make his career. But it wouldn't necessarily give him the career he wanted. After all, he had found himself drawn to Nixon because he was sick of corporate law and was intrigued by high-level presidential politics.

There were no longer any doubts among his intimates at the firm that Nixon planned on making another run for the White House. As the Supreme Court was setting its calendar for the oral argument, Nixon was already deeply involved with Congress '66. Garment knew that arguing a case before the Supreme Court would be good for his public partner's presidential prospects.

For Nixon, the appeal of doing the *Time v. Hill* oral argument was obvious. "[Nixon] saw that his emergence as a Supreme Court advocate could become part of people's perception of him as a 'new Nixon,' a disciplined advocate respectful of constitutional principles, not the bitter politician lashing out at journalists," Garment said.[22] Plus, the prestige of arguing before the Supreme Court would help distinguish him from his rivals for the presidential nomination and lend Nixon a layer of *gravitas* and credibility that others lacked. Arguing before the Court would confirm his exalted status as a top lawyer and prove that he could succeed in the legal field, thereby burying his "loser" label once and for all (assuming he won the case, of course).

There was also the rather obvious appeal of finally getting a chance to take on one of his biggest and most enduring enemies, the press. As a public figure, he wouldn't be affected too much by whatever the Supreme Court did in *Time v. Hill*. However, in a way, that made the case even more appealing to Nixon. Without self-interest being a factor, as well as the fact that his clients were private citizens who felt that they had been bullied and mistreated by the media, Nixon had a golden chance to paint himself as a man of the people less than two years before the 1968 presidential primaries would begin. And even though he wouldn't be directly affected by the ruling, a strong victory for the Hills could fundamentally transform the way media outlets did their jobs. For someone who had long complained that the media didn't cover him fairly, this was quite an enticing prospect.

Another reason was the Genovese affair. According to Witcover, a Nixon Mudge member told him that one of the main reasons Nixon agreed to argue the case was because he believed his views on individual freedom and the role of the media had been obscured during the Genovese kerfuffle. "In the academic community, and in the law firm and the liberal New York legal fraternity, as well, that case had left a cloud hanging over Nixon's views on individual freedom," Witcover wrote.[23] "*The Desperate Hours* case offered an ideal opportunity to dispel the cloud in a forum certain to receive national attention."

The drawbacks were also obvious. For one thing, there was a legitimate question as to whether or not the client was best served by benching Garment, the lead attorney at trial and on the prior appeals, in favor of a man who was not a courtroom lawyer. After all, Nixon had never, in his entire legal career, argued in an appellate court.[24] Furthermore, during his time at Nixon Mudge, he had yet to bring a major case to trial.[25] Instead, he had focused on bringing in business and helping run the firm—tasks that he and his partners had agreed upon when they had discussed him joining. When it came to the clients that Nixon brought into the firm, the modus operandi at the firm had been to reassign them to another partner or lawyer (usually Garment, Guthrie, or Evans)—especially if there was actual litigation involved.

Even some of his own associates were skeptical. "I didn't think it was the best idea," Zoeller recalled.[26] "I had respect for Nixon, but Len was so much into the case and he was very smart, as well as a good oral advocate." Roger Milgrim, an associate at the firm who did much of the basic research for the appellate brief and helped Nixon prepare for the oral argument, also had misgivings. "I remember thinking 'what the hell does Nixon know about this area of the law?'" said Milgrim, who had joined the firm after a stint in the Paris office of Baker & McKenzie where he became the first American associate in that office.[27] "Even as we were walking up the steps of the Supreme Court, I remember thinking that the best thing would be if he fell down and handed the case off to me."

There was another concern. Nixon was worried about the judges he would be appearing in front of, telling Garment that "some of his ideological enemies now sat on the Court and would have their knives out for him."[28] On the onc hand, this seemed valid. Five of the nine justices on the Court had been appointed by Democratic presidents, while a sixth, liberal Democrat William Brennan, had been appointed by Eisenhower in a show of bipartisanship. On the other hand, the most powerful and influential justice on the Court happened to be a former GOP elected official and someone who had once been on the national ticket for the party. For Nixon, however, this justice was probably the last Republican he wanted to see.

Earl Warren and Richard Nixon hadn't interacted much since they left California—and it was safe to say that absence hadn't made either man's heart grow fonder. This was especially the case with Warren. "There's no question that the one person the Chief [Warren's nickname after he became Chief Justice of the Supreme Court] held in absolute contempt was Richard Nixon," a former Warren clerk recalled.[29]

The roots of their rivalry stretch back to the 1940s and 1950s when they were both rising political stars in California. Along with William Knowland, the three were all seen as potential presidential candidates, although Warren was, by far, the most senior and well known of the bunch, having run as Thomas Dewey's running mate in 1948. By the time 1952 rolled around, it seemed as if any one of Nixon, Warren, or Knowland could have been on the presidential ticket. The three men all ended up playing important roles at the 1952 GOP National Convention, with Warren going for the top job while Knowland and Nixon jockeyed for the second slot. While the California delegation was solidly behind its governor, Warren, many people thought that Nixon was secretly in the pocket of the Eisenhower camp. Most importantly, both Warren and Knowland had felt this way.

"Nixon paid his respects to me and said if any of his friends got out of line to let him know," Warren recalled.[30] "He then visited throughout the train [that took the California delegation to Chicago for the GOP convention]. I do not remember if I saw him again before he left us prior to our arriving in Chicago. Anyway, during the night, the Nixon delegates—but not the [junior] senator as far as I know—held caucuses and urged other delegates to vote for General Eisenhower on the first ballot." Nixon worked quietly, encouraging California delegates to support Eisenhower by touting the general's wide-ranging popularity and appeal. Nixon argued that Eisenhower's closest rival, Senator Robert Taft, could not win in a general election and believed that Eisenhower was the only candidate who could break the Democrats' twenty-year stranglehold on the presidency. Warren was incensed when he found out and flatly called Nixon a traitor and accused Eisenhower of using Nixon as a spy within the California delegation. Knowland had also felt betrayed by Nixon, telling his wife that Nixon had confessed his intentions to help Eisenhower.[31]

In any event, Nixon's decision to boost the general at the expense of his fellow Californian paid dividends. Nixon got the vice presidential nomination and even asked his "personal friend" Knowland to deliver the nominating speech. With the enthusiasm of a man watching his ex-girlfriend marry another man, Knowland took one for the team and agreed to nominate his rival. "I could tell he would have rather had a beating than had to do that," said Keith McCormac, a close Knowland associate who saw the speech on television.[32] "You could tell by looking at him. Knowing Knowland like I did, you could tell that he would rather have been anywhere but there, nominating Nixon."

By the time Nixon ran for president in 1960, however, Warren was finished in California politics (Knowland was also done after losing his gubernatorial race against Brown in 1958). In exchange for his support, Warren had made a deal with Eisenhower for the first vacancy on the Supreme Court—a promise Ike kept when Chief Justice Fred Vinson died suddenly in September 1953.

Despite being out of politics, Warren still maintained his antipathy toward Nixon. At a cocktail party in July 1959, the normally genteel and friendly Warren shocked the D.C. establishment when he angrily confronted one of Nixon's biographers at a party. "You are a damned liar!" Warren yelled at Earl Mazo, whose *Richard Nixon: A Political and Personal Portrait* had been published earlier that year. "It's a dishonest account to promote the Presidential candidacy of Nixon!" Warren had worked himself up into such a fury that he seemed like he wanted to punch Mazo. "You people are persecuting me because you know I can't strike back," Warren said angrily.[33] Warren would later deny that it happened, but the anecdote was widely reported. One of Warren's clerks eventually recalled that not only did it happen but also that Warren remained angry about how he felt he had been misrepresented in Mazo's book, which he called a "whitewash of Nixon."[34]

By the time Nixon returned to California to run for governor, Warren seemed to have learned his lesson and realized that he could do more damage to Nixon by ignoring him or even crossing party lines to buddy up to his opponent. Warren didn't endorse Pat Brown, but it certainly seemed like he wanted to. The two went on a highly publicized hunting trip together, and Warren effusively praised Brown for his accomplishments as governor. Warren even confirmed to a reporter, off the record, that he was backing Brown, saying, "Nixon has to be stopped."[35] Meanwhile, his son, Earl Jr., actually volunteered for the Brown campaign and went so far as to switch his party affiliation to Democrat. The younger Warren wasn't shy about his distaste for his father's old rival. "Nixon, through backdoor tactics and political gain for himself, pulled the rug out from under us in 1952," Warren Jr., said.[36] "He wronged my father and the whole state." When Nixon lost and threw his tantrum, Warren watched with glee—literally. Days after the election, Warren found himself on board Air Force One alongside the president to attend Eleanor Roosevelt's funeral at Hyde Park, New York. According to Mary McGrory of the *Washington Star*, Warren shared some of his news clippings about the "last press conference" with Kennedy, and the two men laughed like a couple of kids reading the comic strip together.[37]

When he wasn't keeping tabs on his home state, Warren was busy leading a liberal revolution on the Supreme Court that drastically expanded the rights of individuals, especially in the areas of civil rights, civil liberties, voting rights, and rights of the accused. And they weren't shy about wading into controversy and flexing their muscle. With one stroke of the pen, Warren, writing for a unanimous Court in *Brown v. Board of Education* (1954), outlawed segregated public schools throughout the country. He did the same thing in *Loving v. Virginia* (1967), writing for a unanimous Court that anti-miscegenation laws were unconstitutional. On a host of criminal law cases, the Court attracted the ire of many, especially from law enforcement, for consistently siding with defendants and expanding their rights under the Fourth, Fifth, and Sixth Amendments. Perhaps his most controversial opinion came in *Miranda v. Arizona* (1966), in which a divided Court ruled that police had to read suspects their rights and inform them of their right to be silent and their right to counsel before they could conduct a custodial interrogation. Warren, already an unpopular figure in certain parts of the country as a result of *Brown*, became even more disliked—especially among law enforcement officials who now felt like they were now the ones wearing the handcuffs.[38] When Nixon ran for president in 1968, he spent a significant amount of time campaigning against Warren and his Court while trumpeting his "law and order" theme.[39]

As Nixon immersed himself in preparations for his oral argument, however, he became convinced that he could actually win Warren's support. Douglas Parker, a young appellate litigation associate at the firm who was part of the team working on the case, recalled a strategy session at Nixon's apartment when Nixon predicted how certain justices would vote. Warren "hated me," Parker recalled Nixon saying, but he was also a family man and would appreciate how destructive this had been to the Hills.[40] Warren's jurisprudence as Chief Justice saw him, consistently, side with the little guys against those with power in society, be it the government, big business, or even society as a whole. The Nixon Mudge team thought that Warren might be "predisposed to protect an individual injured by a more powerful social force"—in this case, *Life*.[41]

Nixon knew he was facing an uphill battle, however. The two most senior justices, Hugo Black and William O. Douglas, were First Amendment absolutists and would, likely, reject Nixon's arguments out of hand. Justices William Brennan and Abe Fortas, the latter a recent appointment by good friend and close confidant Lyndon Johnson, were also consistent liberals and often voted with Warren. Nixon went so far as to dismiss Fortas as a quintessential partisan Democrat.[42] Even the so-called moderate and conservative justices, Potter Stewart, John Marshall Harlan, Byron White, and Tom Clark, sometimes found themselves agreeing with Warren or, at least, voting with him. For instance, in the landmark First Amendment case of *New York Times v. Sullivan* (1964) that promised to loom large when it came to the *Hill* case, those four moderate-to-conservative justices, along with Warren, signed onto Brennan's majority opinion that created the "actual malice" standard for public figures trying to prove that they had been defamed—a very high threshold that requires proof that the person publishing the allegedly defamatory statement either knew it was false or showed a reckless disregard for the truth.[43]

Nevertheless, Nixon threw himself into preparing for the case. He devoured the entire case record, memorizing trial transcripts and appellate arguments, as well as relevant case law. He supplemented his reading with some law review articles, treatises, and philosophical essays about libel and privacy. He jotted down notes and wrote out drafts of his oral argument on yellow legal pads, and it became common to see him scribbling away on a pad while sitting in his seat on the plane to go from one campaign stop to the next during his Congress '66 tour.[44] As Garment later reflected, the yellow legal pad was, in many ways, a "do not disturb" sign that Nixon used to close himself off from the outside world and lose himself in his deepest thoughts. "His closest friend was the always available, always compliant, always silent yellow pad," Garment said.[45] "When Nixon took out his yellow pad and unscrewed his pen, you knew it was time to move on." To provide another buffer from the outside world, either Garment or another aide would usually sit next to Nixon, taking the aisle seat so that Nixon could work in peace.

Perhaps the biggest sign that Nixon was taking this seriously was that, in the weeks leading up to the argument, he locked himself away and crammed as if he were studying for the bar exam again. "I locked myself up in my office for two weeks," said Nixon.[46] "No phone calls. No interruptions. It [took] a tremendous amount of concentration."

He and his team of attorneys at the firm worked hard to prepare for the oral argument. Garment supervised a group of associates that worked almost round the clock to arm Nixon with the facts and legal arguments he would need to make a credible showing before Warren and his fellow justices. They prepared detailed analyses of First Amendment law and recounted the statutory history and judicial interpretation of the New York privacy statute in question. Like Nixon, they also studied law review articles, treatises, and works of philosophy when it came to libel and the rights of newspapers and media outlets.

Garment even wrote out suggested answers to possible questions that the justices might ask Nixon. Predicting that the justices would spend a lot of time asking about the connection between *The Desperate Hours* and the Hill incident, Garment sketched out several arguments for Nixon to use to reinforce his main argument that the *Life* article was patently false and outside the realm of First Amendment protection. Garment proposed, for instance, that Nixon respond to questions about whether or not *The Desperate Hours* had been based, at least partially, on the Hill incident as: "*The Desperate Hours* was based on or inspired by a number of news stories, including the Hill incident, but was the story of no one of them," while citing Hayes's trial testimony to that effect.[47] As to whether or not there was a similarity between "Hill" and "Hillard," Garment suggested that Nixon contest this point, too, stating "an author actually basing his work on a true life incident would steer clear of giving his fictional character a name similar to the real-life person" and that Hayes had testified that "Hillard" came from a car dealer in Bradenton Beach, Florida, where he wrote the book.[48] As to Time, Inc.'s assertion that Hayes had testified that the Hill incident "triggered the book in a very direct way," Garment suggested that Nixon argue that Time, Inc., had left out the part of the quote where Hayes said he had been "unconsciously" triggered by the Hill incident and that, even if this were true, it was a "a long way from even being based specifically on the Hill incident, much less being a re-enactment of that incident."[49]

As to Time, Inc.'s other arguments, Nixon's team at Nixon Mudge spent time drafting a mock argument that they might hear from opposing counsel Harold Medina Jr. of Cravath, Swaine & Moore. Parker turned in a memo that Garment praised in a letter to Nixon, telling his public partner: "Medina will do well, if he even comes close to it."[50] Parker broke Time, Inc.'s position down into four major points: it was newsworthy, there was a "substantial and relevant connection" between the play and the Hill incident, *Life* was entitled to point out the connection between the two, and whatever inaccuracies were present in the story, there was no actual malice behind them. Parker, as Medina, argued further:

> To prohibit the imposing of liability, for negligent misstatements made in the telling of news would not, as [Hill] suggests, destroy the right of privacy. It would leave untouched the remedy for the exploitation of persons in commercial advertising, which was, after all, the principal purpose of the New York statute. It would leave open, for future decision by this court, whether liability

> may be imposed for publications which are shocking or indecent, or which have no relation to a subject of public interest . . . The real clash between privacy and the First Amendment occurs only where, as here, the law of privacy is expanded far beyond the interests which it was originally designed to protect. In such a case it must yield to the demands of the First Amendment.[51]

Nixon's team didn't just focus on legal arguments. They also read up on the Supreme Court to learn as much as about the justices as they could. One associate's memo, for instance, synthesized all of the various factoids gleaned from reading about the Warren Court to support the idea that the justices "had unprecedented solicitude for individuals."[52] The memo also hinted that Justice Fortas could be there for the taking, noting that as a lawyer, he once expressed pride in getting several newspapers, including the *Washington Star* and the *Chicago Tribune*, not to run news stories about LBJ aide Walter Jenkins's 1964 arrest for having sex with another man inside a Washington, D.C., YMCA.[53]

"AN AREA OF THE LAW WHICH DESERVES A PARAMOUNT MEASURE OF PROTECTION."

When Nixon arrived at the Supreme Court building on the morning of April 27, 1966, he was perhaps dismayed to see the intimidating, black-robed visage of his longtime rival lording over him and his legal (and possibly political) future. Once the argument started, however, Nixon's prediction that Warren would be sympathetic to the Hills proved prescient. Medina went first and, during his oral argument, both Warren and Fortas peppered the Cravath lawyer with questions about the right to privacy.

"Well, do you suggest that if there was publicity concerning some event in a person's life particularly when he had done nothing wrong that a publication could follow him every place he went in the country and over a period of years, dig that up to his detriment?" Warren asked Medina after a long colloquy over the scope of the New York privacy statute in question. After a couple of answers that didn't seem to satisfy him, Warren asked him, once again: "Can they follow him around the country and when he tries to forget it and have his family forget it, can they keep publishing it on him to his detriment wherever he goes?" Medina then replied that an intentional act to cause harm is a different cause of action than invasion of privacy, while admitting that *Life* may have made a mistake but that it wasn't intentional and didn't trigger the privacy statute.[54]

This then caused Fortas to jump in, demanding clarification as to whether or not *Life* had the right to dredge all of this stuff up for the Hills, years after it ceased being a newsworthy event. Fortas asked multiple times throughout

Medina's argument whether *Life* could just go to the Hills' former home and run a story about the family two years after the incident ceased being newsworthy—especially if the Hills wanted nothing to do with revisiting the glare of the public spotlight. "That's really the problem that we have," Fortas intoned.[55] "And then you have to add to that the fact that there is a New York statute that on its face seems to say that this is a tort."

When Nixon stood up to give his oral argument, he spoke much slower and more deliberately than Medina. Clad in a dark, conservative suit, Nixon displayed a mastery of the facts at hand, as well as deep knowledge of the relevant law. Speaking slowly and meticulously, Nixon gave an effective, albeit workmanlike argument that was later praised by many in the media and in the legal industry—to say nothing of some of the justices themselves.

In true litigator style, Nixon began his argument with a counterfactual. "Let me read from the reply brief of [Time]," said Nixon.[56] "'*The Desperate Hours* in a very fundamental way was the reenactment of the Hill incident and the *Life* article was accurate and substantially more accurate than it needed to be to gain First Amendment protection. And later on, the differences are superficial differences.' Now, as my argument will develop, if those statements or conclusions are correct, this decision by this Court of New York should be reversed both on constitutional grounds and also, I would say parenthetically that this case would not qualify for liability under the law of New York."

This argument, according to Nixon, was fallacious, and he intended to show that Time, Inc. was liable under the privacy statute. "If it is a true account of a newsworthy event then even though it goes back many, many years referring earlier to Mr. Justice Fortas' question then a true account incurs no liability," Nixon argued.[57] "But it's only when the publisher falsifies, fictionalizes the term that is used in the New York cases, the relationship between a past event and the plaintiff and falsifies for the purposes of trade in order of course to make it a more newsy saleable article—it is then, only, that liability incurs."

Indeed, his constant theme was that *Life* had lied, so the statute applied. He also took the opportunity to cast himself as an ardent defender of privacy rights. Arguing that this was an issue of first impression for the Court, Nixon underscored the importance of what was at stake. "[Privacy], it seems to me, is an area of the law which deserves a paramount measure of protection," Nixon said.[58] "It's an area where you have the fundamental problem that confronts all Americans today and that is how does an individual remain an individual in our mass communication society?"

Warren, mostly, steered clear of his old rival. Other than a brief exchange where he corrected Nixon on a point involving California law, Warren seemed content to take a back seat during Nixon's argument. Predictably, it was the First Amendment absolutist, Hugo Black, who challenged Nixon the most. "How can a newspaper publish anything except for purposes of trade?" Black wondered.[59] "Why wouldn't [the privacy statute] cover every news item they have or every editorial? Doesn't any publication made about a human being affect his privacy?"

"Any publication does in the general sense but I should point out that in 60 years, the New York courts had been—have followed a very narrow line of definition in this particular field because of their concern for First Amendment problems," Nixon responded.[60]

By the time he was finished, Nixon received the plaudits he was looking for. The *New York Times* actually praised Nixon, observing that he seemed "as comfortable in his role as a lawyer as he did in politics."[61] The *Washington Post* also heaped acclaim on him, saying that he delivered "one of the better oral arguments of the year."[62] The justices also seemed impressed by Nixon's effort, and Fortas later remarked that he thought Nixon's argument had been "one of the best arguments that he heard since he had been on the Court" and that he thought Nixon had the potential to be a great oral advocate—maybe even one of the best of his time.[63]

Garment, himself, was full of praise for Nixon's effort. "This was Nixon's first argument in any appellate court, but he sounded like a polished professional of the bar," Garment said,[64] "his footing confident, his language lawyerlike, his organization clear." Milgrim, Parker, and Zoeller agreed, although Zoeller believed that Garment would have been better.[65] "On the night of the argument, I stayed with an acquaintance of mine, Owen Fiss [who was to become a prominent professor at Yale Law School], who was then clerking for Justice Brennan," recalled Milgrim.[66] "I asked him what the reaction to Nixon was, and he told me that the Justices and clerks got together after the argument and Justices, including Warren, thought Nixon's argument was the best that any of them had heard."

Nixon, on the other hand, was a little harder on himself and felt as if he could have done better in certain areas. On the plane ride back to New York, Nixon had written up a five-page memorandum chronicling the things he had done wrong and what he could have done better and left it on Garment's desk for him to read the morning after the argument. There were a couple of moments where he wished he had been more forceful and asserted more facts in favor of the Hills. He also believed he should have spent more time highlighting how this case was different from *Times v. Sullivan* in order to win over Brennan, that opinion's author. While he thought that he had done a good job presenting his theme about how the article had been false, he also highlighted a different point of attack that they could have taken:

> This is a First Amendment case. It is generally agreed that neither false statements nor commercial statements deserve First Amendment protection. We therefore could have pointed out that our case did not present a First Amend-

> ment problem, not only because the statements were "commercial" but also on the independent ground that they were false . . . I think in view of the fact that Fortas zeroed in on this point, it might have been quite effective to emphasize it in the oral argument. The heart of the case, in other words, is that false statements invading privacy just like false statements injuring reputation in private libel cases should not have First Amendment protection, whether the falsehood was negligent or with malice.[67]

He also regretted that he wasn't able to deliver one of the zingers he had been practicing: "If this had been a documentary, it would have been the shortest play in history!"[68]

Nixon also expressed disappointment that he didn't see more reporters covering the argument. While the *New York Times*, *Washington Post*, the *Associated Press*, and *United Press International* were on hand in court, Nixon had counted on more reporters being there. According to his memo, Nixon blamed Safire for not delivering on his promise to publicize the argument and instructed Garment to find out what had happened. "First, if he did not follow through, we will have guidance in the future as to how much we can rely on him when we have a similar assignment," Nixon wrote.[69] "Second, if he did follow through, this could well be an indication of an attempted 'blackout' by the 'press establishment.'" Nixon's reference to "the future," with regard to Safire, showed where Nixon's head was at with regard to national politics. "It will not help us, in terms of getting the publicity which we deserve which might bring us more clients in the future who have possible Appellate problems and naturally it does not helps us in terms of *other considerations* [emphasis added] which are broader than our purely 'commercial interests,'" Nixon wrote.[70]

Milgrim remembered meeting with Nixon the morning after the oral argument to give his take on how it had gone. "I told him that his presentation was magnificent but in my view, wasted because I thought Medina had done a terrible job," Milgrim said.[71] Milgrim noted that several partners that had attended the argument thought that Medina had been rude at points during his argument and chided him for a serious breach of protocol by refusing to answer two of Brennan's questions. Nixon, according to Milgrim, didn't agree and insisted that Medina had actually done better than Nixon had. He also didn't think that Medina had been rude by refusing to answer Brennan and commended Medina for sticking to his presentation, which Nixon thought had been well organized. Nixon then engaged in some introspection as he took stock of his own abilities. "I know I have a certain bardic gift," Nixon said.[72] "I don't know exactly what it is, but I wish I did so maybe I could sell it. I have a way of speaking that pleases a live crowd. In person, I can hold an audience and be very persuasive. But as you and I know, that doesn't translate to TV."

In later years, Nixon recalled that the experience had been a profoundly stressful one. "I've prepared for press conferences, speeches and so forth, but there is nothing which certainly exceeds the tension and the preparation requirements as compared to the Supreme Court, because you have nine of the ablest lawyers and legal minds in the country up there," Nixon said.[73] "And in the period of one hour or so, you've got be able to answer all their questions. It was an ordeal. I wouldn't want to do it again."

Unfortunately for Nixon, he would have to do it again. The reason why wouldn't become known for many years—and it helped cost him a victory that he had desperately wanted and believed he had deserved.

"THEY DO NOT CONFER A LICENSE FOR POINTLESS ASSAULT."

After Nixon's bow before the Court, both he and Garment believed they had come away with a narrow majority. Warren and Fortas seemed like they had been on Nixon's side, and Clark, who had been mostly silent during the argument, was another vote they were counting on. Nixon later said that he understood why Fortas and Warren had seemed sympathetic. "These two men had been in the political arena and knew firsthand how fierce and lacerating the press could be when it fastened on a target," Garment recalled.[74] "They would see that for private persons, such unwanted and false exposure could be, in Nixon's words, 'as traumatic as a physical blow.'"

Black, meanwhile, had been the most hostile to Nixon—a move that was hardly surprising given Black's views on the First Amendment. His fellow absolutist, William O. Douglas, had stayed quiet during the argument—as he was wont to do. Nevertheless, it was obvious to any Court watcher that Douglas would side with Black, his longtime ally. That left Harlan, White, Stewart, and Brennan up for grabs with Nixon only needing two to win.

According to Bernard Schwartz, Nixon's side had, indeed, won a majority—at least, at first. At the justices' regular Friday conference to vote on cases heard earlier in the week, Nixon's side had won a 6–3 majority as Warren, Clark, Fortas, Harlan, Stewart, and a reluctant Brennan voted to uphold the lower court rulings in favor of the Hills. Black, Douglas, and White dissented.

Warren, as the senior justice in the majority, assigned Fortas to write a majority opinion. At the beginning of June, several weeks before the end of the Court term, Fortas took *Life* to the proverbial woodshed when he circulated a strident and contemptuous draft opinion that was full of invective and criticism over the magazine's conduct. "The facts of this case are unavoidably distressing," the opinion began.[75] "Needless, heedless, wanton and deliberate injury of the sort inflicted by *Life*'s picture story is not an essential instrument of responsible journalism."

It turns out that Nixon had pushed the correct buttons when it had come to Fortas. "Magazine writers and editors are not by reason of their high office relieved of the common obligation to avoid deliberately inflicting wanton and unnecessary injury," Fortas wrote[76] in a line that was fairly consistent with what Nixon would cover in his academic freedom speech that he delivered at Rochester at around the same time. Another line in Fortas's draft opinion dealt with limits on freedom and the delicate balance between liberty and license—albeit from a different angle than the one Nixon had taken in his Rochester speech. "The prerogatives of the press—essential to our liberty—do not preclude reasonable care and avoidance of casual infliction of injury to others totally unexplainable by any purpose or circumstances related to its function of reporting or discussing the news or publishing matters of interest to its readers," wrote Fortas.[77] "They do not confer a license for pointless assault."

Fortas also wholeheartedly endorsed the notion that there was a constitutional right to privacy. The right to privacy had been previously recognized in *Griswold v. Connecticut*, but there was disagreement among the justices in the majority as to where the right came from in the US Constitution. (Douglas had argued that there were "penumbras" of privacy that were derived throughout the Bill of Rights such as the right against self-incrimination and the right against unlawful searches and seizures, Justice Arthur Goldberg had argued that the Ninth Amendment had created a right to privacy, while Harlan and White took a narrower view and cited the due process clause of the Fourteenth Amendment.) Fortas (who had not been on the Court when the *Griswold* case had been decided) endorsed, in broad and sweeping language, a constitutional right to privacy that would have gone further than *Griswold*.[78]

> There is . . . no doubt that a fundamental right of privacy exists, and that it is of constitutional stature. It is not just the right to a remedy against false accusation . . . it is not only the right to be secure in one's person, house, papers, and effects . . . it is more than the specific right to be secure against the Peeping Tom or the intrusion of electronic espionage devices and wire-tapping. All of these are aspects of the right to privacy, but privacy reaches beyond any of its specifics. It is, simply stated, the right to be let alone; to live one's life as one chooses, free from assault, intrusion, or invasion except as they can be justified by the clear needs of community living under a government of law.

When it came to privacy rights, Fortas had gone beyond what Nixon had hoped for. Nixon had been critical of the penumbras approach to privacy and had told Garment in his postargument memo that he had regretted not "clearing up Medina's fuzzy reference to a right of privacy being a constitutional right emanating from the Fourth, Fifth, Ninth and other Amendments (in other words, using the *Griswold* analogy)," and he called the penumbras approach "both inaccurate and potentially dangerous from a constitutional standpoint."[79] Nixon also criticized the approach that had been favored by some others on the Court to recognize a constitutional right to privacy in the Ninth Amendment:

> A parallel danger, perhaps presenting even greater problems as far as the Court is concerned, is that if we should contend that there is a constitutional right to privacy emanating from the Ninth Amendment, the Court would then have the problem in every case to determine whether the right of privacy under the Ninth Amendment or the right of free expression under the First Amendment should prevail where the two come into conflict.[80]

The problem Nixon saw coming would come to fruition in, perhaps, the most ironic way imaginable. During his campaign for president, Nixon made the Warren Court an issue and promised to appoint "strict constructionists" to the Supreme Court. In 1973, the Court (which included four Nixon appointees) extended *Griswold*'s framework in two landmark and controversial cases that legalized a woman's right to have an abortion (*Roe v. Wade* and *Doe v. Bolton*). Three of Nixon's justices were in the majority, and one of them, Harry Blackmun, wrote both majority opinions.

Fortas's opinion, had it become law, would have strengthened privacy rights considerably and could have fundamentally changed the way newspapers, magazines, TV stations, and other members of the press did their jobs. Under Fortas's framework, the right to privacy would have extended, not just to victims of false publicity, like the Hills, but potentially anyone who had ever been thrust into the spotlight—regardless of how newsworthy the story might be.

Hugo Black, however, had other ideas.

"ONE OF THE MOST BASIC ANIMOSITIES ON THE COURT."

As expected, Black was horrified by Fortas's opinion. He marked up his copy of the draft opinion and let loose with a bevy of criticisms and grievances toward Fortas and his conclusions. Calling it "the worst First Amendment opinion he had seen in a dozen years," Black accused Fortas of having a "vendetta against *Time*" and grossly exaggerating the facts in order to make *Time* look like an "ogre." Worse, Black was stunned by Fortas's privacy analysis and thought what he was trying to do was unprecedented and dangerous. The "power to change the Constitution," Black stated, was what you might see from a "totalitarian regime."[81]

Were it anyone else, Black might have been content to simply accept defeat. Black, however, didn't just hate Fortas's opinion. He also hated Fortas.

It hadn't always been that way. Fortas and Black had once been friends—a pair of New Deal Democrats who had ascended to the top of the legal industry and had warmth and respect for one another. Elected to the US Senate in 1927, the Alabaman Black had quickly established himself as one of FDR's most loyal and outspoken allies in the Senate. Black had voted for almost every piece of New Deal legislation and, after the Supreme Court had ruled several of those bills to be unconstitutional, Black supported the president's ill fated and ultimately futile move to add more justices to the Court. When FDR finally got his first chance to fill a vacancy on the Court, he rewarded Black for his loyalty and stuck with him even after it was revealed, shortly after his confirmation by the Senate, that Black had once been a member of the Ku Klux Klan. Black gave a live radio address where he admitted he had once been a member but had resigned before running for Senate.

"I believe that my record as a senator refutes every implication of racial or religious intolerance," Black said during his radio address.[82] "It shows that I was of that group of liberal senators who have consistently fought for the civil, economic and religious rights of all Americans, without regard to race or creed." That may not have been completely true. As a senator, Black led the battle to defeat an antilynching bill during his first term in office.[83] What is true, however, is that as an associate justice, Black consistently supported civil rights and was one of the strongest opponents of public school segregation on the Court.

Fortas, meanwhile, had made his reputation as one of the finest advocates of his generation. The famed litigator had argued several important cases before the Supreme Court, although none were as famous as *Gideon v. Wainwright*. The Supreme Court issued a unanimous opinion, authored by Black, that established the right to counsel in all cases, both state and federal (previously, the Sixth Amendment right to counsel had only applied to federal cases).

Fortas had also made a powerful friend during his time as a lawyer. When Lyndon Johnson ran for Senate in 1948, he had defeated incumbent Texas governor Coke Stevenson in the Democratic primary by a mere eighty-seven votes (the razor-thin margin led to Johnson receiving the somewhat derogatory moniker of "Landslide Lyndon"—a nickname Johnson embraced). The result, which was tantamount to election in those days, was challenged by the Stevenson campaign due to alleged voter fraud. Stevenson had succeeded in getting Johnson's name stricken from the ballot, only for Fortas to appeal on behalf of Johnson. Fortas ultimately got Black to overturn the ruling, allowing Johnson's victory to stand.

In fact, if it hadn't been for Black, Fortas might never have joined the Supreme Court. Fortas never had a desire to be a justice, mainly because he loved being a Washington insider and having the ear of President Johnson, who relied on his lawyer's counsel on a wide range of domestic and international issues, including the Vietnam War. Fortas was also especially happy running his successful law firm, Arnold, Porter & Fortas (the firm, now known as Arnold & Porter Kaye Scholer, is one of the largest and most prestigious firms in the country).[84] Known for living the high life and enjoying the finer things, Fortas and his wife, Carolyn Agger, a successful tax attorney at Arnold, Porter & Fortas, were both upset about the fact that Abe would go from earning over $200,000 a year to just under $40,000. They worried about being stretched financially—something that came back to haunt them later on. Agger had even tried to talk her husband out of joining the Court, only for Black, who had been friends with the Fortases since the 1930s, to intercede and convince Agger to drop her objections.[85]

When Fortas joined the Court, most observers expected the two to become close allies. Fortas and Black were both seen as liberals, but the judicial and ideological differences between the two men could not have been more stark. Whereas Black had once been the most influential justice on the Court—a man whose previous dissents and minority viewpoints had become the law of the land as the Court tilted left during the 1950s and 1960s—he became more and more isolated as his formalistic approach clashed with those of his colleagues. Fortas's jurisprudence, especially, seemed to anger Black, who saw his junior colleague as opportunistic and results oriented.[86] The two found themselves on different sides on a number of highly charged cases, including *In Re Gault* (juvenile defendant rights), *Tinker v. Des Moines* (rights of students), *Powell v. Texas* (scope of the Eighth Amendment), and *Epperson v. Arkansas* (teaching of religion in public schools). In *Brown v. Louisiana*, Fortas had written a plurality opinion setting aside the convictions of five African Americans for "trespassing" in a segregated public library. Black had issued a blistering dissent accusing Fortas of bias against the South that he insisted on reading in open court. The hiding was such that Warren even apologized to Fortas afterward. "I am somewhat saddened by Hugo's dissent," Warren said to Fortas.[87] "It does not reflect the better part of his nature." According to Roger Newman, however, Fortas had given as well as he had gotten on that case. "Look, Hugo was in the Klan and now he's coming to the aid of southern white womanhood," Fortas noted scornfully to his clerks.[88]

Eventually, the two had gone from feuding over jurisprudence to simply feuding. Black started refusing to join Fortas's opinions as a matter of principle—even if the two agreed on the result. "Just because Fortas is writing," his clerks noted when asked why their boss insisted on doing this.[89] During the 1968 term, a Warren clerk noted the breakdown in relations between Fortas and Black, calling it "one of the most basic animosities on the Court."[90] Douglas, who was friends with both, observed that things seemed to get worse between the two as time went on, and that Fortas became angrier and more aggrieved with each Black salvo.[91] In 1969, their mutual contempt and hostility was obvious to anyone who showed up to the Court to watch the justices in action, as bitter exchanges in open court between the two were becoming more commonplace. "I blame that on Black," one of their fellow justices said.[92] The *Hill* case played a major role in getting Black and Fortas to the point where their feud became "an almost unprofessional version of judicial warfare that did nobody any good."[93]

Black was determined not to let Fortas win and rewrite First Amendment law. Fortas had actually issued another draft, which included some extensive revisions to his original majority opinion. Because all cases that were not decided before the end of the term would have to be reargued in the next Supreme Court term, Black decided to stall for time and give himself the summer to write a First Amendment treatise/dissent that would systematically dismantle Fortas's opinion and, hopefully, sway any vacillating justices over to his side. The others agreed to hold the case over until the next term, and Medina and Nixon were ordered to come back and do it all again.

Over the summer, Black worked hard on his dissent. According to his wife, Black worked until 1:30 every morning and seemed invigorated by his task at hand.[94] Black pulled no punches in attacking Fortas's opinion, criticizing his colleague for creating rights out of thin air and accusing him of distorting the facts of the case. "Neither the 'right to be let alone' nor the 'right to privacy,' while appealing phrases, were enshrined in our Constitution, as was the right to free speech, press, and religion," Black wrote in a condescending tone.[95] "If the judges have . . . by their own fiat today created a right of privacy equal to or superior to the right of a free press that the Constitution created, then tomorrow and the next day and the next the judges can create more rights that balance away other cherished Bill of Rights freedoms."

Fortas was stunned and hurt by Black's dissent and even went to Black's house to try to clear the air.[96] Nevertheless, the dissent had served its purpose. When Nixon and Medina reargued the case on October 18 and 19, 1966, the tide had dramatically turned against Nixon and the Hills. Nixon was annoyed that he had to take three weeks out of his campaign schedule—especially with less than a month before Election Day.

Despite that, he seemed more relaxed and effective during the reargument than he had six months earlier, according to Garment[97] and Parker.[98] Not everyone agreed, however. One justice later said that it seemed clear that Nixon was distracted during the October reargument.[99] Nixon, himself, seemed like he just wanted to get it over with. Toward the end of his allotted time, when Warren asked him if he wished to respond to an earlier question from Justice Harlan, Nixon actually demurred and said: "I don't want to take up Mr. Medina's time."[100] Ultimately, Nixon did respond to Harlan's question after Warren graciously granted him a few extra minutes.

The reargument had given Nixon an opportunity to execute some of the suggestions he had enumerated in his memo to Garment following the initial argument in April. "It is our contention that in this case, it was argued by the plaintiff, it was established by the evidence, it was charged by the Court, it was found by the jury and it was held by the courts of New York in their Appeals Courts that *Life* Magazine lied," Nixon argued.[101] "And that *Life* Magazine knew that it lied."

This time, however, it seemed as if a clear majority of justices were against Nixon. Black, in particular, went after Nixon, spending nearly ten minutes grilling the man who would eventually appoint his replacement. Garment was especially impressed that his public partner held his own and refused to give in under intense questioning from the venerated judge.[102]

Black, though, had some backup. Brennan and White also spent extended periods of time asking Nixon skeptical questions about his position. "I do not think that it's the responsibility of this Court," Brennan opined.[103] "Indeed, I have some serious question on whether—really we have the power to resolve conflicts among the New York cases to arrive at an independent conclusion of what the New York law is."

Unfortunately for Nixon, his performance seemed not to sway a majority of the justices. When it came time to vote, only Warren, Fortas, and Clark held fast to their position from six months ago and backed the Hills. Brennan and Stewart had switched their votes while Harlan staked a middle position where he concurred in part and dissented in part. Perhaps in a maneuver designed to solidify Brennan's support, Black assigned him to write the majority opinion, and Brennan took the opportunity to extend the First Amendment test he first enunciated in *Times v. Sullivan*. "Now we find applicable here the standard of knowing our reckless falsehood, not through blind application of our decision in *New York Times v. Sullivan*, which related solely to liable actions by public official," Brennan wrote in his majority opinion.[104] "But only upon consideration of the factors which arise in the particular context the application to the New York statute in cases involving private individual."

Brennan's majority opinion was not the paean to privacy the way Fortas's draft opinion had been. Instead, Brennan held that freedom of speech was paramount and that privacy was, sometimes, a necessary sacrifice in order to have a truly free society. "The guarantees for speech and press are not the preserve of political expression or comment upon public affairs, essential as those are to healthy government," Brennan wrote.[105] "One need only pick up any newspaper or magazine to comprehend the vast range of published matter which exposes persons to public view, both private citizens and public officials. Exposure of the self to others in varying degrees is a concomitant of life in a civilized community. The risk of this exposure is an essential incident of life in a society, which places a primary value on freedom of speech and of press."

The decision came down on January 9, 1967. Two days before, Nixon had held a very important meeting in New York that will be covered in the next chapter, in which he announced to those present that he was running in 1968. Though in his mind he was already looking ahead to the ensuing presidential campaign, Nixon was, nevertheless, disappointed that he had lost the *Hill* case. He put on a brave face in public, telling reporters after the decision came down that he saw the ruling as "a historic vindication of fundamental rights of the individual as against abuses of freedom of the press."[106]

Privately, however, he was bitterly disappointed. "I always knew I wouldn't be permitted to win a big appeal against the press," Nixon told Garment, having no idea just how close he had come to winning. [107] Nixon even told Garment that he never wanted to talk about the case again. In fact, Nixon did not see fit to write, at length, about the case in either of his memoirs, outside of one line in his *In the Arena* autobiography where he said he got to argue before the Supreme Court twice. *In the Arena* even contains an entire chapter on the right to privacy, and doesn't mention *Time v. Hill* at all. Ultimately, the case settled in May 1967 with Time, Inc. agreeing to pay $75,000 to James Hill rather than going to trial on the remaining claims. [108] It wasn't until Schwartz's book came out in 1985 that Nixon seemed willing to revisit the matter, as he asked Garment to launch an investigation.

Perhaps, after finding out about everything that had happened and how his majority had been taken away from him, Nixon came away with a greater appreciation for what Fortas had done—and regret over what happened next. In the summer of 1968, with Nixon's presidential hopes looking pretty good, Warren hastily sent Johnson a letter announcing his intention to retire as Chief Justice. Warren included a curious clause at the end, saying that the retirement was "effective at your pleasure." The obvious inclination was that Warren wanted to give Johnson a shot at filling his seat before Nixon could become president—although Warren denied it strenuously. "One thing I knew was that Warren had a much better feel for American politics than I did," one of his clerks that term, Larry Simon, said.[109] "And it was at that point that I became pretty sure Nixon was going to be the next President of the United States."

Johnson already had a replacement in mind. His old friend, Fortas, clearly deserved the promotion, Johnson believed, and the president thought he had enough political capital, even as an unpopular lame duck, to get the nomination through the Senate. To sweeten the pot for the southern Democrats that Johnson would need to help push the Fortas nomination through, the president nominated a southerner for Fortas's seat—US Circuit Court Judge for the Fifth Circuit Court of Appeals and another longtime Johnson friend, Homer Thornberry. Johnson, a renowned vote counter, believed he could get as many as seventy-four votes in favor of Fortas—easily beating a possible filibuster.[110] Even better for him, influential senators Richard Russell and Everett Dirksen promised to support Fortas and Thornberry.[111]

Once Fortas's confirmation hearings started, however, it was clear that he was in for some rough sailing. The hearings had turned into a referendum on the Warren Court, and Fortas found himself fending off questions from outraged senators involving cases he had participated in, as well as ones that had predated his time on the Court. There were also a number of questions about the continuing friendship between Johnson and Fortas and whether the justice was too close to the president (Fortas still had a direct line to the Oval Office—even as a member of the Court).[112] After candidate Nixon expressed his opinion that the next president should fill the vacancy, Senate Republicans started stalling on the nomination, and Dirksen felt as if he had to abandon Johnson for the sake of his caucus. Russell also turned on Johnson, but he had more personal reasons. Angered after the president dithered over a federal judicial appointment Russell wanted for one of his men, the influential Georgian turned on his former protégé, signaling to the rest of the southern Democratic caucus that it was okay to fight the White House on this nomination.[113]

One betrayal that Fortas might not have seen coming was from his longtime enemy, Black. The senior justice called his former friend and eventual successor in the Senate, Lister Hill of Alabama, to encourage him to come out against Fortas's nomination.[114] Once close friends, the two Alabamans had fallen out over the *Brown v. Board of Education* case,[115] and Black hadn't spoken to Hill for over a year before he called about Fortas. The "enemy of my enemy approach" worked, and the influential Hill, who had been on the fence about the nomination, announced his opposition.[116]

In the end, Johnson had to work overtime in order to secure a floor vote for Fortas—and the embattled justice did win a bare majority. However, it wasn't enough to beat back a filibuster, and Fortas dutifully withdrew his nomination. Warren's retirement went over to Nixon and, in one of his first major decisions as president, Nixon would appoint D.C. Circuit Court judge Warren Burger to be the next chief justice of the Supreme Court.

Fortas still had his seat as associate justice, but even that would soon be gone. On May 9, 1969, Fortas's old friends at *Life* published a story that would lead to the justice's undoing.[117] In "Fortas: A Question of Ethics," the magazine revealed that the justice had a contract to serve as a consultant to a foundation created by a former client, financier Louis Wolfson. Fortas had accepted a $20,000 fee from Wolfson in January 1966, during which time Wolfson was under investigation by the Securities and Exchange Commission. Fortas returned the $20,000 in December 1966—after Wolfson had already been indicted for fraud (he would be convicted of securities fraud in 1967 and 1968).[118]

Republicans called for Fortas to be impeached while Nixon's Justice Department, now led by Attorney General John Mitchell, opened a criminal investigation into the embattled justice. Whatever personal regards Nixon may have had for Fortas took a back seat to the political considerations, to say nothing of getting a chance to fulfill a campaign promise by reshaping the Court immediately. He dispatched Mitchell to have a sit-down with Warren in order to convince the chief to nudge Fortas out the door. Mitchell even indicated that the criminal probe would "die of its own weight" if Fortas were to resign immediately.[119]

This was no idle threat. Mitchell, evidently, had information that *Life* did not—and it was far more damaging to Fortas. Mitchell showed up to his meeting with Warren with the full contract between Fortas and Wolfson, and it revealed that Wolfson had agreed to pay Fortas $20,000 per year for the rest of his life, and if Fortas died before his wife, Wolfson would then pay her for the rest of her life. The entire arrangement smacked of influence peddling—especially given Fortas's close relationship with Johnson.[120] While Fortas denied he had done anything wrong, the damage to his reputation was unquestionable. "My God, how did Abe do such a stupid thing?" Douglas wondered after Warren informed the rest of the Court what he had learned from Mitchell.[121]

With his options dwindling and the feeling of the proverbial noose tightening around his neck, Fortas became desperate. He even turned to Black, his longtime nemesis, to ask for his advice. Black didn't say much, except that if it were him, he'd resign for the good of the Court. Ultimately, Fortas took Black's advice and resigned less than a fortnight after the *Life* article was published. Black actually seemed saddened by it, telling his wife: "I don't think Abe had any criminal intent."[122] After two unsuccessful nominations, Nixon would appoint US Circuit Court Judge Harry Blackmun of Minnesota to replace Fortas.[123]

Until the day Fortas died, he believed *Life* had pursued a vendetta against him as a result of the *Hill* case.[124] In January 1969, *Life* ran a column naming its "Winners and Losers" of 1968, and Fortas was listed in the latter category for his jurisprudence and his failed nomination as chief justice. "This man [Fortas], in the considered judgment of the U.S. Congress, condoned dirty movies, accepted extravagant fees and befriended you-know-who [LBJ], Justice Fortas was fortunate not to have been arrested."[125] Fortas thought this extraordinarily mean spirited and wrote out, but did not mail, an angry response where he wondered whether *Life*'s motivation was due to his *Hill* dissent.[126]

After Fortas resigned, *Life* took a victory lap, of sorts. In its June 6, 1969, issue, *Life* published a self-congratulatory memo at the front of the book highlighting its recent investigations. Titled "A Memo on Muckraking from the Publisher of *Life*," the magazine took issue with the notion that it had only recently gotten into the investigative journalism business with the Fortas matter (as well as with an article about Ohio's governor James Rhodes and his finances) and maintained that it had always been involved in "the discovery and exposure of wrongdoing affecting the public weal."[127] The magazine also highlighted its Fortas investigation multiple times throughout the one-page memo before closing with praise from a competitor. "*Newsweek Magazine* called the report on Justice Fortas 'an expose that marked *Life*'s arrival as perhaps the most important investigative journal of the day . . . ' These comments are gratifying. And we plan to continue probing behind events—accurately and honestly—for a long time to come."[128]

As for Fortas, the case—to say nothing of *Life*'s treatment of him—continued to haunt him, even as he made his way back into private practice. Shunned by the law firm he had helped build into a powerhouse, Fortas started his own D.C. firm, Fortas and Koven, and even appeared before his old colleagues on the Court from time to time. He also became a friend to Garment, telling him in 1970—a year or so after Garment joined Nixon's White House staff—that he had wished he could have been more effective in the *Hill* case. "It was a bad result, and terribly unfair to the Hill family," Fortas said.[129] Years later, Fortas even extended an invitation to Garment to become his law partner at Fortas and Koven, an offer a flattered Garment turned down.[130]

Parker recalled a similar incident with Fortas several years later. Parker had left Mudge in 1969 to start his own firm, Lankler & Parker, in Washington, D.C. One of his clients, Dun & Bradstreet, was looking for a libel lawyer, and Lankler had recommended former justice Arthur Goldberg, who had joined Paul Weiss in 1968. Parker, remembering the *Hill* case, suggested Fortas. Parker took the D&B general counsel to see Fortas at his new firm and, eventually, the two started talking about the *Hill* case. "I told Fortas how much his dissent had meant to us," said Parker.[131] "I'll never forget that case," Fortas responded. "And *Life* never forgot it, either."

As for Nixon, the case may have been a sore subject for decades, but from a political perspective, Nixon's bow before the Supreme Court had accomplished what he had wanted it to. He had stood up to the big, bad media and refashioned himself as a champion for the individual. Arguing before the Supreme Court on a matter of such importance also gave him a huge boost in confidence and stature as he embarked on his ultimate quest for the White House. "Nixon's appearance before the Supreme Court marked the zenith of his legal career," Aiken wrote in his biography of Nixon.[132] "In his own mind he had now proved himself on the fast track of the New York bar. This made him feel ready to return to the even faster track of national politics." Barbas, meanwhile, pointed out that even though he had already planned on getting back into politics, Nixon's confidence levels were always fluctuating, and the praise he got for his argument put him in the black at just the right time.[133]

Garment, too, got what he had wanted. In his postargument memo in April 1966, Nixon had expressed his gratitude to Garment and his staff for all their help and singled Garment out for graciously stepping aside and letting Nixon take the argument in the first place. "Your stepping aside when you, yourself could have handled the matter in brilliant fashion demonstrated a selflessness which is very rare in our firm, or in any other firm for that matter," Nixon wrote.[134] "I only hope that you will get some much deserved 'dividends' in the future!" While Nixon followed that sentence by expressing hope that Garment would get his own turn before the high court soon, it was clear that Garment preferred a different type of "dividend." After playing a marginal role during the 1966 midterms, Garment would become one of Nixon's point men during the 1968 campaign.

Hill, obviously, had some important long-term ramifications for Nixon. Legal scholars have opined that *Hill* helped lead to an era where media outlets act with carte blanche and are answerable to no one. As Barbas pointed out, in the years immediately following *Hill*, courts around the country consistently sided with the press and found that newsworthiness trumped privacy concerns. Courts also cited *Hill* in libel cases, even though *Hill* had not been a libel case. In subsequent years, the Supreme Court cut back on this approach, culminating in *Gertz v. Robert Welch* (1974), which held that states could establish their own standards when it came to libel or defamation cases brought by private citizens.[135]

Nevertheless, the power of the media continued—fueled, in large part, by Nixon himself. "What might have happened if Watergate had not apotheosized the investigative journalist and made the idea of restraint, self-imposed or court-imposed, anathema to dominant journalistic opinion?" Garment opined.[136] Perhaps the more profound question would be what if Nixon had won the *Hill* case and his victory led to an industrywide chilling effect where reporters were reluctant to pursue stories relating to both public and private figures for fear of litigation?

NOTES

1. Samantha Barbas, "When Privacy Almost Won: *Time, Inc. v. Hill*," *University of Pennsylvania Journal of Constitutional Law* 18, no. 2 (December 2015). Also: Samantha Barbas, *Newsworthy: The Supreme Court Battle over Privacy and Press Freedom* (Stanford, CA: Stanford University Press, 2017).
2. Barbas, "When Privacy Almost Won"; Barbas, *Newsworthy*.
3. Perhaps demonstrating the enduring appeal of this story, *The Desperate Hours* was remade, once again, in 1990. This version, despite boasting the talents of Academy Award winner Anthony Hopkins, Mickey Rourke, and director Michael Cimino, was not as well received as its predecessors.
4. Barbas, "When Privacy Almost Won."
5. "True Crime Inspires Tense Play: The Ordeal of a Family Trapped by Convicts Gives Broadway a New Thriller: 'The Desperate Hours,'" *Life*, February 28, 1955.

6. Barbas, "When Privacy Almost Won."
7. Leonard Garment, *Crazy Rhythm: From Brooklyn and Jazz to Nixon's White House, Watergate and Beyond* (Cambridge, MA: Da Capo Press, 1997), 80–81.
8. Barbas, "When Privacy Almost Won." By the time *Time v. Hill* rolled around, the firm had lost a few libel/privacy cases; however, the majority of those cases had been for nominal damages.
9. Barbas, "When Privacy Almost Won."
10. Barbas, "When Privacy Almost Won."
11. Garment, *Crazy Rhythm*, 81.
12. Barbas, "When Privacy Almost Won."
13. Garment, *Crazy Rhythm*, 81.
14. Garment, *Crazy Rhythm*.
15. Garment, *Crazy Rhythm*, 82.
16. Garment, *Crazy Rhythm*.
17. Garment, *Crazy Rhythm*.
18. Garment, *Crazy Rhythm*.
19. Garment, *Crazy Rhythm*, at 83.
20. Barbas, "When Privacy Almost Won."
21. Barbas, "When Privacy Almost Won."
22. Garment, *Crazy Rhythm*, 83.
23. Jules Witcover, *The Resurrection of Richard Nixon* (New York: G. P. Putnam's Sons, 1970), 128
24. Garment, *Crazy Rhythm*, 87.
25. Witcover, *The Resurrection of Richard Nixon*, 127.
26. Donald Zoeller, interview by Victor Li, February 1, 2016.
27. Roger Milgrim, interview by Victor Li, October 29, 2016.
28. Garment, *Crazy Rhythm*, 83.
29. Bernard Schwartz, *Super Chief: Earl Warren and His Supreme Court—A Judicial Biography* (New York and London: New York University Press, 1983).
30. Gayle Montgomery and James Johnson, One Step from the White House : The Rise and Fall of Senator William F. Knowland (Berkeley: University of California Press, 1998), 110.
31. Montgomery and Johnson, One Step from the White House , 110–11.
32. Montgomery and Johnson, One Step from the White House , 120.
33. Schwartz, *Super Chief*, 337–38.
34. Schwartz, *Super Chief*.
35. Jim Newton, *Justice for All: Earl Warren and the Nation He Made* (New York: Riverhead Books, 2006), 396.
36. "Political Ghost of Warren Stalks Nixon in 1962 Race," *Los Angeles Times*, May 13, 1962.
37. Newton, *Justice for All*, 397.
38. Victor Li, "50-Year Story of the Miranda Warning Has the Twists of a Cop Show," *ABA Journal*, August 1, 2016, accessed March 30, 2017, http://www.abajournal.com/magazine/article/miranda_warning_history.
39. Li, "50-Year Story of the Miranda Warning."
40. Douglas Parker, interview with Li, May 18, 2016.
41. Memorandum, Wilderness Years Collection, Series VI, Legal Papers, *Time, Inc. v. Hill* (March 14, 1966) (on file with the Nixon Presidential Library).
42. Parker, interview by Li.
43. *New York Times Co. v. Sullivan*, 376 U.S. 254 (1964).
44. Garment, *Crazy Rhythm*, 84.
45. Garment, *Crazy Rhythm*, 111.
46. Barbas, "When Privacy Almost Won."
47. Richard Nixon, Memorandum from Leonard Garment, April 25, 1966, Pre-Presidential Papers, Richard Nixon Presidential Library and Museum.
48. Nixon, Memorandum from Leonard Garment, April 25, 1966.
49. Nixon, Memorandum from Leonard Garment, April 25, 1966.

50. Richard Nixon, Memorandum from Leonard Garment, October 6, 1966, Pre-Presidential Papers, Richard Nixon Presidential Library and Museum.

51. Nixon, Memorandum from Leonard Garment, October 6, 1966.

52. Richard Nixon, Memorandum to Leonard Garment, March 23, 1966, Pre-Presidential Papers, Richard Nixon Presidential Library and Museum.

53. Nixon, Memorandum to Leonard Garment, March 23 memo. Also James Warren, "On the Brink of Scandal, LBJ Showed How to Act Very Fast," *Chicago Tribune*, March 28, 1999, accessed March 30, 2017, http://articles.chicagotribune.com/1999-03-28/news/9903280124_1_walter-jenkins-johnson-presidential-library-conversation.

54. "*Time, Inc. v. Hill*," Oyez, accessed March 31, 2017, https://www.oyez.org/cases/1965/22.

55. *Time, Inc. v. Hill.*"

56. *Time, Inc. v. Hill.*"

57. *Time, Inc. v. Hill.*"

58. *Time, Inc. v. Hill.*"

59. *Time, Inc. v. Hill.*"

60. *Time, Inc. v. Hill.*"

61. "High Court Hears Argument by Nixon, His First Before It," *New York Times*, April 28, 1966.

62. "Nixon Upholds Rights of Privacy in Arguing First High Court Case," *Washington Post*, April 28, 1966.

63. Garment, *Crazy Rhythm*, 87. However, according to Schwartz, Fortas was quoted as saying he thought Nixon's performance had been mediocre immediately following the argument.

64. Garment, *Crazy Rhythm*, 87.

65. Zoeller, interview by Li.

66. Milgrim, interview by Li.

67. Richard Nixon, Memorandum to Leonard Garment, April 28, 1966, Pre-Presidential Papers, Richard Nixon Presidential Library and Museum.

68. Nixon, Memorandum to Leonard Garment, April 28, 1966.

69. Nixon, Memorandum to Leonard Garment, April 28, 1966.

70. Nixon, Memorandum to Leonard Garment, April 28, 1966.

71. Milgrim, interview by Li.

72. Milgrim, interview by Li.

73. Richard Nixon, interview by Tom Evans, March 15, 1983, transcript.

74. Garment, *Crazy Rhythm*, 87.

75. Barbas, "When Privacy Almost Won."

76. Barbas, "When Privacy Almost Won."

77. Bernard Schwartz, *Unpublished Opinions of the Warren Court* (New York: Oxford University Press, 1985), 251.

78. Barbas, "When Privacy Almost Won."

79. Memo to Garment, April 28, 1966.

80. Memo to Garment, April 28, 1966.

81. Barbas, "When Privacy Almost Won."

82. "I Quit Klan: Black's Defense," *Chicago Tribune*, October 2, 1937, accessed March 31, 2017, http://archives.chicagotribune.com/1937/10/02/page/1/article/i-quit-klan-blacks-defense.

83. "Justice Black Dies at 85: Served on Court for 34 Years," *New York Times*, September 25, 1971, accessed March 31, 2017, http://www.nytimes.com/learning/general/onthisday/bday/0227.html.

84. Linda Greenhouse, "Ex-Justice Fortas Dies at 71; Shaped Historic Rulings on Rights," *New York Times*, April 7, 1982, accessed March 31, 2017, http://www.nytimes.com/1982/04/07/obituaries/ex-justice-abe-fortas-dies-at-71-shaped-historic-rulings-on-rights.html?pagewanted=all.

85. Laura Kalman, *Abe Fortas: A Biography* (New Haven: Yale University Press, 1990), 320.

86. Kalman, *Abe Fortas*, at 321.

87. Howard Ball, *Hugo L. Black: Cold Steel Warrior* (New York: Oxford University Press, 1996), 156.
88. Roger Newman, *Hugo Black: A Biography* (New York: Fordham University Press, 1994), 589.
89. Newman, *Hugo Black*, 590.
90. Kalman, *Abe Fortas*, 321.
91. Ball, *Hugo L. Black*, 156.
92. Ball, *Hugo L. Black*.
93. Ball, *Hugo L. Black*.
94. Barbas, "When Privacy Almost Won."
95. Barbas, "When Privacy Almost Won."
96. Barbas, "When Privacy Almost Won."
97. Garment, *Crazy Rhythm*, 90.
98. Parker, interview by Li.
99. Schwartz, *Super Chief*, 642–43.
100. "*Time v. Hill*," Oyez.
101. "*Time v. Hill*," Oyez.
102. Leonard Garment, "Annals of Law: The Hill Case," *New Yorker*, April 17, 1989.
103. "*Time v. Hill*," Oyez, supra.
104. *Time, Inc. v. Hill*, 385 U.S. 374 (1967).
105. *Time, Inc. v. Hill*.
106. Ronald Ostrow, "High Court Backs Press in False Report Cases," *Los Angeles Times*, January 10, 1967.
107. Garment, "The Hill Case."
108. Richard Nixon, Memorandum from Leonard Garment to Richard Nixon, May 18, 1967, Pre-Presidential Papers, Richard Nixon Presidential Library and Museum.
109. Ed Cray, *Chief Justice: A Biography of Earl Warren* (New York: Simon and Schuster, 1997), 497.
110. Cray, *Chief Justice*, 499.
111. Kalman, *Abe Fortas*, 331.
112. Cray, *Chief Justice*, 500–1.
113. Andrew Glass, "Senate Spikes Abe Fortas' Supreme Court Nomination, Oct. 1, 1968," *Politico*, October 1, 2015, accessed March 31, 2017, http://www.politico.com/story/2015/10/senate-spikes-fortas-supreme-court-nomination-oct-1-1968-214129.
114. Kalman, *Abe Fortas*, 349.
115. Newman, *Hugo Black*, 444.
116. Newman, *Hugo Black*, 596.
117. William Lambert, "Fortas: A Question of Ethics," *Life*, May 9, 1969.
118. Bob Woodward, "Fortas Tie to Wolfson Is Detailed," *Washington Post*, January 23, 1977, accessed September 1, 2017, https://www.washingtonpost.com/archive/politics/1977/01/23/fortas-tie-to-wolfson-is-detailed/0b15ab1b-ca34-4a99-be65-51967ea123a6/?utm_term=.fdfa34ebb4e2.
119. Bob Woodward and Scott Armstrong, *The Brethren* (New York: Simon & Schuster, 1979), 19–20.
120. Woodward, "Fortas Tie to Wolfson Is Detailed." According to the article, which was based on transcripts from a phone call to Fortas that Wolfson had secretly recorded, Wolfson had asked Fortas to talk to the president about a pardon. When Wolfson brought up asking for a pardon, he noted that "apparently nothing happened." "No," was Fortas's response.
121. Woodward and Armstrong, *The Brethren*, 20.
122. Newman, *Hugo Black*, 596–57.
123. Woodward and Armstrong, *The Brethren*, 56–57, 74–75. Nixon was determined to nominate a southerner and picked South Carolina jurist Clement Haynsworth, chief judge of the US Court of Appeals for the Fourth Circuit, to take Fortas's seat. Haynsworth was well respected, and both Black and Brennan believed he would have been a good justice. Labor unions and civil rights groups, however, opposed Haynsworth, and liberal senators, who were spoiling for a fight after the Fortas affair, helped defeat the nomination. Nixon then nominated

another southerner, G. Harrold Carswell, of the US Court of Appeals for the Fifth Circuit. Carswell's nomination came under fire after it came out that, as a candidate for public office in 1948, he had made a number of prosegregation speeches. Judges and lawyers also questioned his competence, leading to a memorable, and unintentionally damaging, speech from a supporter, Senator Roman Hruska, in which the conservative Republican argued: "There are a lot of mediocre judges and people and lawyers, and they are represented to a little representation, aren't they? We can't have all Brandeises, Frankfurters and Cardozos." The Senate also rejected Carswell. Nixon then gave up and nominated a northerner, Harry Blackmun of the US Court of Appeals for the Eighth Circuit. Blackmun was confirmed 94–0.

124. Kalman, *Abe Fortas*, 361–62.
125. "Winners and Losers, '68," *Life,* January 10, 1969.
126. Kalman, *Abe Fortas*, 361–62.
127. "A Memo on Muckraking from the Publisher of Life," *Life,* June 6, 1969.
128. "A Memo on Muckraking from the Publisher of Life."
129. Garment, "The Hill Case," 107.
130. Garment, *Crazy Rhythm*, 97.
131. Parker, interview by Li.
132. Jonathan Aitken, *Nixon: A Life* (Washington, DC: Regnery History, 1993), 314.
133. Barbas, "When Privacy Almost Won."
134. Nixon, April 28, 1966 memo.
135. Barbas, "When Privacy Almost Won."
136. Garment, "The Hill Case," 109.

Chapter Ten

"The Purpose of This Group Is to Begin Planning, Now, to Win the Nomination."

On January 7, 1967, seven men descended upon the famed Waldorf-Astoria Hotel in New York City for a secret meeting. Boasting an average age of forty years old, these seven young men were smart and highly accomplished in their respective fields. And they all had a pretty good idea as to why they had been summoned to the famous Suite 31-A of the Waldorf—otherwise, they probably wouldn't have been invited.

They were there to meet with Richard Nixon to begin formal preparations for the 1968 presidential campaign.

The choice of suites had not been an accident. Suite 31-A was most famous for having housed former president Herbert Hoover ever since he left the White House in disgrace in March 1933. Nixon was well acquainted with the suite, having paid numerous visits to the ex-president over the years to seek his counsel and advice. Furthermore, Nixon had always admired and respected Hoover in spite of Hoover's failures and defeats. Indeed, Suite 31-A was an apt metaphor for Nixon's impending political comeback.

Of all the Republican presidents that Richard Nixon could have chosen as a role model, Herbert Hoover probably wasn't the most obvious choice. Hoover is routinely ranked among the worst presidents in American history and serves as a cautionary tale for presidents who resist acting aggressively to combat economic meltdown. A self-made millionaire and world traveler who had widely been considered to be one of the most intelligent, able, and successful governmental figures in the country when he ran for president in 1928, Hoover seemingly turned into an incompetent, uncaring, and out-of-touch weakling overnight, as the stock market crash of October 1929 helped lead to the worst economic collapse in American history. Hoover resisted using the powers of the presidency to alleviate the suffering of millions of Americans, instead arguing that the business community was better suited to solving the economic crisis than the government. As a result, most of his actions were designed to prop up businesses rather than help individuals. Hoover even refused to pour money into unemployment relief due to his philosophical belief that putting workers on the dole decreased their incentive to work.

Uncharismatic and hard to like even on his best days, Hoover made matters worse with a series of unfortunate comments that made him into the American Marie Antoinette. "Nobody is actually starving," he told a Washington journalist.[1] "The hobos, for example, are better fed than they have ever been." When the International Apple Shippers Association experienced a supply surplus in December 1930, they offered to sell apples to unemployed men on credit and allowed them to resell the apples for a nickel each, leading to an explosion of apple salesmen. Hoover's remark that "many people have left their jobs for the more profitable one of selling apples" [2] made him seem out of touch, at best, and indifferent at worst. Pretty soon, his name became a derogatory phrase. Shantytowns set up by homeless individuals and families were known as "Hoovervilles." "Hoover blankets" referred to the newspapers used by all of those well-fed hobos to wrap themselves up in order to keep warm. The "Hoover flag" was a slang term for empty pockets turned inside out. [3] For many years, the only thing associated with Herbert Hoover that had any positive connotation was the Hoover Dam—and even that went through a fourteen-year period from 1933 to 1947 when it was officially disassociated with Hoover and simply referred to as "The Boulder Dam."

It surprised almost no one when Hoover lost in a landslide to FDR in the 1932 presidential election. Roosevelt's popular vote tally was the largest in American history up to that point, and Hoover's electoral vote count went from 444 in 1928 to 59 in 1932. Hoover even received a telegram encouraging him to "vote for Roosevelt and make it unanimous."[4]

Hoover, however, took his defeat in stride and became an active and respected ex-president. After being shut out of the FDR White House, he became an important advisor to presidents Truman and Eisenhower and chaired presidential commissions under both Administrations to examine ways to make government more efficient. He helped with the effort to rebuild war-torn Europe and toured occupied Germany on behalf of the Truman Administration to determine how to combat food shortages there. Whereas during the Depression, the phrase *Hoover Meal* probably would have referred to people eating rotting food from a garbage can—for postwar Germany, a Hoover Meal (*Hooverspeisung*) was a much-needed and welcome program where free meals were given to German schoolchildren.[5]

Hoover also wielded a tremendous amount of influence as a power broker and respected elder within the Republican Party. Associates and friends referred him to as "the Chief," and it became customary for Republican officials to pay their respects to the Chief, whether it be at Suite 31-A or at the Bohemian Grove, a California secret society/social club that was only open to powerful and prominent men where Hoover frequently held court. It was Hoover who had first noticed Nixon, taking the time to write to the brash congressman from Whittier to praise him for getting Alger Hiss. "My dear Mr. Congressman," Hoover wrote to a young Nixon.[6] "[The Hiss conviction for perjury] was due to your patience and persistence alone. At last the stream of treason that existed in our Government has been exposed in a fashion that all may believe."

The Chief had also served as an unofficial advisor to Nixon during the 1960 presidential election. When Nixon came to the Waldorf-Astoria to seek his counsel, Hoover flatly advised the GOP standard-bearer to stop debating Kennedy. "You've had three debates," Hoover told Nixon at the Waldorf-Astoria.[7] "Isn't that enough?" Like many, Hoover knew that the stark differences between the uncharismatic hangdog with the Pinocchio nose and the handsome Greek God only hurt the Republican nominee. Meanwhile, it was Nixon's lack of clear-cut ideological differences with Kennedy that really bothered the Chief. "By every implication, he is determined on a new and greater New Deal," Hoover lamented privately about Nixon.[8]

Despite that, Hoover remained loyal to the cause. He even counseled Nixon during the days after the election and advised Nixon to play ball when Kennedy tried to arrange a photo-op with his defeated opponent in an effort to ensure his legitimacy to the office he had just won. It was Hoover who told Nixon to go to Kennedy, rather than the other way around, and even yelled at Nixon when the defeated candidate tried to wiggle out of it. "This is a generous gesture on his part," Hoover told Nixon.[9] "You ought to meet it with equal generosity."

By the time Hoover died in 1964, he had gone a long way toward rehabilitating his reputation by setting a standard for ex-presidents to continue serving their country long after their terms expired. It was this spirit and determination not to let a devastating defeat define his legacy that inspired Nixon as he looked to do what Hoover could not—win the White House after suffering his repudiation at the hands of the electorate.

Nixon's official comeback started in that suite with those seven young men. "The purpose of this group is to begin planning now to win the nomination," Nixon told the seven in attendance.[10] Two of the seven charged with this task were from the Nixon Mudge firm: Tom Evans and William Safire. There were two holdovers from Congress '66: Bob Finch, the forty-one-year-old newly elected lieutenant governor of California, and Peter Flanigan, the forty-three-year-old investment banker. Rounding out the group were Fred

LaRue, a thirty-eight-year-old Republican who was state party chairman for Mississippi; Jerry Milbank, a forty-six-year-old businessman who had been one of Goldwater's fundraisers in 1964; and Peter O'Donnell, the forty-two-year-old state chairman for the Texas Republicans.[11]

Most of the people present had long known of Nixon's intentions. As Evans noted, the Congress '66 committee had been created with an eye toward 1968, so that Nixon would have an established campaign organization in place in case he decided to run for president.

Now he was making it official. Evans later described the 1968 campaign as a series of concentric circles with Nixon at the center of it all. Stans would head the fundraising circle, which would operate under the formal name of the Nixon for President Committee.[12] Another circle would handle political issues and would include the likes of Garment, Buchanan, and Robert Ellsworth, a Kansas Republican who had just completed three terms in the US House of Representatives and would link up with the Nixon campaign.[13] There would be yet another circle that handled public relations and imaging and was tasked with making Nixon seem as presidential as possible throughout the campaign.

And there was the circle of seven that met at the Waldorf in January 1967. These men represented a small, elite circle that was tasked with the most important task of all—making sure that Nixon won the Republican nomination. "It is important that we keep the existence of this group quiet, not only because of the press, but because we don't want to hurt the feelings of anybody we've left out," Nixon said, emphasizing how important this group was to his plans.[14] "It is not the purpose of this group to help me on the issues." Nixon offhandedly made reference to some issues he thought would be important to the campaign, including Vietnam, inflation, race, and crime. However, his primary instinct was that the 1968 election would be more of a personality-driven race between him and LBJ, and that issues wouldn't really matter as much. Nixon, as Ambrose pointed out, had already taken the position that anything Johnson was for he was against—especially when it came to Vietnam.[15]

Instead, the main task for the seven men in attendance, the "Strategy Board," as Evans called the group, was to figure out how to get rid of Nixon's "loser" label. "My biggest problem," Nixon conceded,[16] "is 'Nixon can't win.'" Finch argued that the Board had to convince delegates that Nixon could win, to which Safire suggested that they promote the "inevitability" of a Nixon nomination.[17] Nixon, however, wasn't sure and pointed out to the Board that he was no normal candidate. "You can't repackage Nixon with PR," Nixon said.[18] "Maybe that's okay with a new man, but not with me. I'm a known quantity. That has its benefits . . . but it has its drawbacks."

Flanigan argued that Nixon had no choice but to enter, and win, the Republican primaries in order to permanently shed his "loser" label. It wasn't lost on any of the men in the suite that it had been seventeen years since Nixon had last won an election on his own—without a certain beloved ex-general standing beside him. In 1968, the vast majority of delegates would be chosen by state conventions; however, there would also be approximately a dozen presidential primaries. Some of the primaries were not worth entering, as they would be in the bag for various favorite-son candidates. Nixon's former home state of California fit that description, as the state would clearly go for Ronald Reagan, its popular, newly elected governor.

Some in the group also believed that the winnable primaries weren't worth entering either. Nixon could only hurt his chances at clinching the nomination—one mistake, one gaffe, or one bad result would reinforce the idea that he couldn't win. Plus, Goldwater had sewn up the nomination in 1964 thanks to his overwhelming popularity with state delegates. Given Nixon's name recognition, as well as his tireless campaigning in both 1964 and 1966, he could have skipped the primaries and simply called in all of his favors accumulated over the previous two election cycles and clinched the nomination before the opening gavel at the 1968 convention.[19]

To Flanigan and the others, however, this was a dangerous route for Nixon to take. Simply put, he would have no momentum going into the convention and would still have that dreaded "loser" label. Instead, Flanigan argued that Nixon should enter primaries in New Hampshire, Wisconsin, Nebraska, and Oregon because there would be no favorite sons to compete with, and Nixon could demonstrate his head-to-head superiority against the rest of the GOP field.[20]

As for who might be part of that GOP field, there had been several names and faces that had entered the void following Nixon's exit from the electoral stage and Goldwater's retreat to the US Senate following his landslide loss to Lyndon Johnson. Nixon was clearly concerned that one of these foes could upend his comeback and beat him to the Republican nomination.

Rockefeller, however, was not one of them. Despite the New York governor's continued prominence within the GOP, Nixon was immediately dismissive, saying that his old nemesis had "no chance at all."[21] Safire recalled being surprised at his boss's casual dismissal of his longtime rival.[22] However, Rockefeller's star had faded considerably after the 1964 election, and he had engendered a tremendous amount of ill will in light of his refusal to lift a finger for Goldwater. Plus, trying to decipher his intentions when it came to the presidency had been a popular parlor game over the last couple of election cycles.[23] Rockefeller always seemed to vacillate between going for the White House and staying out of the race and, like a high-schooler who was afraid of getting turned down for prom, his default mode was to show disinterest while making it known that he would be willing to consider accepting the nomination if the party wanted it badly enough. "When I became insecure because of events getting out of control and beyond my capacity, I always pulled back to a base which was controllable," Rockefeller, himself, noted.[24]

Instead, Nixon seemed more concerned about Reagan. A relative newcomer to politics, Ronald Reagan had made his name as a Hollywood actor and was, perhaps, best known for his starring role in *Knute Rockne: All American*, where he played dying Notre Dame football player George "The Gipper" Gipp who inspires his teammates to go out and "win one for the Gipper." With his acting career winding down, Reagan had begun gravitating toward politics. Formerly a New Deal Democrat who considered FDR to be his political hero, Reagan found himself drifting to the right throughout the 1950s and eventually joined the Republican Party, making the famous statement that he didn't leave the Democrats, the Democrats left him. He built up his right-wing bona fides, touring the country in 1954 and giving probusiness speeches on behalf of General Electric, which had hired him to serve as host of the weekly TV series the *General Electric Theater*. In 1961, with Medicare looming, he created a recording for the American Medical Association where he warned that the United States was in danger of becoming a socialist dictatorship.[25]

But it was Reagan's speeches on behalf of Barry Goldwater during the 1964 campaign that shot him to fame. His most famous speech, titled "A Time for Choosing," was prerecorded and broadcast on television in October 1964. "You and I are told we must choose between a left or right, but I suggest there is no such thing as a left or right," Reagan said in the most oft-quoted portion of his speech.[26] "There is only an up or down. Up to man's age-old dream—the maximum of individual freedom consistent with order or down to the ant heap of totalitarianism." Reagan took full advantage of his "A Star Is Born" moment, winning the California gubernatorial race in a landslide in 1966, and in doing so, defeating Nixon's conqueror, Pat Brown. By 1968, Reagan had assumed the mantle of the conservative wing of the GOP in place of Goldwater and was an intriguing dark horse candidate for president. Nixon gave Reagan four-to-one odds, and the Board brainstormed some ways to negate the threat the former leading man posed. Finch, Reagan's lieutenant governor, suggested using Reagan as a stalking horse while proposing that they lean on him not to run.[27]

Nixon placed himself and Illinois senator Charles Percy in second place at two-to-one odds. Safire recalled being surprised that his boss had given Percy such a good chance at snagging the nomination, but noted that others at the meeting had agreed with Nixon that Percy was a threat.[28] A moderate-to-liberal Republican who had more in common with Rockefeller than Goldwater, Percy was rich, young, handsome, and well liked throughout Washington, D.C. In many ways, he was like the GOP version of John F. Kennedy,[29] and his policies were almost every bit as anathema to conservative Republicans as those of a typical northeastern Democrat. Percy had made his reputation as a champion of affordable housing and was considered a dove on foreign policy issues. He had even compared himself to Eisenhower, self-identifying as "a conservative on money issues but a liberal on people issues."[30] Nixon noted that Percy "had a good forum in Washington" and was "smart" but ultimately concluded that the senator didn't have much of a delegate base.

Ray Price spelled out the strengths and weaknesses of Percy in a strategy memo issued several months after the inaugural Strategy Board meeting. While he identified Percy as Nixon's biggest threat, he threw in a major caveat. "Percy's biggest strength is as the presumed heir to the Romney forces, when Romney fails," Price wrote.[31] "He has the substantial advantage of being acceptable to both the liberal and conservative wings, and of having no particular block of enemies in the party structure." Price, however, believed that Percy's support was soft and that he was, essentially, a fallback option for most moderate GOP voters. "This is our first target of opportunity: The people now leaning to Romney but looking for a place to jump to, and who can be gotten if we can simply erase some of the negative images that are now, in fact, obsolete," Price wrote.[32]

Indeed, it was George Romney that concerned Nixon the most. The moderate governor of Michigan was, according to a November 1966 Gallup poll,[33] the frontrunner for the GOP nomination, and Nixon told the Board that Romney was "even money to get the nomination."[34] Nixon had good reason to worry about Romney, who seemed like the perfect candidate—at least on paper. For one thing, no one looked more presidential than the tall, telegenic, square-jawed Romney. In addition to looking like he came from central casting, Romney had other clear advantages. He was incredibly wealthy thanks to his successful tenure as CEO of American Motor Corporation and had developed a reputation for being a man of principle, especially when it came to civil rights. The Mormon Romney made headlines in 1963 by marching alongside the NAACP in Michigan despite the fact that his church, at the time, saw blacks as "cursed" and banned them from becoming priests.[35] Romney's strong support of the 1964 Civil Rights Act was also cited as a reason why he refused to support Goldwater, who had made his opposition to the act a central part of his platform.[36]

Romney also had the advantage of having the "winner" label. He had knocked off an incumbent Democratic governor in 1962 and had increased his margin of victory in his 1964 reelection before winning a landslide victory in 1966 (Michigan switched to four-year terms for its governor in 1967). His 1966 win immediately put him on the map for the presidential race, and he led both LBJ and RFK in polls taken in November 1966.[37]

Nixon, however, seemed convinced that Romney was out of his depth. Romney held an eight-point lead in the Gallup poll over Nixon at the time the Board met for the first time.[38] Nixon pointed out to the Board that Romney had "never shown an ability to hit big-league pitching" and believed that an early loss for Romney during the primary election season could doom him.[39] Nixon also believed Romney would wilt under the weight of all the extra scrutiny and attention that came with being the prohibitive frontrunner. "Let Romney take the point," Nixon said. Meanwhile he would take a "moratorium" on politics during the first half of 1967. Instead of actively campaigning, Nixon would travel and brush up on his foreign policy credentials, especially with Vietnam looming as a major issue during the upcoming campaign.[40]

While Nixon's moratorium was in effect, it would be up to the Board to walk the line between letting everyone know that Nixon was running but not to be so obvious about it that it would draw attention away from Romney. "If I were to do nothing, Romney would be nominated," Nixon pointed out.[41] "Nobody could stop him in the Midwest. Whoever is running has to start running now, and this group of cynical idealists should be the first to realize it."

Finally, Nixon closed with a call to action. "While I am lying back, I want you to work your tails off getting the job done," Nixon said. "We will have to work harder and better than the other candidates to win." For a man who had long thought that sheer hard work could win over even his fiercest critics, this was merely a reaffirmation of one of his core beliefs. What was different was that now he had a group of young, smart, determined men that was willing to do it for him.

"THE MAN IN THE ARENA."

Before the initial meeting of the Strategy Board ended, Nixon did a quick, informal tally of his presumed delegate count and came up with 603. With 667 needed to clinch the GOP nomination on the first ballot, Nixon was already in good shape to get the nod. However, as he and others with his campaign knew all too well, simply getting the nomination wasn't enough. Nixon needed to look like a winner, and perhaps just as importantly, he needed a way to deemphasize his less attractive features.

As his colleagues and subordinates all attest, Nixon was hardly devoid of charm. Television may not have been his best friend over the years, but in the past, he had demonstrated an ability to be likeable on the small screen—like he had been during that 1963 appearance on *The Jack Paar Program*. But to most of America, he was still the brooding, mean-spirited caricature with the droopy jowls, Pinocchio nose, and perpetual five o' clock shadow that had taken his ball and gone home after things didn't go his way. Despite spending the last several years softening his image while strengthening his credentials as an elder statesman and party leader, to many in America, Nixon was still the same not-so-loveable loser, and no amount of piano playing on late night television would change that.

Nixon needed to undergo a complete repackaging if he wanted to have a chance at winning the White House. So, he did what was starting to become a custom for him: he asked Garment to figure something out. "In his view, I had the requisite credentials," Garment said.[42] "I was trustworthy, politically ignorant and an energetic recruiter. I had experience in persuasion (trial lawyer) and show business (jazz saxophonist)." Admittedly, Garment lacked actual advertising experience, but to Nixon, that was a plus. "Nixon's guidelines were simple: Don't hire an advertising agency," Garment recalled.[43] "They're dinosaurs and devour money."

Garment immediately recruited Frank Shakespeare, the president of CBS Television and a staunch political conservative. Shakespeare seemed on track to be the head of the network; however, his real life's passion was to "destroy liberals"[44]—a quality that must have been music to Nixon's ears. Shakespeare decided that Nixon was his man in 1968 after coming to the realization that his first choice, Reagan, was too inexperienced. In July 1967, Shakespeare met with Nixon at the Mudge offices at 20 Broad Street, after which Nixon asked Garment to find a place for the experienced television executive within the campaign. Garment took Shakespeare to lunch, and the two became fast friends. "At our initial lunch, Shakespeare delivered an illuminating two-hour lecture on the impact of modern television," Garment said.[45] "It was transforming not only politics, he said, but the way the culture received and used information." Calling television "the cruelest of all media," Shakespeare warned that it could sink Nixon in a heartbeat unless he learned how to harness its power to project the image he wanted.

Shortly after their lunch, Shakespeare and Garment met up in a CBS screening room along with Evans and Ray Price. Like a coach breaking down game tape to figure out where the team had gone wrong, the men critiqued six or seven hours worth of Nixon's television appearances stored in the network's vast archives, and what they found was that Nixon's prepared stump speeches brought out the worst in him. When forced to stand up before a crowd and deliver some variation of the usual talking points, Nixon was stiff and awkward. Rarely inspirational, Nixon's overly formal style on the stump made him sound more like a professor giving a lecture or a lawyer trying a case in court. Worse, his tendency to perspire kicked in, making him look deceptive and deceitful. On the other hand, the group found that, in less formal, one-on-one sessions, he was relaxed, easygoing, and even came across as somewhat likeable.

That observation squared with Garment's overall view of Nixon. For a self-described "liberal Democrat," Garment, obviously, had a preconceived notion of Nixon that was largely influenced by his public persona and his prominent facial features, which Garment called "odd-looking." However, he also recalled being surprised that, as he got to know Nixon on a personal level, he found him to be witty, interesting, and even self-deprecating. Garment was profoundly impressed by Nixon's intelligence, an important quality that gave Nixon the foresight to embrace his negative public persona and utilize it to his advantage. "It would give him, in addition to his 99 percent name and face recognition, the capacity to surprise," Garment said.[46] "To set the low public expectations against his large private abilities and permit the press to discover, gradually, some realities that they would dub the 'new Nixon' running again for President."

Sears concurred, observing that Nixon's personality was not conducive to being a great politician. "He was always very anxious," Sears recalled.[47] "He didn't like to be with people he didn't know." Sears also stated Nixon's primary appeal wasn't that he was likeable but that he was someone that could be easily admired. "He was smart—very, very smart," said Sears.[48] "Sometimes, I don't think he even knew how smart he was. You could also admire his doggedness. No one outworked him."

So it was up to Nixon's partners and employees at Nixon Mudge to figure out how best to bring out the side of Nixon that would engender admiration from the voters instead of distrust, discomfort, or outright revulsion. Garment hired Harry Treleaven, an advertising executive who had been at J. Walter Thompson for eighteen years—the same company Haldeman had worked for. The small, thin, gray-haired man looked like the archetype of the 1960s-era ad man, wearing a Brooks Brothers–style suit as if it were a uniform while displaying a stern, stoic demeanor as he ran important ad campaigns for the likes of Ford, Lark Cigarettes, and RCA. Joe McGinniss, who wrote *The Selling of the President* after receiving near-unlimited access to Nixon's media team, compared Treleaven to a high school vice principal and observed that he resembled William Scranton.[49]

Treleaven had cut his teeth working on George H. W. Bush's successful 1966 House of Representatives race. Bush had lost his first electoral race, a 1964 Senate campaign in Texas, against incumbent Democrat Ralph Yarborough, and another defeat for Bush could very well have stopped the future president's political career dead in its tracks. As a politician, Bush had always had some serious handicaps. Like Nixon, he could be awkward in public and hardly exuded charisma. Even worse, in a state that craved authenticity, Bush was about as Texan as Taco Bell. A New England born and bred blue blood whose father had been a prominent moderate Republican senator from Connecticut, Bush, the former Yale first-baseman, had only moved to Texas so that he could get into the oil business. If anyone were a card-carrying member of the very Eastern Establishment that Nixon hated, it was Bush. And like Nixon, Bush was an uninspiring, charismatically challenged campaigner who had a pedantic style of speaking.

Yet Treleaven was able to reinvent his candidate as a casual "man of the people" who cared, deeply, about the problems of everyday Texans and would fight his heart out for them.[50] What issues those were or how he would go about fighting for his constituents was left unsaid. Instead, Treleaven, who sank 80 percent of his campaign budget into advertising, the vast majority of which went to TV, knew that all he had to do was to create the image of Bush as a "fighting underdog," and voters would naturally flock toward him.[51] "People sympathize with a man who tries hard," Treleaven said.[52] "They are also flattered that anyone would really exert himself to get their vote. Bush, therefore, must be shown as a man who's working his heart out to win." In that vein, Treleaven made sure that Bush was constantly on television with his suit coat casually slung over his shoulder and his sleeves rolled up as he worked his tail off to shake as many hands and listen to the concerns of as many voters as possible. Again, it didn't matter what he believed in or if he was even going to help the voters he spoke to. All that mattered was that it looked like he cared.[53] In the end, Bush won with 58 percent of the vote and would become a staunch Nixon backer until the Watergate scandal drove a wedge in their alliance.

In November 1967, Treleaven delivered his report to Garment and identified several of Nixon's negative traits that could be magnified by television. For one thing, Treleaven was concerned about Nixon's lack of humor, but noted that it could be corrected by having professionals write and craft jokes for him. Treleaven also noted that several 1968 hopefuls, particularly Robert Kennedy, projected warmth and caring, two qualities that have never been associated with Nixon. That, too, could be corrected by having professional writers "give him words to say that will show emotional involvement in the issues," as well as staging scenes and situations so that Nixon could show off his (prepared) warmth.[54]

Treleaven's ultimate finding, however, buoyed Garment. Don't worry about creating a "new Nixon," Treleaven argued. He had found that, as far as the voters were concerned, absence had made their hearts grow fonder. The old Nixon was actually doing pretty well with voters, who tended to remember his positive attributes with more specificity and clarity than his negatives.[55]

Ray Price had also come to the same conclusion. "It's not what's *there* that counts, it's what's projected," Price argued.[56] "And carrying it one step further, it's not what *he* projects but rather what the voter receives. It's not the man we have to change, but rather the *received impression* [original emphasis]." To Price, the way to combat the "loser label" when it came to television was simple: the campaign had to portray Nixon as a winner at all times. Eventually, the label would stick because, in Price's words, most voters were "basically lazy" and would vote for Nixon as long as they felt an emotional connection to him. "[Nixon] has to come across as a person larger than life," Price said.[57] "People are stirred by the legend, including the living legend, not by the man himself. It's the aura that surrounds the charismatic figure more than it is the figure itself that draws the followers. Our task is to build that aura."

To accomplish this task, Garment decided to follow through on a suggestion that had come from an unlikely source. William Gavin was a thirty-one-year-old teacher from Pennsylvania, as well as a huge fan of Nixon's. Gavin had hoped that Nixon would run for president in 1968 and wrote him a letter of encouragement in early 1967. Rose Mary Woods, who handled Nixon's mail, had read the letter and flagged it to Garment as something worth following up on:

> Dear Mr. Nixon,
> May I offer two suggestions concerning your plans for 1968? 1. Run. You can win. Nothing can happen to you, politically speaking, that is worse than what has happened to you. Ortega y Gasset says in *The Revolt of the Masses*: " . . . these are the only genuine ideas; the ideas of the shipwrecked. All the rest is rhetoric, posturing, face. He who does not really feel himself lost, is lost without remission . . . " You, in effect, are lost. That is why you are the only political figure with the vision to see things the way they are and not as leftist or rightist kooks would have them. Run. You will win.[58]

The soaring rhetoric grabbed Garment's attention while Gavin's ability to boil it all down to one paragraph impressed the man who had become Nixon's chief recruiter. Meanwhile, it was Gavin's second paragraph that helped Garment and the advertising team conceptualize their approach to controlling Nixon's television presence:

> 2. A tip for television: Instead of those wooden performances beloved by politicians . . . why not have live press conferences as your campaign on television? People will see you daring all, not asking and answering phony "questions" made up by your staff.[59]

The "wooden approach" Gavin referred to was Nixon's use of televised telethons in 1960 and 1962. Along with their stated purpose of raising campaign funds, Nixon's telethons saw him take prescreened questions from callers while interacting with his family, as well as with celebrities like Pat Boone, Ginger Rogers, and Dodgers star Jackie Robinson.[60] Mixed in with the questions that, legitimately, came from outside callers were prewritten questions from Nixon's staff that would allow Nixon to attack his opponent or deliver a memorable one-liner or sound byte. Some of the questions were even designed to show off Nixon's softer side, such as: "If you had your life to live over, what changes would you make?"[61]

According to Paul Keyes, a former head writer for the *The Jack Paar Program* who had taken a leave of absence from his television duties to help Nixon's 1962 gubernatorial campaign, the telethons had been designed to make Nixon appear likeable and charismatic. Keyes decried what he saw as the commoditization of politicians and was critical of politicians using television or other forms of media to sell themselves to the public. Instead, he hoped to use television to stir the grassroots and inspire them to rise up and demand Nixon's service. "In short, we will replace the insensitive selling of a product with the sensitive affection for a candidate," Keyes maintained.[62]

What Gavin envisioned was something different. Instead of getting people to love, or even like, Nixon, Gavin's strategy was to get people to admire or respect him. That argument resonated with Garment and other Nixon friends who found the former vice president to be complicated and difficult to know. Garment invited Gavin to New York and immediately bonded with him over their shared love of jazz. Gavin soon went to work for Nixon's growing speechwriting corps, where he developed a knack for getting a single line or phrase into most of Nixon's speeches, including a line about how a "great philosophy is not one without defeat but one without fear" that Gavin had written into Nixon's draft concession speech on Election Night in 1968, only for Nixon to put it into his victory speech.[63] Nixon even referred to him as the "one-liner man." Gavin went on to have a long career in Washington, serving as a speechwriter for both Nixon and Reagan before embarking on an eighteen-year stint working as a writer for longtime House Minority Leader Robert Michel of Illinois.[64]

Despite his ideas for how the campaign should utilize television, Gavin did not have any role in implementing his strategy. For that, the campaign turned to another young man who would go on to have a bright future in Republican circles.

Twenty-six-year-old Roger Ailes was a producer for *The Mike Douglas Show* when Nixon stopped by in the fall of 1967 for an interview. As Nixon was getting ready in the green room, he complained about how, in order to get elected, politicians like him had to rely on gimmicks like talk show interviews on television. "Television is not a gimmick," Ailes said.[65] "And if you think it is, you'll lose again."

Ailes then told the former vice president that his lack of television presence had cost him the 1960 presidential race and that, in order to win in 1968, he needed people around him who understood television.

"Mr. Nixon, you need a media adviser," Ailes told a stunned Nixon.

"What's a media adviser?"

"I am," Ailes said confidently.[66]

Ailes made a huge impression with the prohibitive candidate.[67] Nixon had Garment reach out to him soon after that green room meeting to offer him a spot with the campaign.[68] For Ailes, a devoted Republican from Ohio, the job was his opportunity to merge his love of politics with his skills as a television producer—as well as his first step toward becoming one of the most influential television executives of his time.

With Ailes in tow, the media team began to implement the "live press conference" ad campaign that Gavin had proposed—with a slight twist. The "press conferences" would not be the usual Q&A sessions where combative reporters would fire questions at a defensive Nixon. Instead, what Nixon and his team had in mind was more of a pretaped program featuring the candidate interacting with a hand-picked panel consisting of five-to-seven individuals each representing a certain demographic or ethnic group before a studio audience, also hand picked, by the Republican Party. The idea was to show Nixon developing a rapport with each panelist, making television audiences realize that Nixon did have some charisma after all. The questions would be preapproved but would not be obvious softballs, either. After all, Nixon was, often, at his most compelling when he was arguing a point and trying to convince his audience to see things his way. Ailes referred to the program as "the man in the arena" session, taking the phrase from a famous Teddy Roosevelt speech that the future Fox News impresario counted as one of his favorites:

> It is not the critic who counts; not the man who points out how the strong man stumbles, or where the doer of deeds could have done them better. The credit belongs to the man who is actually in the arena, whose face is marred by dust and sweat and blood; who strives valiantly; who errs, who comes short again and again, because there is no effort without error and shortcoming; but who does actually strive to do the deeds; who knows great enthusiasms, the great devotions; who spends himself in a worthy cause; who at the best knows in the end the triumph of high achievement, and who at the worst, if he fails, at least fails while daring greatly, so that his place shall never be with those cold and timid souls who neither know victory nor defeat.[69]

Nixon loved the quote, too.[70] After all, there aren't many quotes that capture, perfectly, Richard Nixon's entire ethos than that excerpt from Roosevelt's 1910 speech in France—particularly his relationship with his critics. Nixon saw himself as the prototypical man in the arena—a battle-tested warrior who was a striver and doer (the ultimate Orthogonian) who had learned from his prior failures to become stronger and wiser. It was a compelling narrative and one that would help power his 1968 campaign. Nixon loved the quote so much that he would use some variation of the "man in the arena" line repeatedly over the years. For instance, his presidential

resignation speech contained a reference to "man in the arena," and he even titled one of his memoirs *In the Arena*.

The first of the "Man in the Arena" spots that Ailes conceived of would be recorded in February 1968 from Hillsborough, New Hampshire, on the eve of that state's primary. Perhaps still believing in what he told Ailes about television being a "gimmick," Nixon was in a grouchy mood when he first reported to the studio. He relaxed once the session began and even seemed to enjoy the format. His longtime antagonists, the press, had not been given advance notice of the taping, and Nixon felt secure in knowing that the panelists weren't coming in with an agenda. With private citizens instead of experienced journalists, Nixon could do what he did best—demonstrate his expertise of various issues and cite any number of facts and figures to bolster his argument. Nixon ended up enjoying the session so much he continued answering questions after the allotted two hours had expired.[71]

The media team was ecstatic with the results, with Shakespeare even referring to them as electric and interesting.[72] Garment and Ailes then went to work cutting down the footage into five-minute ads, as well as a half-hour program that could serve as an infomercial for the campaign.

Meanwhile, Nixon found comfort with the controlled format, so his campaign continued with the Hillsborough approach throughout the primary campaign. In July 1968, with the nomination assured but not yet official, Nixon taped a panel session in New York that was then edited down to thirty minutes and shipped off to markets in Ohio, Illinois, and Michigan, three important battleground states for the general election.[73]

Once the nomination was officially his, Nixon took his act on the road. He had committed to doing ten sessions in states ranging from Massachusetts to Texas. His first session would be in Chicago, the site of his disastrous first debate with JFK in 1960 and site of the even more disastrous 1968 Democratic National Convention. Throughout the primary campaign, the press had chafed over not being allowed into the arena and was demanding access as Nixon started his general election campaign. Shakespeare had gone so far as to ban the press from even being in the studio during the Chicago taping. Given Nixon's contentious relationship with the press, the last thing his media team wanted was to show off his defensive and contentious side. According to McGinniss, Treleaven tried to talk Shakespeare out of it, but Shakespeare, backed by Ailes ("Fuck 'em," Ailes said), insisted that they be kept out. "It's a television show," Shakespeare said.[74] "Our television show. And the press has no business on the set." Ultimately, the media team allowed the press to watch from an adjacent studio, but they would not be allowed in with Nixon.

As for the content of the show, Nixon and his staff had upped their games since the primaries and had everything choreographed and planned down to the most minute detail. Typically, the show would open with clips of Nixon doing his trademark "v-for-victory" pose. For the Chicago spot, Treleaven and his team juxtaposed images of the triumphant Nixon with clips of the chaos and destruction the city had experienced during the recent Democratic National Convention. Then, like a gladiator marching out to face his competition, Nixon would stride, confidently, onto the stage while being showered with a warm, enthusiastic standing ovation from the studio audience. Wearing his warmest and brightest smile, Nixon would then banter a bit with the designated emcee, former ABC announcer and former Oklahoma football coach Bud Wilkinson, before he began taking questions—questions Wilkinson assured everyone that Nixon had never seen before and had not prepared for.[75]

Except that he had prepared for them. He and Ailes had crafted a series of stock answers he could utilize in any setting. Ailes believed that political sound bytes were most effective when they were full of descriptive visual phrases that could be hammered home to the viewer or listener with a memorable kicker. "The general public is not sophisticated enough to wade through answers," Ailes wrote in a memo to the campaign.[76] "Therefore, at least some of Nixon's answers should end with a . . . specific, graphic, succinct, memorable comment."

In Chicago, Nixon showed that he had mastered Ailes game plan. One of the first questions was about whether or not Nixon's views had shifted over the years due to political expediency. Nixon started by cracking a joke: "I supposed I could counter by saying, which Humphrey should we listen to today?" After the laughter from the audience, Nixon and even the guy asking the question faded, Nixon then deftly pivoted to a discussion about how much the world had changed since the end of World War II and the advent of the Cold War. "My answer is, yes, there is a new Nixon, if you are talking in terms of new ideas for the new world and the America we live in," Nixon said. "In terms of what I believe in the American view and the American dream, I think I am just what I was eight years ago." There was no follow-up—only a round of applause.[77]

Another audience member asked Nixon what he meant by "law and order"—one of the central pillars of his campaign. Nixon denied that "law and order" was a code word for racism and went back to his tried-and-true answer about the need for freedom and order to be in balance and how revolutions destroy all progress. "The greatness of America, with few exceptions over the period of our history, is that we have had the combination of having a system in which we could have peaceful change, peaceful progress, with order," Nixon said.[78] "Now that's what I want for America." Once again, he got a loud ovation for his response.

Even when things didn't go as planned, Nixon showed that he had finally grasped what TV was about. In Philadelphia, a few weeks after the Chicago taping, Nixon was confronted with a question that he hadn't prepared for as a local journalist sitting in the audience asked him why he was avoiding the Sunday news programs and their professional journalists in favor of these pretaped programs with amateur questioners. Nixon got angry and stared a hole through his questioner. "You talk about these quiz shows that take place on Sundays," Nixon said contemptuously.[79] "I've done *Meet the Press* and *Face the Nation* until they were running out of my ears."

Ailes and Shakespeare were thrilled. The spots had been going a little too well and things were coming a little too easy for Nixon. Having a bit of conflict, especially on a minor point like Sunday talk shows, was just what they needed to show voters that Nixon hadn't lost his backbone. Plus, it reinforced one of their main narratives of the campaign: Nixon never got a fair shake from the mainstream media, so he had to resort to other means in order to get his message out. From the control room, Shakespeare couldn't contain his glee. Thanks to Paul Keyes, who had moved on from Nixon's gubernatorial campaign to eventually become head writer of the popular sketch comedy show *Rowan & Martin's Laugh-In*, Nixon had recently made a well-received cameo on the show where he delivered the show's trademark catchphrase, albeit with his usual awkwardness, as well as a strangely inquisitive tone at the very end of it ("Sock it to meee?").[80] The bit had gone over well and was still fresh on everyone's mind, giving Shakespeare a ready-made punch line that perfectly illustrated his mood. "That socks it to him, Dickie Baby!" Shakespeare shouted.[81]

"HE JUST DECIDED TO DO IT."

Nixon's young staff did more than just work on his image. They also served as a conduit for new ideas. Martin Anderson, the young conservative professor from Columbia University who had joined the campaign as issues director and had been one of the men featured in the "Why Are These Men for Nixon?" piece, had drafted a memo calling for the abolition of the draft and the creation of an all-volunteer armed forces. In April 1967, when Anderson sent his fairly radical proposal to Nixon, he had good reason to assume that it would be summarily rejected. After all, conscription had existed in some form since the founding of this country. Furthermore, with the war in Vietnam showing no signs of slowing down, ending the draft seemed completely antithetical to Nixon's public statements about doing whatever was necessary to win.

Anderson recalled that, at the time he made his proposal, Nixon seemed like he was heading in the complete opposite direction. "At the time Nixon, I believe, had supported universal military training because that's exactly what Eisenhower supported when [Nixon] was Vice President," Anderson said.[82]

In his memo, Anderson laid out a case for why Nixon should embrace a voluntary military. Influenced by the work of economist Milton Friedman, Anderson argued that the entire draft process smacked of "involuntary servitude" that was "inimicable to the basic principles of freedom that are the moral foundations of our Republic."[83] Anderson also pointed out that there was little upside to having a military where the vast majority of soldiers were itching to get out as soon as possible—in fact, Anderson claimed that 93 percent of draftees left the armed forces immediately after their commitments were up. Instead, Anderson asserted that having professional soldiers who were motivated and dedicated to the cause would result in a better fighting force.

Politically, Anderson felt like the issue could be a winner for Nixon. "The attainment of both increased military protection and increased personal freedom should gain support from Republicans, Independents and Democrats, from Conservatives to Liberals," Anderson wrote.[84] He also argued that an all-volunteer force would insulate the government from claims of social or racial inequity, as no one group would bear the burden of providing soldiers to the American armed forces.

It was the latter point that, especially, intrigued Nixon. By eliminating the threat of being drafted into combat, Nixon reasoned that he could cripple the antiwar movement.[85] As such he forwarded Anderson's memo to several national security experts to get their input. He also asked a couple of his Mudge colleagues to weigh in. Partner Franklin B. Lincoln Jr., a former naval officer during World War II who went on to serve as civilian counsel in the navy and assistant secretary of defense under Eisenhower,[86] agreed with Anderson's conclusions but cautioned that the transition from an army of conscripts to an army of volunteers should be slow. "Under the Draft, rotation in Vietnam is indispensible," Lincoln observed, calling the elimination of the draft a "vote getter."[87] "This results in unnecessary expense and . . . high casualties. This seems to be the consensus of military commanders in Vietnam."

Buchanan had also come to the same conclusion. "I started pushing for it in 1966," Buchanan recalled.[88] "One of the reasons why I did was because this country was split. Antiwar radicals were prevalent on campuses everywhere, and you couldn't draft these kids and bring them into the barracks. It would destroy morale. You couldn't keep drafting soldiers to fight and die in a war they didn't believe in." In October 1967, he wrote a memo suggesting that Nixon come out in favor of a volunteer army only when the Vietnam War ended for fear of looking like he was caving to the "anti-war peaceniks" and giving them "the means to avoid service."[89]

Another veteran at the firm, Tom Evans, agreed with Lincoln that an all-volunteer force was desirable. Evans, however, had a couple of concerns, including whether or not ending the draft would decimate the manpower pool for available officers. He was also concerned that the armed forces would have trouble recruiting and holding onto specialists in the face of competition from the private sector.[90]

Anderson heard nothing from Nixon about his memo for months. Then, in November 1967, Nixon was giving a speech at the University of Wisconsin when a student asked him about the draft. Nixon stunned the audience, the *New York Times* reporter covering his speech, and Anderson himself, by reciting Anderson's talking points about eliminating the draft and creating a professional corps.[91] "He just decided to do it, announced it to the *New York Times*, and that became the policy," Anderson said.[92] The promise to eliminate the draft soon became an important and highly popular part of Nixon's stump speeches, although, as Ambrose pointed out, Nixon seemed not to notice that the cheers would get loudest when he promised to use his highly skilled and motivated professional army to bring about an end to the Vietnam War.[93] Nixon would keep his campaign promise and, after a long transition period, finally ended the draft in 1973.

Anderson didn't always agree with Friedman. One idea that engendered passionate opposition from Anderson related to welfare reform. Nixon had made reforming welfare a central part of his campaign platform but had been light on specifics. While on the campaign trail, Nixon had spoken of the need to streamline and improve existing programs and to provide incentives for those on welfare to find employment and get themselves away from being dependent on the government. As Anderson pointed out, that was a much more moderate position than many conservatives had taken, and he assumed that Nixon was merely trying to take an issue away from Democrats.[94]

Instead, Nixon sought to carve out a fairly radical position. As Roger Milgrim recalled, Nixon asked him to write a position paper concerning the negative income tax. Based on Friedman's teachings, the negative income tax created an income threshold whereby individuals or families making less than that amount would receive money from the government to supplement their existing income. For people over the threshold, they would be taxed based on how far over the minimum they were. In theory, the negative income tax is supposed to provide a safety net for all Americans, obviating the need for welfare, minimum wage, food stamps, Medicare, Medicaid, and many of the other Great Society and New Deal programs. "[Nixon] was very taken with the idea of supplanting the demeaning welfare system, which made it impossible for people to get out, with something more pragmatic," said Milgrim.[95]

The negative income tax proved to be a more divisive issue within the Nixon ranks than the draft had been. Anderson hated it and believed that it was simply another way of redistributing wealth in violation of free market principles.[96] Buchanan, likewise, was against it.[97] Milgrim recalled that the issue caused controversy within the firm. "I liked my position paper, but [Nixon] instructed me to talk to John Alexander to see what he thought," Milgrim said. Alexander, the head of the firm's tax practice, was not a fan of the proposal and let Milgrim have it. "It was a disaster," Milgrim said.[98] "We got into a heated shouting match." As Milgrim recalled, Alexander claimed that governmental programs that sent money to the poor, however sensible and reasonable they were, always got out of hand, and cited the Sixteenth Amendment to the Constitution as an example. According to Alexander, the income tax was, originally, supposed to be limited to a small number of individuals, and the rates mentioned were under 5 percent. Obviously, things had changed, considerably, since the Amendment was first adopted in 1913.

Ultimately, Nixon would propose the Family Assistance Plan, a modified version of the negative income tax, during his first year in the White House. The bill passed the House but died in the Senate.

"PANNING GOLD IN A SWIMMING POOL."

In June 1964, right as Nixon was in the middle of plotting a possible last-minute coup at the GOP National Convention in San Francisco in order to steal the nomination from Barry Goldwater, prominent political journalists Rowland Evans Jr. and Robert Novak published a story that underlined his biggest weakness. "The Achilles Heel of Richard M. Nixon's quiet campaign for another crack at the White House is the total lack of visible financial support," they wrote.[99] According to GOP fundraisers they interviewed, Nixon needed at least $12 to $15 million to make a credible run for the White House—a near impossible task that would be like "panning gold in a swimming pool."[100] To make matters worse for Nixon, as Evans and Novak reported, he was old news, which meant that he wouldn't have the kind of enthusiastic backers as someone like Goldwater. Nixon would have to dip into his own funds, and he hardly had that kind of money.

Come 1968, Nixon was richer than he had ever been but was hardly swimming in gold. However, things had changed in the intervening four years. Through his tireless campaigning, as well as his perception that Johnson's landslide win in 1964 had been more illusory than permanent, he was, once again, the leading Republican candidate for president.

His lofty status loosened donors' purse strings, considerably. Thanks to Tom Evans, Nixon's donors had many different ways of helping the cause. Evans's experience during the Congress '66 days had given him some insight into how campaign finance worked, as well as what was allowed under the law. "I set up the umbrella account entitled Issues Research Council, but initially concluded that our efforts were restricted by campaign laws, which prohibited donors from contributing more than $5000 'in the aggregate' to any candidate," said Evans.[101] "Then I was handed a gift from Lyndon Johnson's Justice Department." Evans received a DOJ opinion letter that interpreted the phrase *to any candidate* to mean a campaign committee, not the candidate him/herself. "So much for the 'plain meaning' rule of statutory interpretation which I had been taught at law school," Evans thought to himself as he set up thirty-four committees with names like Citizens for Good Government or The Committee for a Better Executive.[102]

Finance chair Maurice Stans was able to take advantage, fulfilling his stated intent to raise so much money that Nixon would never have to worry about his finances and could, instead, concentrate on political and substantive matters. Stans spent $9 million to secure the nomination[103] and then raised a record $25.4 million for the general election—a mark that stood until the following election when Nixon's campaign raised $61.4 million for the general election.[104] "Ours was, by far, the most expensive campaign ever," Stans recalled,[105] "and I never once had to go to him to ask him to do anything."

Stans's go-to fundraising device was a series of $1,000-a-plate dinners, and he wasn't shy about scheduling as many as humanly possible. On September 16, for instance, he had dinners in twenty-two different cities, with Nixon speaking to each one via closed-circuit television.[106] Stans also sent out tens of thousands of fundraising letters to wealthy Republicans asking for a $1,000 contribution.

Stans wasn't the only one keeping the post office busy. The campaign had also enlisted the services of Walter Weintz, a *Reader's Digest* circulation director who had become famous in political circles for using direct mail to help Ohio senator Robert Taft win reelection in 1950 in the face of virulent opposition from organized labor as a result of his authorship of the Taft-Hartley Act. "In direct mail you are able to test almost anything, including political appeals," Weintz recounted.[107] "We mailed out, as I recall, several different letters, each one putting forward a different central idea on why the recipient of the letter should support Sen. Taft." Weintz found that Taft's most effective message was to tell Ohio's labor force why the Taft-Hartley Act was actually good for them. A short rejoinder at the end asking for a donation, however small, was similarly effective for Taft. "Much to our surprise, we received a substantial number of small contributions, which helped us finance the direct mail campaign," Weintz said.[108] "Indeed, the campaign paid for itself!"

According to Evans, *Reader's Digest* general manager Al Cole, who raised funds for Congress '66, brought Weintz into the campaign.[109] True to his words, Weintz tested several different letters and approaches. In most cases, Evans and Garment did not see anything special about his letters, and neither saw anything that would make recipients want to part with their hard-earned money. Evans and Garment were wrong. Nixon ended up raising $6.6 million from small donations solicited through direct mail, including $2.2

million for the primaries.[110] Weintz, for his part, was immediately snapped up by the Republican National Finance Committee to overhaul their direct mail campaign.

Nixon's law clients proved to be a good source for campaign contributions. During the prenomination period, Robert Abplanalp of Precision Valve Corporation and Elmer Bobst of Warner-Lambert each gave $7,000 for Nixon to spend in for the Wisconsin, Oregon, and Nebraska primaries. Eugene McGovern, meanwhile, gave $10,000 for Nixon to spend in those three primaries.[111]

According to Herbert Alexander, a large of number of Nixon's clients and friends donated to Republican-affiliated campaigns and/or committees during the 1968 election. Abplanalp gave a total of $28,000 to Republicans, Bobst handed out $63,250, and McGovern contributed $19,000. Several additional Nixon clients donated at least $10,000 to Republicans in 1968, including Cliff Folger ($19,000), William Pawley ($22,000), and Jack Dreyfus ($76,000—although he and his wife also donated over $169,000 to Democrats).[112] Oil magnates John M. Shaheen and Robert Anderson, both Nixon clients, also gave liberally to the Republicans, with Shaheen contributing $16,500 and Anderson donating $44,000. Meanwhile, Richard Buck, head of brokerage firm Richard J. Buck & Co. and, like Nixon, a fellow board member for Harsco Corporation, chipped in with $25,000 while Witco Corporation executives Robert Wishnick and his son, William, contributed $36,625 and $17,625, respectively.[113]

In fact, during the 1968 election cycle, Republicans raked in significant amounts of money from executives in several different industries. Shaheen and Anderson weren't the only oil executives who donated to the GOP, as Harold McClure Jr. of McClure Oil contributed $90,000; J. Howard Pew, CEO of Sun Oil Co., gave $64,733; and Waller Royal Davis, former president of Primian Corp., chipped in with $25,000. According to Alexander, officials at several major oil trade associations gave, overwhelmingly, to the Republicans. For instance, American Petroleum Institute officials donated $429,366 to the GOP compared to $30,606 to Democrats. Alexander also found that officials at the American Gas Association, the Independent Natural Gas Association of America, the Independent Petroleum Association of America, and the Natural Petroleum Refiners Association gave a combined $99,000 to the GOP and only $18,000 to Democrats.[114]

Business organizations also favored the GOP. Officials with the Business Council donated $280,913 to Republicans, as opposed to $83,000 to Democrats, while their counterparts at the Chamber of Commerce handed out $40,000—all to the GOP. In particular, Robert Dowling, chairman of City Investing Co. in New York, gave $102,754 to the GOP while J. Willard Marriott, chairman of Marriott Corp., gave $103,500.[115]

The insurance industry also gave heavily to the GOP. Alexander found that, of the donors that gave more than $10,000 and identified themselves as working in the insurance sector, the vast majority of their contributions ($340,000 out of $378,500) went to the Republicans. The biggest donor in the insurance industry was Clement Stone, founder of Combined Insurance Company of America. Four years before he would pledge an unprecedented $2 million for Nixon's reelection campaign, Stone would give over $200,000 to Republicans in 1968, making him one of the biggest individual donors to the party that year.[116] Stone, an ebullient force of nature who had preached the power of positivity as a means of getting rich, was known to begin each day by affirming: "I feel happy! I feel healthy! I feel ter-r-r-ific!"[117]

He also was known to be very generous with his money. Guided by one of his other affirmations—"All I want to do is change the world"—the Chicago native gave over $275 million to charities during his lifetime.[118] Evans recalled how Stone, in his own inimitable way, made known his fervent support for Nixon in 1968. "Stone's introduction to the other principal Nixon financial supporters came at the January 1968 meeting of the group that had emerged from Congress '66," Evans recalled.[119] After a rousing call to arms on behalf of the candidate he called "Richard Jay Nixon," Stone shocked the crowd even more by pledging fifty cents to the cause. "Fifty cents for every dollar contributed by everyone else in the room—combined," he said to the relief and joy of the assembled audience.[120]

What was it about Nixon that caused all these donors and members of industry to flock to him with their checkbooks out? Like most Republicans, Nixon claimed to be against excessive government regulations. During his very first congressional campaign, Nixon had attacked his opponent, Jerry Voorhis, as a regulation-loving authoritarian, while portraying himself as an opponent of excessive governmental regulation.[121] In subsequent campaigns, Nixon would frequently beat the drum in favor of fewer regulations while on the stump. During his acceptance speech at the 1960 GOP National Convention, for instance, he stated emphatically:

> The way to assure maximum growth in America is not by expanding the functions of government, but by increasing the opportunities for investment and creative enterprise for millions of individual Americans. At a time when the Communists have found it necessary to turn to decentralization of their economy and to turn to the use of individual incentives to increase productivity—at a time, in other words, when they are turning our way—I say we must not and we will not make the mistake of turning their way.[122]

Approximately a month before the election, Nixon made clear that he intended to put his money where his mouth was. In a letter to three thousand financial and business executives, including law firm clients and longtime friends Donald Kendall and Elmer Bobst, Nixon had criticized the Johnson

Administration over its attempt to "establish bureaucratic domination over the competitive relations and everyday activities of banks, savings institutions, insurance companies and institutional investors."[123] Nixon then claimed that the best way to reverse this trend was "through the appointment of men to the regulatory commissions whose views of the proper relationship between government and business correspond with my own." Nixon then solemnly promised: "That I will do."[124]

When the *LA Times* asked him about the letter and whether they represented his plans as president, Nixon doubled down and told the paper that he would look for regulatory appointees that shared his views, which he claimed were well known. As a result, newspapers and journalists pointed out that several of Nixon's clients stood to benefit as a result his "well known" views. The *LA Times* reported that, in his letter to the business and financial executives, Nixon had singled out for criticism a bill that cut fees for mutual fund salesmen that had been unanimously endorsed by the SEC and supported by President Johnson. The *Times* pointed out Nixon's ties to several mutual funds, including his board membership of four IDS funds, as well as his firm's representation of two major mutual funds: Hornblower & Weeks and D. H. Blair.[125]

There were other firm clients that stood to benefit from having a noninterventionist like Nixon in the White House. Drew Pearson reported that Nixon, in his letter, had specifically addressed concerns from Kendall and Bobst concerning the Johnson Administration's restrictions on overseas investments. Kendall and Bobst had told shareholders that they hoped the controls would be "temporary," and Nixon seemed willing to oblige.[126] Pearson, a longtime muckraker who Nixon disliked and considered to be unfair, coauthored a column with his protégé, Jack Anderson, bringing up firm clients El Paso Natural Gas. The pipeline giants had been fighting an antitrust action originally brought by the Eisenhower Administration blocking its purchase of Pacific Northwest Pipeline Corp. The case had gone up the Supreme Court multiple times and was still kicking around in 1968. The Mudge firm had been active in defending El Paso over the years, earning over $771,000 in fees from 1961 to 1967.[127] Nixon's arrival at the firm, however, seemed to put an extra hop in their step. "I remember that Howard Boyd, president of El Paso, was in my office and went out of his way to brag about the fact that Richard Nixon was now representing him," recalled William Bennett, a California Public Utilities Commissioner who had challenged the merger all the way to the Supreme Court.[128] It was understandable why Boyd would feel the need to brag. After all, if his lawyer entered the Oval Office, then he had to like his chances concerning the long-delayed merger and antitrust action.

"THIS TERRIBLE THING."

As 1967 drew to a close, Nixon's decision to run again may have been a fait accompli to the people at the firm who had spent the better part of three years getting ready for the 1968 presidential contest—especially considering Nixon's quote about being "mentally dead in two years and physically dead in four" if all he had to look forward to, for the rest of his life, was his law practice.

According to Nixon, however, he had a crisis of confidence as 1967 came to a close. After a Christmas Party at his New York apartment, he even drew up a list of pros and cons for running and found that the list was overwhelmingly negative. "A good candidate must have five qualities: brains, heart, judgment, guys and experience," Nixon wrote in his memoir.[129] "I felt that I measured up to four of them. But I was not sure whether I still had the heart—whether I had not reached the time in life when I lacked the zeal to continue a political career." Nixon also recalled writing down that he was sick of dealing with the media, he was afraid of losing again, and he did not want the presidency in order to feel important. "Finally, I startled myself again by writing at the bottom of the page a thought that I had never expected to have: 'I don't give a damn.'"[130]

Nixon even told his children that he had decided not to do it. "Christmas vacation this year, Daddy called Tricia and me in separately and told us that he had decided—almost definitely—not to run," Julie Eisenhower Nixon wrote in her diary.[131] "He was very depressed. I had never known him to be depressed before—not even after 1962."

According to Nixon, it was his children that, ultimately, changed his mind. Julie told him he had to run for the good of the country, while Tricia told him: "If you don't run, Daddy, you really will have nothing to live for."[132]

Pat, however, remained ambivalent about another White House run. More than anyone else in the family, living in comparative anonymity in New York City had really agreed with her, and she was happy being out of the political spotlight. In fact, her antipathy toward presidential politics was such that some of her husband's associates were explicitly told not to bring up politics in her presence.[133] Despite that, she seemed resigned to her fate and told her husband that she'd help out.

Nixon still felt the need to get away for a few days and agonize over his decision a bit longer. On December 28, he went to Key Biscayne where Bebe Rebozo and the Reverend Billy Graham both urged him to run. "I think it is your destiny to be President," Graham told his longtime friend.[134] Finally in mid-January, he called for a family dinner back at the Fifth Avenue apartment that even included his live-in servants Fina and Manolo Sanchez. "Daddy called Fina and Manolo in, since they are part of the family too, and asked

Fina why she thought he must 'do this terrible thing,'" Julie Nixon Eisenhower wrote in her diary.[135] "She said that in the world there are few men that are born to do something and that [Nixon] was one of them. It brought tears to his eyes and to Mother's too." It was only then that Nixon decided to put his misgivings to the side and heed the call of destiny.

Or not. "For Nixon, this sort of thing was a necessary part of gearing up for the campaign," Ambrose wrote.[136] "For Nixon, every decision had to be a crisis, every decision had to be part of a larger drama, even where there was none. He pretended, evidently even to himself, that he was in an agony of indecision." Nixon's personal passion play was an appropriate denouement for a man who had, long ago, realized that it was better to be the reluctant candidate dragged back into the arena by popular demand instead of the guy who didn't know when to quit. His family proved to be a good test audience for him. After all, if he could convince his wife and daughters, so devastated after 1960 and 1962, to support one more presidential campaign, then why wouldn't the rest of the country get on board?

NOTES

1. Jean Edward Smith, *FDR* (New York: Random House Trade Paperbacks, 2008), 286–87.
2. William Manchester, "Rock Bottom in America," *New York Magazine*, August 5, 1974, accessed March 31, 2017, https://books.google.com/books?id=kukCAAAAMBAJ&printsec=frontcover&source=gbs_ge_summary_r&cad=0 -v=onepage&q&f=false.
3. Manchester, "Rock Bottom in America."
4. "FDR," PBS.org, accessed March 23, 2016, http://www.pbs.org/wgbh/americanexperience/features/transcript/fdr-transcript/.
5. Richard Norton Smith, *An Uncommon Man* (New York: Simon & Schuster, 1984), 362.
6. Jeffrey Frank, *Ike and Dick: Portrait of a Strange Political Marriage* (New York: Simon & Schuster Paperbacks, 2013), 18.
7. Smith, *An Uncommon Man*, 423.
8. Smith, *An Uncommon Man*.
9. Smith, *An Uncommon Man*.
10. William Safire, *Before the Fall: An Inside View of the Pre-Watergate White House* (Garden City, NY: Doubleday & Company, Inc., 1975), 42–44.
11. Safire, *Before the Fall*.
12. Thomas Evans, "Nixon Mudge," unpublished manuscript, 1994, 171–72. Also "The Accounting Hall of Fame," The Ohio State University, Fisher College of Business, accessed April 30, 2016, http://fisher.osu.edu/departments/accounting-and-mis/the-accounting-hall-of-fame/membership-in-hall/maurice-h.-stans/.
13. Safire, *Before the Fall*, 43. Evans, "Nixon Mudge," 173–74.
14. Safire, *Before the Fall*; Evans, "Nixon Mudge."
15. Stephen Ambose, *Nixon: Volume 2: The Triumph of a Politician, 1962–1972* (New York: Simon & Schuster, 1989), 102.
16. Safire, *Before the Fall*, 42–43.
17. Safire, *Before the Fall*, at 43.
18. Safire, *Before the Fall*.
19. Ambrose, *Nixon: Volume 2*, 104–5.
20. Ambrose, *Nixon: Volume 2*, 104–5.
21. Ambrose, *Nixon: Volume 2*.

22. Ambrose, *Nixon: Volume 2*.
23. Michael Cohen, "Nelson Rockefeller Enters Presidential Race," OUP Blog—Oxford University Press, accessed April 30, 2016, http://blog.oup.com/2016/04/rockefeller-1968-presidential-race/.
24. Sam Roberts, "Capturing the Life of a Striver Who Fell Short of the White House: Richard Norton Smith Dissects Nelson Rockefeller," *New York Times*, October 14, 2014, accessed April 1, 2017, http://www.nytimes.com/2014/10/18/books/richard-norton-smith-dissects-nelson-rockefeller.html?_r=0.
25. Victor Li, "Leaning Left: The AMA at a Crossroads," *Huffington Post*, May 25, 2011, accessed April 1, 2017, http://www.huffingtonpost.com/victor-li/leaning-left-the-ama-at-a_b_422556.html.
26. "Ronald Reagan: A Time for Choosing," American Rhetoric, accessed April 1, 2017, http://www.americanrhetoric.com/speeches/ronaldreaganatimeforchoosing.htm.
27. Safire, *Before the Fall*, 43.
28. Safire, *Before the Fall*.
29. Adam Clymer, "Charles Percy, Former Ill. Senator, Is Dead at 91," *New York Times*, September 17, 2011, accessed April 1, 2017, http://www.nytimes.com/2011/09/18/us/politics/charles-percy-former-illinois-senator-is-dead-at-91.html?_r=0.
30. "Charles H. Percy Dies at 91; Moderate Former GOP Senator," *Los Angeles Times*, September 18, 2011 accessed April 1, 2017, http://www.latimes.com/local/obituaries/la-me-charles-percy-20110918-story.html.
31. Memo from Ray Price, 17 May 1967 (TWE).
32. Memo from Ray Price, 17 May 1967 (TWE).
33. Rhodes Cook, "Like Father, Like Son? The Romneys Run for President," Larry Sabato's Crystal Ball, September 20, 2007 accessed April 1, 2017, https://web.archive.org/web/20080606225654/http://www.centerforpolitics.org/crystalball/article.php?id=FRC2007092001.
34. Cook, "Like Father, Like Son?"
35. Edward Blum and Paul Harvey, "How (George) Romney Championed Civil Rights and Challenged His Church," *The Atlantic*, August 13, 2012, accessed April 17, file://localhost/2017, http/::www.theatlantic.com:national:archive:2012:08:how-george-romney-championed-civil-rights-and-challenged-his-church:261073..
36. Blum and Harvey, "How (George) Romney Championed Civil Rights."
37. Evans, "Nixon Mudge," 179.
38. Cook, "Like Father, Like Son?".
39. Safire, *Before the Fall*, 43.
40. Safire, *Before the Fall*, at 46.
41. Safire, *Before the Fall*, at 44.
42. Leonard Garment, *Crazy Rhythm: From Brooklyn and Jazz to Nixon's White House, Watergate and Beyond* (Cambridge, MA: Da Capo Press, 1997), 129.
43. Garment, *Crazy Rhythm*.
44. Rick Perlstein, *Nixonland: The Rise of a President and the Fracturing of America* (New York: Scribner, 2008), 234.
45. Garment, *Crazy Rhythm*, 130.
46. Garment, *Crazy Rhythm*.
47. John Sears, interview by Victor Li, February 16, 2016.
48. Sears, interview by Li.
49. Joe McGinniss, *The Selling of the President* (New York: Penguin Books, 1969), 41.
50. Perlstein, *Nixonland*, 234.
51. McGinniss, *The Selling of the President*, 45.
52. McGinniss, *The Selling of the President*.
53. McGinniss, *The Selling of the President*.
54. McGinniss, *The Selling of the President*, 34–36.
55. Garment, *Crazy Rhythm*, 132.
56. McGinniss, *The Selling of the President*, 37.
57. McGinniss, *The Selling of the President*, at 38.
58. Garment, *Crazy Rhythm*, 108.

59. Garment, *Crazy Rhythm*.
60. David Coleman, *The Fourteenth Day: JFK and the Aftermath of the Cuban Missile Crisis* (New York: W. W. Norton & Company, 2012), 96.
61. Richard Nixon, Memorandum from Paul Keyes, June 1, 1962, Pre-Presidential Papers, Richard Nixon Presidential Library and Museum.
62. Richard Nixon, Memorandum from Paul Keyes, June 13, 1962, Pre-Presidential Papers, Richard Nixon Presidential Library and Museum.
63. William Gavin, *Speechwright: An Insider's Take on Political Rhetoric* (East Lansing, MI: Michigan State University Press, 2011).
64. "William Gavin, "Speechwriter for Nixon, Reagan, Lawmakers, Dies at 80," *Washington Times*, June 30, 2015, accessed April 1, 2017, http://www.washingtontimes.com/news/2015/jun/30/william-gavin-speechwriter-for-nixon-reagan-lawmak/.
65. McGinniss, *The Selling of the President*, 63. Also Tom Dickinson, "How Roger Ailes Built the Fox News Fear Factory," *Rolling Stone*, May 25, 2011, accessed April 1, 2017, http://www.rollingstone.com/politics/news/how-roger-ailes-built-the-fox-news-fear-factory-20110525?page=3.
66. Gabriel Sherman, *The Loudest Voice in the Room: How the Brilliant, Bombastic Roger Ailes Built FOX News—and Divided a Country* (New York: Random House, 2014), 32–33.
67. Kerwin Swint, *Dark Genius: The Influential Career of Legendary Political Operative and Fox News Founder Roger Ailes* (New York: Union Square Press, 2008), 16–17.
68. Garment, *Crazy Rhythm*, 132.
69. "The Man in the Arena," Theodore-Roosevelt.com, accessed April 1, 2017, http://www.theodore-roosevelt.com/trsorbonnespeech.html.
70. Evans, "Nixon Mudge," 198–99.
71. Evans, "Nixon Mudge," 139–40.
72. Kathleen Hall Jamieson, *Packaging the Presidency: A History and Criticism of Campaign Advertising* (New York: Oxford University Press, 1996).
73. Jamieson, *Packaging the Presidency*.
74. McGinniss, *The Selling of the President*, 65–66.
75. Sherman, *The Loudest Voice in the Room*, 48–49.
76. Sherman, *The Loudest Voice in the Room*, 40.
77. McGinniss, *The Selling of the President*, 70–71.
78. Sherman, *The Loudest Voice in the Room*, 51.
79. Sherman, *The Loudest Voice in the Room*, 53–54.
80. Noel Murray, "Nixon Gets Socked in Laugh-In's Most Famous, and Influential, Five Seconds," The A.V. Club, September 13, 2012, accessed April 1, 2017, http://www.avclub.com/article/nixon-gets-socked-in-ilaugh-inis-most-famous-and-i-84881.
81. Sherman, *The Loudest Voice in the Room*, 54.
82. Martin Anderson, interview by Jim Young, Stephen Knott, and Allison Asher, December 10–11, 2001, accessed April 14, 2017, Oral History Project, UVA Miller Center, https://millercenter.org/the-presidency/interviews-with-the-administration/martin-anderson-oral-history-assistant-president.
83. "Outline of Factors Involved in Establishing an All Volunteer Armed Force," The Nixon Foundation, accessed April 14, 2017, https://www.nixonfoundation.org/2015/02/towards-volunteer-force/.
84. "Outline of Factors Involved in Establishing an All Volunteer Armed Force."
85. Ambrose, *Nixon: Volume 2*, 264–65.
86. Wolfgang Saxon, "Franklin B. Lincoln, Aide in Transition of Nixon, Dies at 85," *New York Times*, November 5, 1993, accessed April 14, 2017, http://www.nytimes.com/1993/11/05/obituaries/franklin-b-lincoln-aide-in-transition-of-nixon-dies-at-85.html.
87. Tom Evans, Copy of Memorandum from Frank Lincoln, August 17, 1967, Tom Evans collection.
88. Patrick Buchanan, interview with Victor Li, June 21, 2017.
89. Buchanan, 147–48.
90. Tom Evans, Evans Memorandum to Richard Nixon, August 18, 1967, Tom Evans collection.

91. Robert Semple Jr., "Nixon Backs Eventual End of Draft," *New York Times*, November 17, 1967.
92. Anderson oral history.
93. Ambrose, *Nixon: Volume 2*, 190.
94. Martin Anderson, *Welfare: The Political Economy of Welfare Reform in the United States* (Palo Alto, CA: Hoover Institution Press Publication, 1978), 4.
95. Roger Milgrim, interview with Li, October 29, 2016.
96. Rutger Bregman, "The Bizarre Tale of President Nixon and His Basic Income Bill," *The Correspondent*, accessed April 20, 2017, https://thecorrespondent.com/4503/the-bizarre-tale-of-president-nixon-and-his-basic-income-bill/173117835-c34d6145.
97. Buchanan, interview with Li.
98. Milgrim, interview with Li.
99. Rowland Evans and Robert Novak, "Nixon's Big Weakness Is Lack of Financing," *Los Angeles Times*, June 3, 1964.
100. Evans and Novak, "Nixon's Biggest Weakness."
101. Thomas Evans, "The Education of Richard Nixon: The Wilderness Years on Wall Street," unpublished manuscript, 139.
102. Evans, "The Education of Richard Nixon," at 139.
103. Ambrose, *Nixon: Volume 2*, 179.
104. Andre Tartar and Eric Benson, "The Forever Campaign," *New York Magazine*, October 14, 2012, accessed April 1, 2017, http://nymag.com/news/politics/elections-2012/timeline-2012-10/.
105. Ambrose, *Nixon: Volume 2*, 179.
106. Ambrose, *Nixon: Volume 2*, 179.
107. Denny Hatch, "Obama's $750 Million Juggernaut," *Target Marketing*, December 16, 2008, accessed April 1, 2017, http://www.targetmarketingmag.com/article/the-father-direct-mail-political-fundraising-401158/all/.
108. Hatch, "Obama's $750 Million Juggernaut."
109. Evans, "Education of Richard Nixon," 140.
110. Laurence Jaeger, "Can McGovern Be Sold through the Mails?" *New York Magazine*, September 18, 1972.
111. Herbert Alexander, *Financing the 1968 Election* (Lexington, MA: Lexington Books, 1971), 20–21.
112. Alexander, *Financing the 1968 Election*, 268–300. Donations were reported per household, so in some cases, they were made in the names of both husband and wife—for simplicity's sake, I referred to a single spouse (e.g., the one that had a relationship with Nixon).
113. Alexander, *Financing the 1968 Election.*
114. Alexander, *Financing the 1968 Election*, at 346–50.
115. Alexander, *Financing the 1968 Election.*
116. Alexander, *Financing the 1968 Election.* Also: Douglas Martin, "Clement Stone Dies at 100: Built Empire on Optimism," *New York Times*, September 5, 2002, accessed April 1, 2017, http://www.nytimes.com/2002/09/05/business/clement-stone-dies-at-100-built-empire-on-optimism.html.
117. Martin, "Clement Stone Dies at 100."
118. Martin, "Clement Stone Dies at 100."
119. Evans, "Education of Richard Nixon," 144.
120. Evans, "Education of Richard Nixon."
121. Conrad Black, *Richard M. Nixon: A Life in Full* (New York: PublicAffairs, 2007), 78, 85.
122. "Richard Nixon: Address Accepting Presidential Nomination at the Republican National Convention in Chicago," July 28, 1960, accessed April 1, 2017, http://www.presidency.ucsb.edu/ws/?pid=25974.
123. Murray Seeger, "Nixon Pledges to Restrict Regulatory Agency Moves: Would Appoint New Officials to Reverse Trend," *Los Angeles Times,* October 17, 1968.
124. Seeger, "Nixon Pledges to Restrict Regulatory Agency Moves."
125. Seeger, "Nixon Pledges to Restrict Regulatory Agency Moves."

126. Drew Pearson, "Now a Word about Nixon's Sponsors," *Los Angeles Times*, October 15, 1968.
127. Drew Pearson and Jack Anderson, "What Are Nixon's Regulatory Views?" *Washington Post*, October 25, 1968.
128. Pearson and Anderson, "What Are Nixon's Regulatory Views?"
129. Richard Nixon, *RN: The Memoirs of Richard Nixon* (New York: Simon & Schuster, 2013).
130. Nixon, *RN*.
131. Julie Nixon Eisenhower, *Pat Nixon: The Untold Story* (New York: Simon & Schuster, 1986), 233.
132. Nixon, *RN*. And Eisenhower, *Pat Nixon*, 233–34.
133. Eisenhower, *Pat Nixon*, 218–19.
134. Nixon, *RN*.
135. Eisenhower, *Pat Nixon*, 234.
136. Ambrose, *Nixon: Volume 2*, 131.

Chapter Eleven

"He Wanted Prestige."

Nixon still needed someone to run his campaign. Garment had the respect of Nixon's staffers but lacked political connections. Garment also recognized that Nixon needed a "heavyweight" to serve as his commander-in-chief—someone with the experience and credentials to keep Nixon in line and prevent him from repeating his mistakes from prior campaigns. "Although Nixon was highly disciplined when analyzing abstract issues, he was deeply ambivalent when faced with personal decisions," Garment said.[1] "He made costly mistakes when he listened to his inner voice, which did not always have his best interests at heart."

Evans recalled that one of the only times he's ever seen Nixon lose his temper came as a result of one of these meetings where he had to answer for his conduct during previous campaigns. Shortly after the Strategy Board's inaugural meeting, Nixon had flown to Los Angeles to speak with Haldeman and some others. During that meeting, LaRue and O'Donnell hit Nixon with an ultimatum: hire a real campaign manager with real authority or else they would walk away. Pointing out how Nixon had micromanaged his campaign in 1960 to his own detriment, LaRue and O'Donnell were determined not to see that happen again. They even told Nixon that his 1960 cocampaign manager, Leonard Hall, had defected to the Romney campaign and was telling Republican officials around the country that Nixon was an incompetent manager.[2]

After Nixon got back to New York, he flew into a rage. "He was ranting, red-faced and kicking furniture," Evans recalled.[3] "He was mad—more than mad. He had just come from the airport and was shouting phrases like 'those little bastards' and 'those shitheels,' to recall some of the less profane epithets." Ultimately, Nixon felt he had no choice but to accept their terms, and he instructed Evans to start interviewing potential campaign managers.

The first man to get the job was Dr. Gaylord Parkinson, an obstetrician and prominent California Republican who, as state GOP chairman, had helped oversee an impressive sweep in the 1966 elections. Republicans had won five of six statewide races that year, including Reagan's triumph over Brown for the Governor's Mansion. Parkinson, meanwhile, had made a name for himself as a unifier and bridge builder within the still badly split GOP by coining the now famous "Eleventh Commandment" for the party: "Thou shalt not speak ill of a fellow Republican." Parkinson had been one of the names mentioned by LaRue and O'Donnell as possibilities for the job, and Evans flew to San Diego in February 1967 to interview him.

Evans had doubts about him from the beginning. For one thing, Parkinson seemed ambivalent about the job—accepting it one day and then backing out or vacillating the next. Later on, Evans and the others found out that Parkinson had been negotiating with Romney at the same time as Nixon.[4] Buchanan, meanwhile, didn't trust Parkinson. Within hours after his initial meeting with Nixon, Parkinson leaked it to the *Washington Post*, which published a front-page story stating that Nixon had offered him the job. "I never trusted these hired guns who talked to the press to get their names in the paper," Buchanan said.[5]

It didn't take long for the rest of the Nixon Mudge contingent to sour on Parkinson. The California Republican had already ruffled some feathers after his assistant, Bob Walker, designed what he thought was a flashy logo for Nixon that consisted of parallel lightning bolts in the shape of the letter *N*. "It worked well for the Nazis," Garment deadpanned, pointing out that the logo looked like the one used by the Schutzstaffel (SS).[6] The logo was immediately discarded.

Meanwhile, the Nixon Mudge contingent never shook the feeling that Parkinson was out for himself. Nixon was in the middle of his political moratorium which, as he and the Strategy Board had agreed on, was designed to allow him to lay low while the press trained its fire on Romney. However, Parkinson pressed him to declare for the presidency—an idea that was rejected, out of hand, by Nixon and almost all of his staffers.[7] When Parkinson made trips to New Hampshire, he had the subtlety of a used car salesman as he tried to build up his undeclared candidate's field operations in the vital primary state. "Parky was a salesman," one Parkinson partisan told Witcover.[8] "But he came on a little strong for them. He went up there once to meet a group of old Republicans, and all he talked about was young people and 'pizzazz.'"

By late March, the Nixon Mudge contingent was openly campaigning for Parkinson and Walker to go. "No one in the office trusts them," Buchanan wrote in a memo to Nixon.[9] "Not Sears or Evans or Buchanan or Rose [Woods] or Garment." They weren't alone with their feelings toward Parkinson. Frank Jorgensen, a fellow California Republican who worked on all of

Nixon's campaigns until 1962, also had doubts about Parkinson. "Somehow, my exposure to this fellow does not breed a lot of confidence," he told Woods.[10] After watching Parkinson show off and run his mouth about raising a million dollars for the primaries during a luncheon, Jorgensen seriously doubted that he could be trusted. Nixon, eventually, saw things the way his charges did, and, suspicious that Parkinson was keeping his options open with the Reagan folks, cut ties with Parkinson in August 1967. In a statement explaining his departure, Parkinson cited familial issues—in fact, his wife was suffering from cancer at the time.[11]

His replacement, Governor Henry Bellmon of Oklahoma, took the job on an interim basis and would leave after only a couple of months to run an ultimately successful campaign for US Senate. Once Bellmon quit, Ellsworth and Sears handled day-to-day matters for the campaign while looking for yet another campaign manager. According to press reports, the campaign considered senators John Tower of Texas and Clifford Hansen of Wyoming,[12] before it ultimately realized that the right person for the job was just down the hall from them.

"I'VE FOUND THE HEAVYWEIGHT!"

At first glance, John Newton Mitchell wasn't an obvious choice for campaign manager. The bald-headed, gruff-mannered, perpetually pipe-smoking bond lawyer had never even worked on a political campaign before, let alone run one. Unlike many of Nixon's political intimates, Mitchell had no longstanding relationship with the former vice president—they had met, briefly, during Nixon's congressional days but didn't get to know each other until after Nixon moved to New York.

It wasn't even clear what Mitchell's political ideology was, let alone whether it was consistent with Nixon's. In a 1973 profile of Mitchell in the *New York Post*, one longtime associate couldn't recall ever having a single political conversation with him.[13] In fact, he could have easily gone to work for the Democrats. Mitchell's former press secretary, Jack Landau, would reveal in 1993, five years after his old boss's death, that Mitchell had been offered an interesting opportunity in 1960: helping run Jack Kennedy's campaign. According to Landau, Bobby Kennedy had met with Mitchell and tried to convince his fellow future attorney general to join the team. Mitchell demurred, but years later, after everything that had happened with Nixon, he seemed to have second thoughts. "If I had it all over to do," Mitchell said with a smile on his face,[14] "I'd run Jack Kennedy's campaign."

Yet Mitchell quickly became the only choice for Nixon and his campaign staff.

A look at Mitchell's life and career made it understandable as to why Nixon and his staffers would see him as the ideal heavyweight—and why Nixon would respect Mitchell enough to let him run the campaign. Like Nixon, who was a mere eight months his senior, Mitchell was a self-made man who was as out of place within the Eastern Establishment as Nixon. Born in Detroit, Michigan, in 1913, Mitchell grew up in Long Island, New York. He earned his bachelor's degree and his JD from Fordham University. After graduating from law school in 1938, he married his high school sweetheart, Elizabeth "Bette" Shine, with whom he had a daughter and a son.

During World War II, Mitchell served in the navy and, when it came to his war record, the evidence suggests that Mitchell was a different type of self-made man. As James Rosen revealed in *The Strong Man: John Mitchell and the Secrets of Watergate*, Mitchell's military exploits have been heavily exaggerated over the years, and in some cases, they were outright fiction. Mitchell, like JFK, commanded a PT Boat unit, although a popular misconception at the time (perpetuated by a September 1968 story in *New York Times* magazine) was that Mitchell had been Kennedy's commanding officer. As Rosen found, there's no evidence that Mitchell had any interaction with Kennedy during the war, let alone given him orders. In later years, Mitchell would claim that he had earned a Silver Star and two Purple Hearts, although Rosen would find no evidence of any of those honors being bestowed upon Mitchell.[15] "When you spill blood for America," Mitchell once said, "that's the highest sacrifice you can make."[16]

On the other hand, his record as a lawyer was indisputable. Mitchell may have been only eight months younger than Nixon, but when it came to experience on Wall Street, Mitchell had decades on him. While in law school, Mitchell had worked as an "office boy" with the Wall Street firm of Caldwell & Raymond. The firm, which specialized in state and local bonds, traced its history back to 1887 when James Caldwell set up his own practice in New York City. In 1938, six years before he would enlist in the navy, Mitchell officially joined the law firm as an associate. During that stretch of time, he became so successful and generated so much revenue for his firm that they put his name on the shingle within four years after he started practicing law—an unheard of feat on Wall Street. "We were getting all of the business from all over the country," Mitchell said.[17] "So Caldwell, one day, decided to give me a percentage of the retainer. And within a year I was making more money than all the other partners, so it was cheaper for them to make me a partner." As he was living the high life, he decided to divorce his wife, Bette, and agreed to pay her 35 percent of his gross annual income even if she chose to remarry.[18] Mitchell, himself, chose to remarry and didn't waste much time. Eleven days after his divorce, there was a new Mrs. Mitchell: Martha Beall Mitchell, who would go onto become an extremely colorful—and controversial—figure during Watergate.

The secret of his success lay in his creativity. Even before he officially joined the firm as an associate, he found that Caldwell & Raymond's lawyers were flummoxed by some of FDR's New Deal policies—especially his initiative to provide low-income housing to the poor. One of Mitchell's first assignments was one that no one else at the firm wanted. Caldwell gave him a folder containing some paperwork for a bond program in Syracuse to fund low-income housing. "Take this damn fool New Deal idea and work it out," he told Mitchell.[19] Caldwell, like many of his fellow bond lawyers, saw very little money to be made in such bonds due to the fact that the rental income to be made off the properties would be so low.

However, Mitchell smelled an opportunity and came up with a proposal for a tax-exempt municipal housing bond. As his colleagues recognized, the bond, itself, was nothing new. Mitchell's wrinkle was that the federal government would pledge its intention to repay the bond (even though it had no legal obligation to do so) and, as a sign of its commitment, back up each bond with monetary reserves. "In other words, this was not a guarantee by the government, but they would promise to make annual contributions," William Madison, a former colleague and partner of Mitchell's, told Rosen.[20] "It was a—sort of like a gimmick."

What Mitchell was really selling was security and peace of mind. "When the bonds were issued, you knew damn well that they were going to get paid, and of course, Moody's and Standard and Poor's felt that way because they rated the bonds Triple-A," Francis Maloney, another former partner of Mitchell's, told Rosen.[21] Mitchell generated so much business for his firm that he had clients coming to him even before he passed the bar. "They sold like hotcakes," Mitchell later recalled.[22]

He was also making himself indispensible to the state and local governments that wished to take advantage of these bonds. As Carl Person, a former Mudge associate who left the firm in 1963, pointed out, municipal bonds were highly attractive to state and local governments because they did not have to be registered as securities with the SEC under the Securities Act of 1933.[23] Mitchell soon became their point man, researching existing statutes, codes, and constitutions of the various states where the bonds were to be issued and drafting bills for the legislatures to enact so that they could start issuing the bonds. He would also have his firm issue opinions vouching for the legality of the bonds.[24] As a result, during the course of his work, he would travel extensively around the country, meeting with government officials and working closely with them. Before he knew it, he had built up an enviable network of governmental contacts throughout the country.

One of his biggest contacts happened to be Nixon's biggest and longest-standing intraparty rival, Nelson Rockefeller. The two had worked together when Rockefeller was undersecretary of Health, Education and Welfare during the Eisenhower Administration to finance the building and construction of schools throughout the country using a form of the "moral obligation bonds" that Mitchell had utilized for the Syracuse housing project. In 1960, with New York State facing a housing boom, now-governor Rockefeller turned to Mitchell and his moral obligation bonds to deal with the increase of going from building 90,000 units annually to 125,000.[25] Acting on Mitchell's suggestion, Rockefeller secured the creation of the New York State Housing Agency, a semiautonomous state agency that would underwrite the bonds to fund New York's housing boom. Rockefeller loved the moral obligation bond because it enabled the state to raise money without having to submit the project for approval by voters via statewide referendum. Mitchell, when asked if moral obligation bonds undermined popular will, was honest: "That's exactly the purpose of them!"[26]

The moral obligation bond soon caught on with other state and municipal governments throughout the country, making Mitchell a wealthy, and politically well connected, man. His firm, now called Caldwell, Trimble & Mitchell, began handling similar bond issues in over forty states, including multiple projects in New Jersey and Florida.[27] Mitchell's legal work forced him to work with Republicans and Democrats alike, and he developed a reputation as a bipartisan dealmaker. In a bit of hyperbole that was, nevertheless, easy to believe, *BusinessWeek* reported that Mitchell knew or had dealt with more governmental officials throughout the country than most professional politicians.[28]

Several firms were itching to get on the municipal bond gravy train, including Nixon Mudge. As Mitchell's deals became more complicated, the bond underwriters began looking for their own counsel to advise them, and Nixon Mudge was one of the firms they turned to. "We spent quite a bit of time with Bob [Guthrie] and Dick Nixon," Mitchell recalled.[29] "Not so much with Dick on the business, but on the social side of it." Meanwhile, some of Mitchell's bond clients began asking him and his firm to handle some of their other legal work. In order to accommodate his clients, Mitchell would have to either expand the capabilities of his firm or look for a merger partner.[30]

He decided to go with the latter. Caldwell, Trimble & Mitchell had no shortage of suitors, but Guthrie, who worked hard to recruit Mitchell into the Nixon Mudge fold, believed he had the inside track. As Martha Mitchell, John's controversial wife, later put it: "My husband's greatest desire was to build the biggest law firm in the country."[31] The merged firm, which became official in the beginning of January 1967, would boast thirty-three partners, putting it behind the likes of Sullivan & Cromwell, Shearman & Sterling, Davis Polk and Cravath.[32] However, with 120 lawyers on staff, the proposed firm of Nixon, Mudge, Rose, Guthrie, Alexander & Mitchell would be a force to be reckoned with on Wall Street.[33]

There was, of course, another consideration for Mitchell. "John Mitchell, personally, wanted to be close to Richard Nixon," said Evans.[34] "That was a major motivator in his bringing his firm into [Mudge]." Garment agreed, writing that while he believed Mitchell when he said that he was joining Nixon Mudge in order to expand his practice, he assumed that Mitchell's primary reason was to establish a relationship with the man who would be president. "I think he came primarily because of the larger possibilities of a political partnership with Richard Nixon, who he knew, from his life in the heart of American politics, had a substantial chance to become president," noted Garment.[35] "This prospect, I thought and still believe, was exciting to the publicly unexcitable John Mitchell."

Guthrie, for his part, believed that Nixon was the deciding factor in getting Mitchell to sign on the dotted line. "He wanted prestige," Guthrie said.[36] "He actually took a reduction in income to come." It was true that Mitchell was sacrificing equity by moving into the Nixon Mudge partnership structure where he'd have to share profits with twenty other partners instead of only three. His slice may have shrunk, but Mitchell was now eating from a much larger pie. Indeed, the move paid dividends for Mitchell almost immediately. In his first year at the firm, his salary actually increased.[37] In 1968, according to his tax returns, he had his best year ever, taking home $495,000.[38]

The merger paid huge dividends for Nixon Mudge, as well. Mitchell and his three partners from Caldwell, Trimble & Mitchell (John Trimble, William Cannon, and William Madison) generated several hundreds of millions of dollars worth in business and new matters within their first six months at Nixon Mudge. From January to July 1967, the four Caldwell, Trimble & Mitchell partners brought in new bond matters with a total value in excess of $750 million for their new firm, including a $140 million industrial development revenue bond project for the Northwest Aluminum Company, a $100 million bond project in Mississippi for construction of shipyards, and nearly $200 million in various bond projects for the New York State Housing Finance Agency, the agency Mitchell had proposed to Rockefeller. Additionally, the new partners brought in multiple bond matters for cities and towns in New York, New Jersey, and Florida, as well as several bond issues for Chase Manhattan Bank worth nearly $22 million.[39]

Garment would later say that it was his idea to name Mitchell campaign manager and described the discussion where he and Nixon realized that the answer to their prayers was down the hall from them as a "Eureka!" moment.[40]

> I remember the Mitchell moment. It was the end of 1967, and we were in Nixon's office. He was nattering to me about the perennial campaign manager problem. Suddenly, the lightbulb clicked on over my head and I announced: "The answer to our problem is sitting twenty feet away from us, in the next office, a guy who looks, walks and sounds like a campaign manager, knows more about politics than all the other guys you've been talking about and his name is John Mitchell." Nixon reacted by doing something he did only when

> he heard a fresh thought about politics—in other words, very rarely. He abruptly stood up—shot up, actually—and started pacing the room. Mitchell. But of course.

However, others with the firm noted that the two seemed to gravitate toward one another from the very beginning. Within days of the merger, Evans sent his new partner a memo that helpfully identified various members of Nixon's political staff and recommended that "during the next few days, you may want to set up conferences with none or all of" them.[41] Evans also had a different recollection of Garment's "Eureka!" moment, recalling that Garment had approached Mitchell about it in December 1966 during a dinner party prior to the pending merger between the two firms.[42]

Others at the firm did their best to bring Nixon and Mitchell together. Guthrie tried to go the metaphoric route, quoting a famous speech by Russell Conwell titled "Acres of Diamonds," which called on people to utilize the riches around them that they might, otherwise, take for granted. In some cases, the signs were even more obvious. Chapin pointed out that, of all the offices in the firm, Mitchell happened to get the one that was next to Nixon's. "I think, in retrospect, that it was by design," Chapin said.[43] "After all, you name any governor or high-ranking official in any part of the country, and they were dealing with Mitchell. I don't think Nixon would have been elected president without him."

Nixon wasn't oblivious. Safire recalled that Nixon knew, right away, that Mitchell was the right guy for him. "I've found the heavyweight!" Nixon gushed to Safire during the beginning of 1967.[44] However, Nixon also realized that he couldn't just turn over the reins to Mitchell without seeing if his purported heavyweight could actually punch at that level.

Mitchell's inauguration into Nixon's campaign started slowly. Nixon sent him to Wisconsin, an important primary state that he was counting on winning. Mitchell had plenty of contacts and connections in the state, having, almost literally, written the law that created the state's borrowing agency. He turned to that agency's head, Jerris Leonard, a prominent state Republican who was running for US Senate in 1968, to help recruit the top political operatives in the state. Meanwhile, to run the campaign's state operations, Mitchell tapped fellow bond lawyer John MacIver, a partner at Milwaukee-based firm Michael Best & Friedrich. By late July 1967, Mitchell's Wisconsin office had nearly forty-two experienced politicos running it. He had also forged a coalition among the most prominent GOP officials in the state, including Leonard and a number of individuals who had helped Republican Warren Knowles win the Governor's Mansion in 1965. Mitchell's plan included having campaign chairs in each of the state's seventy-two counties and retaining a Milwaukee public relations firm to produce a slick advertising campaign emphasizing Nixon's foreign policy credentials.[45]

Mitchell's approach wowed the Nixon team—many of whom were still unsure who this newcomer was and whether he was up to the job of helping Nixon win the White House. Indeed, it was Mitchell's organization in Wisconsin that helped push Parkinson out the door. Parkinson had decided on a different approach for Wisconsin, relying on private organizations and citizens to organize the state for Nixon, and had gone far enough to tell Mitchell not to proceed with his plans. Mitchell, however, ignored him and even had plans to expand his model to many other states. "To summarize a fairly complex series of events, Parkinson feels that his prerogatives have been usurped by Mitchell," Evans wrote in a memo to Nixon.[46] "John, on the other hand, is completely surprised by this attitude and wants to clarify the method of operation before proceeding in the other states previously discussed with him (Florida, Kansas, Nebraska, New Jersey, West Virginia and New York)."

A few weeks later, Garment tried to make it official by cornering Mitchell in the restroom at a black-tie function at New York's University Club. "Say, John," Garment said, "how would you feel about managing a presidential campaign?" Mitchell, puffing away on his pipe per usual, sounded less than enthused. "Are you out of your fucking mind, Garment?"[47]

Garment, however, came to realize that this was Mitchell's way of saying "yes." Mitchell, meanwhile, had a different recollection of how he came to join the campaign. "One day I was invited up to Nixon's apartment up on Fifth Avenue, and they had somepeople like Garment and Ellsworth and Rose Woods and I don't know who all," Mitchell recalled.[48] "Anyway, at that meeting he announced I was the new campaign manager without any prior consultation. So that's how that started."

Frank Sorg had his own recollection. According to him, the job was originally going to be split between him and Mitchell. Sorg, like Mitchell, had no prior political experience. However, Sorg was very good at glad-handing with the rich and powerful, something Nixon still wasn't comfortable doing. Sorg recalled that, during his years in New York, Nixon would throw a Christmas party at his home on Fifth Avenue for "fat cats" and wealthy, prominent individuals such as Roger Bough, the chairman of US Steel, and Claire Booth Luce, a prominent conservative and publishing executive. Sorg made a reputation for himself as the life of the party. He would often dress as Santa Claus and entertain the "fat cats" in attendance before changing out of his costume and entertaining the audience some more by playing the piano. After Sorg donned the suit for the first time at the 1965 party, Nixon sent his friend a letter the following day thanking him and pointing out that it was "the first occasion on which Santa Claus honored us with his presence." Nixon also added that "everyone was thoroughly delighted with your appearance in that time-honored role" and that "they will be true believers in the most beloved Saint Nick as a result of your convincing performance."[49]

Sorg recalled that he was such a hit that, in subsequent years, his invitation to Nixon's "fat cat" party always contained the postscript that he shouldn't forget to invite Santa Claus. For the 1967 Christmas party, he chose not to bring the Santa suit and Nixon got upset with him. "I was sick and tired of wearing the Santa Claus suit, so I came in with my wife without the Santa Claus suit, and you'd think the man who became President was hit over the face with a fish," Sorg said.[50] "He was appalled. He said: 'Where's Santa Claus? Where's Santa Claus?' He was very, very upset."

Nixon even went so far as to explicitly request Santa's presence at another party at his home during the following evening. Sorg took the not-so-subtle hint and was in his Santa suit when he arrived the next night. "There were a lot of faces there that I didn't know, like Bob Haldeman, John Ehrlichman and Dwight Chapin and all these people that I'd never met before," Sorg said.[51] It was at that party when Sorg finally asked Nixon whether he was going to run for president again.

"By a way, are you set on going for the brass ring?" Sorg asked, referring to the presidency.

"Yes," Nixon responded.

"Well, who's going to run things for you?" Sorg asked.

"You and John Mitchell," Nixon said to a shocked Sorg. "I want you to get closer to John."[52]

Sorg claimed that he did try to get close to Mitchell, as Nixon requested. According to Sorg, he and Mitchell met a few times after that Christmas party and began talking about the upcoming campaign. However, Sorg was skeptical that he and Mitchell could work together. For one thing, Sorg admitted that he didn't like Mitchell very much. For another, the two didn't seem to share the same philosophy when it came to running the campaign. According to Sorg, Mitchell looked at Nixon as a product to be molded and even referred to him as such. "'The product,' hell," Sorg told Mitchell.[53] "The product is a man—flesh and blood."

Ultimately, Sorg did not assume the role of cocampaign chair. According to him, he suffered a financial calamity right around the time he was going to devote himself full time to the campaign. "I was embarrassed about the fact that I was suddenly broke, and I was fighting for my absolute economic life—and it seemed like for about two months I didn't even take my shoes and socks," Sorg recalled.[54] "I just sort of dropped out of sight, and I suppose to this day Dick Nixon thinks that I probably reneged on him."

Sorg's assertion that he was supposed to comanage the campaign is not confirmed by either Nixon or any of the available scholarship concerning the 1968 election. Indeed, his name isn't even mentioned by Ambrose, Witcover, or Garment in their respective books. Buchanan, meanwhile, said in an interview that Sorg's name wasn't familiar to him.[55] "Frank Sorg was a terrific guy," Chapin recalled.[56] "But, I don't think he was ever a co-chair, or even close to that, with Mitchell. Maybe in Frank's mind—but not Nixon's."

With or without Sorg, Mitchell proved to be just the right heavyweight for the job. Right off the bat, Mitchell showed off his managerial skills by implementing his Wisconsin playbook in various other states. In California, for instance, Mitchell and Peter Flanigan demonstrated flexibility by building up their offices in the state despite the fact that it was Reagan's home turf.[57] Similarly, Mitchell built up the campaign's organization in Arizona by recruiting Richard Kleindienst, a brilliant young lawyer and partner at Shimmel, Hill, Kleindienst & Bishop who had run field operations for Goldwater in 1964.[58]

Most importantly, Nixon actually listened to Mitchell. During a lunch with Republican members of Congress shortly after assuming the job, Mitchell faced down skeptical questions about his ability to lead the campaign. "I'm the only man who can say 'no' to Richard Nixon," Mitchell declared,[59] admitting later that his statements had been a bluff on his part to hide his inexperience.[60] "I've made more money in the practice of law than Nixon, brought more clients into the firm, can hold my own in an argument with him, and as far as I'm concerned, I can deal with him as an equal." Haldeman agreed, noting: "Nixon saw him as a peer rather than as an employee, which is what he saw most of the rest of us that he worked with politically."[61]

Mitchell was known to be less charitable toward Nixon in private, mocking him and even referring to him by his hated middle name of "Milhous" while questioning his intelligence. "Nixon couldn't piss straight in the shower if I wasn't there to hold him!" Mitchell once told his press secretary at the DOJ, Jack Landau.[62] Meanwhile, when Tennessee senator Howard Baker introduced his wife to Mitchell at the 1968 GOP National Convention, she mentioned that she had heard of him and identified him as a member of Nixon's firm. "No, madam," Mitchell replied.[63] "Mr. Nixon has joined my law firm."

"GENTLEMEN, THIS IS NOT MY LAST PRESS CONFERENCE."

In order to serve as Nixon's campaign manager, Mitchell would need to take time off from the firm he had just joined. As with all of Nixon's other campaign staff requests to date, the public partner's colleagues accommodated him. Word came down in mid-January 1968—two months before the all-important New Hampshire primary—that Mitchell would be given time off to serve as Nixon's "personal chief of staff."[64] "This was the first time most of the nascent Nixon organization had heard of Mitchell," Evans recalled.[65]

"In time, John Mitchell would provide stability to the management of the campaign."

Mitchell immediately went to work in New Hampshire, a state where the campaign had already spent a considerable amount of time. Prior to Mitchell's appointment, Nixon had tapped Evans to lead the ground effort in the state, and the two had already lined up an impressive coterie of New Hampshire Republicans to their cause. Evans had strong connections in the state as a result of his father-in-law, Harlan Logan,[66] a former majority leader of the New Hampshire State House of Representatives. Logan had introduced Evans to the various movers-and-shakers in the state, making Evans a natural choice to serve as liaison between the campaign and its state operations. Meanwhile, Nixon landed former New Hampshire governor Wesley Powell and eventually installed one of Powell's protégés, a state legislator named David Sterling, as chairman of New Hampshire's Nixon for President Committee. Nixon had also lined up Lane Dwinell, Powell's predecessor as governor, as well as longtime state legislator Stewart Lamprey, longtime diplomat Robert Hill, and several other New Hampshire luminaries.[67]

The campaign may have done a little too well when it came to winning the support of prominent Republicans in the state. Presidential primaries are really about choosing delegates who are pledged or committed to a particular candidate at the national convention. Mitchell immediately realized that the campaign had too many choices for delegates—there were only eight delegate slots at stake, yet some fifty individuals had filed or intended to file as Nixon delegates. It was possible the Nixon delegates could dilute their votes, thereby giving Romney or another candidate an advantage in the all-important delegate count, even if Nixon ended up winning the popular vote. Mitchell wanted to run a single slate of eight delegates so there would be no dilution and no confusion over who would represent the candidate at the convention.

In his first public appearance as Nixon's campaign manager, Mitchell paid a visit to the Granite State in order to cull some of the fat from his slate of delegates. In one meeting, Evans recalled that he and Herbert Brownell accompanied Mitchell as he had a sit-down at the Highway Hotel in Concord with Chester Jenks. The seventy-four-year-old Jenks was a dedicated and loyal soldier to the GOP cause, having served as a delegate to the National Convention for Eisenhower in both 1952 and 1956, and for Nixon in 1960. Jenks had been a Goldwater delegate in 1964 but didn't get to attend the Convention in San Francisco that year because Henry Cabot Lodge had won the New Hampshire primary. Jenks was desperate to go to the Convention for Nixon but was devastated after his employer received an anonymous phone call advising that Jenks not run as a delegate this time around. "His gray head was bowed, his shoulders shook uncontrollably. He was in tears," Evans said.[68] "I listened to his story, feeling embarrassed for him. John Mitchell sat, puffing on his pipe, not saying a word."

Ultimately, Jenks got to run as an alternate delegate and, according to Evans, seemed thrilled to do so. "While I was never absolutely certain as to who called Chester Jenks's employer, John Mitchell and I were the only people dealing with him," Evans said,[69] "and I knew I had not made the call."

The only thing left to do was to make it official. On February 1, 1968, the campaign released a statement announcing that Nixon would enter the New Hampshire primary. Nixon argued that the fate of peace and prosperity was at stake and that new leadership was needed in Washington. He also cast his eight years in the political wilderness as a moment of growth for him, and that his time away from public office had given him the necessary prospective to be a better president. "During the last eight years, I have had a chance to reflect on the lessons of public office, to measure the nation's tasks and its problems from a fresh perspective," Nixon said.[70] "I have sought to apply those lessons to the needs of the President . . . and I believe have found some answers."

One day later, he held a news conference at the Holiday Inn in Manchester, New Hampshire to officially, kick off his campaign. He strode to the microphone and, like he had done five-and-a-half years before at the Beverly Hilton, stared down the gaggle of reporters that, he believed, had tried their hardest to prevent him from being in this position again. This time, though, there was no temper tantrum. Instead, he tapped into his well of self-effacement, something he had done more of during the intervening six years. "Gentlemen," he intoned.[71] "This is *not* my last press conference!"

"BEST CAMPAIGN STAFF ANY CANDIDATE EVER HAD"

As the New Hampshire primary approached, Nixon's campaign staff had a problem on their hands. George Romney, as predicted, couldn't hit major league pitching and shot himself in the proverbial foot before he could really make a dent in the 1968 race. The man who, at one point, had been the favorite for the nomination, essentially committed political *hara-kari* when he sat down for a interview with a TV station in Detroit in August 1967 about the Vietnam War. "When I came back from Vietnam [in November 1965], I'd just had the greatest brainwashing that anybody can get," Romney said, trying to make a point about how the United States should not have gotten involved in Vietnam in the first place.[72] The comment conjured up images of films like *The Manchurian Candidate* and was devastating to Romney's campaign. In one poll, he dropped sixteen points immediately after his "brainwashing" statement.[73]

While Romney's struggles were, obviously, good news for the Nixon campaign, they had come at an inopportune time. Because Romney was hemorrhaging support, he decided that he wouldn't make it to New Hampshire and withdrew from the race two weeks before the opening primary. Nixon was now certain to win, but by default rather than on his own merits. "Knowing he was far ahead in the polls, he felt deprived of a certain, smashing victory in the primary, and also in Wisconsin," Witcover wrote.[74] "Now the press would be saying Nixon may have lost his loser image, but he still hadn't beaten anybody."

Ultimately, Nixon's longtime rival, Rockefeller, made a last-minute push for New Hampshire—although he refused to officially declare his candidacy, fearing a backlash from GOP voters still angry about his refusal to help Goldwater four years before. Rockefeller also realized that Nixon had the state wrapped up and getting in now would only allow his rival to claim his scalp. In the end, some voters in the state tried to undertake a last-minute write-in campaign for Rockefeller, and Nixon egged them on, hoping to create a little bit of suspense so that his inevitable victory would look better. "New Hampshire becomes a very significant race with a massive, well-financed write-in for Rockefeller," Nixon said with a straight face.[75] "He has the money and the men to do it."

In the end, Nixon won New Hampshire in a rout. With 79 percent of the vote in his column, Nixon had obliterated the field. His closest opponent ended up being Rockefeller, who had garnered a mere 11 percent in write-in votes.[76] Nixon had earned a stunning 84,005 votes—a far larger tally than either Eugene McCarthy or Lyndon Johnson had earned in the Democratic primary (Johnson, as was traditional for incumbents then, did not actually appear on the ballot—his voters were expected to write in his name).[77]

Johnson's smaller-than-expected victory ended up overshadowing Nixon's resounding win. The president was held under 50 percent and only managed to defeat McCarthy by seven points. Nixon, however, didn't seem to mind as it gave him a chance to join the crowd and pile on to Johnson's miseries—something he was used to doing after casting himself as the anti-LBJ for the better part of the previous two years. "The people of the nation don't want four more years of Johnson in the White House," Nixon said in his victory speech.[78] Calling the primary results "the first referendum on Lyndon B. Johnson," Nixon expressed confidence that his win in New Hampshire meant that "we are going to win in August, and that America is going to get new leadership in November."[79]

He also took the opportunity to spread around the credit for his resounding victory to the people who had helped him accomplish it. "The staff did it," Nixon told the Associated Press after the New Hampshire primary.[80] "Best campaign staff any candidate ever had."

With his heavyweight in place and his Nixon Mudge–dominated staff running on all cylinders, it seemed like Nixon had finally changed his ways. His micromanaging style and domineering presence seemed to be a thing of the past, and the injection of new blood into his political operation seemed to rejuvenate him. His staffers were happy and exhilarated to be involved in such an important undertaking, and Nixon seemed more relaxed and confident after his years away from electoral politics. After Johnson shocked the world and announced on March 31 that he would not run for reelection, Nixon was, suddenly, the favorite to win the presidency. He solidified his status as the man to beat with a resounding victory in Wisconsin, and it seemed like Nixon's new staff would continue to hold sway over its candidate as the National Convention in Miami approached, and beyond.

Unfortunately for the Nixon Mudge contingent, they would soon find out that old habits died hard.

"THE HAPPY, CAREFREE ENVIRONMENT CAME TO A SCREECHING HALT."

On April 29, 1968, the tone and tenor of the campaign changed, irrevocably, with a simple announcement. Mitchell called a staff meeting and announced that two of Nixon's old stalwarts, H. R. Haldeman and John Ehrlichman, would be officially joining the campaign. The two West Coast–based men had been holding back, waiting to see how things shook out before committing to another Nixon campaign. Now, they seemed ready to get involved. "By 1967, I had an eight-year investment in Nixon's political career, and 1968 looked like the year when he might win one," Ehrlichman said.[81] "By now, I had an equity in his candidacy, and he was my only entrée into the big political game I had learned to play."

Haldeman and Ehrlichman have become almost inseparable in American political history—and for reasons beyond the fact that their names sounded similar and produced a nice, rhythmic quality when you said them in succession. Dubbed "Nixon's SOB," the crew-cut-wearing, hard-charging Haldeman had an abrasive personality and take-no-prisoners attitude that endeared him to almost no one. Ehrlichman was more reserved but almost always wore a serious-looking expression on his face that bordered on a scowl. In time, Mitchell would distrust and even dislike Ehrlichman, calling him a "conniving little SOB."[82]

Once Haldeman and Ehrlichman came onto the scene, the campaign seemed to lose its sense of fun and adventure, with one staffer telling Rosen that the "happy, carefree environment came to a screeching halt."[83] Hobart Lewis, the *Reader's Digest* CEO who had been a part of Congress '66 and had traveled with Nixon in 1960 and 1962, was so disillusioned after spending a few days under the new regime that he went home and, after a couple of days, phoned Rose Mary Woods to tell her that "the fun's gone."[84]

For instance, one thing that Haldeman and Ehrlichman did was place themselves as buffers between Nixon and the rest of his staff. With memories of Nixon's reputation as a micromanager, Haldeman and Ehrlichman made sure there wouldn't be a repeat, keeping all but the most important stuff from their candidate. During Nixon's presidency, the two men would be nicknamed "The Berlin Wall" as a play on their German surnames, as well as their reputation for isolating Nixon, carefully controlling who got access to the president and what information got through to him. The initial bricks in the wall were laid during the campaign, as Nixon's closest aides no longer had unfettered access to their boss.

Buchanan experienced the isolation up close. During the course of several foreign excursions and countless campaign trips throughout the previous two-plus years, the speechwriter had become accustomed to being able to talk to Nixon whenever he wanted. After the Oregon primary in May, he was told to start sending his memos and speeches through Haldeman as "a curtain fell between the candidate in the front of the plane and the staff and press to the rear."[85] "Haldeman was between me and the candidate," said Buchanan.[86] "Haldeman was an honest broker and [my memos] got to Nixon. But there started to be a bulwark between Nixon and me, even though I had been face-to-face with him and dealing directly with him for two-and-a-half years."

Even as Haldeman and Ehrlichman kept Nixon walled off from his staffers, the Nixon Mudge aides continued to handle important tasks, including vetting for Nixon's vice presidential running mate and recruiting future Nixon Administration secretary of state Henry Kissinger into the fold. Kissinger, in particular, was a major "get" for the campaign. The Harvard professor had been hoping for an opportunity to shape or influence US foreign policy, and had hitched his wagon to Nelson Rockefeller, backing the New York governor in 1960, 1964, and during the early part of the 1968 campaign. Now, with Nixon on the verge of securing the nomination, Evans and Garment dispatched a young volunteer named Michael Saperstein to meet with Kissinger to see if he might be willing to transfer his loyalties.

There were some significant fences to be mended. Kissinger had called Nixon "unfit to be President" while predicting that, if elected, he would be "a disaster in the White House."[87] Nevertheless, after meeting with Kissinger, Saperstein predicted to Evans and Garment that the professor would be receptive to joining the campaign. "Mr. Kissinger expressed concern over the fact that Mr. Nixon has not publicly identified himself with foreign policy advisors, although he admitted that he is, essentially, in agreement with Mr. Nixon's views on Vietnam and conceded Mr. Nixon's knowledge in foreign affairs," Saperstein wrote.[88] "He gave every assurance that he is anxious to have a Republican as our next President."

Kissinger's former loyalty to Nixon's nemesis proved to be no obstacle—at least as far Nixon was concerned. Evans pointed out that while Nixon was obsessed with loyalty, he also liked winning over people from an opposing camp. Mitchell, given his history with Rockefeller, could be seen as one such person—although Mitchell had never supported him politically. Nevertheless, Rockefeller had always been somewhat territorial over Mitchell, telling Nixon at a cocktail party shortly after the 1968 campaign: "John is my lawyer."[89]

The vice presidential search was another area where Nixon seemed to relish collecting one of Rockefeller's old men. According to Evans, Buchanan, Garment, and others, the selection of Agnew was a stunner that caught all of them off guard. "I cannot recall any discussion of Agnew, nor was there any consensus on a candidate," Buchanan said.[90] Nixon's staff was split in many different directions. Buchanan and Sears wanted to secure the right flank and pick Reagan, Price thought liberal New York mayor John Lindsay was necessary to win votes in the North,[91] and Evans pushed for Percy as well as a surprise pick: John Gardner, Johnson's secretary of Health, Education and Welfare, that had been strongly recommended by conservative leader William F. Buckley Jr.[92] "None of the possible candidates appear to me to add significant strength to a Nixon ticket," wrote Evans, whose short-list included senators Mark Hatfield of Oregon, Howard Baker of Tennessee, and John Tower of Texas, as well as Governor Dan Evans of Washington and Representative John Rhodes of Arizona.[93] Other names bandied about included George H. W. Bush, Governor John Volpe of Massachusetts, and Nixon's friend and Strategy Board member Bob Finch.[94]

Nixon surprised them all by selecting Agnew. Even Haldeman was at a loss to explain Nixon's reasoning; decades later, he stated, emphatically, that he still didn't know why Nixon chose Agnew. In the end, Haldeman figured that the governor of Maryland had been a close ally to Rockefeller, and Nixon's decision to put him on the ticket was more about tying down the Rockefeller wing of the party.[95] There may have also been a personal reason. As White pointed out in *The Making of the President 1968*, Agnew had seemed put out when Rockefeller withdrew from the 1968 race without telling him, leaving the Maryland governor feeling "humiliated" and made to feel "too unimportant to be taken into the know." "Agnew was never to come back to Rockefeller; his orientation to Richard Nixon began at that moment," White said.[96]

The Maryland governor had made his reputation as a "tell-it-like-it-is" type who could reach across the aisle to craft bipartisan solutions. As governor, he and the Democratic state legislature enacted the state's first open-housing laws and repealed an antimiscegenation statute. Agnew, however, also had a reputation for being a "law and order" type, and during the riots that followed the assassination of Martin Luther King Jr. in the spring of 1968, he called several noted civil rights leaders to his office and yelled at them for not being able to control their followers. The leaders, who thought they were there to try to forge a consensus were, instead, subjected to a laundry list of insults that would soon become Agnew's trademark: "circuit-riding, Hanoi-visiting . . . caterwauling, riot-inciting, burn-America-down type of leaders[s]." Eighty of the civil rights leaders walked out while the others listened in stunned silence.[97]

Despite his later comments that he couldn't remember any discussion of Agnew, it was Buchanan who, reportedly, brought this piece of information to Nixon. "That guy Agnew is a really impressive fellow," he told Nixon.[98] "He's got guts! He's got a good attitude!" One aide later told Witcover that Nixon seemed impressed by Agnew, calling him a "very tough guy."[99] There was also little inkling of what was to come with Agnew, who resigned from the vice presidency in 1973 amid corruption charges (he eventually pleaded no contest to tax evasion and was sentenced to probation and a fine). "Today, you'd say: 'Didn't they know he was a crook?'" Herbert Brownell said.[100] "But that is hindsight. At the time, Agnew had a good reputation."

Good reputation or not, the more moderate staffers were aghast. Garment, for one, did not hide his distaste for Agnew. Ordered by Mitchell to help Agnew with his speech at the Convention, Garment called it a "depressing assignment" that was only surpassed by trying to explain Agnew's selection to the world. "Agnew proceeded to make matters progressively worse with his love of alliteration and his peculiar penchant for politically poisonous prose, viz., 'if you've seen one slum, you've seen them all,'" Garment said.[101]

According to some historians, Agnew's nomination was a reward to southerners,[102] particularly South Carolina senator Strom Thurmond, who had switched to the GOP in 1964 and had been an early supporter of Nixon's in 1968. Nixon and Mitchell had spent months lining up Thurmond's support and were counting on the influential South Carolinian to help stave off any last-minute southern revolts at the Convention. That nearly happened when Ronald Reagan, working alongside Rockefeller, made a last-minute attempt to deny Nixon the nomination. Thurmond, who personally preferred Reagan but felt he wasn't ready for the presidency, helped Mitchell put down the proposed insurrection, and Nixon won the nomination, easily, on the first ballot.

Thurmond's help, however, had come at a steep price. Nixon had to reassure the one-time standard-bearer for the prosegregation Dixiecrats that he would not turn into Lyndon Johnson on civil rights and that, while he supported desegregation, he would oppose forced busing and would give states some latitude in enforcing civil rights laws. Thurmond also wanted

Nixon to look members of several southern delegations in the eye and repeat his promises. One of them ended up wearing a wire for the *Miami Herald* and recorded Nixon vowing never to forget about the South and to refrain from using them as a "whipping boy" for the rest of the country.[103] He also assured them that they would have a voice in the running mate selection process and steadfastly denied reports that he had already made deals with others, notably liberals Rockefeller or Percy.[104]

Mitchell went further and personally assured southern state chairs that Nixon was open to selecting a running mate who would "bring peace" on civil rights and "lay off pro-Negro crap."[105] Agnew, as a border-state governor who wasn't a segregationist but, clearly, distrusted civil rights leaders, was the perfect poster boy for a Republican Party looking to pick up votes in the South.

"THE MECHANISTIC STAGES"

The GOP National Convention in Miami seemed to mark a demarcation point for the campaign—at least as far as the Nixon Mudge contingent were concerned. With the obvious exception of Mitchell, Nixon's law firm–based staff would find itself increasingly marginalized and isolated as the campaign wore on. Evans noted that the process began almost immediately after the Convention ended. "We were all being slotted into specific assignments which, while significant, were further limitations over our former access to the candidate," Evans said.[106]

For instance, Garment was put in charge of African American outreach. In other campaigns, it might have been an important assignment. However, for Nixon's 1968 campaign, which placed an emphasis on winning over southern white voters disenchanted with the Democratic Party, it was a token task. According to Evans, Garment and others at the firm handled this assignment with aplomb—at one point, they even landed an audience with Wilt Chamberlain. The basketball legend supported Nixon and volunteered to help out with the campaign, including public appearances and serving as a liaison to the African American community. "Wilt was the center of attention in our African-American suite at the convention, with receptions every evening," Evans recalled.[107] "Our Citizens for Nixon operation had other suites devoted to similar entertaining (e.g., Lawyers for Nixon, Veterans for Nixon, etc.), but none was more spirited than this one." The enthusiasm for Wilt, obviously, didn't lead to any real in-roads into the African American community, and as Evans noted, it was probably never going to happen anyway, especially after Johnson's vice president, civil rights icon Hubert Humphrey, secured the Democratic nomination.

Sears also felt like he had been shunted away from Nixon. After the Convention, Sears found himself in Agnew's camp, minding the VP candidate and handling his side of the campaign. Originally, the plan had been for Sears to function as a go-between for Nixon and Agnew in order to ensure that the presidential and vice presidential campaigns were well coordinated, thereby avoiding a repeat of 1960 when Nixon and his then–running mate, Henry Cabot Lodge, had made a number of contradictory statements. However, as time went on, that plan seemed to fall by the wayside as Sears was, more or less, exiled to Agnew's camp permanently—an assignment Witcover termed "American Siberia."[108]

There may have been a personal reason why Sears remained stuck in Agnewland. Buchanan noted that Mitchell disliked Sears and blamed an incident during the Convention where Mitchell believed Sears had disrespected him. "At the 1968 convention, where he was a delegate hunter, Sears took to calling campaign chairman John Mitchell by his first name, while instructing him on convention politics," Buchanan recalled, noting that Sears had also done this with Ray Bliss, the national chairman of the Republican Party.[109] "A smoldering Mitchell directed me to follow him into his suite, spun around, stuck a finger in my face, and went into a rant about 'your goddamn friend Sears.' J. P. Sears had made a bad enemy."

Sears confirmed that he and Mitchell didn't get along, although he downplayed their lack of rapport as the reason for his move to Agnew's camp. "I don't know why we didn't get along," Sears said.[110] "I think, maybe, he thought that Nixon talked to me more than he should." Sears also underlined the fact that Nixon believed he had been burned by Lodge in 1960 and was worried that an inexperienced and outspoken candidate like Agnew could be a headache for the campaign. "He needed someone to take charge of Agnew, who had already made a lot of mistakes," said Sears.[111] "And I was out of a job because delegate hunting was over after the Convention, so I was available."

The Nixon Mudge folks weren't the only ones who felt a growing sense of isolation. Nixon had also started ignoring the TV and advertising group. "We can't even get through to [Nixon] anymore," Treleaven, Nixon consultant, complained.[112] "There's two groups of people in the way: one on the plane [Haldeman with the candidate] and one at headquarters [Mitchell] and between them, we can't get through."

Haldeman justified the move by pointing out: "As [we shifted] from the early stages of engineering a comeback to the mechanistic stages of running the actual operation of a campaign, [Nixon] turned, tended to turn back, to those of us who had been through that routine before."[113] Haldeman and Mitchell had, essentially, agreed to split their duties so that Haldeman ran the candidate and Mitchell ran the campaign.[114] As such, there wasn't much room left for anyone else. Ehrlichman agreed, pointing out that many of the

Nixon Mudge staffers, other than Mitchell, Evans, and Sears, had to worry about their day jobs and weren't always around.[115]

"THIS IS TREASON."

The 1968 presidential campaign is, obviously, one of the most interesting and monumental events in American history. It's also been written about from many different angles by many different historians and writers. As such, this book won't cover the general election campaign in much depth.

There is one incident involving Mitchell that merits a look.

The phrase *October Surprise* gets thrown around a lot, but perhaps the archetype of the term occurred during the 1968 contest. After a catastrophic Democratic National Convention in Chicago where Hubert Humphrey's moment of glory was overshadowed by gory and graphic scenes of anti–Vietnam War protestors clashing, violently, with Mayor Richard Daley's police force, the Democrats were, for all intents and purposes, dead in the water. Humphrey was also being weighed down by Johnson's continuing unpopularity as the incumbent president had made clear that he intended for his vice president to remain loyal to the administration's policies on Vietnam.

There was also a personal element. Johnson loved to brag about having Hubert's "pecker in my pocket" and was known to call his vice president "weak" and "disloyal" in private.[116] Both Johnson's and Humphrey's aides wondered whether the president even wanted his vice president to win. "A number of us felt like Johnson never really rallied people for Humphrey," said Stuart Eizenstat,[117] Humphrey's research director in 1968 who later went onto a long career in government where, among other things, he helped secure nearly $8 billion in compensation on behalf of Holocaust victims.[118] "I think he had doubts about whether or not Humphrey would be a strong President and whether he would follow Johnson's Vietnam policies." Joseph Califano, Johnson's top domestic aide, confirmed that Johnson's ambivalence toward Humphrey ran so deep that, before Nixon secured the nomination, Johnson was considering crossing party lines and supporting Nelson Rockefeller for the presidency. "He wanted Rockefeller to run," Califano said.[119] "He urged him to run. We brought him into the White House secretly . . . and tried to talk him into it."

Nixon had taken advantage of this dysfunctional relationship between the two Democrats by cozying up to the president and currying favor with his one-time rival. "I don't give a goddamn what the politics is," Nixon had told Johnson in August.[120] "But we've got to stand very firm. And I won't say a damn word that's going to embarrass you. You can be sure of that." Nixon then asked LBJ whether Humphrey would stand firm with them, and Johnson responded that he didn't know. The following month, Nixon continued his campaign to drive a wedge between Johnson and his vice president, sending a confidential message to the president through mutual friend Reverend Billy Graham. "I will never embarrass him after the election," Nixon vowed.[121] "I respect him as a man as the President. He's the hardest working and most dedicated President in 140 years." Finally, playing to Johnson's concerns over his legacy, Nixon promised that, if he brought the Vietnam War to its conclusion, he would give Johnson the lion's share of the credit and that he would "do everything" to ensure Johnson "a place in history."[122]

Nixon's charm offensive seemed to be working. As summer turned to autumn, Johnson seemed to be covertly favoring Nixon over Humphrey. According to Nancy Gibbs and Michael Duffy, Johnson sat on numerous pieces of information that could have been harmful to Nixon had they leaked to the press. Johnson even told one of Humphrey's advisors that "Nixon is following my policies more closely than Humphrey."[123] The embattled vice president, who was fifteen points behind Nixon in a late September Gallup poll,[124] was stuck between a rock and a hard place. If he continued to stick with the unpopular Johnson, then his campaign would remain stuck in neutral and he would lose in a landslide. If he broke with Johnson, his poll numbers would improve but he would turn Johnson into an implacable enemy.

Humphrey went with the latter option, giving a well-publicized speech in Salt Lake City on September 30 where he put some daylight between him and the White House on Vietnam. Humphrey promised that he would end the bombing campaign in North Vietnam and push for peace. To Humphrey and several Johnson Administration officials, the speech barely deviated from Johnson's policies and didn't seem worth getting upset about. Johnson, however, stewed with rage and refused to campaign for Humphrey in Texas. The president even snubbed Humphrey after the Democratic nominee requested a meeting with his predecessor to clear the air. "That bastard Johnson," Humphrey seethed to an aide.[125] "You tell the President he can cram it up his ass."

Nevertheless, Humphrey's maneuver worked. His poll numbers and campaign donations immediately started to climb following Salt Lake City, and he began closing the gap with Nixon.

Then came the game-changer. On October 31, Johnson stunned the country when he announced a bombing halt, as well as upcoming peace talks in Paris between the United States and both North and South Vietnam. The maneuver wasn't completely out of the blue—Johnson had laid down his terms for a bombing halt in June. The breakthrough had come in early October when the North Vietnamese dropped its objection to South Vietnam's participation in the proposed peace talks.[126] Johnson now had his chance to end the war on his own terms and salvage his place in history in one fell swoop. There were still some significant hurdles to be cleared before there was any chance of an actual peace treaty, but the news buoyed his spirits considerably.

The news also lifted Humphrey's fortunes. After Johnson's announcement, Nixon's lead vanished almost immediately and Humphrey was now in a dead heat with the GOP nominee. Nixon was irate and convinced that Johnson was trying to steal the election at the last minute in favor of his vice president. Nixon still had the bitter taste of 1962 in his mouth when a race he thought he was winning turned against him in the closing stages as a result of a piece of Democratic foreign policy that he had little respect for. Now he had an unwelcome sense of déjà vu. Luckily for him, however, he had prepared for something like this, and this time, he had an acc in the hole.

Chinese-born Anna Chennault was a well-connected former journalist who had relocated to Washington, D.C., following the death of her husband, Flyer Tigers founder Claire Lee Chennault, in 1958. One of the charter members of the so-called China Lobby, Madame Chennault had long been suspicious of Democrats, blaming Truman, Acheson, Marshall, and others for "losing China" to the Communists.[127] She, naturally, gravitated toward Republicans, and her Watergate apartment soon became a popular hangout for powerful and influential Republicans. In 1964, for instance, Barry Goldwater and several of his advisors became regular fixtures there as they planned his ultimately doomed presidential campaign.[128]

Chennault had been friends with Nixon since the latter's vice presidential days, having met both Dick and Pat during a banquet held in their honor in Taiwan by Chiang Kai-shek. Chennault volunteered for Nixon's 1960 presidential campaign and kept in touch with him during his wilderness years. During one of Nixon's many trips abroad, Chennault even met up with Nixon in Taipei and drove him to the airport.

> As Nixon followed me into my car, he cracked his forehead on the door. It was a hard, resounding blow that left no doubt about the pain. He bit his lip hard, not uttering a sound, and turned pale. Blood was oozing out of his forehead, spilling in a thin trickle across the bridge of his nose. I reached into my purse for a handkerchief and pressed it to his forehead, against the gash. He cupped it hastily in his hands, muttering, "I'm all right, I'm all right." He seemed frantic with embarrassment, looking back everyone once in a while, handkerchief still pressed to brow, at Ambassador [Konsin] Shah [Chiang's chief of protocol tasked with seeing off Nixon] . . . He mumbled apologizes about my dress, which was white and, by now, conspicuously spattered with drops of blood.[129]

With 1968 gearing up, Chennault and Nixon reaffirmed their friendship. According to Chennault, Nixon had told her in the spring of 1967 that he intended to run again, and she had agreed to keep him informed of events in Vietnam, an issue that promised to dominate the upcoming presidential race.

She also agreed to serve as chair of the National Women's Advisory Committee for Nixon.[130] Chennault was an important "get" for Nixon, as she had a lot of friends in Vietnam and was close to several powerful South Vietnamese government officials, including South Vietnamese ambassador to the United States Bùi Diễm and Nguyen Văn Kieu, brother of South Vietnamese president Nguyễn Văn Thiệu.

In July 1968, Chennault and Bùi Diễm flew to Nixon's campaign suite in the Hotel Pierre to meet with Mitchell and Nixon. Diễm, unlike Chennault, was not a dyed-in-the-wool Republican and claimed to want close relations with both parties. However, Diễm was starting to get disillusioned with LBJ and his Administration's handling of the ongoing war in Vietnam. "As the Democrats steered with all due haste away from the Indochinese involvement they had engineered, I was increasingly attracted to the Republican side," Bùi Diễm recalled.[131]

During the meeting, Diễm and Chennault liked what they heard from Nixon regarding his plans to win the war, and the two agreed to act as a secret back channel for the campaign to South Vietnam's government.[132] "If I should be elected the next President, you can rest assured I will have a meeting with your leader and find a solution to winning this war," Nixon promised Diễm.[133] With the entire election on the line, Nixon and Mitchell decided to deploy their secret weapon.

Almost immediately after issuing the bombing halt, Johnson started hearing rumblings about the possibility that the Paris peace talks were being sabotaged. The talks were always going to be a hard sell for the South Vietnamese, who had never formally recognized the North regime, yet Johnson pushed ahead, hoping for the best. Now, he was starting to hear whispers that South Vietnamese officials were stalling and being told to hold out until after the election in the hope of getting a better deal from Nixon. The first such warning came from Alexander Sachs, a well-known and well-respected figure who had a pretty good track record with making predictions, having correctly forecast the Great Depression as well as the Nazi atomic bomb project during World War II. Sachs informed White House officials that he had heard serious chatter among Wall Street figures that Nixon's campaign was going to intervene and prevent a peace deal from happening. "[O]ne of his associates, a fellow named [John] Mitchell, who's running his campaign, who's the real [Eisenhower's chief of staff] Sherman Adams of the operation, in effect, said to a businessman that 'we're going to handle this like we handled the Fortas matter,' unquote," Johnson told his old mentor, Senator Richard Russell of Georgia.

Soon, they were more than whispers. Suspicious of their motives, US intelligence agencies had decided to place Chennault and Diễm under surveillance back in April.[134] That was only part of the net that they had set up. The CIA had bugged the office of the president of South Vietnam, and the

NSA was intercepting diplomatic messages from the South Vietnamese embassy in D.C.[135] Mitchell, paranoid that something like this could happen but desperate to be kept in the loop, had established a protocol with Chennault where she would contact him on a different phone number each day so that he could keep the pressure up on the South Vietnamese to rebuff Johnson.[136]

With all that surveillance in place, it was only a matter of time before Johnson heard what he needed to hear. On November 2, three days before the election, Johnson got word at his ranch from the FBI that they had a smoking gun.

> Mrs. Anna Chennault contacted Vietnamese Ambassador Bùi Diễm and advised him that she had received a message from her boss [unidentified], which her boss wanted her to give personally to the ambassador. She said the message was that the ambassador is to "hold on, we are gonna win" and that her boss also said: "Hold on, he understands all of it." She repeated that this is the only message. "He said please tell your boss to hold on." She advised that her boss had just called from New Mexico.[137]

Nixon was not in New Mexico that day, but Agnew was. Later on, Chennault would say that she had meant to say "New Hampshire," which was the home state of Robert Hill, former ambassador to El Salvador, Costa Rica, and Mexico under Eisenhower, and the go-between for the campaign and Chennault.[138] Either way, Johnson felt he had enough to confront the highest-ranking Republican official in D.C. Less than an hour after he received the FBI message, he spoke with his good friend, Senate Minority Leader Everett Dirksen, and read the Illinois Republican the riot act. "Some of our folks, including some of the old China Lobby, are going to the [South] Vietnamese embassy and saying, 'Please notify the President that if he'll hold out till November the 2nd they could get a better deal,'" Johnson told Dirksen.[139] "And they oughtn't to be doing this. This is treason."

Johnson went on, throwing out a not-so-veiled threat to Dirksen, knowing that it would get back to Nixon.[140] "Now, I can identify them, because I know who's doing this," Johnson told Dirksen. "[Dirksen attempts to interject.] I don't want to identify it. I think it would shock America if a principal candidate was playing with a source like this on a matter this important."

Nixon called Johnson the following day and seemed to mollify the president with his "non-denial denials," as Ken Hughes put it. "I just wanted you to know that I feel very, very strongly about this, and any rumblings around about somebody trying to sabotage the Saigon government's attitude there [is] absolutely no credibility as far as I'm concerned," Nixon told Johnson.[141] In private, Nixon hardly seemed bothered at all. After the call, Nixon and his friends "collapsed with laughter," according to the *Sunday Times* of London.[142]

Nevertheless, Johnson wasn't showing his cards in that conversation and did not repeat his threat that he had made to Dirksen about going public. According to Califano, Johnson informed his vice president of the matter and left it to Humphrey to decide whether or not to use it on the eve of the election,[143] which the polls showed was too close to call. A Harris poll taken the Friday before the election had Humphrey winning a plurality of the popular vote and a clear majority of the Electoral College. However, the following day, South Vietnam announced it would not participate in the peace talks, a move that had the side effect of killing Humphrey's momentum dead. "I saw [pollster Lou] Harris after the election and he told me his polls had been accurate," Eizenstat recalled.[144] "What happened was that they had stopped polling on Friday evening/Saturday morning and they didn't poll the weekend. That was when the President of South Vietnam said he wasn't going to the conference. That knocked the air out of our sails pretty badly."

Despite knowing that it could possibly secure his election, Humphrey decided not to leak news of the Chennault affair to the press. According to Eizenstat, Max Kampelman and some other senior aides encouraged Humphrey to go public. "Max told me that he urged Humphrey to do it, but Humphrey refused," said Eizenstat, who didn't find out about the Chennault affair until several years afterward.[145] "I think he would have won if he had leaked it, and probably would have ended up saving tens of thousands of lives." There were other considerations. For one thing, Humphrey would have to reveal all of the wiretaps and surveillance methods being used by the Johnson Administration—some of which were illegal. Several of Humphrey's loyalists maintained that what he had done was for the good of the country, because had Nixon won, he would have come into office under a cloud of suspicion that would have rendered him powerless to rule. "I know of no more essentially decent story in American politics than Humphrey's refusal to [go public]," White wrote.[146] Kampelman would later recount how, after the election, Nixon told him how thankful he was that Humphrey had put his country before the election and compared Humphrey's sacrifice to Nixon's own decision in 1960 not to challenge his defeat to Kennedy.[147]

In the immediate aftermath of the Chennault affair, it wasn't entirely clear what, if any, role Nixon had played in the whole thing. According to Chennault, she had dealt only with Mitchell. In her 1980 book, *The Education of Anna*, Chennault claimed that a frantic Mitchell called her right after Johnson announced the bombing halt and, despite his well-founded paranoid about surveillance, could not have been clearer about what he wanted. "Anna, I'm speaking on behalf of Mr. Nixon," Mitchell told her.[148] "It's very important that our Vietnamese friends understand our Republican position, and I hope you have made that clear to them." Chennault responded that all she had done was relay messages. "If you're talking about direct influence, I have to

tell you it isn't wise for us to try to influence the South Vietnamese," she responded. "I don't think either we or the Democrats can force them to act one way or another. They have their own politics, you know." Later on, she confirmed to Witcover that she had been coordinating with the Nixon campaign. "The only people who knew about the whole operation were Nixon, John Mitchell and John Tower, and they're all dead," Chennault told Witcover. [149] "But they knew what I was doing. Anyone who knows about these things knows I was getting orders to do these things. I couldn't do anything without instructions."

Nixon campaign staffers have maintained that they did not know about the Chennault affair at the time. Indeed, some still doubt whether it actually occurred. "Didn't know anything," Garment said when asked about Chennault.[150] "Anna Chennault was a mystery to me." Sears, who was assigned to Agnew's detail at the time, also said he wasn't aware of anything involving Chennault. "I don't know what role she actually played," Sears said, noting that he had been warned by the Secret Service about making telephone calls due to the possibility that his phone could be tapped.[151] "Maybe they thought I would have met her at some point, but I didn't know her." Buchanan said that he "did not believe it then" and does not believe it now. "Nixon would never have taken the insane risk of opening a back channel through Mrs. Chennault to Saigon to torpedo a peace agreement negotiated to end the war in Vietnam," Buchanan maintained.[152] In his manuscript, Evans does not mention Chennault's name once, although his papers contain an August 1967 memo to Nixon referencing "the Anna Chennault appointment." The memo also references Robert Hill,[153] the man who, according to Anthony Summers, had escorted her to Nixon's Fifth Avenue apartment in 1968 when she first met John Mitchell.[154]

The questions surrounding Nixon's involvement with the Chennault affair continued to swirl until 2014, when the Richard Nixon Presidential Library and Museum released a declassified interview with Tom Charles Huston. The national chairman of Young American for Freedom, Huston first got involved with Nixon in 1966 when the former vice president was traveling around the country speaking on behalf of Republican candidates. During the 1968 campaign, Huston set up the Youth for Nixon group and then took a job at the White House doing research and speechwriting immediately after Nixon was inaugurated in 1969.[155] Huston would attain greater infamy as architect of the Huston Plan, a 1970 domestic surveillance proposal that advocated burglarizing, eavesdropping, and even opening the mail of antiwar radicals.[156]

In September of that year Nixon approached Huston to conduct an investigation into LBJ's bombing halt the previous year. "He believed, incorrectly in my judgment, but nevertheless, he believed that the whole bombing halt thing had been a Johnson ploy to elect Humphrey," Huston said.[157] His investigation, inevitably, led to the Chennault affair. "I've concluded that there was no doubt that Nixon was—would have been directly involved, that it's not something that anybody would've undertaken on their own," Huston said.[158] As for Mitchell, Huston found that there was "no question" that the campaign manager "was directly involved" and was the one "meeting with her."[159] "I think my understanding of the way in which—having been in the '68 campaign, and my understanding of the way that campaign was run, it's inconceivable to me that John Mitchell would be running around, you know, passing messages to the South Vietnamese government, et cetera, on his own initiative," Huston said.[160]

Then in 2017, John A. Farrell published *Richard Nixon: The Life*, which uncovered written notes from Haldeman in which his boss ordered Haldeman to "keep Anna Chennault working on the [South Vietnamese]." Haldeman also recalled Nixon asking if there were "any other way to monkey wrench" the peace talks and weighed the possibility of bringing in others to try to communicate to the South Vietnamese the benefits of holding out until after November 1968.[161] While the notes would seem to be a "smoking gun," the *New York Times* pointed out that there's no evidence that Haldeman actually carried out Nixon's orders.[162]

Additionally, the chance of a peace deal was so remote that Nixon's actions, if any, probably made no difference. As Jack Torry, Washington bureau chief of the *Dayton Daily News* and the *Columbus Dispatch*, wrote in his review of Farrell's book: "Nothing Nixon said that night had the slightest impact on any deal which could have ended U.S. involvement in the war. The undisputed fact is there was no chance for a peace agreement in 1968 which would have been accepted by any American president."[163]

In any event, John Mitchell had proven that he would do just about anything to get Richard Nixon elected president. His vindication came with Nixon's. In 1968, Richard Nixon defeated Hubert Humphrey in one of the closest presidential races in American history (third-party candidate George Wallace, governor of Alabama, turned in a strong third-place showing that contributed to the closeness of the race). Nixon won a clear majority in the Electoral College but defeated Humphrey by less than 1 percent in the popular vote. Much like in 1960, a few close states could have swung the election in the other direction. In this case, had Humphrey won Ohio, Illinois, and California (he lost all three by less than 3 percent), he would have won the presidency.

Nixon's victory, which wasn't confirmed until the following morning, was a tremendous accomplishment for both the candidate and his campaign manager. For Nixon, it was the culmination of an incredible comeback that seemed like a pipe dream after that fateful morning in 1962 when he behaved like a sore loser. For Mitchell, it was confirmation that he was one of the smartest, savviest lawyers in the country. The two men shared a moment right after the networks declared Nixon the winner. "Well, John, we had better get down to Florida and get this thing planned out," Nixon said, putting his hand on his campaign manager's shoulder. "Mr. President," Mitchell responded, eyes welling up with tears. "I think I'd better go up and be with Martha." As Nixon would later reflect, this was the first time anyone would ever call him "Mr. President."[164]

Those bonds of loyalty between the two would only be strengthened in the coming years. As Mitchell found out, however, those bonds really only went one way.

NOTES

1. Leonard Garment, *Crazy Rhythm: From Brooklyn and Jazz to Nixon's White House, Watergate and Beyond* (Cambridge, MA: Da Capo Press, 1997), 117.
2. Thomas Evans, "The Education of Richard Nixon: The Wilderness Years on Wall Street," unpublished manuscript, 147–48.
3. Evans, "The Education of Richard Nixon."
4. Evans, "The Education of Richard Nixon," at 149–50.
5. Buchanan, 110.
6. Evans, "Education of Richard Nixon," 151.
7. Evans, "Education of Richard Nixon," at 152.
8. Jules Witcover, *The Resurrection of Richard Nixon* (New York: G. P. Putnam's Sons, 1970), 208.
9. Buchanan, 110.
10. Tom Evans, Copy of Message from Frank Jorgensen to Rose Mary Woods, May 3, 1967, Tom Evans Collection.
11. "Dr. Parkinson Quits as Nixon Group's Chief," *Chicago Tribune*, August 17, 1967, accessed April 1, 2017, http://archives.chicagotribune.com/1967/08/17/page/4/article/dr-parkinson-quits-as-nixon-groups-chief.
12. David Broder, "Bellmon to Quit Nixon's Command; Sen. Tower Is Prime Prospect for Job," *Washington Post*, October 22, 1967.
13. James Rosen, *The Strong Man: John Mitchell and the Secrets of Watergate* (New York: Doubleday, 2008), 14.
14. Rosen, *The Strong Man*, 498.
15. Rosen, *The Strong Man*, 16.
16. Rosen, *The Strong Man*.
17. John Mitchell, interview by Tom Evans, February 7, 1985.
18. Rosen, *The Strong Man*, 20–21.
19. Rosen, *The Strong Man*, 10–11.
20. Rosen, *The Strong Man*, at 11.
21. Rosen, *The Strong Man*.
22. Rosen, *The Strong Man*.
23. Carl Person, *Self Employment and No College* (Bookbaby, ebook, 2015).
24. Rosen, *The Strong Man*, 11.
25. Rosen, *The Strong Man*, at 24
26. Rosen, *The Strong Man*, at 26.
27. Rosen, *The Strong Man*.
28. "The Sharp New Line on Antitrust," *BusinessWeek*, June 21, 1969.
29. Mitchell, interview by Evans.
30. Evans, "Education of Richard Nixon," 101.
31. Rosen, *The Strong Man*, 30.

32. Richard Nixon, "Nixon Mudge Partnership Agreement," Pre-Presidential Papers, Richard Nixon Presidential Library and Museum. Also: Evans, "Education of Nixon," 102.
33. Rosen, *The Strong Man*, 30.
34. Rosen, *The Strong Man*.
35. Garment, *Crazy Rhythm*, 118–19.
36. Evans, "Education of Richard Nixon," 102.
37. Rosen, *The Strong Man*, 510, n. 2.
38. Rosen, *The Strong Man*, 20.
39. Richard Nixon, New Matters, 1967, Pre-Presidential Papers, Richard Nixon Presidential Library and Museum.
40. Garment, *Crazy Rhythm*, 118–19.
41. Tom Evans, memorandum to John Mitchell, January 4, 1967, Tom Evans Collection.
42. Evans, "Nixon Mudge," 197.
43. Dwight Chapin, interview by Li, May 9, 2016.
44. Rosen, *The Strong Man*, 34.
45. Stephen Ambrose, *Nixon: Volume 2: The Triumph of the Politician, 1962–1972* (New York: Simon and Schuster, 1989), 124–25. And Witcover, *The Resurrection of Richard Nixon*, 209–10.
46. Tom Evans, memorandum from Tom Evans to Richard Nixon, April 24, 1967, Tom Evans Collection.
47. Garment, *Crazy Rhythm*, 119–20.
48. Mitchell, interview by Evans.
49. Richard Nixon, Letter to Francis Sorg, December 21, 1965, Pre-Presidential Papers, Richard Nixon Presidential Library and Museum.
50. Frank Sorg, interview by Tom Evans, December 6, 1989, transcript.
51. Sorg, interview by Evans.
52. Sorg, interview by Evans.
53. Sorg, interview by Evans.
54. Sorg, interview by Evans.
55. Patrick Buchanan, interview by Victor Li, June 21, 2017.
56. Chapin, interview by Li, supra.
57. Rosen, *The Strong Man*, 38.
58. Rosen, *The Strong Man*. Kleindienst would succeed Mitchell as attorney general in 1972.
59. Rosen, *The Strong Man*, 35.
60. Ken Adelman, "What I've Learned: You Do What Has to Be Done," *Washingtonian*, April 1988.
61. H. R. Haldeman, interview by Tom Evans, January 26, 1988.
62. Rosen, *The Strong Man*, 36.
63. Rosen, *The Strong Man*, 35.
64. Evans, "Education of Richard Nixon," 155.
65. Evans, "Education of Richard Nixon."
66. "Harlan Logan, 90, Editor and Publisher," *New York Times*, January 5, 1995, accessed April 1, 2017, http://www.nytimes.com/1995/01/05/obituaries/harlan-logan-90-editor-and-politician.html.
67. Evans, "Nixon Mudge," 199.
68. Evans, "Education of Richard Nixon," 156–57.
69. Evans, "Education of Richard Nixon."
70. Glen Elsasser, "Nixon Announces Candidacy for Nomination for President," *Chicago Tribune*, February 2, 1968, accessed April 1, 2017, http://archives.chicagotribune.com/1968/02/02/page/1/article/nixon-announces-candidacy-for-nomination-for-president.
71. Frank Gannon, "2.2.68," Richard Nixon Foundation, accessed April 1, 2017, https://www.nixonfoundation.org/2009/02/2268/.
72. Eric Black, "Politics by Gaffe: Recalling the 'Brainwashing' of George Romney," *MinnPost*, December 2, 2011, accessed April 1, 2017, https://www.minnpost.com/eric-black-ink/2011/12/politics-gaffe-recalling-brainwashing-george-romney.

73. Rick Perlstein, *Nixonland: The Rise of a President and the Fracturing of America* (New York: Scribner, 2008).
74. Witcover, *The Resurrection of Richard Nixon*, 251.
75. Witcover, *The Resurrection of Richard Nixon*, 257.
76. Witcover, *The Resurrection of Richard Nixon*, 259.
77. Larry Sabato Jr., "The Ball of Confusion That Was 1968," University of Virginia Center for Politics, March 16, 2016, accessed April 1, 2017, http://www.centerforpolitics.org/crystalball/articles/the-ball-of-confusion-that-was-1968/.
78. Ambrose, *Nixon: Volume 2*, 145.
79. Witcover, *The Resurrection of Richard Nixon*, 259.
80. Rosen, *The Strong Man*, 41.
81. John Ehrlichman, *Witness to Power: The Nixon Years* (New York: Simon Schuster, 1982), 39.
82. Rosen, *The Strong Man*, 42–43.
83. Rosen, *The Strong Man*, at 43.
84. Julie Nixon Eisenhower, *Pat Nixon: The Untold Story* (New York: Simon & Schuster, 1986), 240.
85. Buchanan, 262.
86. Buchanan, interview by Li.
87. Robert Dallek, *Nixon and Kissinger: Partners in Power* (New York: Harper Collins e-books, 2007).
88. Tom Evans, Memorandum from Michael Saperstein to Leonard Garment and Tom Evans, Re: Meeting with Henry Kissinger, June 13, 1968, Tom Evans Collection.
89. Rosen, *The Strong Man*, 27.
90. Buchanan, 314–35.
91. Witcover, *The Resurrection of Richard Nixon*, 351.
92. Witcover, *The Resurrection of Richard Nixon*, 351.
93. Tom Evans, Memorandum to Richard Nixon, July 31, 1968, Tom Evans Collection.
94. Witcover, *The Resurrection of Richard Nixon*, 352.
95. Strober and Strober, 21.
96. White, 269.
97. Ambrose, *Nixon: Volume 2*, 163.
98. Witcover, *The Resurrection of Richard Nixon*, 321, 350.
99. Witcover, *The Resurrection of Richard Nixon*, 350.
100. Strober and Strober, 20.
101. Garment, *Crazy Rhythm*, 125–26.
102. John A. Farrell, *Richard Nixon: A Life* (New York: Doubleday, 2017), 332–33. Also: Jack Bass and Marilyn Thompson, *Strom: The Complicated Personal and Political Life of Strom Thurmond* (New York: PublicAffairs: 2005), 214–15.
103. Rosen, *The Strong Man*, 43–45.
104. Bass and Thompson, *Strom*, 211–12.
105. Farrell, *Richard Nixon: A Life*, 332–33.
106. Evans, "Education of Richard Nixon," 178.
107. Evans, "Education of Richard Nixon," at 179
108. Witcover, *The Resurrection of Richard Nixon*, 367.
109. Buchanan, 59–60.
110. John Sears, interview by Victor Li, February 16, 2016.
111. Sears, interview by Li.
112. Evans, "Education of Richard Nixon," 186.
113. Haldeman, interview by Evans, 5.
114. Haldeman, interview by Evans. Also Rosen *The Strong Man*, at 42.
115. John Ehrlichman, interview by Tom Evans, January 28, 1988, transcript.
116. Perlstein, *Nixonland*, 267–28. Also Nancy Gibbs and Michael Duffy, *The Presidents Club: Inside the World's Most Exclusive Fraternity* (New York: Simon and Schuster, 2012).
117. Stuart Eizenstat, interview by Li, October 29, 2016.

118. Victor Li, "Lifetime Achiever: Stuart Eizenstat," *The American Lawyer*, September 20, 2013, accessed April 1, 2017, http://www.americanlawyer.com/id=1202616216359/Lifetime-Achiever-Stuart-Eizenstat?slreturn=20161019132657.
119. Califano, interview by Timothy Naftali, April 3, 2007, Richard Nixon Oral History Project, Richard Nixon Presidential Library and Museum.
120. Gibbs and Duffy, *The Presidents Club*, 229.
121. Gibbs and Duffy, *The Presidents Club*, 223.
122. Gibbs and Duffy, *The Presidents Club*.
123. Gibbs and Duffy, *The Presidents Club*, at 233.
124. "Hubert Humphrey Presidential Campaign, 1968," Wikipedia, accessed April 1, 2017, https://en.wikipedia.org/wiki/Hubert_Humphrey_presidential_campaign,_1968.
125. Gibbs and Duffy, *The Presidents Club*, 235.
126. Ken Hughes, *Chasing Shadows: The Nixon Tapes, The Chennault Affair and the Origins of Watergate* (Charlottesville, VA: University of Virginia Press, 2014), 26–27.
127. Hughes, *Chasing Shadows*, 7.
128. Anna Chennault, *The Education of Anna* (New York: Times Books, 1980), 167.
129. Chennault, *The Education of Anna*, at 169–70.
130. Chennault, *The Education of Anna*, at 170–73.
131. Bùi Diễm with David Chanoff, *In the Jaws of History* (Bloomington and Indianapolis: University of Indiana Press), 238.
132. Tim Weiner, *One Man against the World: The Tragedy of Richard Nixon* (New York: Henry Holt and Company, 2015), 19.
133. Chennault, *The Education of Anna*, 175–76.
134. Rosen, *The Strong Man*, 54.
135. Hughes, *Chasing Shadows*, 6.
136. Rosen, *The Strong Man*, 54.
137. Hughes, *Chasing Shadows*, 46.
138. Anthony Summers, *Arrogance of Power: The Secret World of Richard Nixon* (New York: Viking, 2000), 518.
139. "Lyndon Johnson and Everett Dirksen on 2 November 1968," Presidential Recordings, Digital Edition, accessed April 1, 2017, http://prde.upress.virginia.edu/conversations/4006123.
140. "Lyndon Johnson and Everett Dirksen."
141. Hughes, *Chasing Shadows*, 50–51.
142. Thomas, *Being Nixon: A Man Divided* (New York: Random House, 2015), 2015.
143. Califano, Oral History.
144. Stuart Eizenstat, interview with Li, October 29, 2016.
145. Eizenstat, interview with Li.
146. Theodore H. White, *Making of the President 1968* (New York: Atheneum Publishers, 1965), 444.
147. Daniel Schorr, "The Secret Nixon-LBJ War," *Washington Post*, May 28, 1995, accessed April 1, 2017, https://www.washingtonpost.com/archive/opinions/1995/05/28/the-secret-nixon-lbj-war/78bb77c3-e2e7-4261-b4d7-9aaad200ccde/?utm_term=.d6acfe5ea3aa. Also: Ambassador Max M. Kampelman, interview by Charles Stuart Kennedy, June 24, 2003, Association for Diplomatic Studies and Training Foreign Affairs Oral History Project, http://adst.org/OH TOCs/Kampelman, Max.toc.pdf.
148. Chennault, *The Education of Anna*, 190–91. Also: Rosen, *The Strong Man*, 54.
149. Jules Witcover, *The Making of an Ink-Stained Wretch: Half a Century Pounding the Political Beat* (Baltimore: Johns Hopkins University Press, 2005), 131.
150. Garment, interview by Timothy Naftali, April 6, 2007, Richard Nixon Oral History Project, Richard Nixon Presidential Library and Museum.
151. Sears, interview by Li.
152. Buchanan, 357
153. Tom Evans, Memorandum to Richard Nixon, August 23, 1967, Tom Evans Collection.
154. Summers, *Arrogance of Power*, 298–99.
155. Tom Charles Huston, interview by Timothy Naftali, April 30, 2008, Richard Nixon Oral History Project, Richard Nixon Presidential Library and Museum.

156. Christopher Lydon, "Conservative Architect of Security Plan Tom Charles Huston," *New York Times*, May 24, 1973, accessed July 4, 2017, http://www.nytimes.com/1973/05/24/archives/conservative-architect-of-security-tom-charles-huston-man-in-the.html.

157. Lydon, "Conservative Architect of Security Plan Tom Charles Huston."

158. Lydon, "Conservative Architect of Security Plan Tom Charles Huston."

159. Tom Charles Huston, interview by Timothy Naftali, June 27, 2008, Richard Nixon Oral History Project, Richard Nixon Presidential Library and Museum.

160. Huston, interview by Timothy Naftali.

161. Farrell, *Richard Nixon: A Life*, 342–43.

162. Peter Baker, "Nixon Tried to Spoil Johnson's Vietnam Peace Talks in '68, Notes Show," *New York Times*, January 2, 2017, accessed June 11, 2017, https://www.nytimes.com/2017/01/02/us/politics/nixon-tried-to-spoil-johnsons-vietnam-peace-talks-in-68-notes-show.html.

163. Jack Torry, "Did Nixon Deliberately Prolong Vietnam War?" *Dayton Daily News*, April 17, 2017, accessed June 11, 2017, http://www.daytondailynews.com/news/national-govt--politics/did-nixon-deliberately-prolong-vietnam-war/qU6DC0sEQcTfxxjTSOfnIK/.

164. Richard Nixon, *RN: The Memoirs of Richard Nixon* (New York: Simon & Schuster, 2013).

Chapter Twelve

"The Word Is Out That Mudge Rose Is In."

As Richard Nixon took the oath of office on January 20, 1969, he was surrounded by enemies. The man who administered the oath of office to him was outgoing Supreme Court Chief Justice Earl Warren, a man whose enmity toward Nixon stemmed, in large part, because he blamed the man standing in front of him for costing him a chance to be the one receiving the oath of officc. Standing behind Warren was the outgoing president, with whom Nixon's longstanding love-hate relationship had crossed into hate on several occasions during the election. Meanwhile, standing behind Nixon and trying to put a brave face on the proceedings was the outgoing vice president and the man Nixon had beaten by a razor-thin margin for the right to stand in front of Warren.

With that in mind, the conciliatory tone Nixon struck in his inaugural address took on greater meaning.

> We are caught in war, wanting peace. We are torn by division, wanting unity. We see around us empty lives, wanting fulfillment. We see tasks that need doing, waiting for hands to do them. To a crisis of the spirit, we need an answer of the spirit. To find that answer, we need only look within ourselves. [1]

So it must have been a welcome diversion for him when, during the inaugural parade, he found himself surrounded by a cheering throng of well-wishers and supporters. When the presidential procession passed by 1701 Pennsylvania Ave, a stone's throw from Nixon's new residence, the newly sworn-in president looked up, as if by habit, and started waving to a group of especially ecstatic individuals hanging out along the fourth floor of a building he had known so well. It was the Nixon Mudge D.C. office (the firm would be renamed Mudge, Rose, Guthrie & Alexander upon the departure of Nixon and Mitchell). Until a few months ago, he had been their public partner and face of the firm.

Now he was the most powerful man in the world. And his former firm was poised to reap the benefits.

"EVERYBODY WAS TO SWEAT A LITTLE."

As Nixon was preparing to assume the presidency, he turned to his firm to help him out one last time. Nixon appointed Mudge partner Frank Lincoln to head his presidential transition team. The sixty-year-old Lincoln had extensive governmental experience, having served in various capacities within the Armed Services, as well as a stint as assistant secretary of defense from 1959 to 1961.[2] Together with another Nixon Mudge partner, William Harman, Lincoln had been working full time since the early fall to plan Nixon's transition "on the happy assumption that the election would be a successful one for Nixon."[3] Johnson had designated a full-time liaison to handle transition matters and to meet, regularly, with Lincoln and representatives from the Humphrey and Wallace campaigns. Lincoln later said that Johnson's commitment to starting the transition process early "saved weeks of precious time and removed any embarrassment on the part of the candidates to embark upon overt preparation for taking over the duties of the Presidency."[4]

Meanwhile, Lincoln kept Nixon informed of what had to be done in the event of victory. Two weeks before Election Day, the Mudge partner delivered a detailed memorandum to the candidate under the assumption that they would be victorious despite the fact that the actual electoral race was starting to tighten. In his memo, Lincoln covered several important matters to be dealt with between the election and the inauguration, including key appointees, crisis management, briefing materials, and proposed meeting dates between Nixon and Johnson.

The most important administrative task, according to Lincoln, was to staff the administration and fill various cabinet and subcabinet posts. "Of almost 3,000,000 government workers, approximately 3,000 are subject to appointment by the incoming administration," Lincoln noted.[5] "To locate, process and place this number of executive personnel in less than three months is no small task."

It didn't help that Nixon, himself, dragged his feet when it came to dishing out the plum spots in his administration. Safire pointed out that it was because Nixon didn't want his prominent campaign staffers to feel as if they were entitled to a job in the incoming Administration. "Everybody was to sweat a little," Safire recalled.[6]

Ultimately, most of his top lieutenants were rewarded. Rose Mary Woods was, obviously, the only choice for Nixon as far as who his secretary in the White House would be. As for Chief of Staff, Nixon wanted someone who would serve as a gatekeeper to the Oval Office, so there was no better choice than Haldeman, who did such an effective job of controlling access to the candidate during the campaign. Ehrlichman, who worked so well with Haldeman, was named White House Counsel.

Not all of Nixon's close allies got what they felt was coming to them. Herb Klein, Nixon's longtime press secretary and an experienced journalist, didn't get the job as White House press secretary, to the surprise of many within the Nixon inner circle. Instead, Klein was given the newly created post of director of communications that had no clearly defined duties. Ambrose wrote that the snub of Klein had more to do with Nixon's vision of an adversarial press and the need to control the flow of information from the White House to the public. As such, he appointed twenty-nine-year-old Ronald Ziegler, a protégé of Haldeman's who had a background in advertising and was otherwise inexperienced and unprepared for the demanding job as press secretary.[7]

Garment was another Nixon loyalist that found himself on the outside looking in. Garment recalled that he waited for months to hear from Nixon what position he had in mind for his now-former law partner. Meanwhile, he continued to give advice to Nixon about how to shape his cabinet. According to Garment, he was the one that suggested that Nixon choose Democrat Daniel Patrick Moynihan for his Administration. Haldeman asked Garment to speak to Moynihan to see if he might be interested in coming aboard. Garment recalled that Moynihan asked to be secretary of transportation, but the job had already been promised to Governor John Volpe of Massachusetts. Ultimately, Moynihan settled for becoming Nixon's adviser on urban affairs.[8]

Then one day, Garment finally got the call he had been waiting for. He recalled that, during the cab ride over to the Pierre Hotel in New York, the site of Nixon's transition headquarters, his heart "beat a little faster" than usual as he had been reduced to a pile of nerves.[9] Nixon had made him sweat it out for long enough, and now, at long last, he was going to get his just reward. Garment, as well as his partners at the firm, had hoped that he would be named White House Counsel, only for Ehrlichman to get the job. That left attorney general.

Garment quickly realized that the top job at the Department of Justice had already been earmarked for someone else. And true to form, it was going to be up to Garment to convince that person to take the job. Nixon wanted John Mitchell as his attorney general, but Mitchell was resistant. "We have the same old problem, Len, and I need your help," Nixon said, before making it clear that he needed Mitchell in his administration.[10] "You've got to talk to him and make him understand how important this is. He trusts your judgment on things like this."

Garment agreed to do his best before Nixon got to the matter at hand. Nixon told his former partner that he wanted him to stay with the firm, but to relocate to the D.C. office so that he could advise the president whenever possible. He would have a White House pass and take on assignments from the president that he didn't want to run through the usual channels. "What does *that* mean?" Garment wondered.[11] Ultimately, Nixon said that he saw Garment as a potential "Clark Clifford of the Republican Party," referring to the influential D.C. lawyer who became an important counselor to several Democratic presidents despite spending part of that time practicing law in the private sector. Garment was dejected and hurt by Nixon's stance, but decided to do as he suggested. He relocated to Mudge's D.C. office and, within six months of Nixon's inauguration, he finally did get that White House job he had coveted when Nixon named him special consultant. Eventually, Garment would work his way up to become White House Counsel in 1973, when the dark cloud of Watergate had overtaken the Nixon Administration.

Garment would also become a balkanization point for some of the Nixon Mudge crowd when they tried to figure out what went wrong in the White House. "Haldeman and Ehrlichman came in and gave him terrible advice," says Zoeller.[12] "Had Nixon listened to Garment instead of those two phonies, he wouldn't have had to step down." Evans noted that Garment had been completely isolated from Nixon's political operatives as the Watergate scandal unfolded, and wondered whether things might have turned out better had Nixon listened to his old law partner instead of his political staff. In 1973, after taking over the White House Counsel job from Ehrlichman, Garment's first order of business was getting up to speed on Watergate so that he could more effectively advise the president. "I told him that based on what I already knew, I was convinced his survival depended on removing every official who was actually or potentially implicated in any aspect of the scandal (including, I said illogically, me)," Garment said.[13] "He had to sweep clean so that he could show the country an administration with a fresh face." Ultimately, Nixon dismissed Garment's warnings as overly dramatic while complaining to Haldeman that he had wanted his former law partner to focus, solely, on legal issues.[14] "What if [Garment] had never been isolated from the President, a process which began when the concentric circles moved during the campaign of 1968?" Evans wondered.[15] "What if their relationship had been what it was when they were together at the firm in the late 1960s, when they had met on almost a daily basis?"

Instead, it was clear that Nixon preferred the counsel of his other former law partner. Unlike Garment and the others, Mitchell had not been eager to serve. Nixon had asked him to take the job the day after the election, but Mitchell had demurred. He had several reasons for wanting to avoid Washington, D.C. His wife, Martha, had been struggling with psychiatric problems, and John wasn't sure she would be able to survive living under the microscope in D.C. "[Martha's psychiatric issues] were discernible to everyone," Garment recalled.[16] "[Mitchell] knew that and he knew that would present a problem, bringing her down to this heady hothouse atmosphere of Washington. Sort of like carrying an explosive substance into a very hot area."

Mitchell had another reason for not wanting to go to D.C. "John Mitchell was adamant in stating that neither he, Len Garment or I should go into the Administration," Evans said.[17] "With a former partner in the White House, he predicted (accurately, as it turned out) that we would become 'the firm to see.'"

"THERE'S NO QUESTION IT'S BEEN BENEFICIAL."

Mitchell was only able to hold out for so long. Nixon would not take "no" for an answer, and Mitchell couldn't really refuse a request from the president of the United States. After satisfying Mitchell's condition that he wanted Kleindienst as his deputy attorney general, Mudge was now down two named partners.

Despite the loss of their two most well-known partners, the firm thrived throughout most of the Nixon Administration. Immediately after the election, the heads of the firm offered Evans the role of firmwide managing partner. In his new role, he would still practice law, but he would also spend about half of his time running the day-to-day operations of the firm, including hiring and budgeting. To better reflect his increased status at the firm, Evans took one of the offices that was next to Nixon's former office. The "President's Room" would be preserved so that the firm would have something to show off to visitors and clients, as well as a place to hold receptions and firm events.

For better or worse, the firm was mostly known as "Richard Nixon's law firm," and despite Guthrie's claims that Mudge was not a political firm, the firm was perceived as having access to the White House, if not influence. After all, it wasn't just Nixon, Mitchell, and Garment that were ensconced in the executive branch. According to the *New York Times*, Nixon and Mitchell had taken approximately a half-dozen or so of the firm's brightest political minds with them, leaving behind a law firm that was less interested in politics and just wanted to do their jobs.[18] Associates Douglas Parker, Gerald Parsky, Lee Pickard, Martin Pollner, Gordon Strachan, and J. Curtis Herge would all make their way over to the White House in the intervening years, while the likes of Buchanan, Chapin, Price, and Safire joined Nixon's White House staff immediately after the election.

As for the ones who didn't make it to the Administration, several members of the firm still found themselves in positions of influence. In addition to Garment, Nixon continued to call on his former partners for advice from time to time, particularly Guthrie and Alexander, who were frequent guests in the Oval Office. Ehrlichman, one of Nixon's gatekeepers, noted that Alexander was especially helpful to the president on tax policy. Another Mudge attorney, Richard Ritzel, was on hand to help the president with his estate plan.[19] "[Mudge] continued to be very helpful and very influential through the first couple or three years of the Administration," Ehrlichman said.[20]

Penn Central Railroad had that relationship in mind when it turned to Mudge for help in securing a $200 million government loan to stave off bankruptcy. Bob Guthrie, along with other lawyers at the firm, had represented Penn Central for years. However, he had never had occasion to set foot inside the corporate boardroom until this matter, whereupon he was introduced as "a member of the Nixon firm" and someone who was "close to the White House."[21] US Representative Wright Patman, a Democrat from Texas, led the effort to block the loan and, during a speech on the floor of the House of Representatives, cried crony capitalism. He maintained that Penn Central had only hired Mudge because of its connection to Nixon and pointed out that the firm also represented Investors Diversified Services, a major shareholder in the railroad and one of the corporate boards Nixon sat on during his tenure at the firm.[22] Patman wasn't the only one who had reservations. Transportation Secretary John Volpe wasn't happy about Mudge's involvement, either, and worried that it could hurt Nixon.[23] Ultimately, the government chose not to issue the loan.

As Guthrie pointed out to journalist Paul Hoffman, Nixon's election had placed the firm in a bind. "We obviously don't want to refuse to handle the matters of clients because of problems with the Administration," Guthrie said.[24] "On the other hand, we don't want to hold ourselves out to clients, either substantially or optically, because of our relations with the Administration. Generally, we don't take on any job relating to the Government from a new client." Another partner was more open with the *National Journal*, telling them: "There is no question that some people come here because of the President and the Attorney General. There is no question that it has been beneficial."[25] That partner also said that the firm had to turn down a request from client Eastern Airlines to help them secure more routes from the government.

At first, it looked like Mudge's mergers and acquisitions team would be in for a tough go. One of Mitchell's primary objectives as attorney general was to maintain a stringent antitrust enforcement policy—especially when it came to large mergers. During his first three months in charge, Mitchell's DOJ blocked a number of mergers, including a proposed union between Mudge client International Telephone and Telegraph (ITT) Corporation and food vending company Canteen Corp.[26] Mitchell made his position clear, saying "the Department of Justice will probably oppose any merger by one of the top 200 manufacturing firms of any leading producer in any concentrated industry."[27] In fact, Mitchell had even criticized the Johnson Administration over what he deemed lax antitrust enforcement, while questioning whether mergers were even profitable or efficient. Mitchell went so far as to argue that "the future vitality of our free economy may be in danger because of the increasing threat of economic concentration."[28]

Despite that, several mergers, including a few involving Mudge clients, managed to get the DOJ's blessing. The moves resulted in controversy for both Mudge and the Nixon Administration and furthered the growing narrative that the executive branch was helping the president's old firm. Within two months after the inauguration, the DOJ announced that it would dismiss the antitrust case against El Paso Natural Gas over the utility company's purchase of Pacific Northwest Pipeline Corp. Public utilities lawyers were stunned by the move. "Attorney General Mitchell could merely have said that the case was filed by the Democrats and it's their baby," said William Bennett, former chair of the California Public Utilities Commission who took the case against El Paso Natural Gas to the Supreme Court.[29] "He could have let the courts decide it, which was the proper procedure, rather than taking the matter in his own hands. If he had left it to the courts, there would have been no criticism of the Nixon Administration." Bennett went so far as to accuse El Paso Natural Gas's attorneys of having made a "sweetheart deal" with their old law partner. Mitchell, however, claimed that he had recused himself from the matter, leaving it to Solicitor General Erwin Griswold (a holdover from the Johnson Administration and the highest-ranking DOJ official after Mitchell and Kleindienst) to make the call.[30]

Controversy followed another longtime Mudge client as it tried to navigate the DOJ's antitrust policies. In 1970, Elmer Bobst hoped to merge his Warner-Lambert Company with Parke-Davis, creating a behemoth of a pharmaceutical company that promised to produce more than $1 billion in annual sales. Richard McLaren, the antitrust head at the DOJ, recommended that the merger be rejected only for Kleindienst to overrule him and approve the merger (Mitchell, once again, recused himself). Evidently, McLaren refused to let the matter drop and continued to object to the merger, forcing the DOJ to send the matter over to the Federal Trade Commission.[31] The FTC would, eventually, sign off on the deal, giving its stamp of approval in 1976.[32]

Even more controversy came in the form of ITT. The company had submitted two merger deals to the DOJ in addition to the aforementioned Canteen union: a proposed pact with Grinnell Corporation, as well as one with Hartford Insurance Co. McLaren had blocked all three deals, only for Kleindienst to overrule him on the Hartford acquisition. This time, it was clear who was calling the shots. "My order is to drop the goddamn thing—is that clear?" Nixon told Kleindienst in a tape-recorded conversation.[33] "I want something understood, and if it's not understood, McLaren's ass is to be out of there within one hour. The ITT thing—stay the hell out of it. Is that clear? That's an order . . . I do not want McLaren to run around prosecuting people, raising hell about conglomerates, stirring things up . . . I don't like the son of a bitch."

The ITT incident nearly drove a wedge between him and the president and almost triggered a mass resignation at DOJ, presaging the Saturday Night Massacre that would take place two years later at the height of the Watergate scandal. In this instance, Kleindienst, McLaren, and Griswold all threatened to resign and it was up to Mitchell to smooth things over with the president. "[W]e have a situation—and [U.S. Treasury Secretary John] Connally has spoken to me about it—but where the business community, for, for—believes that we're a hell of a lot rougher on them in the antitrust than our predecessors were," Nixon told Mitchell at their sit-down two days after the Kleindienst call.[34] Mitchell defended his men and warned Nixon that there would be massive political consequences if he insisted on enforcing his ultimatum. Nixon, who was about to run for reelection, decided to defer to his attorney general and soon-to-be returning campaign manager.[35] By the end of the year, however, McLaren was gone from the Justice Department, albeit with a federal judgeship as his going-away present.

As for Mitchell's old municipal bond practice at Mudge, business was booming. His departure had left a huge void in the practice area he had once dominated. However, Mitchell's perch at the DOJ had given Mudge's bond lawyers additional credibility and weight as they bid for various projects all over the country. "The opinion of counsel was always printed right in the bond offering documents," Evans stated.[36] "Unless buyers recognized the name of the firm providing the opinion, they would not purchase the bonds." And most buyers recognized Mudge because of its former association with Mitchell. The *Wall Street Journal* reported that, within a year of Mitchell's ascension to the DOJ, Kentucky, Nebraska, New Jersey, Washington, D.C., West Virginia, and the US Virgin Islands moved a large part of their municipal bond work over to Mudge.

> It's suggested that the President and the Attorney General have found occasion to let the states know that their old firm was available, or that Mudge Rose is not averse to reminding potential clients who the firm's old partners are. It's also speculated that some states figure a Mudge Rose connection will provide them with favors from the Federal bureaucracy or that Republican officials involved in at least four of the states wanted to repay political debts owed to the President and the Attorney General.[37]

The *Wall Street Journal* noted that everyone involved was quick to deny such speculation. White House and Justice Department officials maintained that neither Nixon nor Mitchell did a thing to help their old firm land this work. The firm, meanwhile, argued that neither Nixon nor Mitchell had any reason to help their old firm because "neither man retains any financial connection with the firm, and neither has any understanding about returning to it later on."[38] The firm also pointed out that it had recently hired two lateral partners from Hawkins, Delafield & Wood, one of Mudge's main rivals in the municipal bond area. The two lawyers, Nicholas Capozzoli and future named partner Robert Ferdon, brought in those states and territories with them as clients when they joined the firm in 1969.

Another high-profile bond assignment brought the firm some more unwanted attention. As a result of the US postal strike of 1970, Congress had passed, and Nixon had signed into law, the Postal Reorganizational Act of 1970. The Act abolished the cabinet-level US Post Office Department and created the US Postal Service, an independent agency that was structured more like a corporation and had a legal monopoly over mail delivery.

As part of the Act, the Postal Service was allowed to issue up to $10 billion in postal bonds, and plenty of firms wanted in on that action. In 1971, for the first series of issuings, the Postal Service decided to offer $250 million in postal bonds. The bond underwriters retained Mudge for the issue, and the firm pocketed $100,000 in legal fees before Congress intervened, once again. This time, it was influential Democratic congressman Morris Udall of Arizona who started raising questions about the propriety of the firm's involvement. Udall, the chair of the House Postal Services Subcommittee, claimed that underwriters had been pressured into hiring Mudge. "But there is no way that this appointment of a law firm with close ties to both the President and the Attorney General can be explained or, defended to the many Congressional critics who are already calling for repeal of the Postal Reorganization Act," Udall said.[39] "Surely, somewhere among the 250,000 lawyers in the country, there is someone else who can handle this. And surely, with all its other business, this barefoot firm in New York can survive without this particular multimillion-dollar contract." The firm denied any wrongdoing but ultimately withdrew from the matter.

"I know there were published reports from time-to-time that Mudge Rose was taking advantage of its connections with Mitchell and Nixon and had beefed up the Washington office, which really wasn't true," said then-associate David Vaughn.[40] "We had basically a maritime litigation practice there and most of our activities were actually related to New York. I remember that we spent most of our time travelling to New York on business, as opposed to the other way around."

Despite all of the controversy, there was no denying that the firm's bottom line was healthier than ever. The number of attorneys at the firm increased from 105 when Nixon left to 120 by 1971. The New York office expanded from three floors at 20 Broad Street to five and even had to rent additional space around the corner at 71 Broadway to handle the overflow. The firm was among the ten largest firms in the United States by head count, and the lawyers all took home quite a bit of money. When it came to associate salaries, the firm matched the highest law firm salaries on Wall Street. Mudge partners, meanwhile, made out even better during this period. In 1969, the firm ranked eighteenth out of thirty-six firms in terms of net income per partner when surveyed by Price Waterhouse & Company before rocketing up the charts the following year. The firm finished second in 1970, slipped to third in both 1971 and 1972, before inching back up to second in 1973.[41]

REELECTION

Richard Nixon's first term was, on the whole, a rousing success. After escalating the Vietnam War by invading the neighboring country of Cambodia, Nixon began withdrawing US troops and reducing American involvement in the region, setting the stage for the signing of the Paris Peace Accords in 1973. Nixon also orchestrated a clear foreign policy triumph by establishing relations with the People's Republic of China. Domestically, Nixon established the Environmental Protection Act, moved the country off the gold standard, and helped slow inflation by instituting wage and price controls. Despite his overtures to southern Democrats during the 1968 election, Nixon quietly worked with local officials in the South to integrate public schools and enforced desegregation orders from the Supreme Court.

Nixon's popular standing reflected these and other accomplishments from his first term. As he set about running for reelection in 1972, Nixon's approval rating hovered at or near 60 percent.[42] He was also helped by the fact that the Democrats were in disarray. Senator Edward Kennedy of Massachusetts had been expected to follow in his brothers' footsteps and run for president but chose not to after he became embroiled in a scandal where he had driven his car off a bridge at Chappaquiddick Island in Martha's Vineyard, killing his passenger. Nixon had been concerned about Humphrey's 1968 running mate, Senator Edmund Muskie of Maine, but Nixon's dirty tricks campaign had neutralized Muskie as a threat by the start of the 1972 New Hampshire primary. One of their tricks ended up going down in political lore as "The Canuck Letter," in which they forged a letter from Muskie that was full of derogatory remarks about French Canadians, thereby guaranteeing an angry response from the large population of French Canadian immigrants living in New England. Muskie, broken down by all of the tricks, as well as a newspaper story questioning the character of his wife, appeared to cry during a press conference on the eve of the primary. That spelled the end for him, and Nixon no longer had to worry about the one Democrat (other than George

Wallace, who would withdraw after an assassination attempt a few months later) that concerned him the most.[43]

Eventually, Democrats would nominate Senator George McGovern of South Dakota, but Nixon was never in any real danger throughout the campaign. Despite that, Nixon took no chances. The reelection campaign raised a stunning $61.4 million—shattering Nixon's record haul in 1968.[44]

He also recalled some of his old Mudge colleagues to action. Evans served as deputy finance chairman for the Committee to Re-Elect the President (abbreviated "CRP" but, in time, would be hit with the derogatory acronym of "CREEP"). And of course, he called on his heavyweight, John Mitchell, who had returned to the firm after resigning as attorney general in early 1972 to manage Nixon's reelection campaign. The firm had sent out cards on March 1, announcing Mitchell's return and its impending name change to Mudge, Rose, Guthrie, Alexander & Mitchell. It was understood within the firm that Mitchell would have as much time off as he needed in order to serve as chairman of CRP—much like what had happened in 1968 when Nixon named him campaign manager.

The move was not without controversy—both inside and outside the firm. Several unnamed partners and associates told reporters in advance of Mitchell's return to their firm that they had opposed the move. A former partner even went so far as to tell the *New York Times* that "Mitchell was never really well liked" at the firm, in contrast to Nixon.[45] Rosen, meanwhile, noted that the firm had hired fourteen new partners since Mitchell was last at the firm, and most of them were in their thirties and were not likely to be Nixon Administration admirers.[46]

In the end, it was all academic, as Nixon won a forty-nine-state landslide and earned 60 percent of the popular vote. He had nearly broken Johnson's popular vote percentage record from 1964 and, in one fell swoop, confirmed the South as solid Republican territory—a reputation it continues to enjoy as of this writing. Nixon had barely even campaigned—preferring to stay above the fray and concentrate on doing his job. He had never even mentioned McGovern by name[47] —until the evening of November 8, 1972, when he declared victory and congratulated his vanquished opponent on a hard-fought campaign that had, in reality, been anything but.

A few weeks later, Nixon and his old colleagues at Mudge had one last happy moment together. Still basking in the glow of his extraordinary triumph, Nixon decided, during a trip to New York City, that he wanted to "visit his lawyers" at Mudge.[48] En route to his old office, which he had not set foot in since 1968, the conquering hero exited the motorcade and shook hands with a throng of supporters and well wishers, even cracking a few awkward jokes along the way. "I'm bullish on America," Nixon said, quoting a popular Merrill Lynch commercial tagline.[49] And since it was Wall Street, he felt the need to add that he wasn't a stockholder.

Nixon, with Garment, several journalists, and a full Secret Service security detail in tow, reflected on how much had changed since the last time he had walked the halls at 20 Broad Street. It certainly wasn't like old times—something Nixon made note of to the reporters covering his visit. He would spend a couple of hours at the Mudge headquarters, meeting with his former partners Guthrie, Rose, Alexander, Lincoln, and Mitchell, as well as hundreds of associates, staffers, and other employees.[50] He also spoke with Goldthwaite Dorr, who had joined Mudge the same year as Nixon after Mudge had acquired his firm, Dorr, Hand & Whittaker. In a show of warmth, the president invited Dorr, who had just celebrated his ninety-sixth birthday the previous October, to spend his next one at the White House. And in a moment that he surely must have relished, Nixon visited his old office—his unofficial vice presidential library. Even during the dark times following his electoral humiliations and public act of political *seppuku*, Nixon had never given up hope that he would, one day, require an official presidential library that was exponentially larger and grander than a Wall Street corner office would ever be. Now, as he was back in his old office at Mudge, he finally had the dilemma he had always wanted for himself. How big would his future library and museum be?

In time, however, a much more serious question with far greater implications for Nixon, his law firm, and the entire country would threaten to consume them all.

"*ATTEMPT* AT A BURGLARY."

On the evening of June 17, 1972, five men were caught, red-handed, breaking into the Democratic National Committee office at the Watergate Hotel in D.C. White House Press Secretary Ron Ziegler immediately labeled it as a "third-rate burglary," and Nixon thought that was giving them too much credit. "*Attempt* at a burglary," he wrote in a memo immediately after the break-in.[51] "Bizarre business. There was no involvement whatever by [White House] personnel."

While historians and Watergate figures, themselves, continue to debate what Nixon knew and when he knew it, it certainly seems odd that, in the immediate aftermath of the break-in, he would be able to state, categorically and without the benefit of a full-scale internal investigation, that there was no White House involvement. Either way, the cover-up was on and it would have staggering, devastating consequences for Nixon, Mitchell, White House officials, and the country as a whole.

Mudge did not escape the firing line. While it had prospered from its association with Nixon, Watergate helped bring about a severe decline in the firm's fortunes.

The downturn began shortly after what was supposed to be Mitchell's triumphant return to the firm. In July 1972, FBI agents interviewed Mitchell at his Mudge office and trapped him after he issued a categorical denial of knowledge, saying that he had no knowledge of the break-in other than what he had read in newspapers. Mitchell would later admit that he had known of the cover up, while others would point the finger at him as the one who had approved the plans for the break-in.[52] In any event, Mitchell's misstatement to the FBI that day in his office would eventually form the basis for one of the counts in the indictment against him.[53]

Meanwhile, the firm started bleeding lawyers. As Hoffman put it, the firm to see had become the firm to flee.[54] After several years of unprecedented growth, Mudge's attorney ranks began to decline as Nixon's fortunes (and standing) took a tumble. According to the *New York Law Journal*, most of the departures were in the associate ranks, as Mudge went from ninety-two associates in 1973 to sixty-nine in 1975. The firm's D.C. office, in particular, took a major hit, going from two partners and thirteen associates in 1973 to just one associate two years later. The firm also had trouble recruiting associates, as many students chose not to interview with Nixon's old firm due to Watergate, Vietnam, and other controversial topics associated with the Nixon White House.[55]

Mitchell, himself, was one of the lawyers who headed for the exit ramp. His circumstances, however, were unique. In early March 1973, Nixon, Haldeman, Ehrlichman, and John Dean had decided that the best way to protect the presidency (and their own hides) was to have Mitchell take one for the team. Nixon had decided to "prick the boil and take the heat" but that the buck would stop with Mitchell, whose final act of loyalty to the president would entail admitting responsibility for authorizing the break-in and absolving the White House. Mitchell, however, refused to sacrifice himself. "There is no way that I'm going to do anything except staying where I am," Mitchell vowed to Ehrlichman, the man who was tasked with getting Mitchell to agree to walk the plank for the others.[56] "The fact of the matter is that I got euchred into this thing, when I say, by not paying attention to what these bastards were doing."

Meanwhile, his legal problems were just beginning. He was forced to resign from the firm after he and Stans were indicted in 1973 for obstructing a federal investigation into fugitive financier Robert Vesco after the latter donated $200,000 to Nixon's reelection campaign. They were acquitted; however, Mitchell would not escape the long arm of the law for long. In 1975, he was indicted for his role in Watergate, and this time, there would be no escape. Mitchell was found guilty of conspiracy, obstruction of justice, and perjury and would become the first attorney general to be convicted and imprisoned.[57]

Mitchell's fall from grace affected his former firm in a number of ways. Authorities scrutinized the ties between the firm and the Nixon Administration and the lawyers who had traversed those two worlds. "I had been Richard Nixon's partner and had held key positions in both the 1968 and 1972 campaigns," Evans recalled.[58] "For any inquisitive, aggressive juror, this could appear to be very fertile ground." Evans was called to testify before a federal grand jury, and was interviewed by a member of Senator Sam Ervin's Watergate Committee.

Ultimately, Evans was not charged with anything and, by his own admission, managed to preserve much of his reputation. He didn't get out unscathed, though. Evans had brought in George Steinbrenner, a longtime friend and college classmate, as a client of the firm's and represented the colorful tycoon when he purchased the New York Yankees for $10 million in 1973.[59] A year beforehand, Steinbrenner had told the influential US Representative Tip O'Neill, a Democrat from Massachusetts and future Speaker of the House, of a blackmail scheme and pointed the finger at Evans, Stans, and Nixon's personal attorney, Herbert Kalmbach.[60] According to O'Neill, Steinbrenner, a Democrat, was facing scrutiny from the US Department of Labor and the Department of Justice, and was told that a donation of $100,000 to the Committee to Re-Elect the President could ease the pressure. Evans, for his part, denied all of those allegations and maintained that Steinbrenner had admired Nixon and had volunteered to make the donations. "Of course, it was clear that he was covering his bets," Evans recalled.[61] "Having been active in Democratic politics, he wanted to have a foot in the other camp, as well. I put him in touch with fund-raiser Herb Kalmbach." In 1974, Steinbrenner was convicted of making illegal political contributions to Nixon's reelection campaign. His relationship with Evans and Mudge had seemingly deteriorated by then. When Steinbrenner tried to hire manager Dick Williams from the rival Oakland Athletics, Evans had warned him that Williams was still under contract and could only be signed with the consent of the A's owner, Charlie Finley. Steinbrenner pressed ahead and even went so far as to hold a press conference announcing Williams as his new manager (as expected, Williams was blocked from taking the job and the Yankees hired Bill Virdon, instead). Evans noted that there was an unfamiliar face on stage with the two and soon realized it was Steinbrenner's new lawyer. "It was then that we at Mudge realized that we no longer represented the Yankees."[62]

Mitchell's downfall also threw the firm's carefully laid succession plans into disarray. According to the *New York Law Journal*, Mitchell had been the heir apparent to Guthrie and Alexander as head of the firm, only for that plan to go up in smoke after Mitchell's first indictment.[63] Mitchell's forced departure had left a power vacuum at the firm. With Guthrie and Alexander in their seventies, the firm had to turn to a number of younger partners in the hope that some of them would be able to fill the void. Richard Ritzel, a member of the governing committee at the firm and a top estates lawyer who had handled Nixon's estate planning needs while president, was the new heir apparent. He would have plenty of help from a newly created executive committee that would include the likes of Evans and a returning Garment, as well as Matthew Herold, Donald Zoeller, and Robert Ferdon.[64]

Meanwhile, one of the few matters Mitchell handled during his short-lived return to the firm had come back to haunt the firm in a big way. California businessman C. Arnholt Smith was a multimillionaire banker whose vast holdings had included Westgate-California Corporation and the United States National Bank of San Diego. Smith, a proud San Diegan, had helped bring the expansion San Diego Padres to the city and had served as the club's original owner until selling it in 1973. He had also been a close friend of Nixon's and was among the group of friends and family inside Nixon's hotel suite on Election Night in 1968.

According to authorities, Smith's interest in Nixon might have been more than just friendly. Accused of making illegal campaign contributions to Nixon's 1968 campaign, Smith found himself with a much bigger problem by the time 1974 rolled around. His bank had collapsed in October 1973, and Westgate-California Corporation went bust a few months later. The SEC accused Smith of unlawfully withdrawing millions from both entities for personal reasons and was looking at him for securities fraud. Smith tapped into his Nixonian network and asked Mitchell and Mudge Rose to represent Westgate. Joseph Daley, a former SEC official who had joined Mudge, took charge of the case and recommended to Mitchell that Westgate make more detailed and complete disclosures about certain transactions between Westgate and US National Bank. The firm would, essentially, be throwing US National Bank under the bus by possibly "exposing the officers of the corporation, and possibly of the bank, to liability under the securities laws, or under the banking laws."[65] But that wasn't Mudge's concern, since it represented Westgate and not US National Bank.

So when Mudge then decided to represent US National Bank as well, it suddenly had a conflict-of-interest problem on its hands. When the firm billed the Westgate bankruptcy trustee for $338,416 in legal fees, the trustee angrily rebuffed Mudge and accused the firm of misconduct. The trustee even demanded that Mudge repay $225,000 in fees that had already been paid to the firm.[66]

The case ultimately went to trial in 1977, with Mudge's attorneys arguing that there was no conflict and that Daley's memo to Mitchell had merely been Daley fulfilling his obligation to "to disclose to proper authorities his discovery of criminal violations committed by his client."[67] Mudge was also accused of cutting a secret deal with the Nixon Administration to transfer funds from Westgate to US National Bank without approval from shareholders. The firm denied the allegations.[68] Despite plenty of fanfare and attention early on, the trial would, eventually, fade away from people's consciousness—so much so that when the presiding judge handed down his decision in favor of Mudge, finding that there had not been a conflict of interest and praising the firm for maintaining its "honest or good intentions,"[69] the opinion went unnoticed by reporters for months.

Mudge was in the clear, but another problem was taking hold at the firm. Firm mergers are always tricky, and the most successful ones usually come down to effective integration of two separate entities into one. At Mudge, the merger that had brought Mitchell and his firm into the fold may have been paid dividends on the balance sheets, to say nothing of Richard Nixon's presidential campaign. However, after nearly a decade into their union, the sense of factionalism between the bond lawyers from Mitchell's old firm and the Mudge lifers in the corporate department was still present. According to the *New York Law Journal*, this rivalry caused at least two bond partners to depart the firm to set up shop at a rival firm.[70]

Lawyers weren't the only ones leaving Mudge. Major clients were taking their work to other firms, notably PepsiCo, which moved much of its business to Cravath.[71] The firm was able to hold onto most of its big clients, however, including Stone & Webster, Studebaker-Worthington, and Warner-Lambert.[72]

Despite the uncertain times, the firm continued to perform well throughout the 1970s and early 1980s. After Watergate, the firm rebounded and returned to its prescandal size. The firm even cut its last tie to the Nixon era by breaking a longstanding tradition and giving Nixon's old office to Robert Ferdon.

In fact, Mudge was in expansion mode. In 1984, the firm set up a second office in New York City to accommodate its growing real estate department. That same year, it acquired Daniels, Houlihan & Palmeter, a Washington, D.C., international trade boutique firm.[73] The following year, the firm opened an office in West Palm Beach[74] before expanding to Tokyo in 1991.[75] By 1987, Mudge was comfortably ensconced in the middle of the pack when compared to other big firms. *The National Law Journal* ranked Mudge fifty-second on its annual list of the 250 largest law firms in the country by lawyer head count with 278 lawyers—well behind the leaders, 946-lawyer Baker & McKenzie.[76] Meanwhile, the inaugural Am Law 50 rankings of 1985, which ranked the top fifty firms based on gross revenue, had Mudge in a five-way tie for last place with $44 million, nearly a third of what top-ranked firm Skadden Arps took in that year.[77] Two years later, the firm took in more ($64 million), but its standing hadn't improved much, as top-ranked firm Skadden took in nearly four times as much.[78]

Much like when it had been known as "Mudge, Sludge, Fudge & Won't Budge," the firm seemed to have accepted the malaise that had crept into its culture. In 1980 Garment recalled that he and Zoeller had negotiated a merger between Mudge and D.C. powerhouse firm Dickstein Shapiro & Morin only to be summarily rebuffed by the aging, but still powerful, Guthrie. "This is a smart, tough crowd," Guthrie warned his partners.[79] "If you merge, in three-to-five years, half of you will be gone. Face it, boys, you're just not good enough." Garment ended up moving to Dickstein on his own that year, where he, once again, became a power player in D.C. upon the election of Ronald Reagan. Garment would carve out a niche as a go-to lawyer for Republican politicians facing legal problems, representing the likes of Attorney General Ed Meese, National Security Adviser Robert McFarlane, and US Information Agency head Charles Wick, among others.[80]

"HE'S BACK"

Richard Nixon didn't see much of his old staff once he unceremoniously resigned the presidency in 1974. As with many adults, Nixon and his staffers didn't have much reason to see each other on a regular basis once the common bond of employment was broken. In their case, Watergate proved to be a convenient excuse. Haldeman and Ehrlichman were imprisoned for eighteen months. Stans pleaded guilty to violating the Federal Election Campaign Act and accepting illegal campaign contributions but didn't serve prison time. Chapin also went to prison, after being convicted of making false or misleading statements.

In many cases, Nixon's reunions with large numbers of former staffers and colleagues came at major events like weddings and funerals. In 1979, Nixon threw a birthday/get-out-of-jail party for his former attorney general and gave him a generous toast: "John Mitchell has friends—and he stands by them."[81]

Nixon saw more of his old New York friends and acquaintances when he moved back to the Big Apple in 1980. Living in a twelve-room brick and stone house that was once owned by respected judge Learned Hand and was a stone's throw away from Nixon's former residence at 810 Fifth Avenue, Nixon maintained an active social life. The ex-president would often eat meals with his former secretary of state, Henry Kissinger, and occasionally met up with former law firm partners like Garment and ex-clients like Robert Abplanalp.[82]

When Mitchell died nine years later, his funeral marked another major gathering of Nixon's former Administration. The occasion brought Nixon together with the likes of Kleindienst, Garment, Safire, Chapin, Ziegler, and Woods as they gathered together to say goodbye to the heavyweight. Nixon was in the midst of yet another comeback as he had reinvented himself as an elder statesman and respected foreign policy thinker. *Newsweek* had even devoted a 1986 cover story to him with the headline: "He's Back: The Rehabilitation of Richard Nixon." Perhaps knowing that he needed to avoid generating controversy, or reminding people of his disgraceful resignation, Nixon kept a low profile at Mitchell's funeral. He gave no public words or statements and, inside St. Alban's Episcopalian Church, where the funeral was being held, he was heard uttering a fairly innocuous and emotionally detached sentence: "He was a friend of ours."[83]

Pat Nixon's funeral was a different story. When Nixon's wife passed away in June 1993, Nixon stunned longtime friends, associates, and observers when he dropped the stoic and solemn veil that most former presidents never remove in public and Nixon almost always wore, even in private, by sobbing openly and uncontrollably. "Oh dear," Woods said as Nixon broke down in convulsive sobs while longtime friend Rev. Billy Graham tried, in vain, to comfort him.[84] Nixon recovered enough to give an impromptu speech about how much his wife had meant to him and how his favorite campaign had been in 1952 because the band would play "You Are My Sunshine" at whistle stops and it reminded him of Pat because she was the sunshine of his life. His poise disguised the fact that he was utterly devastated without his wife, and many of his friends and associates privately bet that Nixon wouldn't live a year without her.[85]

Turns out, they were right. Richard Nixon died on April 22, 1994. His funeral would provide one last opportunity for many of his friends, supporters, intimates, subordinates, and colleagues to get together and reflect on the man who could be complex and hard to love but nevertheless inspired loyalty and admiration. Reflecting on the collection of luminaries gathered to pay their final respects, including then-president and eulogist Bill Clinton, as well as every living former president, Garment couldn't help but wonder whether, in death, Nixon had finally received the approval he had always wanted. "Here were the members of the country's political leadership, gathered en masse, ritually marking their acceptance of the great fact of modern American political life—the fact that the flawed, furiously human Richard Nixon, a man of dark nightmares and optimistic dreams, was part of each of them, as mysterious to them as he was to himself," Garment said.[86]

LAST HURRAH

Law firm failures have many different root causes. Big-time clients can move their business to another firm. Productive rainmakers can leave for better jobs elsewhere. There can also be larger factors at play, like economic recessions or certain sectors going bust.

Despite the myriad causes, law firm failures usually unfold the same way. The firm takes in far less money than expected in a given year, causing partners to get skittish and start looking for better, more stable situations elsewhere. This causes the firm to lose even more money, sending a signal to even more partners to leave. Maybe the law firm tries a Hail Mary and looks for a larger, more stable firm to merge with, but the lengthy process causes still more partners to leave, scaring off potential suitors. The cycle repeats itself before all that's left of a law firm are debts, bankruptcy filings, and memories.

Commentators have dubbed this "the law firm death spiral," and Mudge was about to experience this in a big way. But before that, the firm experienced one last major triumph. In 1987, longtime Mudge client Toshiba found itself in the crosshairs of the US government after the feds accused the company of selling a milling machine to the Soviet Union in violation of an international embargo. What turned Toshiba into public enemy number one was the allegation that Soviet naval officials used the machines to make their submarine propellers quieter, thereby giving their nuclear subs a pronounced advantage.

In the ensuing outcry, US officials seemingly tripped over themselves to emphasize how much they hated Toshiba and wanted to see the company punished. Several sledgehammer-wielding legislators made headlines for smashing a Toshiba radio on the steps of the Capitol. Senator Jake Garn of Utah, meanwhile, represented a more serious threat, as he proposed a bill to ban Toshiba's imports into the United States. According to the *Washington Post*, the threats didn't sit well with the Japanese government and, as a result, relations between the two countries hit their lowest point since World War II.[87]

To help its client stave off the feds, Mudge turned to an old friend. After joining Dickstein Shapiro, Leonard Garment had continued to work with Mudge on certain matters, including a prior antitrust case involving Toshiba. When Garment went to New York to meet with the other lawyers and lobbyists that had been hired to help Toshiba, he found that the temperature in the crowded conference room was at a boiling point. Armed with several facts that put Toshiba's position in a better light, including the fact that the Soviets had long had the technology for quieter sub propeller blades thanks to a French company, as well as the fact that the subsidiary that had signed off on the sale to the Soviet Union had not gotten authorization from the parent company, Toshiba's army of lawyers were ready to fight to the death on behalf of their client.

Garment, however, thought this was a mistake and counseled a more accommodating approach. "It was too late for an aggressive strategy," Garment said.[88] "Yes, the company was not guilty as charged. But blaming things on the French was unlikely to deflect Jake Garn or neutralize the general protectionist, anti-Japanese sentiment in Congress." Instead, Garment suggested a general strategy of public penitence coupled with behind-the-scenes lobbying in order to stave off any legislative sanctions.

Toshiba decided to go with Garment's strategy and took out full-page ads in American newspapers apologizing and accepting responsibility for what had happened. Meanwhile, Mudge and Toshiba's other lawyers and lobbyists went to work in D.C., hammering home the point to various lawmakers that American industries and companies relied heavily on Toshiba's products, so if they punished Toshiba, they would also punish American workers. They put relentless pressure on legislators, especially those in states where Toshiba America had offices or manufacturing plants, such as California, Tennessee, New York, and Oklahoma. "They came in waves, first the Washington lobbyists and then people from companies in my district," said Rep. Donald Lukens (R-Ohio).[89] Garn, for his part, called the lobbying effort "the most intense" he had seen in his fourteen years in Washington.[90]

In the end, Toshiba agreed to a three-year ban on sales to the federal government. Considering they were facing a permanent ban on all commercial products into the United States and a loss of $10 billion in annual sales, the sanction was one that Toshiba gladly accepted. Toshiba's lobbying efforts, which cost a reported $9 million, more than paid off—especially for Mudge, which got $4.3 million.[91]

It was a nice chunk of change for a firm that was starting to see money go out the door. The first sign that the death spiral was about to begin at the firm came in 1990, when a project finance group that, reportedly, brought in $8 million a year went to White & Case.[92] The big blow, however, came when the firm's bread-and-butter practice hit a slowdown. Falling interest rates throughout the 1990s sank the municipal bonds market, and Mudge paid a price for its lack of diversification. According to *Bond Buyer*, the firm served on 104 issues totaling more than $7.5 billion in 1994. The following year, the firm's numbers had dropped to thirty-eight deals totaling more than $3 billion.[93]

To turn around their fortunes, Mudge tried to go back to the well and bring in some political heavy-hitters. As one law firm consultant told *The National Journal*, Mudge seemed to have adopted the "Field of Dreams" approach to lateral partner recruitment. "Mudge Rose is a firm of dreams," said the consultant.[94] "If you hire the big names, then the business will come." Garment returned to the firm in 1993 from Dickstein Shapiro to try to expand Mudge's D.C. presence.[95] The following year, Carla Hills, a former secretary of Housing and Urban Development under President Gerald Ford, joined after her previous firm, Shea & Gould, went out of business.[96] Perhaps the biggest name to join was Jim Florio, the former governor of New Jersey. In 1993, Florio had agreed to join the firm in the weeks following his narrow reelection defeat to Christine Todd Whitman and, according to the *New York Times*, the outgoing governor had signed on the dotted line for an estimated $1 million per year.[97] These partners represented a major investment from the firm that didn't immediately pay dividends. "The approach was to try to expand the practice by bringing in people with political reputations," one partner told *The Lawyer.*[98] "Unfortunately, they were not proven producers of revenue."

In the case of Florio, he may have cost the firm far more than he could ever bring in. As he was about to leave office, Florio had signed a bill into law that Mudge client Cigna Corporation, and some other casualty insurance companies in the state, had adamantly opposed. Almost immediately after the controversial former governor joined Mudge, Cigna yanked its business from the firm in a move that saw nearly $15 million in annual income (14 percent of the firm's annual take) walk out the door and into the arms of rival firm O'Melveny & Myers.[99] At the time, Cigna's stated reason for sending its work to O'Melveny was so that it could consolidate its outside legal work.[100]

Mudge didn't just lose the work. According to *The Lawyer*, twenty-eight Mudge partners and associates moved to O'Melveny as part of the deal—pointedly, Florio was not one of them. Several years later, a former Mudge partner would sue Cigna alleging that, as Florio contemplated whether or not to sign the bill in question, Cigna had demanded that Mudge use its pending job offer to Florio as leverage to get him to veto the bill.[101] According to ex-partner Michael Petrucci, Cigna was incensed when Mudge lawyers refused to do something this unethical and retaliated by sending its business to O'Melveny. The case was dismissed in 1997.[102]

The lack of harmony at the firm wasn't isolated to Florio or the so-called political partners. The firm's dwindling finances became a major point of contention for many. According to *The American Lawyer*, the firm's net profits declined 37.5 percent, to $15 million, in 1994. The firm also lost over twenty-eight partners from January 1994 to summer 1995, costing the firm nearly $25 million in income. The problem got worse in late September 1995 when John Kirby, the former chairman of the firm, took twelve partners, twenty associates, and nearly $20 million in business to Latham & Watkins.[103] Kirby's departure was especially devastating to the lawyers still at Mudge. In June 1995, the influential Kirby had given a rousing lunchtime speech to his partners telling them that the firm's worst days were behind it and that things were on the upswing. "The firm has made the right moves in the last six months," he had assured his partners while projecting higher profits than the previous year.[104] Two months later, he announced his departure, citing, among other things, poor financial performance.

With the overall size of the firm's pie shrinking, partners began to clash over who got to take home the biggest pieces. Several of the younger, more productive partners resented the fact that their older, less productive counterparts in the partnership were still making more than them. They were also upset that celebrity partners like Florio and others were on huge contracts despite the fact that they weren't bringing in business. "In good years, money papers over all your problems," Zoeller told the *New York Times*.[105] "Down years tell you whether people like each other and trust each other."

In Mudge's case, the down years showed that its partners didn't really like or trust one another. Clashes of egos were commonplace among the partnership, and the partners in charge differed over how best to grow the firm. Prior to their departures, Kirby and Ferdon had been the two most powerful partners at the firm, and the two had fought over philosophy, with Kirby leading the charge to diversify the firm's practice, in particular moving away from municipal bonds in favor of corporate finance. Ferdon, a top municipal bonds lawyer by trade and reputation, was more focused on keeping costs down and running an efficient firm. "It was a push-pull between two prominent partners," Zoeller said about Ferdon and Kirby.[106] "It was a personality thing and one of those things that people should have been able to work out. There was such a dislike for one another."

The writing was on the wall, and Mudge's leaders tried, desperately, to save the firm by merging with a larger, more stable firm. There were preliminary talks between Mudge and Coudert Brothers, another firm that had been hurt by a number of high-profile partner defections. Mudge chairman Zoeller acknowledged the talks, but nothing became of them. Instead, Coudert would wait until Mudge went under before announcing the hiring of three corporate partners from the fallen firm.[107] Mudge also, reportedly, held emergency merger talks with Kelley Drye & Warren and the New York office of Graham & James.[108] A potential merger with Squire, Sanders & Dempsey, which Zoeller believed was going to happen, fell through after rumors surfaced that Ferdon intended to leave and join his old comrades at O'Melveny.[109]

The partner defections continued, unabated, to the point where there was soon no firm left. "Too many partners apparently concluded that the prior management of the firm was not pursuing policies which were in the best interests of the majority of the partners and likely to reduce the downward trend in revenue and profits," said Malcolm Schade, the firm's executive partner who moved to Thacher, Proffitt & Wood after Mudge's demise.[110]

By October 1995, time officially ran out for the firm. After 126 years, Mudge was no more. "I felt very badly about it," said Zoeller.[111] "I felt like it was my responsibility to handle the wind down, which took several years. It was very embarrassing that we weren't able to hold the firm together."

For Garment, it was clear to him why the firm had failed. He had seen it during the failed merger talks with Dickstein Shapiro back in 1980—indeed, it had been the firm's biggest problem during the pre-Nixon era and the reason why Guthrie, Alexander, and Rose had brought the future president on board in the first place. "At the heart of it, [the firm's leadership] didn't stay in touch with changes in the law world and didn't develop a generation of people capable of getting business," Garment said.[112] "They were too comfortable. They should have been sent to Hustle Academy."

Indeed, one of the things that Kirby had been pushing for before his departure was to ship out unproductive partners and create a more incentivized system of compensation in order to hold on to productive partners and recruit talented lawyers into the fold. Unfortunately for him, most of the firm seemed content to maintain the status quo. As it became clear that Mudge was about to join the law firm graveyard, some began circulating a parody version of the firm's internal newsletter. On one of the pages was a poem that contained the lines: "I thought that I would never budge/From these oh fabled halls of Mudge."[113] Like many great lines, there was plenty of subtext involved. Did those lines refer to the halcyon days of the firm when it was one of the biggest and most powerful law firms in the country that rebuilt a shattered presidential candidate and got him ready for his date with destiny? Or did they refer to the years when the firm seemed stuck in the mud and unable to move forward? Or did they even refer to the country-club atmosphere at the firm where lawyers could often stay as long as they wanted to even if they stopped being productive?

In the end, it was probably all three.

NOTES

1. "Richard Nixon, Inaugural Address, January 20, 1969," The American Presidency Project, accessed April 1, 2017, http://www.presidency.ucsb.edu/ws/?pid=1941.
2. Frank Lincoln Jr., "Presidential Transition, 1968–1969," *ABA Journal*, June 1969.
3. Lincoln Jr., "Presidential Transition."
4. Tom Evans, Frank Lincoln Memorandum to Richard Nixon, March 28, 1969, Tom Evans Collection.
5. Lincoln, "Presidential Transition."
6. Stephen Ambrose, *Nixon: Volume 2, The Triumph of a Politician, 1962–1972* (New York: Simon and Schuster, 1989), 228.
7. Ambrose, *Nixon: Volume 2*, 228–29.
8. Leonard Garment, *Crazy Rhythm: From Brooklyn and Jazz to Nixon's White House, Watergate and Beyond* (Cambridge, MA: Da Capo Press, 1997), 144–45.
9. Garment, *Crazy Rhythm*.
10. Garment, *Crazy Rhythm*, 145–46.
11. Garment, *Crazy Rhythm*, at 146.
12. Donald Zoeller, interview by Li, February 1, 2016.
13. Garment, *Crazy Rhythm*, 254.
14. "Transcript of A Meeting Between the President and H. R. Haldeman in the Oval Office on April 16, 1973 from 12:00 to 12:31," Richard Nixon Presidential Library and Museum, accessed April 1, 2017, https://www.nixonlibrary.gov/forresearchers/find/tapes/watergate/wspf/897-011.pdf.
15. Thomas Evans, "The Education of Richard Nixon: The Wilderness Years on Wall Street," unpublished manuscript, 276–78.
16. James Rosen, *The Strong Man: John Mitchell and the Secrets of Watergate* (New York: Doubleday, 2008), 66.
17. Evans, "Education of Richard Nixon," 200.

18. Fred Graham, "Nixon's Former Law Firm Here Prospers Amid Unwanted Public Attention," *New York Times*, September 26, 1970.
19. John Ehrlichman, interview by Tom Evans, January 28, 1988, transcript. Also: Folder: 53-36-Staff Secretary Paper Project, Richard Nixon Library, accessed September 14, 2017, https://www.nixonlibrary.gov/virtuallibrary/documents/contested/contested_box_53/Contested-53-36.pdf.
20. Ehrlichman, Iiterview by Evans.
21. Evans, "Education of Richard Nixon," 211–12. Also: Joseph Daughen and Peter Binzen, *The Wreck of Penn Central* (Washington, DC: Beard Books, 1999), 281.
22. Paul Hoffman, "Mudge Rose Guthrie & Alexander: The Firm to See?" *New York Magazine*, April 26, 1971.
23. Daughen and Binzen, *The Wreck of Penn Central*, 281.
24. Hoffman, "The Firm to See?"
25. Dom Bonafede, "Profile/John Mitchell, Nixon's Legal Adviser, Plays Policy Role Far Beyond His Office," *National Journal*, October 2, 1971.
26. "The Sharp New Line on Antitrust," *BusinessWeek*, June 21, 1969.
27. "The Sharp New Line on Antitrust." Also Eileen Shanahan, "Curbs Likely on Giant Mergers," *New York Times*, June 6, 1969.
28. Shanahan, "Curbs Likely on Giant Mergers."
29. Shanahan, "Curbs Likely on Giant Mergers."
30. Hoffman, "The Firm to See?"
31. Hoffman, "The Firm to See?"
32. "Warner Lambert: A History," Pfizer, accessed April 1, 2017, http://www.pfizer.com/about/history/pfizer_warner_lambert.
33. "Richard Nixon Presidential Recordings, Nixon Conversation 002-002," Miller Center, University of Virginia, accessed April 1, 2017, http://archive.millercenter.org/presidentialrecordings/rmn-002-002.
34. Rosen, *The Strong Man*, 193–94.
35. Rosen, *The Strong Man*.
36. Evans, "Education of Richard Nixon," 212.
37. John Pierson, "Former Law Partners of Nixon and Mitchell Add New Clients," *Wall Street Journal*, September 14, 1970.
38. Pierson, "Former Law Partners of Nixon and Mitchell Add New Clients."
39. Marjorie Hunter, "Role of Nixon's Old Firm in Bond Issue Criticized," *New York Times*, July 30, 1971, accessed April 1, 2017, http://www.nytimes.com/1971/07/30/archives/role-of-nixons-old-firm-in-bond-issue-criticized.html.
40. David Vaughn, interview by Evans, September 5, 1989, transcript.
41. Evans, "Education of Richard Nixon," 214–15.
42. David Coleman, "Nixon's Presidential Approval Ratings," History in Pieces, accessed April 1, 2017, http://historyinpieces.com/research/nixon-approval-ratings.
43. Ambrose, *Nixon: Volume 2*, 522.
44. Brent Cox, "How Much More Money Do Presidential Candidates Raise Today?" *The Awl*, November 6, 2012, accessed April 1, 2017, https://theawl.com/how-much-more-money-do-presidential-candidates-raise-today-8bfcbcdd8960.
45. Michael Jensen, "Mitchell and His Law Firm: Mudge Rose Beneficiary of New Business," *New York Times*, May 7, 1972.
46. Rosen, *The Strong Man*, 326–27.
47. Ambrose, *Nixon: Volume 2*, 635.
48. Francis Clines, "Nixon, on Visit to City, Greets 'Old Friends,'" *New York Times*, November 25, 1972, accessed April 1, 2017, http://www.nytimes.com/1972/11/25/archives/nixon-on-visit-to-city-greets-old-friends-nixon-and-family-greet.html.
49. "Nixon Flies to N. Y., Visits Old Law Firm," *Chicago Tribune*, November 25, 1972.
50. "President Richard Nixon's Daily Diary, Nov. 16–30, 1972," The Richard Nixon Library and Museum, accessed April 1, 2017, https://www.nixonlibrary.gov/virtuallibrary/documents/PDD/1972/088 November 16-30 1972.pdf.
51. Ambrose, *Nixon: Volume 2*, 560.

52. "John N. Mitchell Dies at 75: Major Figure in Watergate," *New York Times*, November 10, 1988, accessed April 1, 2017, http://www.nytimes.com/1988/11/10/obituaries/john-n-mitchell-dies-at-75-major-figure-in-watergate.html?pagewanted=all.
53. Rosen, *The Strong Man*, 327.
54. Paul Hoffman, *Lions of the Eighties: The Inside Story of Powerhouse Law Firms* (Garden City, NY: Doubleday & Company, Inc., 1982), 60–61.
55. Alan Kohn, "Effects of Nixon Legacy on Mudge, Rose," *New York Law Journal*, January 19, 1978.
56. Rosen, *The Strong Man*, 373.
57. He was sentenced to serve two-to-eight years in a minimum-security prison but was released after nineteen months due to ill health.
58. Evans, "Education of Richard Nixon," 234.
59. Evans, "Education of Richard Nixon," 216–22.
60. Tip O'Neill and William Novak, "The 1st Tip-Off about Nixon," *Washington Post*, September 14, 1987, accessed July 15, 2017, https://www.washingtonpost.com/archive/lifestyle/1987/09/14/the-1st-tip-off-about-nixon/73159c31-9212-4d3b-b22d-3a995b914f31/.
61. Evans, "Education of Richard Nixon," 238.
62. Evans, "Education of Richard Nixon," at 237.
63. Kohn, "Effects of Nixon Legacy on Mudge, Rose."
64. Kohn, "Effects of Nixon Legacy on Mudge, Rose."
65. Morton Mintz, "Law Firm Accused of Aiding One Client over Another," *Washington Post*, August 30, 1977, accessed April 2, 2017, https://www.washingtonpost.com/archive/politics/1977/08/30/law-firm-accused-of-aiding-one-client-over-another/e425b76b-6b24-425e-903a-e4861838cfc3/?utm_term=.efd0aa39bdd0.
66. Mintz, "Law Firm Accused of Aiding One Client over Another."
67. Mintz, "Law Firm Accused of Aiding One Client over Another."
68. Holcomb Noble, "C. Arnholt Smith, 97, Banker and Padres Chief Before Fall," *New York Times*, June 11, 1996, accessed April 12, 2017, http://www.nytimes.com/1996/06/11/us/c-arnholt-smith-97-banker-and-padres-chief-before-a-fall.html.
69. Tom Goldstein, "Business and the Law," *New York Times*, March 9, 1979, accessed April 2 2017, http://www.nytimes.com/1979/03/09/archives/business-and-the-law-mudge-rose-a-quiet-ruling.html.
70. Kohn, "Effects of Nixon Legacy on Mudge, Rose."
71. Hoffman, *Lions of the Eighties*, 60–61.
72. Hoffman, *Lions of the Eighties*, at 62.
73. Saundra Torry, "Leonard Garment Finds a Challenge in Expansion Puzzle," *Washington Post*, November 22, 1993, accessed April 1, 2017, https://www.washingtonpost.com/archive/business/1993/11/22/leonard-garment-finds-a-challenge-in-expansion-puzzle/901bf63f-7513-455a-9611-a41e78a30820/?utm_term=.2eae5d70a743.
74. "Bond Counsel Proposal May Be Hard to Meet," *Palm Beach Post*, July 28, 1985.
75. "W. H. Hogeland, 68, Lawyer and Analyst," *New York Times*, July 7, 1996, accessed April 1, 2017, http://www.nytimes.com/1996/07/07/nyregion/w-h-hogeland-68-lawyer-and-analyst.html.
76. "The NLJ 250," *National Law Journal*, September 28, 1987.
77. "The Am Law 50," *The American Lawyer*, July/August 1985, http://amlawdaily.typepad.com/AmLaw50-1985.pdf.
78. "The Am Law 50."
79. Garment, *Crazy Rhythm*, 337–38.
80. James Dickenson, "Leonard Garment: Legal Adviser to the Powerful Spans Watergate, Iran Drama," *Washington Post*, December 22, 1986, accessed April 1, 2017, https://www.washingtonpost.com/archive/politics/1986/12/22/leonard-garment-legal-adviser-to-the-powerful-spans-watergate-iran-drama/693b6344-7304-40ff-bdd0-b081185676c6/?utm_term=.a03476779f80.
81. Rosen, *The Strong Man*, xii.
82. Julie Baumgold, "Nixon's New Life in New York," *New York*, June 9, 1980.
83. Rosen, *The Strong Man*, 488.

84. Evan Thomas, *Being Nixon: A Man Divided*. New York: Random House, 2015).
85. Garment, *Crazy Rhythm*, 383–84. Also Thomas, *Being Nixon*.
86. Garment, *Crazy Rhythm*, 386.
87. John Burgess, "Japan Worries That Scandal Has Hurt Relations with U.S.," *Washington Post*, July 16, 1987, accessed April 2, 2017, https://www.washingtonpost.com/archive/business/1987/07/16/japan-worries-that-scandal-has-hurt-relations-with-us/07b09895-5fd1-4bc1-a8f3-33d61bc4504f/?utm_term=.1bd2d8672050.
88. Garment, *Crazy Rhythm*, 355.
89. Robert Rosenblatt, "H ow 'Swat Team' of Toshiba Lobbyists Took on Congress—and Won," *Washington Post*, May 1, 1988.
90. Rosenblatt, "H ow 'Swat Team' of Toshiba Lobbyists Took on Congress—and Won."
91. Stuart Auerbach, "Toshiba Corp.'s Costly Lobbying," *Washington Post*, October 13, 1988, accessed April 2, 2017, https://www.washingtonpost.com/archive/business/1988/10/13/toshiba-corps-costly-lobbying/aee9d12e-5ea4-4fbb-914c-d80c8be21b27/?utm_term=.700fb070a534.
92. Carey Goldberg, "The Mudge Rose Firm Enters the Tar Pit of Legal History," *New York Times*, October 1, 1995, accessed April 1, 2017, http://www.nytimes.com/1995/10/01/nyregion/the-mudge-rose-firm-enters-the-tar-pit-of-legal-history.html?pagewanted=all.
93. Christina Pretto, " Mudge Rose Votes to Disband Firm by End of the Year," *Bond Buyer*, October 3, 1995.
94. John W. Moore, "Thinking Big: A Tale of Two Law Firms," *National Journal*, September 17, 1994.
95. Torry, "Leonard Garment Finds a Challenge in Expansion Puzzle."
96. "Washington Insight," *Los Angeles Times*, April 18, 1994, accessed April 1, 2017, http://articles.latimes.com/1994-04-18/news/mn-47309_1_carla-hills.
97. Jerry Gray, "Florio's Spotlight Dims, but Stage Widens," *New York Times*, May 29, 1994, accessed April 1, 2017, http://www.nytimes.com/1994/05/29/nyregion/florio-s-spotlight-dims-but-stage-widens.html.
98. "Could Mudge Rose Have Been Rescued?" *The Lawyer*, October 17, 1995.
99. Goldberg, "The Mudge Rose Firm Enters the Tar Pit of Legal History."
100. Amy Stevens, "Mudge Rose Ills Mount as Clients and Partners Leave," *Associated Press*, March 31, 1995, accessed April 1, 2017, http://www.apnewsarchive.com/1995/Mudge-Rose-s-Ills-Mount-as-Clients-And-Partners-Leave/id-2172000fb025c6918e1e5a3148500247.
101. Frances McMorris, "Former Mudge Partner Sues Cigna over Firm's Demise," *Wall Street Journal*, May 9, 1997, accessed April 1, 2017, http://www.wsj.com/articles/SB86313633544372500.
102. "Judge Dismissed a Lawsuit over Firm's Firing by Client," *Wall Street Journal*, September 25, 1997, accessed April 1, 2017, http://www.wsj.com/articles/SB875159260286297000.
103. Goldberg, "The Mudge Rose Firm Enters the Tar Pit of Legal History."
104. Amy Stevens and Edward Felsenthal, "Law Firm Finds Complacency Can Kill—U.S.'s Venerable Mudge Will Be Liquidated," *Wall Street Journal*, Oct 3, 1995.
105. Stevens and Felsenthal, "The Mudge Rose Firm Enters the Tar Pit of Legal History."
106. Zoeller, interview by Li.
107. "Coudert Brothers Acquires Corporate Group from Mudge, Rose, Guthrie, Alexander & Ferndon," *The Free Library*, October 3, 1995, accessed April 1, 2017, https://www.thefreelibrary.com/COUDERT+BROTHERS+ACQUIRES+CORPORATE+GROUP+FROM+MUDGE,+ROSE,+GUTHRIE,...-a017511223.
108. "Could Mudge Rose Have Been Rescued?"
109. Zoeller, interview by Li.
110. "Could Mudge Rose Have Been Rescued?"
111. Zoeller, interview by Li.
112. Stevens and Felsenthal, "The Mudge Rose Firm Enters the Tar Pit of Legal History."
113. Stevens and Felsenthal, "The Mudge Rose Firm Enters the Tar Pit of Legal History."

Epilogue

As the previous chapters have shown, there have been plenty of politicians who, at one time, called the venerated halls of Mudge "home." In addition to Nixon, Mitchell, Buchanan, Florio, and Hills, several other prominent national figures have spent time at Mudge, including ex New York mayor John Lindsay,[1] federal judge and DOJ official Harold Russell ("Ace") Tyler Jr., former New York State Supreme Court justice William Lawless, former Dick Cheney aide I. Lewis ("Scooter") Libby, and Manhattan federal district judge Jed Rakoff. More recently, in 2016, Democrat Tim Canova, a former Mudge Rose associate, unsuccessfully ran for US House of Representatives in Florida. Perhaps Mudge's most prominent politico after Nixon, however, was a New Yorker who spent almost no time at the firm.

In 1967, two twenty-three-year-olds who would go on to bigger and better things would report to Nixon Mudge as summer associates. Peter King, a working-class Irish Catholic from Queens who would become a longtime US Representative from Long Island, was a rising 3L at Notre Dame Law School when he met his future GOP colleague on the first day of orientation: Rudy Giuliani. The future mayor of New York City and unsuccessful presidential candidate was, at first glance, an odd choice for Nixon Mudge. For one thing, the NYU Law student considered himself to be a liberal Democrat in the vein of Bobby Kennedy. In fact, one could argue that, when it came to politics, the proud Italian Catholic Giuliani's holy Trinity consisted of JFK, RFK, and Teddy. According to a 1997 *Daily News* profile, Giuliani cried when JFK was assassinated, distributed RFK fliers during Bobby's victorious 1964 Senate campaign against incumbent Kenneth Keating, and once yelled at his aunt for making a joke about Teddy and Chappaquiddick.[2]

So it was strange to see him working at Nixon's law firm. To be fair, it's not like he crossed paths with the future president regularly. The annual summer associates' lunch with Nixon was one of the only occasions where they would have a chance to meet. And as one of Giuliani's colleagues pointed out, it's not like Nixon would have identified the future mayor as a potential political star the way he had with Donald Riegle. "I didn't view him as having any leadership skills," said fellow summer associate Fred Lowther to the *Daily News*. "If you told me Rudy would become mayor, I would've laughed. Rudy Giuliani? You got to be kidding."

But become mayor he did. Giuliani switched to the Republican Party during the Reagan Revolution in 1980 and went onto a storied career as a federal prosecutor, winning convictions in a number of high-profile cases, including the Mafia Commission trials. After an unsuccessful first run for mayor in 1989, he defeated incumbent David Dinkins in 1993. His tenure saw a sharp decrease in crime (although the decline had actually begun under Dinkins[3]) and a large-scale urban redevelopment, particularly in Times Square as the sex shops and peep shows of yore were swept away in favor of Virgin Megastores and Hard Rock Cafes. Additionally, Giuliani was mayor of New York City during 9/11 and emerged as a unifying figure in the aftermath of the attack. Dubbed "America's Mayor," Giuliani set his sights on the presidency in 2008, emerging as front runner in polls taken in the summer of 2007.[4]

But before that, he proved that he had learned something from Nixon, after all. In 2005, Giuliani joined forces with Texas-based law firm Bracewell & Patterson, signing on as the firm's new public partner. The firm, which rechristened itself Bracewell & Giuliani, had desperately wanted name recognition and business for its new office in the Big Apple, and if anyone could do that for them, it was Rudy. He knew all the big players in New York City, and many still held him in high regard as a result of his eight-year run as mayor. In return, he got a nice salary (*The American Lawyer* reported that the firm paid $10 million, up front, for Giuliani and two of his partners to join) and some flexibility (he would be allowed to continue working at Giuliani Partners, the security consulting business he set up in 2002).

Both Giuliani and his new law firm's managing partner, Patrick Oxford, denied that the alliance was made with an eye toward the 2008 presidential campaign. Instead, the two talked about how it was a mutual love of the law that brought them together, and Giuliani even claimed that he was more concerned about making sure he liked the people at his new firm than anything else. "That would be a pretty silly way to run for President. You don't join a law firm to run for President," Giuliani said, ignoring the fact that Nixon had done just that.[5] Oxford agreed, noting that the two had never even spoken about the presidency.

No one bought it. For one thing, Oxford was a well-known political force in Texas. He had played leading roles on campaigns for prominent state Republicans in the state going back more than thirty years, including George

H. W. Bush, John Tower, Kay Bailey Hutchison, and John Cornyn. He had also been a major fundraiser and bundler for then-president George W. Bush and counted both the president and his chief adviser, Karl Rove, as good friends. For another, as *The American Lawyer* pointed out, Giuliani could have had his pick of jobs with well-known, established firms in New York City. Instead, he chose a three-hundred-plus lawyer firm from Texas full of people that he hardly knew or had never met before and was barely known outside of the Lone Star State. Bracewell wasn't even considered to be the best or biggest firm in Texas. A former partner told *The American Lawyer* that he was shocked the firm was able to land someone of Giuliani's stature while another ex-partner figured Rudy had to be getting something big in return for lending his name and prestige to the firm.

Ultimately, Oxford and Giuliani dropped the façade. When Giuliani formed his presidential exploratory committee in 2007, Oxford came aboard as chairman. Giuliani's war chest quickly filled up, as he raised over $17 million in the first quarter of 2007, with $2.2 million coming from Texas sources—far outpacing his rivals, including eventual nominee senator John McCain. Giuliani's nascent presidential campaign received donations from a number of Texas-based donors, including billionaire T. Boone Pickens Jr., who gave $500,000 according to the *Wall Street Journal*; Richard Kinder, CEO of Bracewell client Kinder Morgan, Inc.; and Tom Hicks, owner of the Texas Rangers and the Dallas Stars.[6]

Those halcyon days of 2007 ended up being the high point of Rudy Giuliani's 2008 presidential campaign. When primary season got underway, Giuliani contested the traditional first three contests in Iowa, New Hampshire, and South Carolina. However, the bulk of his time and resources went into several big state primaries that took place later, such as Florida, California, Illinois, and New York.[7] Whether this was a decision that was forced upon Giuliani based on falling poll numbers,[8] especially in Iowa and New Hampshire, or whether it was part of a concerted strategy to play to Giuliani's strengths and emphasize his electability in a general election,[9] is debatable.

Either way, it was a stunning decision that had many political analysts scratching their heads. Long gone were the days when a candidate didn't have to enter a single primary in order to win the nomination (as Nixon had contemplated doing in 1968). In fact, since 1980, it was vital for a candidate to do well or even win one or two of the first three contests in order to have any shot at the nomination. As a result, Giuliani had no momentum heading into the Florida primary and had boxed himself into a situation where he not only had to win in the Sunshine State but also win big. After finishing a disappointing third, Giuliani bowed to the inevitable and withdrew.

In retrospect, it's clear that winning the GOP nomination was always going to be a Herculean task for the ex-mayor. Given how conservative the

Republican Party has become, it's doubtful that GOP voters would have ever backed a twice-divorced man who had, previously, advocated on behalf of abortion rights, gun control, and gay rights—or at least it was that way in 2008. In fact, some influential social conservatives like James Dobson had stated that they would never support Giuliani under any circumstances.[10]

Giuliani also learned about the drawbacks of being the early front runner—something Nixon had worked, assiduously, to avoid in 1967. By peaking with more than a year before Election Day, voters had plenty of time to get reacquainted with Rudy's skeletons, including his messy personal life, his controversial reign as mayor, and his mentorship of Bernard Kerik, the disgraced former NYPD chief and unsuccessful nominee as Secretary of Homeland Security who went to prison on tax fraud charges. In a memorable December 2007 interview on NBC's *Meet the Press*, Giuliani seemed on the defensive for the entire episode after host Tim Russert asked the former mayor about several of those skeletons. Russert had even devoted an entire segment to Giuliani's relationship with Kerik, as well as the use of taxpayer money to protect and drive around Giuliani's then-mistress and future wife, Judith Nathan.

Giuliani also faced tough questions about his law firm. In that same 2007 interview, Russert brought up work that Bracewell & Giuliani had done for the US subsidiary of Citgo, the state-run oil company owned by Venezuela and its controversial leader, Hugo Chavez. "[My] law firm did—never represented Hugo Chavez," Giuliani responded, indignantly.[11] "They represented—wait, wait—they represented an American company, Citgo, in Texas, that employs maybe 100,000 people, 120,000 people, that sells gasoline, needs to comply with the law. They represented them just in Texas, and then they stopped representing them. And they—not a direct representation of Hugo Chavez. That's a very unfair way to say it." The firm would cut ties with Citgo, citing legal conflicts, and Oxford reiterated to *The American Lawyer* that political calculations did not play a role.

Other law firm clients that came back to bite Giuliani included Yousef Jameel, a Saudi businessman who was sued, along with over two hundred others, by victims of the 9/11 attacks for allegedly funding and supporting Al Qaeda. Jameel's case was ultimately dismissed, but not before Oxford told Kenneth Caruso, the Bracewell partner handling the case, to get rid of it. "We had a little bit of a misunderstanding with Ken," Oxford told *The American Lawyer*.[12] "When I found out about it, I said, 'Look, buddy, you need to wind this up.'" In the end, the marriage between Giuliani and Bracewell lasted over a decade before the ex-mayor left for a partnership with another Am Law firm,[13] Greenberg Traurig, in 2016. That same year, a twice-divorced man from New York who had, previously, supported abortion rights, gay rights, and gun control would, indeed, win the presidency as a Republican. That man, Donald Trump, had several big-name media supporters and campaign surrogates—however, few of them would defend him with the same type of fervor and devotion as Giuliani.

In recent years, questions about law firm affiliations have dogged other high-profile lawyers-turn-politicians. When Republican Ted Cruz first ran for Senate in 2012 in Texas, his primary opponent actually ran an attack ad pointing out Cruz's status as a partner at "liberal" law firm Morgan, Lewis & Bockius. The ad alleged that lawyers at the firm had given far more money to Barack Obama and Democrats over an unspecified period of time and questioned why Cruz "has chosen to partner with liberal activists that fund Democrats."[14] Another ad blasted Cruz for representing Shandong Linglong Tyre Company, a Chinese company, accused of stealing intellectual property from an American company. "The Chinese keep stalling in court, they keep counterfeiting, and Ted Cruz keeps getting paid," the ad's narrator intoned ominously.[15]

At the time, the ads didn't seem to do much damage. Cruz won his race handily and immediately set his sights on the White House in 2016. When the presidential race got underway, however, the Chinese ad stuck with him, and he had to answer questions about it during presidential debates and TV interviews. "You can't go around saying you're tough on China but then have a legal record in which you were paid a lot of money to defend the Chinese who had taken a product away from an American unjustly, unfairly and illegally," Florida senator Marco Rubio and 2016 rival stated about Cruz.[16]

The Texas senator, who called the attacks "bogus," also came under fire for having defended several multimillion-dollar damage awards to personal injury victims on appeal during his time at the firm. Despite that, upon becoming a senator, Cruz adhered to the GOP party line about the need for tort reform, even going as far as to say that a Texas law, which caps punitive damages at $750,000, should be a national law.[17] "Lawyers have an ethical responsibility to zealously represent their clients, and Sen. Cruz endeavored to do so both in public service and in private practice," a Cruz spokesperson told *Mother Jones*. "Tort reform is primarily a question of state law, and the judgments entered by the New Mexico juries were pursuant to New Mexico law."

Ultimately, these cases weren't the reason why Cruz lost the GOP nomination. Instead, there were plenty of external factors and surprises unique to the 2016 presidential race that historians and political scientists will study for the next several decades and beyond. In fact, many have already started comparing Donald Trump to Richard Nixon, noting that both men had thin skin, hated the press, tapped into dark forces to win the presidency, had a liberal definition of the truth, and were obsessed with leaks. As former Nixon White House counsel John Dean pointed out, it was Nixon's obsession with leaks that, in many ways, led to Watergate.[18] Time will tell if that same obsession will do in Trump.

In the meantime, what is clear is that using law firm representations to attack someone is not going away. In that same 2016 presidential race, both Democratic presidential nominee Hillary Clinton and vice presidential nominee Tim Kaine were attacked for their work as defense attorneys. Plenty of other candidates have had to play defense because of prior representations, including Indiana senator Dan Coats[19] and South Carolina gubernatorial nominee Vincent Sheheen.[20]

Perhaps that explains why no politician has been able to replicate what Nixon did at Mudge. Lawyers often have to take on tough cases that may cut against their own ideals and morals. Moreover, lawyers have to make money, and in an increasingly global economy, that often means doing business with companies in China, Russia, and other countries that aren't necessarily allies. Plus, many people just don't like lawyers. After all, those lawyer jokes didn't write themselves.

Then again, the vast majority of American presidents have been lawyers, so having "Esq." next to your name is hardly the modern-day equivalent to a scarlet letter. Perhaps the answer lies not with Nixon but with the partners, associates, employees, and aides that all marched in lockstep in order to fulfill their common goal of helping him win the White House. It wasn't enough for Nixon to have access to deep-pocketed clients or a big salary. He needed young, smart, dedicated, and determined people (including ones that might, otherwise, have worked for his opponents) to take care of all the details that he didn't want to handle, provide him with different perspectives, and save him from his own worst impulses. He needed people who believed in him and his cause and were willing to sacrifice themselves and their own careers in order to help him further his own. He needed thinkers who were unburdened by past failure and willing to think outside the box to come up with the best strategy for a two-time loser who looked like he had not only burned his bridge with the voters but had dropped the entire nuclear arsenal of the United States on it.

"The firm played an indispensible role because it provided a base," Nixon reflected when interviewed by his former aide and fellow Mudge alumnus, Tom Evans, in 1983.[21] "We ran [the 1968] campaign out of the modest quarters we had—you compare that with even what a Congressman has today—I don't see how we did it. We did it with very little money, but we had very dedicated people."

In short, he needed a bunch of amateurs.

NOTES

1. Robert McFadden, "John V. Lindsay, Mayor and Maverick, Dies at 79," *New York Times*, December 21, 2000, accessed June 30, 2017, http://www.nytimes.com/2000/12/21/nyregion/john-v-lindsay-mayor-and-maverick-dies-at-79.html.

2. Paul Schwartzman, "Love and the Law," *New York Daily News*, May 13, 1997, accessed April 1, 2017, http://www.nydailynews.com/archives/news/love-law-article-1.754969.

3. Mason B. Williams, "Yes, David Dinkins Was a Criminal Justice Pioneer: Hillary Clinton Was Right to Praise the Former Mayor as 'a Leader We Can Look To' as We Reform Policing in America," *New York Daily News*, April 30, 2015, accessed August 26, 2017, http://www.nydailynews.com/opinion/williams-yes-david-dinkins-criminal-justice-pioneer-article-1.2204993.

4. Lydia Saad, "Giuliani Leads GOP Race; Huckabee, Others Tie for Second," Gallup, December 18, 2007, accessed September 1, 2017, http://www.gallup.com/poll/103348/giuliani-leads-gop-race-huckabee-others-tie-second.aspx.

5. Susan Beck, "Lone Star," *The American Lawyer*, June 2007.

6. Beck, "Lone Star."

7. Michael Cooper and Marjorie Connelly, "Giuliani Has Decided to Zag While the Other Candidates Zig," *New York Times*, December 20, 2007, accessed April 1, 2017, http://www.nytimes.com/2007/12/20/us/politics/20giuliani.html?mtrref=en.wikipedia.org&gwh=2CD450DFCD2DA607BEAD70A4B6F76844&gwt=pay.

8. "'Meet the Press' Transcript for Dec. 9, 2007: Rudy Giuliani," *NBC News*, December 9, 2007, accessed April 1, 2017, http://www.nbcnews.com/id/22170668/ns/meet_the_press/t/meet-press-transcript-dec/ -.WLBwgG8rKHs.

9. Ewen MacAskill, "Giuliani's Diastrous Strategy," *The Guardian*, January 30, 2008, accessed April 1, 2017, https://www.theguardian.com/world/2008/jan/30/usa.rudygiuliani.

10. "Christian Right Leader Writes Off Giuliani," *CNN*, May 17, 2007, accessed April 1, 2017, http://www.cnn.com/2007/POLITICS/05/17/giuliani.dobson/index.html.

11. "'Meet the Press' Transcript for Dec. 9, 2007: Rudy Giuliani."

12. Beck, "Lone Star."

13. Susan Beck, "Rudy Giuliani Jumps to Greenberg Traurig," *The American Lawyer*, January 19, 2016, accessed April 1, 2017, http://www.americanlawyer.com/id=1202747344859/Rudy-Giuliani-Jumps-to-Greenberg-Traurig?slreturn=20170124160858.

14. Victor Li, "Texas GOP Senate Hopeful Attacked by Primary Foe for Being Partner at 'Liberal' Morgan Lewis," *The American Lawyer*, March 8, 2012, accessed April 1, 2017, http://amlawdaily.typepad.com/amlawdaily/2012/03/tedcruzmorganlewisad.html.

15. W. Gardner Selby, "David Dewhurst Says Ted Cruz Represents a Chinese Company Found Guilty of Stealing U.S. Blueprints," *Poltifact*, April 19, 2012, accessed April 1, 2017, http://www.politifact.com/texas/statements/2012/apr/19/david-dewhurst/david-dewhurst-says-ted-cruz-represents-chinese-co/.

16. Elizabeth Koh, "Rubio: Cruz, Who Once Defended Chinese Company, Can't be 'Tough on China,'" *Dallas Morning News*, January 25, 2016, accessed April 1, 2017, http://www.dallasnews.com/news/politics/2016/01/25/rubio-cruz-who-once-defended-chinese-company-cant-be-tough-on-china.

17. David Corn, "As a Lawyer, Ted Cruz Defended Huge Jury Awards. As a Politician, He Opposed Them," *Mother Jones*, February 11, 2015, accessed April 1, 2017, http://www.motherjones.com/politics/2015/02/ted-cruz-tort-reform-2016.

18. Eric Nelson, "John Dean: White House Is in a 'Cover-Up Mode,'" *Daily Kos*, March 20, 2017, accessed April 8, 2017, https://www.dailykos.com/story/2017/3/20/1645584/-John-Dean-White-House-is-in-a-cover-up-mode.

19. Li, "Texas GOP Senate Hopeful Attacked by Primary Foe for Being Partner at 'Liberal' Morgan Lewis."

20. Victor Li, "Republican Governors Association Doubles Down on Negative Ad Campaign against Lawyer," *ABA Journal*, May 1, 2014, accessed April 8, 2017, http://www.abajournal.com/news/article/republican_governors_assocaition_doubles_down_on_negative_ad_campaign_again/.

21. Nixon, interview by Evans, supra.

Bibliography

BOOKS

Aitken, Jonathan. *Nixon: A Life*, (Washington, D.C.: Regnery History, 1993).
Alexander, Herbert, *Financing the 1968 Election* (Lexington, MA: Lexington Books, 1971).
Ambrose, Stephen, *Nixon: Vol. 1- The Education of a Politician, 1913-1962* (New York: Simon & Schuster, 1987).
Ambrose, Stephen, *Nixon. Volume 2: The Triumph of a Politician, 1962-1972*, (New York: Simon & Schuster, 1989).
Anderson, Martin, *Welfare: The Political Economy of Welfare Reform in the United States* (Palo Alto, CA: Hoover Institution Press Publication, 1978).
Baker, Peter, "Nixon Tried to Spoil Johnson's Vietnam Peace Talks in '68, Notes Show," *The New York Times*, January 2, 2017.
Ball, Howard, *Hugo L. Black: Cold Steel Warrior* (New York: Oxford University Press, 1996).
Barbas, Samantha, *Newsworthy: The Supreme Court Battle Over Privacy and Press Freedom* (Stanford, CA: Stanford University Press, 2017).
Bass, Jack and Marilyn Thompson, *Strom: The Complicated Personal and Political Life of Strom Thurmond* (New York, PublicAffairs: 2005).
Black, Conrad, *Richard M. Nixon: A Life in Full*, (New York: PublicAffairs, 2007).
Bonsall, Thomas, *More Than They Promised: The Studebaker Story* (Stanford, CA: Stanford University Press, 2000).
Buchanan, Patrick, *The Greatest Comeback: How Richard Nixon Rose From Defeat to Create the New Majority* (New York: Crown Forum, 2014).
Buchanan, Patrick, *Nixon's White House Wars: The Battles that Made and Broke a President and Divided America Forever* (New York: Crown Forum, 2017).
Caplan, Lincoln, *Skadden: Power, Money, and the Rise of a Legal Empire,* (New York: Farrar Straus Giroux, 1993).
Caro, Robert, *Master of the Senate* (New York: Vintage Books, 2003).
Caro, Robert, *The Years of Lyndon Johnson: The Passage of Power* (New York: Alfred A. Knopf, 2012).
Carrozza, Anthony, *William D. Pawley: The Extraordinary Life of the Adventurer, Entrepreneur and Diplomat who Co-Founded the Flying Tigers* (Washington, D.C.: Potomac Books, 2012).
Chennault, Anna, *The Education of Anna* (New York: Times Books, 1980).
Coleman, David, *The Fourteenth Day: JFK and the Aftermath of the Cuban Missile Crisis* (New York: W.W. Norton & Company, 2012).

Cordery, Stacy, *Alice: Alice Roosevelt Longworth: From White House Princess to Washington Power Broker*, (New York: Penguin Books, 2007).

Crassweller, Robert D., *Trujillo: The Life and Times of a Caribbean Dictator* (New York: The MacMillan Co., 1966).

Cray, Ed, *Chief Justice: A Biography of Earl Warren* (New York: Simon and Schuster, 1997).

Critchlow, Donald, *Studebaker: The Life and Death of an American Corporation* (Bloomington, IN.: Indiana Unversity Press, 1996).

Dallek, Robert, Nixon and Kissinger: Partners in Power (New York: Harper Collins e-books, 2007).

Daughen, Joseph and Peter Binzen, *The Wreck of Penn Central* (Washington, D.C.: Beard Books, 1999).

Denton, Sally, *The Pink Lady: The Many Lives of Helen Gahagan Douglas* (New York: Bloomsbury Press, 2009).

Ebert, Robert, *Champion of the Lark: Harold E. Churchill and the Presidency of Studebaker-Packard, 1956-1961* (Jefferson, NC.: McFarland & Co., Inc., 2013).

Ehrlichman, John, *Witness to Power: The Nixon Years*, (New York: Simon Schuster, 1982).

Eisenhower, Julie Nixon, *Pat Nixon: The Untold Story*, (New York: Simon & Schuster, 1986).

Evans, Thomas, "The Education of Richard Nixon: The Wilderness Years on Wall Street," (unpublished manuscript).

Evans, Thomas, "Nixon Mudge," (unpublished manuscript, 1994).

Farrell, John A., "Richard Nixon: A Life" (New York: Doubleday, 2017).

Feldstein, Mark, *Poisoning the Press: Richard Nixon, Jack Anderson and The Rise of Washington's Scandal Culture* (New York: Farrar, Straus and Giroux, 2010).

Foster, Patrick, *Studebaker: The Complete History* (Minneapolis: Motorbooks, 2008).

Frank, Jeffrey, *Ike and Dick: Portrait of a Strange Political Marriage*, (New York: Simon & Schuster Paperbacks, 2013).

Garment, Leonard, *Crazy Rhythm: From Brooklyn and Jazz to Nixon's White House, Watergate and Beyond*, (Cambridge, MA: Da Capo Press, 1997).

Gavin, William, *Speechwright: An Insider's Take on Political Rhetoric* (East Lansing, MI: Michigan State University Press, 2011), ebook.

Gibbs, Nancy and Michael Duffy, *The Presidents Club: Inside the World's Most Exclusive Fraternity* (New York: Simon & Schuster Paperbacks, 2012,) ebook.

Halberstam, David, *The Powers That Be* (New York: Open Road Media, 2012).

Halberstam, David, *The Making of a Quagmire: America and Vietnam During the Kennedy Era* (Lanham, MD: Rowman & Littlefield, 2008),

Hoffman, Paul, *Lions in the Street: The Inside Story of the Great Wall Street Law Firms* (New York: Saturday Review Press, 1973).

Hoffman, Paul, *Lions of the Eighties: The Inside Story of Powerhouse Law Firms* (Garden City, NY: Doubleday & Company, Inc., 1982).

Howe, Marvine, "Henry Stern, Jr., 80, Ex-Insurance Chief Of New York State," *The New York Times*, July 21, 1993.

Hughes, Ken, *Chasing Shadows: The Nixon Tapes, The Chennault Affair and the Origins of Watergate* (Charlottesville, VA: University of Virginia Press, 2014).

Jamieson, Kathleen Hall, *Packaging the Presidency: A History and Criticism of Campaign Advertising* (New York: Oxford University Press, 1996).

Kalman, Laura, *Abe Fortas: A Biography* (New Haven: Yale University Press, 1990).

Langworth, Robert, *Studebaker 1946-1966: The Classic Postwar Years*, (Osceola, WI: Motorbooks International Publishers & Wholesalers, 1979, 1993).

Li, Laura Tyson, *Madame Chiang Kai-Shek: China's Eternal First Lady* (New York: Grove Press, 2006).

Marling, Karal Ann, *As Seen on TV: The Visual Culture of Everyday Life in the 1950s*, (Cambridge, MA: Harvard University Press, 1994).

Martin, Douglas, "Eugene D. Genovese, Historian of the South, Dies at 82," *The New York Times*, September 30, 2012.

Matthews, Chris, *Kennedy & Nixon: The Rivalry that Shaped Postwar America* (New York: Simon & Schuster, 1996).

McGinniss, Joe, *The Selling of the President* (New York: Penguin Books, 1969).

Mintz, Morton, "Law Firm Accused of Aiding One Client Over Another," *The Washington Post*, August 30, 1977.

Montgomery, Gayle and James Johnson, One Step From the White House: The Rise and Fall of Senator William F. Knowland, (Berkeley: University of California Press, 1998).

Morris, Roger, *Richard Milhous Nixon: The Rise of an American Politician,* (New York: Henry Holt & Co., 1991).

Morrow, Robert, *First Hand Knowledge: How I Participated in the CIA-Mafia Murder of President Kennedy* (New York: S.P.I. Books, 1992).

Naylor, R.T., *Hot Money and the Politics of Debt* (Montreal & Kingston: McGill Queen's University Press, 2004).

Newman, Roger, *Hugo Black: A Biography* (New York: Fordham University Press, 1994).

Newton, Jim, *Justice for All: Earl Warren and the Nation He Made*, (New York: Riverhead Books, 2006).

Nixon, Richard, *In the Arena: A Memoir of Victory, Defeat and Renewal*, (New York: Simon & Schuster, 1990).

Nixon, Richard, *RN: The Memoirs of Richard Nixon*, (New York: Simon & Schuster, 2013), Kindle edition.

Noble, Holcomb, "C. Arnholt Smith, 97, Banker and Padres Chief Before Fall," *The New York Times*, June 11, 1996.

Perlstein, Rick, *Before the Storm: Barry Goldwater and the Unmaking of American Consensus* (New York: Nation Books, 2001).

Perlstein, Rick, *Nixonland: The Rise of a President and the Fracturing of America* (New York: Scribner, 2008), Kindle edition.

Person, Carl, *Self Employment and No College* (Bookbaby, ebook, 2015).

Price, Raymond, *With Nixon* (New York: The Viking Press, 1977).

Rosen, James, *The Strong Man: John Mitchell and the Secrets of Watergate* (New York: Doubleday, 2008).

Saenz, Rogelio, Ph.D., Aurelia Lorena Murga. *Latino Issues: A Reference Handbook: A Reference Handbook* (Santa Barbara, CA: ABC-CLIO, 2011).

Safire, William, *Before the Fall: An Inside View of the Pre-Watergate White House* (Garden City, NY: Doubleday & Company, Inc., 1975).

Safire, William, *Safire's Political Dictionary*, (London: Oxford University Press, 2008).

Schatz, Thomas, *Boom & Bust: American Cinema in the 1940s*, (Berkeley, CA. University of California Press, 1997).

Schmitz, David, *Richard Nixon and the Vietnam War: The End of the American Century* (Lanham, MD: Rowman & Littlefield Publishers, 2014).

Schulzinger, Robert D., *A Time for War: The United States and Vietnam, 1941-1975* (New York: Oxford University Press, 1997).

Schuparra, Kurt, Tr *iumph of the Right: The Rise of the California Conservative Movement, 1945-1966* , (Armonk, NY: M.E. Sharpe, 1998).

Schwartz, Bernard, *Super Chief: Earl Warren and his Supreme Court – A Judicial Biography* (New York and London: New York University Press, 1983).

Schwartz, Bernard, *Unpublished Opinions of the Warren Court* (New York: Oxford University Press, 1985).

Sherman, Gabriel, *The Loudest Voice in the Room: How the Brilliant, Bombastic Roger Ailes Built FOX News – and Divided a Country* (New York: Random House, 2014).

Smith, Jean Edward, *FDR* (New York: Random House Trade Paperbacks, 2008).

Smith, Richard Norton, *An Uncommon Man* (New York: Simon & Schuster, 1984).

Smith, Richard Norton, *Thomas E. Dewey and his Times*, (New York: Simon & Schuster, 1982).

Stoll, Ira, *JFK: Conservative* (Boston: Houghton Mifflin Harcourt, 2013).

Stone, Roger, *Nixon's Secrets: The Rise, Fall, and Untold Truth about the President, Watergate, and the Pardon* (New York: Skyhorse Publishing, 2014).

Summers, Anthony, *Arrogance of Power: The Secret World of Richard Nixon* (New York: Viking, 2000).

Swift, Will, *Pat and Dick: The Nixons, An Intimate Portrait of a Marriage* (New York: Threshold Editions, 2014.

Swint, Kerwin, *Dark Genius: The Influential Career of Legendary Political Operative and Fox News Founder Roger Ailes* (New York: Union Square Press, 2008).

Thomas, Evan, *Being Nixon: A Man Divided*, (New York: Random House, 2015), Kindle edition.

Wefing, John, *The Life and Times of Richard J. Hughes: The Politics of Civility* (New Brunswick, NJ: Rivergate Books, 2009).

Weinberger, Caspar with Gretchen Roberts, *In The Arena: A Memoir of the 20th Century* (Washington, D.C.: Regnery Publishing, 2001).

Weiner, Tim, *One Man Against The World: The Tragedy of Richard Nixon* (New York: Henry Holt and Company, 2015).

White, F. Clinton and William Gill, *Suite 3505: The Story of the Draft Goldwater Movement*, (Ashland, OH: Ashbrook Press, 1967).

White, Theodore, *The Making of the President, 1960* (New York: Harper Perennial Political Classics, 2009).

White, Theodore, *The Making of the President, 1964* (New York: Antheneum Publishers, 1965).

White, Theodore, *The Making of the President, 1968* (New York: Atheneum Publishers, 1969).

Witcover, Jules, *The Making of an Ink-stained Wretch: Half a Century Pounding the Political Beat* (Baltimore: The Johns Hopkins University Press, 2005).

Witcover, Jules, *The Resurrection of Richard Nixon*, (New York: G.P. Putnam's Sons, 1970).

Woodward, Bob and Scott Armstrong, *The Brethren* (New York: Simon & Schuster, 1979).

von Tunzelmann, Alex, *Red Heat: Conspiracy, Murder and the Cold War in the Caribbean* (London, Simon & Schuster, 2011), ebook.

ARTICLES

"A Job Offer from Nixon Draws a 'Thanks, but No Thanks' Response," *Arlington Sun Gazette*, June 7, 2010.

"A Memo on Muckraking from the Publisher of Life," *LIFE*, June 6, 1969.

"ABC's Hagerty Defends Use of Hiss on TV Show," *The Evening Independent*, November 19, 1962.

"Academic Rights Defined by Nixon: He Backs Opposing War, but Not Rooting for Foe," *The New York Times*, June 5, 1966.

Adelman, Ken, "What I've Learned: You Do What Has to be Done," *The Washingtonian*, April 1988.

"Albert Wiggin Retires as Head of Chase Bank," *The Chicago Daily Tribune*, December 22, 1932.

"Alf Landon, G.O.P. Stand-Bearer, Dies at 100," *The New York Times*, October 13, 1987.

"Attorney Earl Adams, Architect of GOP Campaigns, Dies," *The Los Angeles Times*, April 2, 1986.

Auerbach, Stuart, "Toshiba Corp.'s Costly Lobbying," *The Washington Post*, October 13, 1988.

Baker, Katie, "Searching for Madame Nhu," *The Daily Beast*, September 24, 2013.

Balkan, Ed, "Helen Douglas Doused in Hay, Water Barrage," *The Daily Trojan*, May 17, 1950.

Barbas, Samantha, *When Privacy Almost Won: Time, Inc. v. Hill*, University of Pennsylvania Journal of Constitutional Law, Vol. 18, No. 2, December 2015.

Barnes, Bret, "Barry Goldwater, GOP Hero, Dies," *The Washington Post*, May 30, 1998.

"Barry Goldwater is Dead at 89; Conservatives' Standard Bearer." *The New York Times*, May 30, 1998.

Baumgold, Julie, "Nixon's New Life in New York," *New York*, June 9, 1980.

Beck, Susan, "Lone Star," *The American Lawyer*, June 2007.

Beck, Susan, "Rudy Giuliani Jumps to Greenberg Traurig," *The American Lawyer*, January 19, 2016.

Beckman, Aldo, "LBJ Surgery is Scheduled Wednesday," *The Chicago Tribune*, November 14, 1966.
Bennington, Ralph, "Nixons Lands in Frankfurt After Look Behind Wall," *Stars and Stripes*, June 26, 1963.
Black, Eric, "Politics By Gaffe: Recalling the 'Brainwashing' of George Romney," *MinnPost*, December 2, 2011.
Blum, Edward and Paul Harvey, "How (George) Romney Championed Civil Rights and Challenged His Church," *The Atlantic*, August 13, 2012.
Bonafede, Dom, "Profile/John Mitchell, Nixon's Legal Adviser, Plays Policy Role Far Beyond His Office," *National Journal*, October 2, 1971.
"Bond Counsel Proposal May Be Hard to Meet," *The Palm Beach Post*, July 28, 1985.
Boyd, James, "Nixon's Southern Strategy, 'It's All in the Charts,'" *The New York Times*, May 17, 1970.
Braden, Tom, "Nixon and Pepsi-Cola," *Boca Raton News*, November 23, 1972.
Broder, David, "Bellmon to Quit Nixon's Command; Sen. Tower is Prime Prospect for Job," *The Washington Post*, October 22, 1967.
Burgess, John, "Japan Worries that Scandal has Hurt Relations With U.S.," *The Washington Post*, July 16, 1987.
Carter, Paul, "Before He Was President, He Was A Local Attorney," *OC Lawyer*, March 2011.
Chambliss, Elizabeth, "The Shoe Still Fits," *Legal Affairs*, September-October 2005.
"Charles H. Percy Dies at 91; Moderate Former GOP Senator," *The Los Angeles Times*, September 18, 2011.
"Christian Right Leader Writes Off Giuliani," *CNN*, May 17, 2007.
Clines, Francis, "Nixon, On Visit to City, Greets 'Old Friends,'" *The New York Times*, November 25, 1972.
Clymer, Adam, *Charles Percy, Former Ill. Senator, Is Dead at 91*, *The New York Times*, September 17, 2011.
Cooper, Michael and Marjorie Connelly, "Giuliani has Decided to Zag While the Other Candidates Zig," *The New York Times*, December 20, 2007.
Corn, David, "As a Lawyer, Ted Cruz Defended Huge Jury Awards. As a Politician, He Opposed Them," Mother Jones, February 11, 2015.
"Could Mudge Rose Have Been Rescued?" *The Lawyer*, October 17, 1995.
Cox, Brent, "How Much More Money do Presidential Candidates Raise Today?" *The Awl*, November 6, 2012.
David, Mark, "Rock it Like a Rockefeller," *Variety*, February 27, 2008.
Denton, Sally, "'Tricky Dick' vs. The Pink Lady," *The Daily Beast*, November 16, 2009.
Dickenson, James, "Leonard Garment: Legal Adviser to the Powerful Spans Watergate, Iran Drama," The Washington Post, December 22, 1986.
Dickerson, John, "Never Goldwater: The Failed Attempt to Wrest the 1964 GOP Nomination From the Arizona Senator and the Birth of the Modern GOP, *Slate*, May 12, 2016.
Dickinson, Tom, "How Roger Ailes Built the Fox News Fear Factory, *Rolling Stone*, May 25, 2011.
"Dominican Military Chief Was a Major at Age 3; His Father Made Trujillo Jr. a Teen-Age General He Drew Criticism in U.S. Over Lavish Entertaining." *The New York Times*, June 2, 1961.
"Dr. Parkinson Quits as Nixon Group's Chief," *The Chicago Tribune*, August 17, 1967.
Drummond, Roscoe, "Pat Nixon Made Decision To Move, Get Out of Political Fire," *The Los Angeles Times*, May 16, 1963.Drummond, Roscoe, "Will Never Run Again, Nixon Insists," *The Boston Globe*. May 14, 1963.
Elsasser, Glen, "Nixon Announces Candidacy for Nomination for President," *The Chicago Tribune*, February 2, 1968.
Evans, Rowland and Robert Novak, "Kuchel Stays Potent Force Even Out of Governor's Race," *Lawrence Journal-World*, September 28, 1965.
Evans, Rowland and Robert Novak, "Nixon's Big Weakness is Lack of Financing," *The Los Angeles Times*, June 3, 1964.
Farrell, John A., "When Nixon Met the Press," *Politico*, August 6, 2014.

Fisher, Ian, "Wayne Dumont, Jr., 77, is Dead; Was Dean of New Jersey Senate," *The New York Times*, March 21, 1992.
"Forbes's Hunt for Richest 400," *The New York Times*, September 11, 1982.
Frappier, Jon, "Invisible Power Brokers: The Nixon-Mitchell Law Firm," *North American Congress on Latin America*, Vol. 7, No. 9, November 1973.
Garment, Leonard, "Annals of Law: The Hill Case," *The New Yorker*, April 17, 1989.
Glass, Andrew, "Senate Spikes Abe Fortas' Supreme Court Nomination, Oct. 1, 1968," *Politico*, October 1, 2015.
Goldberg, Carey, "The Mudge Rose Firm Enters the Tar Pit of Legal History," *The New York Times*, October 1, 1995.
Goldstein, Tom, "Business and the Law" The New York Times, March 9, 1979.
"Goldwater Set to Reveal Plans at Home Friday," *The Bulletin*, December 31, 1963.
Graham, David, "If You Give Me a Week, I Might Think of One," *The Atlantic*, May 20, 2016.
Graham, Fred, "Cuban Says U.S. Knew of Counterfeiting Plan," *The New York Times,* June 10, 1965.
Graham, Fred, "Nixon's Former Law Firm Here Prospers Amid Unwanted Public Attention," *The New York Times*, September 26, 1970.
Gray, Jerry, "Florio's Spotlight Dims, but Stage Widens," The New York Times, May 29, 1994.
Greenberg, David, "It's a Myth That Nixon Acquiesced in 1960," *The Los Angeles Times*, November 10, 2000, accessed June 11, 2017, http://articles.latimes.com/2000/nov/10/local/me-49741.
Greenhouse, Linda, "Ex-Justice Fortas Dies at 71; Shaped Historic Rulings on Rights," *The New York Times*, April 7, 1982.
Gregory, Joseph R., "Madame Nhu, Vietnam War Lightning Rod, Dies," *The New York Times*, April 26, 2011.
Haley, John O., *The New Regulatory Regime for Foreign Lawyers in Japan: An Escape from Freedom*, UCLA Pacific Basin Law Journal, Vol. 1-2 (1986).
"Harlan Logan, 90, Editor and Publisher," *The New York Times*, January 5, 1995.
Henderson, William and Rachel Zahorsky, "The Pedigree Problem: Are Law School Ties Choking the Profession?" *ABA Journal*, July 1, 2012.
"He's a Democrat: Riegle Switches Parties," *The Argus-Press*, February 27, 1973.
"High Court Hears Argument by Nixon, His First Before It," *The New York Times*, April 28, 1966.
Hill, Gladwin, "Nixon Leaves Fate to G.O.P. Chiefs," *The New York Timems*, September 24, 1952.
Hoffman, Paul, "Mudge Rose Guthrie & Alexander: The Firm to See?" *New York Magazine*, April 26, 1971.
Huebner, Lee, "The Checkers Speech after 60 Years," *The Atlantic*, September 22, 2012.
Hunter, Jack, "Linwood Holton's Long Quest for the Governorship of Virginia and its Impact on the Growth of the Republican Party," *University of Richmond*, June 1972, master's thesis, accessed March 28, 2017, http://scholarship.richmond.edu/cgi/viewcontent.cgi?article=1350&context=masters-theses.
Hunter, Marjorie, "Role of Nixon's Old Firm in Bond Issue Criticized," *The New York Times*, July 30, 1971.
"I Quit Klan: Black's Defense," *The Chicago Tribune*, October 2, 1937.
Jackson, Harold, "Howard K. Smith," *The Guardian*, February 19, 2002.
Jaeger, Laurence, "Can McGovern Be Sold Through the Mails?" *New York Magazine*, September 18, 1972.
Jensen, Michael, "Mitchell and His Law Firm: Mudge Rose Beneficiary Of New Business," *The New York Times*, May 7, 1972.
"John Milem Obituary," *The Columbian*, accessed on March 22, 2017, http://obits.columbian.com/obituaries/columbian/obituary.aspx?pid=162415934#sthash.q7VbOTeR.dpuf.
"John N. Mitchell Dies at 75: Major Figure in Watergate," *The New York Times*, November 10, 1988.
Jones, Janice, "Nixon's Law Office," *The Los Angeles Times*, July 18, 1990.

Jones, Tim, "Dewey Defeats Truman," *The Chicago Tribune*, accessed on January 16, 2016, http://www.chicagotribune.com/news/nationworld/politics/chi-chicagodays-deweydefeats-story-story.html.

"Judge Dismissed a Lawsuit Over Firm's Firing By Client," *The Wall Street Journal*, September 25, 1997.

"Justice Black Dies at 85: Served on Court for 34 Years," *The New York Times*, September 25, 1971.

Kihss, Peter, "Nixon, Happy as New Yorker, Says Job is Law, Not Politics," *The New York Times*, December 29, 1963.

Koh, Elizabeth, "Rubio: Cruz, Who Once Defended Chinese Company, Can't be 'Tough on China,'" *The Dallas Morning News*, January 25, 2016.

Kohn, Alan, "Effects of Nixon Legacy on Mudge, Rose," *The New York Law Journal*, January 19, 1978.

Kolesar, John, "Case History of a Political Campaign Issue," *The Tuscaloosa News*, September 2, 1965.

Krusten, Maarja, "Speculating about Slurred Speech," *The Washington Post*, December 7, 1996.

Lait, Matt, "Looking Back at the 1962 Gubernatorial Race: Debate: Edmund G. (Pat) Brown and ex-President's former campaign manager discuss the election at Richard Nixon Library & Birthplace," *The Los Angeles Times*, March 22, 1992.

Lambert, William, "Fortas: A Question of Ethics," *LIFE*, May 9, 1969.

"Lawyers and Legal Events," *New York Law Review*, 7.3 N. Y. L. Rev. 107, 114 (1929).

Leaf, Janet, "'Cleopatra' at Half-Way Point," *Sunday Gazette-Mail*, January 7, 1962.

Lenzner, Robert, "Remember the Admirable Al Gordon," *Forbes*, May 27, 2009. http://www.forbes.com/2009/05/27/kidder-peabody-harvard-personal-finance-investing-ideas-al-gordon.html.

Lewis, Neil, "THE SUPREME COURT: Woman in the News; Rejected as a Clerk, Chosen as a Justice: Ruth Joan Bader Ginsburg," *The New York Times*, June 15, 1993.

Li, Victor, "50-Year Story of the Miranda Warning has the Twists of a Cop Show," *ABA Journal*, August 1, 2016.

Li, Victor, "Golden Parachute," *The American Lawyer*, October 2012.

Li, Victor, "Help Not Wanted," *The American Lawyer*, May 2013.

Li, Victor, "Joseph Flom, Pioneering M&A Lawyer and Skadden Name Partner, Dies at 87," *The Am Law Daily*, February 23, 2011, accessed January 10, 2016, http://amlawdaily.typepad.com/amlawdaily/2011/02/flomobit.html.

Li, Victor, "Leaning Left: The AMA At a Crossroads," *The Huffington Post*, May 25, 2011.

Li, Victor, "Lifetime Achiever: Stuart Eizenstat," *The American Lawyer*, September 20, 2013.

Li, Victor, "Republican Governors Association Doubles Down on Negative Ad Campaign Against Lawyer," *ABA Journal*, May 1, 2014.

Li, Victor "Texas GOP Senate Hopeful Attacked by Primary Foe for Being Partner at 'Liberal' Morgan Lewis," *The American Lawyer*, March 8, 2012.

Lightblau, Eric, "Leonard Garment, Lawyer and Nixon Adviser During Watergate, Dies at 89," *The New York Times*, July 15, 2013.

Lincoln, Jr., Frank, "Presidential Transition, 1968-1969," *ABA Journal*, June, 1969.

Lydon, Christopher, "Conservative Architect of Security Plan Tom Charles Huston," *The New York Times*, May 24, 1973.

MacAskill, Ewen, "Giuliani's Diastrous Strategy," *The Guardian*, January 30, 2008.

Manchester, William, "Rock Bottom in America," *New York Magazine*, August 5, 1974.

Mansel, Tim, "I Shot the Cruelest Dictator in the Americas," *BBC*, May 28, 2011.

Martin, Douglas, "Clement Stone Dies at 100: Built Empire on Optimism," *The New York Times*, September 5, 2002.

Marutollo, Joseph, "Nixon the Lawyer," *Federal Bar Council Quarterly*, June/July/August 2017.

"Marxism and Vietnam Were Issues in 1965 N.J. Gubernatorial Race," *The Observer*, September 29, 2009.

McFadden, Robert, "John V. Lindsay, Mayor and Maverick, Dies at 79," *The New York Times*, December 21, 2000.
"McKeesport: The First Great Debate," *The Pittsburgh Post Gazette*, October 21, 1976.
McMorris, Frances, "Former Mudge Partner Sues Cigna Over Firm's Demise," *The Wall Street Journal*, May 9, 1997.
Mintz, Morton, "Law Firm Accused of Aiding One Client Over Another," *The Washington Post*, August 30, 1977.
Mitchell, Greg, "When JFK Backed Nixon in His Notorious Race vs. Helen Gahagan Douglas," *The Nation*, November 19, 2013.
Moore, John W., "Thinking Big: A Tale of Two Law Firms," *National Journal*, September 17, 1994.
Morris, Roger, "Nixon Goes to Europe," *The New York Times*, April 16, 2009.
Naravez, Alfonso, "L. Nicholas Ruwe, Ex-Ambassador, 56; Assisted Presidents," *The New York Times*, May 4, 1990.
"Nation: California: Career's End," *TIME*, November 16, 1962, accessed 9 January 2016, http://content.time.com/time/magazine/article/0,9171,829391,00.html.
"Nation: Progressive Conservative." TIME, June 15, 1962.
Nelson, Eric, "John Dean: White House is in a 'Cover-Up Mode,'" The Daily Kos, March 20, 2017.
Nelson, Valerie, "Ex-Legislator Challenged Nixon," *The Los Angeles Times*, April 11, 2008.
"New Jersey: The Genovese Campaign," *TIME*, October 22, 1965.
"Nixon Confers in Geneva on Trujillo Estate Suits," *The New York Times*. May 5, 1965.
"Nixon Degree Protest," *The New York Herald Tribune*, April 15, 1966.
"Nixon Essay on U.S. Hailed," *The Chicago Tribune*, December 8, 1963.
"Nixon Flies to N. Y., Visits Old Law Firm," *The Chicago Tribune*, November 25, 1972.
"Nixon, in Texas, asks for polite Kennedy reception," *The Dallas Morning News*. November 22, 1963.
"Nixon Says He May Move to New York," *The Los Angeles Times*, May 2, 1963.
"Nixon Sees GOP Victory in 1966," *Schenectady Gazette*, December 27, 1965.
"Nixon Upholds Rights of Privacy In Arguing First High Court Case," *The Washington Post*, April 28, 1966.
"Nixon Visits Wall: Calls it an 'Ugly Eyesore,'" *The Chicago Tribune*, July 24, 1963.
"Nixon vs. Khrushchev: The 1959 Kitchen Debate," *The Huffington Post*, accessed March 28, 2017, http://www.huffingtonpost.com/adst/nixon-vs-khrushchev--the_b_7857916.html.
Nixon, Richard, "Four Academic Freedoms," *College and University Journal*, Summer 1966.
Noble, Holcomb, "C. Arnholt Smith, 97, Banker and Padres Chief Before Fall," *The New York Times*, June 11, 1996.
O'Connor, Colleen, "'Pink Right Down to Her Underwear': Politics: The 1950 Senate campaign of Richard Nixon against Helen Douglas reached an unequaled low. Comparison is unfair to John Van de Kamp." *The Los Angeles Times*. April 9, 1990.
O'Neill, Tip and William Novak, "The 1st Tip-Off About Nixon," *The Washington Post*, September 14, 1987.
"On the Brink of Scandal, LBJ Showed How to Act Very Fast," *The Chicago Tribune*, March 28, 1999.
Osius, Larry, "361 Delegates Firmly for Barry; 316 Others Favor Him," *Eugene Register-Guard*, June 18, 1964.
Ostrow, Ronald, "High Court Backs Press in False Report Cases," *The Los Angeles Times*, January 10, 1967.
Pace, Eric, "Herbert Brownell, 92, Eisenhower Attorney General, Dies," *The New York Times*, May 2, 1996
"Pat Makes White House 'Live' for Tourists," *The Pittsburgh Press*, September 3, 1970.
Pearson, Drew, "El Paso Case Dismissal Too Hasty," *The Washington Post*, March 26, 1969.
Pearson, Drew, "Now a Word About Nixon's Sponsors," *The Los Angeles Times*, October 15, 1968.
Pearson, Drew and Jack Anderson, "Nixon Called Nasser Wise, Strong," *Washington Post*, October 28, 1968.

Pearson, Drew and Jack Anderson, "What Are Nixon's Regulatory Views?" *The Washington Post*, October 25, 1968.
Peppard, Alan, "Kennedy Rival Nixon Left Dallas as JFK Arrived in November 1963," *The Dallas Morning News*, November 2, 2013.
Pierson, John, "Former Law Partners of Nixon and Mitchell Add New Clients," *The Wall Street Journal*, September 14, 1970.
"Political Ghost of Warren Stalks Nixon in 1962 Race," *The Los Angeles Times*, May 13, 1962.
Pretto, Christina, " Mudge Rose Votes To Disband Firm By End of the Year," *Bond Buyer*, October 3, 1995.
Pringle, Peter, "'We're heading into nut country': President Kennedy said this to an aide as he began his fatal visit to Texas thirty years ago. Here Peter Pringle evokes Dallas as it was then, a hostile place which cared very little for the dream that died there," *The Independent*, November 20, 1993
Reich, Kenneth, "Ex-Senator Kuchel Dies; Last of the State's GOP Progressives," *The Los Angeles Times*, November 23, 1994
Reeves, Richard, "Nixon's Men are Smart But No Swingers," *The New York Times*, September 29, 1968.
"Richard Nixon Goes to Work With Law Firm," *The Deseret News*, March 14, 1961.
Roberts, Sam, "Capturing the Life of a Striver Who Fell Short of the White House: Richard Norton Smith Dissects Nelson Rockefeller," *The New York Times*, October 14, 2014.
Rosenblatt, Robert, "H ow 'Swat Team' of Toshiba Lobbyists Took on Congress-and Won," *The Washington Post*, May 1, 1988.
Safire, William, "The Cold War's Hot Kitchen," *The New York Times*, July 23, 2009.
Salem (MA) Register. Feb. 18, 1861.
Saxon, Wolfgang, "Donald Nixon, 72, Dies In California," *The New York Times*, June 30, 1987.
Saxon, Wolfgang, "Franklin B. Lincoln, Aide in Transition Of Nixon, Dies at 85," *The New York Times*, November 5, 1993.
Saxton, Wolfgang, "John Brosnan: Former Head of State U. and Regents Unit," *The New York Times*, 15 April 1982.
Schorr, Daniel, "The Secret Nixon-LBJ War," *The Washington Post*, May 28, 1995.
Schudel, Matt, "Thomas W. Evans, Early Backer of Nixon in 1968, Dies at 82," *The Washington Post*, June 18, 2013.
Schwartzman, Paul, "Love and the Law," *New York Daily News*, May 13, 1997.
Sears, John, "The Nation: With Nixon: 'Politics Is Great--Except for People,'" *The Los Angeles Times*, April 24, 1994.
Seeger, Murray, "Nixon Pledges to Restrict Regulatory Agency Moves: Would Appoint New Officials to Reverse Trend," *The Los Angeles Times,* October 17, 1968.
Semple, Jr., Robert, "Core of Nixon Advisers and Experts Is Advancing His Cause for 1968," *The New York Times,* Oct 23, 1967.
Semple, Jr., Robert, "Nixon Backs Eventual End of Draft," *The New York Times*, November 17, 1967.
Shanahan, Eileen, "Curbs on Likely on Giant Mergers," *The New York Times*, June 6, 1969.
Shearer, Lloyd, "The Vanishing Playboys," *St. Petersburg Times*, August 15, 1965.
Skelton, George, "Sacramento's Savvy Sophomore," *The Los Angeles Times*, September 4, 2000.
Stall, Bill, "RICHARD NIXON: 1913-1994: Nixon's Relations With California Ran Hot and Cold," *The Los Angeles Times*, April 24, 1994.
Stap, Dan. "Mustache Man." *The Milwaukee Journal*. 28 November 1982.
Stevens, Amy, "Mudge Rose Ills Mount as Clients and Partners Leave," *The Associated Press*, March 31, 1995.
Stevens, Amy and Edward Felsenthal, "Law Firm Finds Complacency Can Kill --- U.S.'s Venerable Mudge Will Be Liquidated," The Wall Street Journal, Oct 3, 1995.
Stout, David, "William P. Rogers, Who Served as Nixon's Secretary of State, Is Dead at 87," *The New York Times*, January 4, 2001.

Sullivan, Casey, "Has Big Law Associate Bonus Season Already Started?" *Bloomberg BNA*, October 16, 2015.
Tartar, Andre and Eric Benson, "The Forever Campaign," *New York Magazine*, October 14, 2012.
Templer, Robert, "Madame Nhu Obituary," *The Guardian*, April 26, 2011.
"The Sharp New Line on Antitrust," *BusinessWeek*, June 21, 1969.
Thomas, Evan, "Did Nixon Start the Politics of Hate?" Newsweek, May 8, 2008.
"Tom Dewey Sticks to His Albany Knitting," *LIFE*, March 20, 1944.
"The Am Law 50," *The American Lawyer*, July/August 1985.
"The Measure of a President," *The New York Times*, October 6, 2008.
"The NLJ 250," *The National Law Journal*, September 28, 1987.
Thimmesch, Nick, "Why Are These Men for Nixon?" *Newsday*. January 27, 1968.
Thomas, Evan, "Why Nixon Hated Georgetown," *Politico*, June 4, 2015.
Thomas, Jr., Robert McG., "Patrick Frawley Jr., 75, Ex-Owner of Schick," *The New York Times*, November 9, 1988.
Torry, Jack, "Did Nixon deliberately prolong Vietnam War?" *The Dayton Daily News*, April 17, 2017.
Torry, Saundra, "Leonard Garment Finds a Challenge in Expansion Puzzle," *The Washington Post*, November 22, 1993.
Triedman, Julie, "The Am Law 100, the Early Numbers: Davis Polk Posts Record-High Revenue, PPP," *The American Lawyer*, February 13, 2015.
"True Crime Inspires Tense Play: The Ordeal of a Family Trapped by Convicts Gives Broadway a New Thriller: 'The Desperate Hours,'" *LIFE*, February 28, 1955.
"Trujillo's Son Now in Switzerland," *The New York Times*. November 25, 1964.
Turtis, Richard Lee. "A World Destroyed, A Nation Imposed: The 1937 Haitian Massacre in the Dominican Republic". *Hispanic American Historical Review*, August 2002.
"W.H. Hogeland, 68, Lawyer and Analyst," *The New York Times*, July 7, 1996.
"Washington Insight," The Los Angeles Times, April 18, 1994.
Wheeler, Keith, "The Campaigns Get Cracking," *LIFE*, October 5, 1962.
"Wife Kept Lee Harvey Oswald from Shooting Richard Nixon," *Lodi News-Sentinel*, September 19, 1977.
"William Gavin, "Speechwriter for Nixon, Reagan, Lawmakers, Dies at 80," *The Washington Times*, June 30, 2015.
Williams, Brian, "The 'Last Press Conference.'" *The Daily Nightly*. November 7, 2007.
Williams, Mason B., "Yes, David Dinkins was a criminal justice pioneer: Hillary Clinton was right to praise the former mayor as 'a leader we can look to' as we reform policing in America," *The New York Daily News*, April 30, 2015.
"Winners and Losers, '68," *LIFE*, January 10, 1969.
Woodward, Bob, "Fortas Tie To Wolfson Is Detailed," *The Washington Post*, January 23, 1977.

ARCHIVAL COLLECTIONS

Richard Nixon – Pre-Presidential Papers
Thomas Evans – Personal Papers

ORAL HISTORIES

Alexander, Lamar, Interview by Timothy Naftali, June 27, 2007, Richard Nixon Oral History Project, Richard Nixon Presidential Library and Museum.
Anderson, Martin, Interview by Jim Young, Stephen Knott and Allison Asher, December 10-11, 2001, accessed April 14, 2017, Oral History Project, UVA Miller Center.

Bull, Stephen, Interview by Timothy Naftali, June 25, 2007, Richard Nixon Oral History Project, Richard Nixon Presidential Library and Museum.
Califano, Joseph, Interview by Timothy Naftali, April 3, 2007, Richard Nixon Oral History Project, Richard Nixon Presidential Library and Museum.
Chapin, Dwight, Interview by Timothy Naftali, April 2, 2007, Richard Nixon Oral History Project, Richard Nixon Presidential Library and Museum.
DeMuth, Christopher, Interview by Timothy Naftali, January 14, 2008, Richard Nixon Oral History Project, Richard Nixon Presidential Library and Museum.
Ellsworth, Robert, Interviewby Timothy Naftali, January 30, 2008, Richard Nixon Oral History Project, Richard Nixon Presidential Library and Museum.
Garment, Leonard, Interview by Timothy Naftali, April 6, 2007, Richard Nixon Oral History Project, Richard Nixon Presidential Library and Museum.
Haldeman, H.R., Interview by Raymond Geselbracht ad Fred Graboske, August 13, 1987.
Huston, Tom Charles, Interview by Timothy Naftali, April 30, 2008, Richard Nixon Oral History Project, Richard Nixon Presidential Library and Museum.
Huston, Tom Charles, Interview by Timothy Naftali, June 27, 2008, Richard Nixon Oral History Project, Richard Nixon Presidential Library and Museum.
Kampelman, Ambassador Max M., Interview by Charles Stuart Kennedy, June 24, 2003, Association for Diplomatic Studies and Training Foreign Affairs Oral History Project.
Klein, Herbert, Interview by Timothy Naftali, February 20, 2007, Richard Nixon Oral History Project, Richard Nixon Presidential Library and Museum.
Price, Raymond, Interview by Timothy Naftali, April 4, 2007, Richard Nixon Oral History Project, Richard Nixon Presidential Library and Museum.
Safire, William, Interview by Timothy Naftali, March 27, 2008, Richard Nixon Oral History Project, Richard Nixon Presidential Library and Museum.

AUTHOR INTERVIEWS

Buchanan, Patrick, Interview by Victor Li, June 21, 2017.
Chapin, Dwight, Interview by Li, May 9, 2016.
Eizenstat, Stuart, Interview by Li, October 29, 2016.
Milgrim, Roger, Interview by Li, October 29, 2016.
Parker, Douglas, Interview with Li, May 18, 2016.
Sears, John, Interview by Victor Li, February 16, 2016.
Steckel, Raymond, Interview by Victor Li, November 2, 2016.
Stone, Richard, Interview by Victor Li, May 24, 2016.
Zoeller, Donald, Interview by Victor Li, February 1, 2016.

OTHER INTERVIEWS

Ehrlichman, John, interview by Tom Evans, January 28, 1988, transcript.
Guthrie, Randolph, interview by Tom Evans, part 1, March 3, 1981, transcript.
Haldeman, H.R., Interview by Tom Evans, January 26, 1988.
Klein, Herbert, exit interview by John R. Nesbitt and Terry W. Good, July 13, 1973, accessed January 29, 2017, http://www.nixonlibrary.gov/virtuallibrary/documents/exitinterviews/klein-exit.pdf.
Mitchell, John, interview by Tom Evans, February 7, 1985.
Nixon, Richard, interview by Tom Evans, March 15, 1983, transcript.
Rose, Milton, interview by Tom Evans, January 27, 1981, transcript.
Rose, Milton, interview by Tom Evans, November 15, 1989, transcript.
Sorg, Frank, Interview by Tom Evans, December 6, 1989, transcript.
Vaughn, David, Interview by Evans, September 5, 1989, transcript.

Whitaker, John, exit interview by Susan Yowell, May 4, 1963, accessed April 16, 2017, https://nixonlibrary.gov/virtuallibrary/documents/exitinterviews/whitaker-exit.pdf.

Woods, Rose Mary, interview by Tom Evans, February 27, 1988, transcript.

WEBSITES

"An Appraisal of Manila," Issuu.com/RichardNixonFoundation, accessed March 29, 2017, http://issuu.com/richardnixonfoundation/docs/an_appraisal_of_manila?e=7983691/12996707

Ansart, Dorothy and Judith Grier, "Inventory to the Records of the Office of Public Information on the Vietnam War Teach-Ins, 1965-1966," Rutgers University, accessed March 28, 2017, http://www2.scc.rutgers.edu/ead/uarchives/teachinsb.html.

"Biography of Richard M. Nixon," Richard Nixon Presidential Library and Museum, accessed January 10, 2016, http://www.nixonlibrary.gov/thelife/nixonbio.pdf

Bregman, Rutger, "The Bizarre Tale of President Nixon and His Basic Income Bill," *The Correspondent*, accessed April 20, 2017, https://thecorrespondent.com/4503/the-bizarre-tale-of-president-nixon-and-his-basic-income-bill/173117835-c34d6145.

Burnett, Jim, "Mount Who? How Did This Famous Park Get Its Name?" *National Parks Traveler*, Accessed on January 16, 2016, http://www.nationalparkstraveler.com/2009/06/mount-who-how-did-famous-park-get-its-name.

"Carter Ledyard Alumnus Franklin Roosevelt Is Featured in PBS's The Roosevelts: An Intimate History," Carter Ledyard & Milburn, accessed on January 16, 2016, http://www.clm.com/newsitem.cfm?ID=2602.

"Cleary Gottlieb Steen & Hamilton," *The American Lawyer*, accessed on January 16, 2016, http://www.americanlawyer.com/law-firm-profiles-result?firmname=Cleary+Gottlieb+Steen+%26+Hamilton.

"Cleopatra," Turner Classic Movies, accessed on February 27, 2017, http://www.tcm.com/this-month/article/102757|102758/Cleopatra.html.

Cohen, Michael, "Nelson Rockefeller Enters Presidential Race," OUP Blog - Oxford University Press, accessed April 30, 2016, http://blog.oup.com/2016/04/rockefeller-1968-presidential-race/.

Coleman, David, "The Fourteenth Day: JFK and the Aftermath of the Cuban Missile Crisis," JFK14thDay.com, accessed January 9, 2016, http://jfk14thday.com/jfk-pat-brown-jerry-brown/.

Coleman, David, "LBJ's Presidential Approval Ratings," History in Pieces, accessed March 27, 2017, http://historyinpieces.com/research/lbj-presidential-approval-ratings.

Coleman, David, "Nixon's Presidential Approval Ratings," History in Pieces, accessed April 1, 2017, http://historyinpieces.com/research/nixon-approval-ratings.

"Confessions of a Republican," Wikipedia, accessed March 27, 2017, https://en.wikipedia.org/wiki/Confessions_of_a_Republican.

Cook, Rhodes, "Like Father, Like Son? The Romneys Run for President," Larry Sabato's Crystal Ball, September 20, 2007 accessed April 1, 2017, https://web.archive.org/web/20080606225654/http://www.centerforpolitics.org/crystalball/article.php?id=FRC2007092001.

Coudert Brothers Acquires Corporate Group from Mudge, Rose, Guthrie, Alexander & Ferndon," *The Free Library*, October 3, 1995, accessed April 1, 2017, https://www.thefreelibrary.com/COUDERT+BROTHERS+ACQUIRES+CORPORATE+GROUP+FROM+MUDGE,+ROSE,+GUTHRIE,...-a017511223.

"Davis Polk & Wardwell Firm Profile," *The American Lawyer*, accessed on January 16, 2016, http://www.americanlawyer.com/law-firm-profiles-result?firmname=Davis+Polk+%26+Wardwell.

Deignan, Tom, "Irish mafia takes another hit with death of JFK aide Ralph Dungan," *Irish Central*, October 17, 2013, accessed March 27, 2017, http://www.irishcentral.com/opinion/

others/irish-mafia-takes-another-hit-with-death-of-jfk-aide-ralph-dungan-228158071-238258461.html.

"Dewey Ballantine LLP Firm History," Dewey Ballantine, accessed on January 16, 2016, http://web.archive.org/web/20030828143512/http://www.deweyballantine.com/history/history_fr.htm.

"Dewey Ballantine LLP History," Funding Universe, accessed on January 16, 2016, http://www.fundinguniverse.com/company-histories/dewey-ballantine-llp-history/.

Edwards, Lee, "Barry M. Goldwater: The Most Consequential Loser in American Politics," The Heritage Foundation, July 3, 2014, accessed March 27, 2017, http://www.heritage.org/research/reports/2014/07/barry-m-goldwater-the-most-consequential-loser-in-american-politics.

"Election Polls -- Vote by Groups, 1960-1964," Gallup, accessed March 28, 2017, http://www.gallup.com/poll/9454/election-polls-vote-groups-19601964.aspx.

"FDR," PBS.org, accessed 23 March 2016, http://www.pbs.org/wgbh/americanexperience/features/transcript/fdr-transcript/.

"Firm History," Hughes Hubbard & Reed, accessed on 16 January 2016, http://www.hugheshubbard.com/aboutus/Pages/FirmHistory.aspx.

Folder: 53-36-Staff Secretary Paper Project, Richard Nixon Library, accessed September 14, 2017, https://www.nixonlibrary.gov/virtuallibrary/documents/contested/contested_box_53/Contested-53-36.pdf.

"Frank Gannon's Interview With Richard Nixon, Part 1," University of Georgia, September 7, 1983, accessed March 29, 2017, http://www.libs.uga.edu/media/collections/nixon/ohms/sept7part1.html.

"Frank Gannon's Interview With Richard Nixon, Part 2," University of Georgia, September 7, 1983, accessed March 29, 2017, http://www.libs.uga.edu/media/collections/nixon/ohms/sept7part2.html.

Gannon, Frank, "2.2.68," Richard Nixon Foundation, accessed April 1, 2017, https://www.nixonfoundation.org/2009/02/2268/.

Hatch, Denny, "Obama's $750 Million Juggernaut," *Target Marketing*, December 16, 2008, accessed April 1, 2017, http://www.targetmarketingmag.com/article/the-father-direct-mail-political-fundraising-401158/all/.

"History," Davis Polk & Wardwell, accessed on 16 January 2016, http://www.davispolk.com/firm/history/.

HelmerReenberg, November 21, 1963 - Richard M. Nixon in Dallas, Texas, YouTube video, 2:03, Posted December 19, 2012, https://www.youtube.com/watch?v=UkeCQWk9ID8.

Heyni, Roboci, "Richard Nixon on 'The Jack Paar Program' (March 8, 1963), YouTube video, 2:47, posted July 4, 2015, https://www.youtube.com/watch?v=PctLLLVqMrM.

"Hubert Humphrey Presidential Campaign, 1968," Wikipedia, accessed April 1, 2017, https://en.wikipedia.org/wiki/Hubert_Humphrey_presidential_campaign,_1968.

"Intelligence-Report on CIA Assassination Plots (1), Ford Library Museum, accessed on March 24, 2017, https://www.fordlibrarymuseum.gov/library/document/0005/7324009.pdf.

Karp, Josh and Tom Barry, "We are Family: Relatives Who Play and Work Well Together," *Wisconsin Super Lawyers*, December 2007, accessed March 27, 2017, http://www.superlawyers.com/wisconsin/article/we-are-family/f2b3e6ff-2139-4e08-81b1-a11fc024de5c.html.

Kates, James, "Kicking Nixon: Howard K. Smith and the Commentator's Imperative," ARNet, accessed on January 24, 2016, http://www.americansc.org.uk/Online/Nixon.html.

"Lyndon B. Johnson, Address Before a Joint Session of the Congress, November 27, 1963," The American Presidency Project, accessed March 26, 2017, http://www.presidency.ucsb.edu/ws/?pid=25988.

"Lyndon Johnson and Everett Dirksen on 2 November 1968," Presidential Recordings, Digital Edition, accessed April 1, 2017, http://prde.upress.virginia.edu/conversations/4006123.

"Manila Summit Conference, Joint Communique," VietnamWar.govt.nz, accessed March 29, 2017, http://www.vietnamwar.govt.nz/sites/default/files/documents/manila-summit-communique.pdf

"The Marriage of Tricia Nixon and Edward Finch Cox," *The Nixon Foundation*, June 12, 2014, accessed June 30, 2016, https://www.nixonfoundation.org/2014/06/welcome-marriage-tricia-nixon-edward-finch-cox/.

"Maurice H .Stans," Accounting Hall of Fame, The Ohio State University Fisher College of Business, accessed September 1, 2017, https://fisher.osu.edu/academic-departments/amis/accounting-hall-fame/membership-hall/maurice-h.-stans.

Meet The Press Transcript for Dec. 9, 2007: Rudy Giuliani," *NBC News*, December 9, 2007, accessed April 1, 2017, http://www.nbcnews.com/id/22170668/ns/meet_the_press/t/meet-press-transcript-dec/#.WLBwgG8rKHs.

"MI District 7 – R Primary," Our Campaigns, accessed March 29, 2017, http://www.ourcampaigns.com/RaceDetail.html?RaceID=758664.

"MI District 7," Our Campaigns, accessed March 29, 2017, http://www.ourcampaigns.com/RaceDetail.html?RaceID=150341.

Montaner, Carlos Alberto, *Trujillo: The Most Insane Dictator*, Real Clear Politics, March 18, 2006, accessed March 24, 2017, http://www.realclearpolitics.com/articles/2006/03/trujillo_the_most_insane_dicta.html.

Murray, Noel, "Nixon Gets Socked in Laugh-In's Most Famous, and Influential, Five Seconds, The A.V. Club, September 13, 2012, accessed April 1, 2017, http://www.avclub.com/article/nixon-gets-socked-in-ilaugh-inis-most-famous-and-i-84881.

Ngô Đình Nhu," Wikipedia, accessed March 22, 2017, https://en.wikipedia.org/wiki/Ng%C3%B4_%C4%90%C3%ACnh_Nhu.

"Nixon vs. Khrushchev — The 1959 Kitchen Debate," Association for Diplomatic Studies & Training, accessed January, 15 2016, http://adst.org/2015/07/nixon-vs-khrushchev-the-1959-kitchen-debate/.

"October 7, 1960 Debate Transcript," Commission on Presidential Debates, accessed March 26, 2017, http://www.debates.org/index.php?page=october-7-1960-debate-transcript.

"Our History," Simpson Thacher & Bartlett, accessed on January 16, 2016, http://www.stblaw.com/about-us/our-history.

"President Richard Nixon's Daily Diary, Nov. 16-30, 1972," The Richard Nixon Library and Museum, accessed April 1, 2017, https://www.nixonlibrary.gov/virtuallibrary/documents/PDD/1972/088%20November%2016-30%201972.pdf.

"Primary Resources: Checkers Speech, 1952," PBS.org, accessed January 9, 2016, http://www.pbs.org/wgbh/americanexperience/features/primary-resources/nixon-checkers/.

"Rejected by the Firm," Makers, accessed January 10, 2016, http://www.makers.com/moments/rejected-firm

"Richard Nixon: Address Accepting Presidential Nomination at the Republican National Convention in Chicago," July 28, 1960, accessed April 1, 2017, http://www.presidency.ucsb.edu/ws/?pid=25974.

"Richard Nixon, Inaugural Address, January 20, 1969," The American Presidency Project, accessed April 1, 2017, http://www.presidency.ucsb.edu/ws/?pid=1941.

"Richard Nixon Presidential Recordings, Nixon Conversation 002-002," Miller Center, University of Virginia, accessed April 1, 2017, http://archive.millercenter.org/presidentialrecordings/rmn-002-002.

"Richard M. Nixon: White House Farewell," The History Place: Great Speeches Collection, accessed February 13, 2016, http://www.historyplace.com/speeches/nixon-farewell.htm.

"Ronald Reagan: A Time for Choosing," American Rhetoric, accessed April 1, 2017, http://www.americanrhetoric.com/speeches/ronaldreaganatimeforchoosing.htm.

Sabato, Jr., Larry, "The Ball of Confusion that was 1968," University of Virginia Center for Politics, March 16, 2016, accessed April 1, 2017, http://www.centerforpolitics.org/crystalball/articles/the-ball-of-confusion-that-was-1968/.

Saad, Lydia, "Giuliani Leads GOP Race; Huckabee, Others Tie for Second," Gallup, December 18, 2007, accessed September 1, 2017, http://www.gallup.com/poll/103348/giuliani-leads-gop-race-huckabee-others-tie-second.aspx.

"Schick and Patrick Frawley," Quixotic Joust, accessed March 22, 2017, http://quixoticjoust.blogspot.com/2011/09/schick-and-patrick-frawley.html.

Selby, W. Gardner, "David Dewhurst says Ted Cruz represents a Chinese company found guilty of stealing U.S. blueprints," *Poltifact*, April 19, 2012, accessed April 1, 2017, http://www.politifact.com/texas/statements/2012/apr/19/david-dewhurst/david-dewhurst-says-ted-cruz-represents-chinese-co/.

Shinners, Matt, "How to Become a Law Firm Partner," The American Bar Association, June 7, 2012, accessed June 11, 2017, https://apps.americanbar.org/litigation/committees/youngadvocate/email/spring2012/spring2012-0612-how-become-law-firm-partner.html.

Stokes, David, "RN and LBJ – An Overlooked Relationship," The Nixon Foundation, May 13, 2011, accessed March 28, 2017, http://www.nixonlegacy.org/the-new nixon/2011/05/rn-and-lbj-an-overlooked-relationship.

Swaine, Robert Taylor, *The Cravath Firm and Its Predecessors, 1819-1947*, (New York: Ad Press, 1946-48). Web. Accessed on 15 January 2016, http://www.houseofrussell.com/legalhistory/alh/docs/rtswayne.html.

"The 1964 Republican Campaign," *PBS*, accessed March 27, 2017, http://www.pbs.org/wgbh/americanexperience/features/general-article/rockefellers-campaign/.

"The Accounting Hall of Fame," The Ohio State University, Fisher College of Business, accessed 30 April 2016, http://fisher.osu.edu/departments/accounting-and-mis/the-accounting-hall-of-fame/membership-in-hall/maurice-h.-stans/.

The LBJ Library, "The President's News Conference, 11/4/66," YouTube video, 33:25, posted March 20, 2013, https://www.youtube.com/watch?v=sZeDR6j7YZ4.

"The Man in the Arena," Theordore-Roosevelt.com, accessed April 1, 2017, http://www.theodore-roosevelt.com/trsorbonnespeech.html.

"The Manila Communique: Nixon's Comeback," The Richard Nixon Foundation, May 20, 2015, accessed March 29, 2017, http://www.nixonlegacy.org/the-new-nixon/2015/05/the-manila-communique-nixons-comeback.

"The Morrow-Kohly-Nixon Connection," Kennedy Assassination Homepage, accessed March 22, 2017, http://mcadams.posc.mu.edu/morrow2.htm.

"The National Security Archive," George Washington University, accessed March 22, 2017, http://nsarchive.gwu.edu/NSAEBB/NSAEBB355/.

"The System's History," *Cravath, Swaine & Moore Homepage*, accessed on January 15, 2016, https://www.cravath.com/systemshistory/.

"Then and Now: A Dewey Timeline," *Reuters*, accessed on January 16, 2016, http://www.reuters.com/article/us-dewey-timeline-idUSBRE84B00V20120512.

"Thomas E. Dewey," *Dewey Defeats Truman: The Single Most Famous Newspaper Error...Ever*, accessed January 16, 2016, http://www.deweydefeatstruman.com/Deweybio.htm.

"Throwing a Ball," *New York Social Diary*, December 29, 2016, accessed June 30, 2016, http://www.newyorksocialdiary.com/social-diary/2016/throwing-a-ball.

"Time, Inc. v. Hill," Oyez, accessed March 31, 2017, https://www.oyez.org/cases/1965/22.

"Transcript: JFK's Speech on his Religion," NPR, December 5, 2007, accessed March 26, 2017, http://www.npr.org/templates/story/story.php?storyId=16920600.

"Transcript of A Meeting Between the President and H.R. Haldeman in the Oval Office on April 16, 1973 from 12:00 to 12:31," Richard Nixon Presidential Library and Museum, accessed April 1, 2017, https://www.nixonlibrary.gov/forresearchers/find/tapes/watergate/wspf/897-011.pdf.

"Transcript of Richard Nixon's 'Last Press Conference,'" The University of Pennsylvania, accessed 4 March 2016, http://languagelog.ldc.upenn.edu/myl/RichardNixonConcession.html.

U.S. Senate Committee on Banking and Currency, *The Pecora Investigation: Stock Exchange Practices and the Causes of the 1929 Wall Street Crash*, (New York: Cosimo Reports, 2010).

"Warner Lambert: A History," Pfizer, accessed April 1, 2017, http://www.pfizer.com/about/history/pfizer_warner_lambert

"Welcome Mr. Kennedy to Dallas," Latin American Studies, accessed March 26, 2017, http://www.latinamericanstudies.org/mrkennedy.htm.

COURT OPINIONS

Brown v. Board of the Education, 347 U.S. 483 (1954).
Brown v. Louisiana, 383 U.S. 131 (1966).
Doe v. Bolton, 410 U.S. 179 (1973).
Epperson v. Arkansas, 393 U.S. 97 (1968).
Gertz v. Robert Welch, 418 U.S. 323 (1974).
Gideon v. Wainwright, 372 U.S. 335 (1963).
Griswold v. Connecticut, 381 U.S. 479 (1965).
In re Gault, 387 U.S. 1 (1967).
Miranda v. Arizona, 384 U.S. 436 (1966).
New York Times Co. v. Sullivan, 376 U.S. 254 (1964).
Powell v. Texas, 392 U.S. 514 (1968).
Roe v. Wade, 410 U.S. 113 (1973).
Time, Inc. v. Hill, 385 U.S. 374 (1967).
Tinker v. Des Moines, 393 U.S. 503 (1969).

Index

About the Author

Victor Li is a Chicago-based journalist. He is currently an assistant managing editor with the *ABA Journal*, covering the business of law and legal technology. Prior to that, he worked at ALM Media Properties in New York City, serving as a staff reporter for *Law Technology News* and *The American Lawyer*. His work has also been featured in *The Utica Observer Dispatch*, *The Huffington Post*, *The Columbia Journalist*, *Amherst Magazine*, and *The Berkshire Eagle*. A former prosecutor in the Bronx, he earned his J.D. from Tulane University Law School, a M.S. from Columbia University School of Journalism and a B.A. in history from Amherst College.